REA: THE LEADER IN TEACHER CERTIFICATION PREP

PRAXIS® CORE

READING (5712)
WRITING (5722)
MATHEMATICS (5732)

Sandra Rush, M.A.
Mathematics Tutor

Julie O'Connell, D. Litt.
Assistant Professor of English
Felician College
Lodi, New Jersey

Research & Education Association

Research & Education Association
61 Ethel Road West
Piscataway, New Jersey 08854
E-mail: info@rea.com

Praxis® Core with Online Practice Tests

Printed in the United States of America

Library of Congress Control Number 2015934932

ISBN-13: 978-0-7386-1180-8
ISBN-10: 0-7386-1180-8

Each state or agency that uses Praxis® Core tests sets its own testing requirements
and passing scores. For details, check with your state education office or visit
the official Praxis® site at *www.ets.org/praxis*. Praxis® and The Praxis Series® are
registered trademarks of Educational Testing Service (ETS). This product is not
endorsed or approved by ETS. All other trademarks cited in this publication are the
property of their respective owners.

Cover image: ©iStockphoto.com/andresr

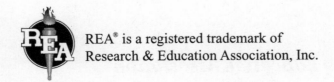

REA® is a registered trademark of
Research & Education Association, Inc.

Contents

PART III: PRAXIS CORE READING REVIEW

CONTENTS

PART IV: PRAXIS CORE WRITING REVIEW

PART V: PRAXIS CORE PRACTICE TEST BATTERY

About Our Authors

Sandra Rush is a best-selling author acclaimed for making mathematics easier to grasp. She has taught math and physics at both the secondary and college levels. As an undergraduate majoring in math at Temple University, Ms. Rush tutored members of the men's basketball team as well as students at Philadelphia public schools, which sparked her interest in teaching. After contemplating a career in the space sciences and receiving her master's degree in ionospheric physics from UCLA, she found fulfillment in teaching in the classroom environment as well as individual tutoring. Ms. Rush has pursued her academic career in Massachusetts, Colorado, and Arizona. She has written test-preparation guides for all ages, with her approach to books continually informed by her one-on-one tutoring and coaching.

Julie O'Connell is an assistant professor of English at Felician College in New Jersey, where she developed and taught a Praxis test preparation course for teacher education students. Dr. O'Connell was chair of Developmental Studies at Felician from 2010 to 2013. From 2000 to 2010, she served as director of the Felician College Writing Lab. She has also worked as a learning specialist at Rutgers University, as a corporate trainer, and as a high school English teacher. Dr. O'Connell received her B.A. in English from Georgetown University, her M.A.T. from Brown University, and her D.Litt. from Drew University.

Authors' Acknowledgments and Dedications

It has been a pleasure to work again on a book with REA, especially with the editorial director, Larry B. Kling. Larry has devoted much time in ensuring that this book is as clear and helpful to the reader as possible, and I appreciate his diligence. I would like to acknowledge those who reviewed the math content and offered some helpful comments. Special thanks go to Trevor Renfro, a student who was my sounding board for many of the math concepts introduced here. Thank you all for the opportunity to help future teachers in their quest for a most rewarding profession. What a profound and lasting influence great teachers have on their students.—**Sandra Rush**

First, I would like to thank REA and its editorial director, Larry B. Kling, for this wonderful opportunity; Alice Leonard for helping me find this project; and Charlie Heinle for his overarching ideas and guidance. I also extend gratitude to Dr. Margaret Gardineer of Felician College for her background information on the Common Core State Standards, and to Professor Karen Pezzolla, also of Felician College, for her expert content editing of the entire manuscript. To Cari Rappaport, thank you for your assistance with the history section; to Nasreen Khan, thank you for your input on the reading passages and test questions as well as for being so smart; and finally, to Sarah Elizabeth O'Connell, my dear niece, thank you for working with me on Saturdays to help me find the voice that would best reach my audience. What a privilege it was to work with all of you! Pax et bene.

I dedicate this book to my daughters, Jennifer and Catherine Juliano. I love you more than words can say and am so proud of you.—**Julie O'Connell**

About REA

Founded in 1959, Research & Education Association (REA) is dedicated to publishing the finest and most effective educational materials—including study guides and test preps—for students of all ages. Today, REA's wide-ranging catalog is a leading resource for students, teachers, and other professionals. Visit *www.rea.com* to see a complete listing of all our titles.

Publisher's Acknowledgments

SVP and Publisher: Pam Weston

VP, Editorial Services: Larry B. Kling

VP, Technology: John Paul Cording

Managing Editor: Diane Goldschmidt

Copywriter and Proofreader: Kelli A. Wilkins

Copy Editor (Reading/Writing): John Kupetz, M.A., Associate Professor, English/Journalism, College of Lake County, Grayslake, Ill.

Copy Editor (Math): Paula Moseley, Ed.D., Instructor, Educational Consultant

Indexer: Sandra Rush

Page Design: Claudia Petrilli

Cover Design: Eve Grinnell

Typesetting: Caragraphics

PART I:
Praxis Core Introduction

Getting Started

So you want to become a teacher. You know it's not an easy path, nor should it be, given what's at stake. Across America, curriculum standards have been stiffened, with the rapidly evolving demands of the Information Age finding their way into the classroom with increasing frequency.

Now, all that stands between you and your admission into a teacher education program and to becoming a licensed professional is an exam battery called the Praxis Core Academic Skills for Educators, better known as the Praxis Core tests.

It may sound overwhelming, but don't worry. Our test prep has everything you need to pass the tests and start your teaching career. Let's start with the basics.

The three tests in the Praxis Core battery gauge academic skills and content knowledge in three areas:

- Reading (5712)

- Writing (5722)

- Mathematics (5732)

You can take each test separately, but if you want to take all three tests at once, register for the Praxis Core Combined Test (5751).

How to Use This Book + Online Prep

Developed with the needs of future teachers in mind, this book, along with REA's online diagnostic tools, helps you customize your prep so you can make the most of your study time. Use all of it or just what you need to brush up in select areas.

Our Praxis Core Book + Online Prep package includes:

- Expert test tips and strategies

- Focused content review for all three Praxis Core tests

- Practice exercises on every selected-response topic

- Extensive essay samples and analyses

- Advice on how to solve math problems quickly

- Three online diagnostic tests (one for each test subject) to help you pinpoint where you need to spend your study time

- Six full-length practice tests (two for each test subject) offered in the book and also online with the added benefit of timed testing conditions and diagnostic score reporting

Test Yourself at the Online REA Study Center

The REA Study Center (*www.rea.com/studycenter*) is where you'll find the online material that accompanies this book—the three diagnostic tests and six full-length practice tests.

We know your time is precious and you want an efficient study experience. Our online content gives you feedback on where you stand right from the start.

- ✓ **Automatic Scoring**—Find out how you did on your test, instantly.

- ✓ **Diagnostic Score Reports**—Pinpoint the areas that challenge you the most, so you can study effectively.

- ✓ **Detailed Answer Explanations**—Learn not just why a response option is correct, but also why the other answer choices are incorrect.

- ✓ **Timed Testing**—Manage your time as you practice, so you'll feel confident on test day.

The Praxis Core tests are computer-based, so practicing online at the REA Study Center will simulate test-day conditions and help you become comfortable with the exam format.

Step One: Take REA's Praxis Core Diagnostic Tests

We've included three online diagnostic tests at the REA Study Center—one for each Praxis Core subject. Our customized diagnostic tools will show you how to spend your time and focus your study, highlighting the areas where you need the most help.

Step Two: Evaluate Your Strengths and Weaknesses

Check your diagnostic score report. Are sentence-correction items your weak spot? If so, you'll know where you need to extend your review. But even where you're already strong, be sure to read our answer explanations. This is a prime opportunity to reinforce key concepts and hone your skills.

Step Three: Create Your Customized Study Plan

Based on your diagnostic feedback, use our self-evaluation chart and sample study plan to create a study schedule. We suggest you start your preparation at least five weeks before test day. This will give you plenty of time to study the review materials and take the practice tests.

Step Four: Review the Content

Improve your weak areas by reviewing the appropriate content areas in this book.

Step Five: Take the Practice Tests

With two REA practice tests for each Praxis Core subject, this book will test your subject knowledge and build your test-day confidence. Taking these tests online at the REA Study Center comes with the benefits of timed testing conditions and automatic score reports. Unlike the diagnostic tests, which are designed to help you identify your problem areas, our practice tests give you a thorough feel for the real exam.

To be assured you're on the path to success on the Praxis Core, you're looking to earn a score of at least 70% correct on your practice test's multiple-choice questions. Think of this as a good approximation of a passing score. We also encourage you to take the interactive practice tests available from Educational Testing Service (ETS), the Praxis Core test developer. For details visit *www.ets.org/praxis*.

Self-Evaluation Chart

Reading	I'm confident	I need to review	When I studied
Key ideas and details			
Craft, structure, and language skills			
Integration of knowledge and ideas			
Writing			
Text types, purposes, and production			
Language and research skills for writing			
Mathematics			
Number and quantity			
Algebra and functions			
Geometry			
Statistics and probability			

Setting Up Your Study Plan

Many people take the Praxis Core tests one test section at a time. Our diagnostic tools can help you decide how to sequence your prep and test-taking.

It's never too early to start studying. The earlier you begin, the more time you'll have to sharpen your skills. We suggest allowing five weeks for preparation, whether you're taking all three tests in one session or splitting your test-taking across three separate sessions. To avoid added anxiety from last-minute prep, we recommend completing your prep about a week before test day.

Sample Study Plan: 5 Weeks till Test Day

Week 1	
Read	Read Part I to familiarize yourself with the book and the three Praxis Core tests.
Diagnose	If you're planning to take the Praxis Core Combined Test, take our three online diagnostic subject tests to pinpoint your strengths and weaknesses. If you've decided to take only one of the Praxis Core tests at a time, take the diagnostic test in that subject and repeat the process for your next Praxis Core test.
Plan	Record the areas you need to focus on in the self-evaluation chart.
Review	Review your results. What questions did you get wrong? Why did you choose the answers that you did? Why did you eliminate the other response options? What is your raw score? Which areas need your attention?
Week 2	
Review	Focus on reviewing the content areas in this book that correspond with the practice items that you got wrong or had to guess. Studying all the content can't hurt! But be sure to pay special attention to your problem areas.
Week 3	
Practice	If you're taking the Praxis Core Combined Test, take our full Practice Test Battery 1,* which contains full-length practice exams of all three Praxis Core tests. This is a format-true test-taking experience in real time (if you take it online). ***If you're planning to take only one subject test at a time, practice only for that test at this time.**
Focus	Check your results from Practice Test Battery 1. Review your score report and the detailed explanations of answers for questions you answered incorrectly. Identify the topics you need to restudy.
Review	Go back to the book and brush up the items you missed by reviewing the corresponding content area.
Week 4	
Practice	If you're taking the Praxis Core Combined Test, take our full Practice Test Battery 2,* which contains full-length practice exams for all three Praxis Core tests. This second battery gives you the opportunity to chart your progress and build your score by focusing your attention on your remaining problem areas. We suggest taking this second test about a week before the actual Core test. ***If you're planning to take only one subject test at a time, practice only for that test at this time.**
Week 5	
Test-Day Checklist	Run through ETS's test-day checklist a week before your test date.

All About the Praxis Core Tests

WHAT'S ON THE TESTS

We'll break down the Praxis Core tests for you in just a minute, but first a little background.

The Praxis Core tests are used to comprehensively assess the academic skills and content knowledge of teacher candidates. They're typically taken early in your college career for entry into educator preparation programs. In addition, many states require Praxis Core scores for you to secure your teaching license.

These tests are used in more than 30 states and territories, the District of Columbia, and the U.S. Department of Defense Education Activity, which serves children of active duty military and DoD civilian families.

The Praxis Core comprises three tests:

- **Reading**—Rich with passages (sometimes presented in pairs), this test asks you to pick out key ideas and details, and to make logical inferences. You'll find questions drawn from informational documents and other nonfiction texts. The test also places emphasis on interpretation of words and phrases based on author intent. Mainly, these are standard multiple-choice questions that ask you to find the "best" answer. However, you'll also see some that have multiple correct answers; you won't be told how many, but such questions may have fewer response options than one-answer items.

- **Writing**—This test is divided into a multiple-choice section and two 30-minute essay sections. The first section puts you through your paces on usage, sentence correction, revision in context, and research skills. The two essays require very different approaches—in the first case, presenting an effective argument; in the second, analyzing a topic based on source material given to you.

- **Mathematics**—This test features mainly standard multiple-choice items with one "best" answer. But, as with the Reading test, be on the lookout for a few questions that require more than one correct answer. The Math test also includes numeric-entry questions. An on-screen four-function (+, −, ×, ÷) calculator that also computes square roots is provided to help you avoid simple arithmetic errors.

A Snapshot of the Praxis Core Tests

Test	Number of Items	Item Format Notes	Actual Testing Time*
Reading	56 selected-response items	• Most questions present five possible responses from which you select the best one. • Some questions direct you to "select *all* [responses] that apply." Such items will give you a box ☐ to mark (for each correct answer) instead of an oval. These items may have as few as three choices. • The stimulus for Reading test questions can be any of the following: 1. Brief passages (perhaps 75 to 100 words) followed by two or three questions whose stems include phrasing such as, "The passage is primarily concerned with . . ." or "Which of the following is an unstated assumption made by the author of the passage?" 2. Short statements (which may be about 50 words) followed by a single question. 3. Paired passages of approximately 200 words combined followed by four to seven questions (e.g., "Which of the following statements best describes the relationship between the two passages?," "Unlike the author of Passage 2, the author of Passage 1 mentions . . . ," or "Which of the following specific strategies mentioned by the author of Passage 1 is exemplified in Passage 2?") 4. Extended passages of about 200 words followed by four to seven questions. These may ask you to find the best description of the passage's organization or identify the statement(s) with which the author would *most* likely agree.	85 minutes

(Continued)

Test	Number of Items	Item Format Notes	Actual Testing Time*
Writing	40 selected-response items and two essay questions	• Selected-response questions ask you to choose one best answer. • The source-based essay requires you to cite specific sources to explain the assigned topic. • The argumentative essay requires you to write persuasively on an assigned topic. Unlike the source-based essay, this one must be "based on your own reading, experience, or observations."	100 minutes (One 40-minute selected-response section and two 30-minute essay sections)
Mathematics	56 selected-response and numeric-entry questions	• Most questions present five possible responses from which you select the best one. • Multiple-selection items direct you to "select *all* [responses] that apply." You must choose all of the correct responses to get credit. • Numeric-entry questions require an answer without the benefit of choices. • An on-screen four-function calculator is provided.	85 minutes

*If you take the Praxis Core tests separately (on separate days), each session lasts two hours (inclusive of a 30-minute tutorial). If you take the Praxis Core Combined Test, which allows you to take all three Core subject tests at once, the full session lasts five hours. Apart from the tutorials on test navigation, each session also includes time for the collection of examinees' background information. During the combined test, you're offered an optional 10-minute break.

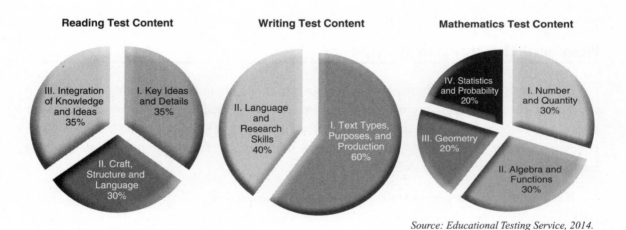

Source: Educational Testing Service, 2014.

The Praxis Core tests are a "regeneration," or rewriting, of the Praxis I Pre-Professional Skills Tests, or PPST, by Educational Testing Service (ETS) to reflect the more demanding Common Core State Standards adopted by most states. The new tests also align with the College and Career Readiness Standards released by the U.S. Department of Education in 2013. Like the PPST battery, these new tests are gateway assessments, designed to evaluate your proficiency in basic academic skills as you prepare to begin your teaching career. Most students take a computer-delivered test. However, students with ADA accommodations may qualify to take a paper-based version. For more information, visit the ETS website at *www.ets.org/praxis*.

ETS has updated its tests to measure better what teachers should know and be able to do as they implement the Common Core State Standards in their classrooms. The Common Core standards were developed by the Council of Chief State School Officers and the National Governors Association Center for Best Practices. These English and Math standards encompass the knowledge and skills high school graduates are expected to master in order to succeed in college or a career. For more details, visit *www.corestandards.org*.

What kinds of test questions will I face?

You'll recognize the questions on any of the three Praxis Core tests as standard multiple-choice items with one best response that you choose by clicking an oval. However, you'll also encounter some questions that ask you to click more than one response to indicate *all* the correct responses. When multiple answers are in play, you may need to click boxes instead of ovals. You must choose all of the correct responses to get credit. Beyond the multiple-choice questions are constructed-response tasks, which take the form of fill-ins and essays.

Over time, ETS may introduce other technology-enhanced item types. These are detailed in ETS's study companions for each test. Be alert to varying commands. But take comfort in knowing that, for the most part, you'll be dealing with more standard multiple-choice items that call for identifying just the one answer that's best.

How will the questions appear?

Each question on the test appears on a separate screen. Instructions for answering each question are given at the bottom of the screen. If, for example, an entire reading passage doesn't fit on your screen, you will need to use the scroll bar to see the directions and stimulus. Stand-alone questions either ask a direct question for which you choose from possible responses, or they may contain incomplete statements for you to complete.

It is possible for one stimulus (e.g., a chart, table, or reading passage) to have several questions associated with it. The computer may use a split screen for this type of question. On a split screen, the graphic or scenario appears on the left side of the screen, and the questions appear page by page on the right screen (the stimulus is repeated on successive pages as necessary). Fortunately, there is a "Previous" button if any of these questions depend at all on a response to a prior question related to the stimulus. Sometimes, the stimulus appears above the questions, so be sure you scroll down to see the type of question and the instructions for answering.

What's on-screen navigation like?

Apart from the on-screen calculator, you'll also have the benefit of these navigation tools and functions.

NEXT: Click NEXT to go to the next screen and next question. You'll see only one question on each screen.

PREVIOUS: Clicking the PREVIOUS button comes in handy when all of a sudden you remember how to do the last question, or when you need the results from the last question to answer the current one.

MARK FOR REVIEW: If you think you want to go back to any question, answer it to the best of your ability and then press the MARK FOR REVIEW button (on the top right of the screen) to return to it later. Remember to use the scratch paper to keep track of which questions you marked for review as well as which answer choices, if any, you already eliminated.

REVIEW: When you have finished all of the questions on any test, pushing the REVIEW button will display a "Review Your Selections" screen, which will show which questions were answered and unanswered as well as those that were marked for review. Clicking on any question number will bring that question to the screen. It is best to do this *after* you have seen every question but *before* you submit your answers.

CONTINUE: When the test ends, clicking the CONTINUE button will take you to two choices: Report or Cancel Scores. Your scores won't be reported until you have clicked the CONTINUE button and then the REPORT button.

Don't let these navigation tools obscure the fact that you should *not* leave any questions unanswered. The scoring on the test is based strictly on the number of correct answers, with no penalty deducted for wrong answers or bad guesses. So forge ahead, but don't skip any questions.

Is a tutorial available on test functionality?

Because it's computerized, the Praxis Core test battery allows you a short dry run on test day to familiarize yourself with test navigation and functionality. That functionality includes a timer displayed in the upper right-hand corner of the computer screen and an on-screen calculator for the math test. You will be able to run the tutorial for up to 30 minutes. The time you spend on the tutorial is solely for that; no scratch paper is permitted.

How are the tests scored?

Each state has its own requirements for how Praxis Core tests are used, as well as what determines passing scores. Based on standard-setting studies done by ETS, the various states' cut scores require you to answer *at least* the following approximate percentages of questions correctly:

- Reading, 58%

- Writing, 56%

- Math, 52%

Our advice, however, is to tread cautiously around these figures. First, because there is variability across states. Second, because the raw score is not a fixed thing, even though what it stands for—the number of items or points earned for correct answers—makes it seem that way.

For the sake of achieving comparability across different versions of each of the three Praxis Core tests, raw scores are converted to scaled scores. Your state teacher-credentialing agency reports a scaled score for each Praxis Core test. The scaled score is calculated based on how raw points for different items are weighted using a method called equating, a computation that shifts from one test version to another as determined by the varying difficulty of different versions of the test.

The reporting scale for the Praxis Core tests ranges from 100 to 200 scaled-score points. Find your state requirements at the ETS Praxis website at *www.ets.org/praxis/states*.

With all that in mind, we suggest you use our *guestimated* benchmark of 70% correct on Praxis Core Reading, Writing, and Mathematics *multiple-choice* practice-test questions. Based on the holistic scoring system used for the essays, we recommend you set as a goal to get at least 8 points out of the available 12.

How are the scores reported?

Scores are reported by the individual test (5712, 5722, 5732), even if you decide to take all three Core exams at the same time. If you wish to take them all at once, select Core Academic Skills for Educators: Combined Test (5751) when registering.

How do I register for the tests?

Before registering, check your state testing requirements to make sure you are taking the right test. You can also locate the nearest testing centers at *http://www.ets.org/praxis* for both the computerized and, for special accommodations, paper-based versions of the test, as well as available test dates.

If you take the tests separately, they each cost $85. If you are taking the Praxis Core Combined test, though, the total cost is only $135.

However you register, you must bring your admissions ticket with you to the test center. You also must bring photo identification with you. If you lose your admission ticket or do not get it within a week before the test, you should call or email ETS and have the testing agency send your ticket.

Contact ETS by phone at 1-800-772-9476 if you're in the U.S., U.S. territories, or Canada. If you're overseas, phone 1-609-771-7395. ETS's email address is praxis@ets.org.

What must I bring to the test center?

Just two items are required when you appear at the test center for computerized testing:

- **Your admission ticket,** which you should receive when you register online.

- **Photo ID,** which must be valid and include your:

  ▶ Full name

  ▶ Signature

  ▶ Recent photograph that's clearly you

Acceptable forms of ID include a passport, government-issued driver's license, state or province ID card, national ID card, or military ID card.

What should be left at home?

Here's a list of what to keep at home on test day:

- Cellphones, smartphones, smartwatches, pagers, calculators, or other electronic, recording, listening, scanning, or photographic device.

- Any books, pamphlets, notes, or other reading material.

- Scratch paper. The test center will offer scratch paper for note-taking, math computations, and outlines.

- Personal items, including food, drink, and tobacco. If you're taking the three tests separately, there's little point to bringing food into the test center. If you're tackling the Praxis Core Combined Test, however, we suggest you bring your favorite energy bar and bottled water.

You may also be asked to remove your watch and empty your pockets when you arrive, so it's best to travel light.

For full, up-to-date ETS test-day guidelines, be sure to read the regulations shared at registration and posted at *www.ets.org/praxis*.

Are there any no-brainers that could help my score?

These tips may seem obvious, but ignoring them could cost you dearly.

- Be sure to wear comfortable clothing that won't be a factor in your performance, such as making you too hot or too cold.

- Use the restroom, if necessary, before the exam. If you have to leave the room at any time, the clock doesn't stop, so you would be wasting precious time.

- Be sure to get a good night's sleep before the test. Often, being well rested helps your score more than any last-minute cramming. In fact, Belgian researchers recently found that students who increased their night's sleep from six to seven hours scored an average of nearly 10% higher on exams.

What are options for retesting?

Test retakes are not as uncommon as you may think. For example, official data show that over a recent five-year period, the first-time passing rate for the CBEST, a California teacher-certification test similar to the Praxis Core, ranged from 69.7% to 71.4% for each year's examinee group.

So if teaching really is your calling, retaking a Praxis Core test should only make you work harder. Praxis Core tests are offered continuously and may be taken once every thirty days. Tests offered during testing windows (i.e., paper-and-pencil tests for students with accommodations), however, can be taken only once per window of opportunity. Before applying for a retest, you should check your state's retest policy to see if retesting is allowed. Moreover, you should reset your study plan to ensure you shore up your weaknesses and build on your strengths, which happens to be exactly what this book is designed to do.

Proven Test-Taking Strategies

All test-taking strategies have the same practical goal: to show you the best way to answer questions so you can improve your score.

The strategies and tips that follow come straight from teacher education students who have passed the Praxis Core tests. We have worked directly with students just like you to see what works best.

Remember: There is no one right way to study. Savvy test-takers sharpen their skills while minimizing obstacles such as poor time management and test anxiety. As you assess these strategies, identify those you already use in your daily life and adapt the approaches that best address your problem areas—you know, the ones for which you'll need to invest more study time.

To make the most of whatever strategies you use, it's best to have an overall plan in mind.

Our strategy list can be adjusted according to your needs, which no one knows better than you. Do what best fits your style of learning and method of study.

FOUR-PART PLAN FOR REASONING SKILLS

The Praxis Core stresses reasoning skills across all three tests. So it's useful to come to the test armed with a systematic way to address test questions across the board. The plan comprises four simple steps:

1. Determine (a) what is known, (b) what is necessary to solve the problem, (c) what information is missing (usually your solution), and (d) what is unnecessary (just because something is mentioned doesn't necessarily mean it has anything to do with your solution).

2. Devise a strategy to solve the problem. This may involve taking notes, making a sketch or a table (use the scratch paper), or looking for a pattern, for example. (See "14 Tips to Boost Your Score" below.)

3. Solve the problem according to your strategy and choose or enter the correct answer.

4. Make sure the answer makes sense.

With this four-step frame of reference in hand, let's look at how this reasoning aspect might play out on the Praxis Math test. Rather than being asked "10 − 3.50 − 4.25 = ?" you may be presented with a problem such as "George bought a gallon of milk for $3.50 and a half-dozen doughnuts for $4.25. How much change should he receive if he pays with a $10 bill?" Same math, but you have to use reasoning to get to the 10 − 3.50 − 4.25 part. This book shows how to get to the arithmetic part of a question on the Math Test, and since the Praxis test supplies you with an online calculator if you need it, you should be able to take it from there.

Once you have your basic battle plan, you're ready to turn your attention to question-level strategies.

14 TIPS TO BOOST YOUR SCORE

When approaching the Praxis Core exams, fear can overwhelm you and make you forget your knowledge and understanding of test-taking. Don't give in to anxiety. Take heart that everything about the test is knowable.

Here are 14 expert tips to help you raise your score.

1. Guess Away

One of the most frequently asked questions about the Praxis Core tests is: Can I guess? The answer: absolutely! There is no penalty for guessing on the Praxis test. That means that if you guess incorrectly, you will not lose any points, but if you guess correctly, you will gain points. Thus, while it's fine to guess, it's important to guess smartly, or as the strategy is called: use process of elimination (see Strategy No. 2). Your score is based strictly on the number of correct answers. So answer all questions and take your best guess when you don't know the answer.

2. Process of Elimination

Process of elimination is one of the most important test-taking strategies at your disposal. Process of elimination means looking at the choices and eliminating the ones you know are wrong, including answers that are partially wrong. Your odds of getting the right answer increase from the moment you're able to get rid of a wrong choice.

3. All in

Review all the response options. Just because you believe you've found the correct answer—or, in some cases, answers—look at each choice so you don't mistakenly jump to any conclusions. If you are asked to choose the *best* answer, be sure your first answer is really the best one.

4. Choice of the Day

What if you are truly stumped and can't use the process of elimination? It's time to pick a fallback answer. On the day of the test, choose the position of the answer (e.g., the third of the five choices) that you will pick for any question you cannot smartly guess. According to the laws of probability, you have a higher chance of getting an answer right if you stick to one chosen position for the answer choice when you have to guess an answer instead of randomly picking one.

5. Use Choices to Confirm Your Answer(s)

The great thing about multiple-choice questions is that the answer has to be staring back at you. Have an answer in mind and use the choices to *confirm* it. You'll need to take an extra moment or two to come up with multiple correct answers, but this won't slow you down to any degree since most multiple-choice questions you'll be facing have only one right answer. This strategy works well on the Reading and Writing tests. For the Math test, you can work the problem and find the match among the choices, or you may want to try the opposite: *backsolving*—that is, working backwards—from the choices given. (We discuss more about how to approach the Math test in the math review in Part II.)

6. Watch the Clock

Among the most vital point-saving skills is active time management. The breakdown and time limits of each section are provided as you begin each test. If you are taking an accommodated paper-based test, bring a watch (as long as it's an ordinary timepiece, without any special digital or "smartwatch" features like a calculator) to keep the overall time in view. With the computerized test, which most candidates take, keep an eye on the timer on your computer screen. Make sure you stay on top of how much time you have left for each section and never spend too much time on any one question. Remember: Most multiple-choice questions are worth one raw point. Treat each one as if it's the one that will put you over the top. You never know, it just might. For the essay section, make sure you have enough time to write a well-organized essay. The last thing you want on test day is to lose easy points because you ran out of time and focused too much on difficult questions. Read more on time management in the chart at the end of this chapter.

7. Read, Read, Read

It's important to read through all the multiple-choice options. Even if you believe answer choice A is correct (or, in the case of the few questions with multiple correct options, choices A *and* C), you can misread a question or response option if you're rushing to get through the test. While it is important not to linger on a question, it is also crucial to avoid giving a question short shrift. Slow down, calm down, read all the choices, verify that your choice is the best one, and click on it.

8. Take Notes

Use the scratch paper provided to you to make notes to work toward the answer(s). If you use all the scratch paper you're initially given, you can get more.

9. Isolate Limiters

Pay attention to any limiters in a multiple-choice question stem. These are words such as *initial, best, most* (as in *most appropriate* or *most likely*), *not, least, except, required,* or *necessary*. Especially watch for negative words, such as "Choose the answer that is *not* true." When you select your answer, double-check yourself by asking how the response fits the limitations established by the stem. Think of the stem as a puzzle piece that perfectly fits only the response option(s) that contain the correct answer. Let it guide you.

10. It's Not a Race

Ignore other test-takers. Don't compare yourself to anyone else in the room. Focus on the items in front of you and the time you have left. If someone finishes the test 30 minutes early, it does not necessarily mean that person answered more questions correctly than you did. Stay calm and focus on *your* test. It's the only one that matters.

11. Confirm Your Click

In the digital age, many of us are used to rapid-clicking, be it in the course of emailing or gaming. Look at the screen to be sure to see that your mouse-click is acknowledged. If your answer doesn't register, you won't get credit. However, if you want to mark it for review so you can return later, that's your call. Before you click "Submit," use the test's review screen to see whether you inadvertantly skipped any questions.

12. Creature of Habit? No Worries.

We are all creatures of habit. It's therefore best to follow a familiar pattern of study. Do what's comfortable for you. Set a time and place each day to study for this test. Whether it is 30 minutes at the library or an hour in a secluded corner of your local coffee shop, commit yourself as best you can to this schedule every day. Find quiet places where it is less crowded, as constant background noise can distract you. Don't study one subject for too long, either. Take an occasional breather and treat yourself to a healthy snack or some quick exercise. After your short break—5 or 10 minutes can do the trick—return to what you were studying or start a new section.

13. Knowledge is Power

Purchasing this book gave you an edge on passing the Praxis test. Make the most of this edge. Review the sections on how the test is structured, what the directions look like, what types of questions will be asked, and so on. Take our practice tests and download the sample Praxis study companions from ETS (*www.ets.org/praxis*) to familiarize yourself with what the test looks and feels like. Most test anxiety occurs because people feel unprepared when they are taking the test, and they psych themselves out. You can whittle away at anxiety by learning the format of the test and by knowing what to expect. Fully simulating the test even once will boost your chances of getting the score you need. Meanwhile, the knowledge you've gained will also will save you the valuable time that would have been eaten up puzzling through what the directions are asking and how some of the oddball question types (ETS calls them "unfamiliar formats") work. As an added benefit, previewing the test will free up your brain's resources so you can focus on racking up as many points as you can.

14. B-r-e-a-t-h-e

What's the worst that can happen when you take a test? You may have an off day, and despite your best efforts, you may not pass. Well, the good news is that a test can be retaken. In fact, you may already be doing this—this book is every bit for you as it is for first-timers. Fortunately, the Praxis test is something you can study and prepare for, and in some ways to a greater extent than other tests you've taken throughout your academic career. Yes, there will be questions you won't know, but neither your teacher education program nor state licensing board (which sets its own cut scores) expects you to know everything. When unfamiliar vocabulary appears or difficult math problems loom, don't despair: Use context clues, process of elimination, or your letter of the day to make your choice, and then press ahead. If you have time left, you can always come back to the question later. If not, relax. It is only one question on a test filled with many. Take a deep breath and then exhale. You know this information. Now you're going to show it.

The following section provides tips for time management as well as corresponding test-taking strategies. However, your approach depends on who you are. Pick the strategies that work best for you and consistently apply them.

PUTTING TIME ON YOUR SIDE

Whatever strategy you choose, and whatever kind of test-taker you are, time management is essential to your success. Pick a strategy that fits you best and try it. Then chart your results.

As you work out the kinks of test timing, realize that the Praxis Core Reading test presents a recurring dilemma. Test candidates wonder whether to read the passage or the questions first. The answer may surprise you: whichever works for you.

Reading the questions first gives some test-takers an idea of what to search for in the passage. However, others find this strategy makes them skip over key information. They get confused and have to reread the passage to remember what they are looking for—a bad idea considering the time constraints. Remember that the passages are relatively short—with none running much more than 200 words. If you can skim them and avoid rereading, you can save a lot of time.

Whatever you do, don't dawdle over the response options. Test items may present a decoy answer that causes you to miss spotting the real answer in the passage.

Using the motto that timing is everything, pay close attention to the time it takes you to get through our practice tests. Then check the chart that follows to see where you stand.

Test Your Timing

The following self-evaluation chart will help you master the clock. Three different scenarios are presented to help you get through each Praxis Core test with time to spare.

Below the Time Limit	Close to the Time Limit	Over the Time Limit
What it means...		
Congratulations! This means you're controlling one of the most critical elements of the test: time itself. Your performance makes it likely you'll have enough time to return to unanswered questions to give them more attention. As a rule, you'll want to finish with about 15 minutes left on the test clock so you can address any questions you skipped or marked for review. Follow your preferred strategy, but stay attuned to the time. Be sure to mark questions on the computer for review so you know which ones you want to revisit. And return to them you should: The test is scored on a "rights-only" basis, which means incorrect answers won't result in any deduction in your score while correct responses will only add to it.	Keep doing what you're doing. If you are close to going over the time limit, look at the strategies in the next box. You want to make sure you don't exceed the time limit on your next test. You should also peek at the strategies in "below the time limit." They can help you gain more time.	Don't panic. See how many questions were left at the end—5? 10? 20? Depending on how many questions you have left, you may want to change your strategy. Diagnose why you're over the time limit. Are you fixating on certain questions? Are you just a slow test-taker? The best way to use time wisely is to find out what's slowing you down. Then practice, practice, practice.
What you should do...		
If you still have time after answering the skipped questions, double-check to make sure the answers you have filled match the right answer you chose for that number. Make sure you are happy with your answers and that you have made no simple mistakes.	Gauge your timing on different sections to see whether there are areas where you can pick up the pace. Make deals with yourself. For example, instead of continuously checking the clock, tell yourself something like this: By 11:30 I should be on No. 10.	If you're over the time limit, don't give in to the urge to skip questions. If you can eliminate even one choice, you increase your chances of getting it right. If not, use your fallback answer position. Bear in mind you're always better off guessing than not answering at all.
The takeaway...		
Keep an eye on how much time you have left and beware of any time-wasting traps.	You're going at a good pace. You may need to tweak your test-taking here and there, but all is well.	You're trying to answer as many questions correctly as you can. Since you won't lose points for an incorrect answer, guess on those that you don't know, and move on.

PART II:
Praxis Core Math Review

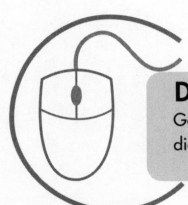

Diagnostic Test

Go to the online REA Study Center to take the diagnostic test to help focus your study.

(www.rea.com/studycenter)

OVERVIEW OF THE MATH TEST

If we give the same math problem to three people, it is very possible that all three will get the correct answer, and it also is possible that they will find that answer three different (and all correct) ways. The following four chapters provide hints for solving math problems on the Praxis Core Mathematics Test quickly and accurately. Each of these chapters is devoted to one of the Praxis Core Math categories:

- Number and Quantity. This chapter presents numbers in more than one way (for example, integers, fractions, and decimals); explains the properties of addition, subtraction, multiplication, and division; and shows how numbers are used in everyday problems, such as those using percentages, ratios, and proportions.

- Algebra and Functions. This chapter takes the mystery out of "What is *x*?" It presents real-life situations that can be solved in multiple ways, among them setting up equations, graphs, and functions to "decode" a problem.

- Geometry. Many common problems can be solved with an understanding of shapes and the relations among them. This chapter shows how applications of geometric shapes appear in our everyday world and how to deal with them, from figuring out how much paint to buy for a room to estimating how tall a building is based on its shadow.

- Probability and Statistics. Information is often given in visual displays (graphs and charts) or in terms of representations of a specific group of data. This chapter explains how to interpret different forms of data presentation and how to use numerical information to predict an outcome.

Questions on the test will come from one or several of these categories in no particular order.

QUESTION FORMATS

Questions in the math section of the Praxis test have one of three formats. Two of these formats are selected-response questions, which ask you to select either one correct answer choice (the usual multiple-choice format), or one or more answer choices (like a "multiple" multiple-choice format). The third format is numeric entry, in which you are asked to fill in a numeric answer to a problem.

Most of the questions on the test are multiple choice. That means you can either work the problem out and match your answer to one of the five answer choices, or you can find a way to pick out the correct answer choice without actually doing all of the calculations.

The second type of multiple-choice question has more than one correct answer choice, and you must choose *all* of them or you get no credit. There are two hints that the question is this type of multiple choice question on the computer-based Praxis test. First, whereas the regular multiple-choice questions have ovals next to the answer choices that you fill in with a click of the computer mouse, multiple multiple-choice questions have squares that you choose. Second, the on-screen instruction will ask you to indicate *all* such values, or to click on the correct response(s).

The third type of question is the numeric-entry, or fill-in question. These problems have boxes in which you place your answer. They require you to do the math to get the final answer and enter it in the box.

Many of the math examples and exercises in this book present solutions in more than one way, labeled "good" for a solution that will present the correct answer, "better" for a solution that has more insight and will save time on the test, and "best" for a solution that will solve the problem based on even more insight and often without much calculation.

The Praxis Math test has 56 questions you must answer in only 85 minutes, which means you have about a minute and a half for each question. Some of that time is spent reading the question and coming up with a method to find the solution, so time is precious. If you can find a quick and easy way to choose the correct answer, you will have more time for the difficult questions.

ITEM FORMATS

As stated above, the multiple-choice questions present five possible answers, and you have to choose the best one (or more than one in the case of multiple multiple-choice questions). On the actual computerized test, each of these choices is preceded by an oval or box to click on. For the sake of convenience, this book presents these choices as a series of lettered choices, A, B, C, D, and E. So for the examples and exercises in this book, instead of "clicking" your answer as you would on the computer version, you must choose the letter or letters for the correct answer. For the fill-in questions, simply place your answer in the box provided. For the practice tests, fill in the oval(s) or blanks on the separate answer sheet.

You can compare your choices to the correct solutions presented after each example or in a separate section following the exercises and practice tests. Every solution is accompanied by a detailed explanation of the steps used for the correct solution, which reinforces the text presentation for that topic. Also presented are explanations for many of the incorrect solutions in the multiple choices. The idea behind these explanations is that "you learn from your mistakes," so you often can see why a wrong answer is incorrect. Explanations of the correct answers for fill-in questions also reinforce what was explained in the text.

As tedious as it may seem, the good news is that filling in letter choices or numbers on an answer sheet in a prep book format such as this one takes more time than simply clicking an answer on a computer screen. Therefore, when you take a practice test in this book by using the answer sheet and you finish all 56 questions within the 85-minute limit, you are doing well.

COMPUTER LITERACY

We just said that computer answers (with a click) take less time than paper-and-pencil answers. This assumes that you are familiar with a computer. It is very important that you be comfortable using a computer and a mouse, and that you know how to navigate around the screen because you must "click" in the correct space to register your answer. If you want to change your answer, a second click removes the prior answer. Take as many online practice tests as you can to become familiar with the computer format. We strongly suggest you purchase the ETS Praxis interactive practice test. You can find it at *www.ets.org/prepare/materials/5732*. Use it after you use the ones at the back of this book.

ON-SCREEN CALCULATOR

The test center will provide you with pencils and scratch paper. Use these for simple problems, if needed, and use the on-screen calculator for more complicated math. A lot of the math that is needed on the test is "mental math," meaning that you won't need the scratch paper or the calculator—you can simply do the problem in your head (the quickest way).

```
Calculator                    X
                         0.
MR  MC  M+  (   )
7   8   9   ÷   C
4   5   6   ×   CE
1   2   3   −   √
±   0   .   +   =
        Transfer Display
```

The on-screen calculator (shown above) is a four-function calculator built into the testing software. Even if you think you are familiar with using a calculator, practice with one like that provided on-screen. Note that the number pads on calculators can vary, so make sure that when you practice, you note where the 0 is, where the four functions (+, −, ×, ÷) and the equal sign are, and how to display the answer.

A vitally important key on the online calculator is the "Transfer Display" key. The display on the calculator can go right into the box in numeric-entry questions that have a single box. This is not only a time-saver during the test—it also assures that you don't copy the answer incorrectly when typing it onto the test. But be careful, though, to be sure that the answer is in the correct form—don't press Transfer Display if the question asks for a fraction and the calculator display is the corresponding decimal. Remember that you can change your answer; a second click in the box deletes the answer.

Another feature of the online calculator is that it uses the correct order of operations, which is explained in both Chapters 4 and 5. This includes doing all multiplications and divisions before additions and subtractions, going left to right. Therefore, the problem $10 - 4 \times 2$ will calculate as the correct answer 2, rather than 12 (if done left to right without regard to the order of operations).

For specific instructions on using the online calculator, download ETS's primer on the on-screen calculator. You'll find it at *www.ets.org/praxis*; search under "on-screen calculator."

You'll find tips on how to use the calculator throughout the math review, but here's some basic advice:

1. Don't use a calculator if you can figure the answer out right away. If the calculation is 5×9, you should know that the answer is 45, so don't waste time using the calculator. It is better used for more complex multiplications such as 35×29, or divisions, such as $368 \div 16$.

2. If you have the time, you can check addition and subtraction with the calculator, but unless an addition problem is very long (involving lots of numbers), you are better off doing it by hand (using some of the hints to eliminate wrong answer choices presented in Chapter 4). For a problem with lots of numbers, there is a risk of entering one digit wrong and therefore wasting time and getting the wrong answer.

3. Use the calculator for square roots only if you don't know them. (Become familiar with perfect squares, see Chapter 4.)

4. Don't use the calculator simply because you can. Many problems can be solved by quickly eliminating the wrong answers instead of actually doing the calculation, as shown throughout this book. Remember that on average each question should take about 90 seconds, so if the calculation seems too complex, perhaps eliminating wrong answers is quicker and more accurate.

5. The calculator is only as accurate as the keys that are pressed, so be careful. As for all answers, make sure your calculations make sense. If you press the wrong function, say $\div$ instead of $-$, you may end up with a nonsensical answer. For example, if Jim has a collection of 27 miniature helmets and gives 5 to his younger brother, how many does he have left? You shouldn't even use the calculator for this (the answer is 22). But if you do use the calculator and press $\div$ instead of $-$, you get an answer of 5.4, which doesn't make sense.

Number and Quantity

THE REAL NUMBER SYSTEM

The Number Line

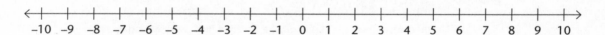

The **number line** actually goes on forever in both directions, so the line above is just part of it. Between the whole numbers shown on this line are actually infinitely many numbers, such as fractions and decimals. Any number is smaller than all of the numbers to the right of it and larger than any number to the left of it. Therefore, all positive numbers are larger than any negative number.

You should know the following symbols:

> < less than

> > greater than

> ≤ less than or equal to

> ≥ greater than or equal to

> ≠ not equal to

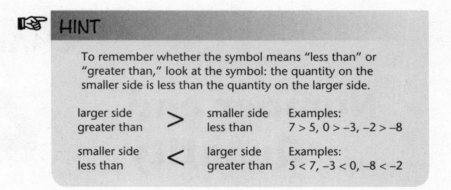

HINT

To remember whether the symbol means "less than" or "greater than," look at the symbol: the quantity on the smaller side is less than the quantity on the larger side.

| larger side greater than | > | smaller side less than | Examples: $7 > 5$, $0 > -3$, $-2 > -8$ |
| smaller side less than | < | larger side greater than | Examples: $5 < 7$, $-3 < 0$, $-8 < -2$ |

What was just written in a sentence as "all positive numbers are larger than any negative number" can be symbolized as

positive numbers > negative numbers   or   negative numbers < positive numbers

For example, $-3,678,295 < 20$.

Notice also on the number line that as the numbers get farther from zero, the digits increase. We are familiar with that on the positive side of the number line, but it takes some getting used to that fact on the negative side of the number line. For example, $-983 < -900$.

HINT

To remember how the digits on the positive and negative sides of zero get larger but the negative numbers themselves (with their – sign) get smaller the farther they are from zero, visualize a thermometer in Fargo, North Dakota.

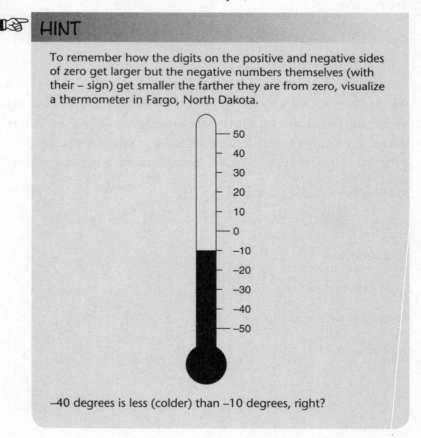

–40 degrees is less (colder) than –10 degrees, right?

The Praxis Core Math test quite often includes one problem in which a group of values has to be put in order, usually smallest to largest, as in Example 4.1.

EXAMPLE 4.1

Arrange the following from smallest to largest:

35, 49, –200, stripes on the American flag, 0, –1 million

(A) 35 < 49 < –200 < stripes on the American flag < 0, <–1 million

(B) –200 < stripes on the American flag < 0 < –1 million < 35 < 49

(C) –1 million < –200 < stripes on the American flag < 0 < 35 < 49

(D) –1 million < –200 < 0 < stripes on the American flag < 35 < 49

(E) –1 million < stripes on the American flag < –200 < 35 < 49 < 0

SOLUTION

The correct answer is (D).

Good solution: You can find the correct answer by going through each answer choice item by item and eliminating any that have one untrue statement (such as 49 < –200, since all positive numbers are greater than any negative number).

Better solution: Instead of going through each choice one by one, glance through all of them for "0" and eliminate any that show positive numbers on the left of (or less than) 0. Therefore, choices (A), (B), (C), and (E) are eliminated right away.

The phrase "stripes on the American flag" is included here to show that problems of this type don't necessarily have to be numbers—they can also be words that represent numbers. Later in this chapter, after we discuss fractions and decimals, this ordering type of problem will get even more interesting.

Absolute Value

Absolute value is defined as the distance of a number from 0 on the number line. It is the value of the number without regard to sign. For example, –6 is 6 units from 0, and +4 is 4 units from 0. Their places on the number line say that $+4 > -6$. However, their absolute values, or distances from 0 on the number line, say that $|-6| > |+4|$ because 6 units is greater than 4 units. The symbol for absolute value is two vertical lines $||$.

EXAMPLE 4.2

What is the distance from −5 to +3 on the number line?

SOLUTION

The correct answer is 8 units.

Good solution: Difference is found by subtracting one value from another, but we have to take the absolute value of that difference to get distance. So the distance from −5 to +3 on the number line is $|-5 - (+3)| = |-5 - 3| = |-8| = 8$ units.

Better solution: Eliminate the possibility of getting the minus signs mixed up if you can visualize the number line and count the units between each number (here, −5 and +3). This will give 5 units on the negative side of 0 plus 3 units on the positive side of 0, or $5 + 3 = 8$.

Notice the difference between the distance from −5 to +3 (8 units, as seen in Example 4.2) and the distance from −5 to −3: $|-5 - (-3)| = |-5 + 3| = |-2| = 2$ units, or the distance from 5 to 3: $|5 - (3)| = |5 - 3| = |2| = 2$ units. Better yet, visualize the points on the number line.

We will see in Chapter 6 how absolute value is used to figure distance between points on the two-dimensional coordinate plane.

Note that since any positive number is greater than any negative number, $1 > -23,896$ because 1 is to the right of −23,896 on the number line. However, there is no doubt that $|-23,896| > |1|$.

Classifying Numbers

This section is about the real number system—but are there any "un-real" numbers? Well, yes, there are, and they are called, not surprisingly, imaginary numbers. We will get to them after we talk about square roots, so let's not get ahead of ourselves here and just concentrate on real numbers, the ones we are used to, for now. **Real numbers** include:

Natural numbers, or counting numbers (1, 2, 3, 4, …)

Whole numbers, which are natural numbers with a 0 (0, 1, 2, 3, 4, …)

Integers, which are whole numbers but also include negative numbers (… ,−3, −2, −1, 0, 1, 2, 3, …)

Between the whole numbers are **fractions** (such as $\frac{3}{4}$) and **decimals** (such as 3.256), which we will discuss later in this chapter.

You should know these classifications for problems such as Example 4.3.

EXAMPLE 4.3

How many whole numbers are there between –4 and +3?

    (A) 8

    (B) 7

    (C) 4

    (D) 3

    (E) 0, 1, 2

SOLUTION

The correct answer is (D), 3.

This example seems innocent enough, but most people get it wrong. First of all, it is asking for whole numbers, so no negative numbers are counted for the answer—forget answer choices (A) and (B). Second, remember that 0 is a whole number, so count it. Then count 1 and 2 in the answer, but do not include 3 because the problem says "between." That means only the numbers 0, 1, and 2 should be included. Finally, the question is asking how *many* of these whole numbers there are, which is answer choice (D), 3. It does not ask *what* these whole numbers are (answer choice (E)). So this seemingly easy question really needs your attention. It isn't difficult, but your analyzing skills must come into play.

Prime Numbers

Another classification is whether the number is prime or composite (the opposite of prime). A **prime** number is not divisible by any positive number except 1 and itself. The first several prime numbers are 2, 3, 5, 7, 11, 13, 17, and 19—no positive numbers divide into any of these numbers, nor the next prime number. Do you know what that is?

All non-prime numbers are called **composite** numbers, and they may be divisible by several numbers. For example, the number 4 is the first composite number, and it is divisible by 1, 2, and 4 because $2 \times 2 = 4$, and $1 \times 4 = 4$. Therefore, we say the *factors* of 4 are 1, 2, and 4. All even numbers (except 2, which is prime) are divisible by 2, so all even numbers are composite numbers.

EXAMPLE 4.4

What are all of the factors of 12?

    (A) 2, 3, 4, 6

    (B) 3×4

    (C) 2×6

    (D) 1, 2, 3, 4, 6, 12

    (E) 12 is prime

SOLUTION

The correct answer is (D), 1, 2, 3, 4, 6, and 12.

To list all of the factors, remember to include the number and 1 as factors.

It's a Fact!

The number **1** is considered to be neither prime nor composite.

NUMBER PROPERTIES

Number properties are well known by anyone who has to add, subtract, multiply, and divide numbers, even though the names may not be as familiar as the properties themselves. Although you should (and probably do) know the properties, you should know both the name and what it means for the Praxis Core Math test.

Properties of Addition and Subtraction

Addition has some very useful properties, all of which come from the fact that you can add numbers in any order.

Commutative Property of Addition

An example of the **commutative property of addition** is $3 + 5 = 5 + 3$. The name *commutative* comes from the word *commute*, which means to change position (like commuting to school—going from home to school). Changing the position of the numbers does not affect the answer. This extends to adding any string of positive numbers:

$$3 + 5 + 6 = 5 + 3 + 6 = 6 + 3 + 5$$

and so on.

Associative Property of Addition

In addition, we can also group numbers by using parentheses, so we can say, for example:

$$3 + (5 + 6) = (5 + 3) + 6 = (6 + 3) + 5$$

as well as a whole lot of other variations of the numbers and groupings. This grouping property has the name **associative property of addition** because we are *associating* numbers with other numbers in different groups.

We can use the associative property to make finding a sum easier. When we add 3 + 6 + 7 + 4, it is faster to add the 3 + 7 together and the 6 + 4 together (mentally) because we recognize 3 + 7 = 10 and 6 + 4 = 10, and the answer is 20. Compare that to adding in the order given: 3 + 6 = 9, then 9 + 7 = 16, then 16 + 4 = 20. Whenever you can group numbers together that add to 10, it makes adding a string of numbers easier than adding them in the order in which they were given.

EXAMPLE 4.5

What is the sum of the numbers 17, 18, 25, 12, 13, and 5?

SOLUTION

The correct answer is 90.

Good solution: If you got 90, you are correct. But how did you get that answer? Did you go down the line, saying 17 + 18 is 35, and 35 + 25 is 60, and 60 + 12 is 72, and 72 + 13 is 85, and finally 85 + 5 is 90? That works, obviously, but is it the best way to do this addition?

Another good solution: Perhaps you wrote the numbers in a column and added the units column first, carrying the tens digit and then adding the tens column:

$$
\begin{array}{r}
\overset{3}{1}7 \\
18 \\
25 \\
12 \\
13 \\
+\ 5 \\
\hline
90
\end{array}
$$

Better solution: Use the column method, but instead of adding the units digits as they appear, group them into tens (7 + 3, 8 + 2, 5 + 5) by using the associative property to get three groups of 10 (which equal 30), write the 0 in the units column and carry the 3 into the tens column to get 3 + 1 + 1 + 2 + 1 + 1 = 9, and finally the answer 90. If you used this method, it actually is faster and less prone to errors than the first method (even though it took a longer time to describe it).

Best solution: Use your calculator and enter the six numbers to get 90. That is the most accurate way to do this problem, and maybe even the fastest. With calculators being so readily available, this last choice is what most people do.

The Praxis Core Math test comes with an on-screen calculator, so this last method works well for this problem. You should not forget, however, how to do problems in your head. A question that requires you to multiply 6×8 should not be done on the calculator unless you are so nervous about the test that you forget $6 \times 8 = 48$ (which can happen). In many cases, problems indeed can be done in your head. In some cases, you are better off using the online calculator, such as when presented with multiplying 68 by 139. Yes, you can do this on scratch paper, and you must be prepared to do so, but if you have a calculator, use it and go on to the next question.

Let's look at a multiple-choice variation of Example 4.5 with five choices for the answer.

EXAMPLE 4.6

What is the sum of 17, 18, 25, 12, 13, and 5?

    (A) 60

    (B) 85

    (C) 87

    (D) 90

    (E) 120

SOLUTION

The correct answer is (D), 90.

Good solution: Use your calculator to get the answer. But be careful to enter the numbers accurately.

Better solution: Often you can save time by eliminating answers that are obviously wrong. Rather than jumping in and completely solving a multiple-choice problem, glance at the choices. Some are obviously not going to work. For this problem, there are six numbers and most are more than 10 and less than 20. That would eliminate answer choices (A) and (E) right away. If you group tens in the units column, you can see that the units digit must be a 0. You don't have to go any further. The only correct answer choice is (D), 90.

Subtraction Properties

Because the order in which the numbers appear makes a difference in subtraction (that is, which number is subtracted from which), the operation of subtraction isn't associative or commutative. For example, $7 - 4 \neq 4 - 7$ and $(5 + 2) - 3 \neq 3 - (5 + 2)$.

Properties of Multiplication and Division

This section discusses three of the most important properties of multiplication, which can simplify problems greatly.

Commutative Property of Multiplication

Just as for addition, multiplication can be done in any order (also called the **commutative property**, this time for multiplication). So $3 \times 8 = 8 \times 3$. And $3 \times 5 \times 2$ is the same as $3 \times 2 \times 5$ or $5 \times 3 \times 2$ or many other combinations of these three numbers. The **products** (answers in multiplication) are the same.

Associative Property of Multiplication

The commutative property allows us to "group" numbers in multiplication. This grouping has the name **associative property**, and it makes finding the product easier.

EXAMPLE 4.7

What is the product of $7 \times 4 \times 25$?

SOLUTION

The correct answer is 700.

Good solution: Multiply the numbers as they appear: $(7 \times 4) \times 25 = 28 \times 25 = 700$.

Better solution: Recognize that $25 \times 4 = 100$, so the problem is really the same as $7 \times (4 \times 25) = 7 \times 100 = 700$.

Distributive Property

Another property of multiplication is that $6(3 + 4) = (6 \times 3) + (6 \times 4)$. This is called the **distributive property** because multiplication by 6 is "distributed" to each term in the parentheses. Parentheses say "do me first," so this problem is viewed easily as $6 \times 7 = 42$. The distributive property is strictly a property of multiplication.

Division Properties

Just as for subtraction, where the order of the terms makes a difference, order makes a difference for division. Obviously, the answer for $4 \div 2$ ($= 2$) is different from the answer for $2 \div 4$ ($= \frac{1}{2}$). The commutative and associative properties don't work for division.

ORDER OF OPERATIONS

- *Parentheses:* Parentheses say "do me first." In other words, evaluate what is in the parentheses ( ) or brackets [ ] or braces { }, working from the inside out, until they are all gone.

- *Exponents:* Evaluate any part of the expression that contains exponents (such as $2^3 = 2 \times 2 \times 2 = 8$; see Chapter 5) next.

- *Multiplication and Division:* Do any multiplication and/or division in order from left to right.

- *Addition and Subtraction:* Do any addition and/or subtraction in order from left to right.

This order is often remembered by the mnemonic word PEMDAS, in which each letter stands for one of the above operations in order. (A **mnemonic** is a method to help memory—it doesn't even have to be a real word.) A mnemonic sentence for the same order of operations is the sentence "**P**lease **E**xcuse **M**y **D**ear **A**unt **S**ally," which uses the first letter of each word. You just have to remember what operations they stand for.

So even if the equation without the parentheses, $x = 7 \times 2 + 4 \times 2$, is evaluated, PEMDAS tells us to do the multiplication, $7 \times 2 + 4 \times 2$, first, and then the addition:

$$x = 7 \times 2 + 4 \times 2 = 14 + 8 = 22.$$

If the operations were done as they appear, without regard to the order of operations, the incorrect answer would be $x = 7 \times 2 + 4 \times 2 = 14 + 4 \times 2 = 18 \times 2 = 36$.

TEST-TAKING STRATEGIES

There are several ways to answer the questions on the Praxis Core Math test, and of course you want to use the fastest and most accurate way. This takes practice, which is why this book presents so many drills and exercises—so that you will be comfortable during the test, and hopefully in the real world, figuring out mathematical problems. The math questions on the Praxis test do not just bombard you with arithmetic. They require analysis, and some require you to see another way to do the problem. Let's look at some more examples and the methods used to solve them.

EXAMPLE 4.8

Find the following sum: $362 + 455 + 608 + 781 =$

(A) 1057

(B) 2201

(C) 2315

(D) 906

(E) 2206

SOLUTION

The correct answer is (E), 2206.

Good solution: Rewrite the numbers in columns and add as usual, starting with the units column and carrying over to the columns to the left. Or use the calculator and enter the numbers and + signs to get 2206 as the answer. Then match your answer to one of the given choices.

Better solution: Look at the units digits of each number and mentally add them by combining the 2 and 8 to get 10. Since the 5 and 1, which equal 6, are left, the last digit in the answer must be 6, which eliminates all answers except (D) and (E). Immediately dismiss (D) as an answer because it clearly isn't big enough. So the answer must be (E).

EXAMPLE 4.9

The product of 34698×4872 is ☐.

    (A) 139,648,292

    (B) 169,048,656

    (C) 169,048,655

    (D) 169,048,654

    (E) 269,048,654

SOLUTION

The correct answer choice is (B), 169,048,656.

Good solution: Multiply these numbers out by hand. Or use a calculator. But what if you got an answer on the calculator that is none of the above choices because you pressed one wrong digit? Well, you have to enter the numbers all over again.

Better solution: Determine that the answer has to end in a 6 because the product of the units digits in the numbers ($8 \times 2 = 16$) ends in a 6. Then the only answer choice is (B). Analysis—it works every time.

Before we get to Example 4.10, notice that the letters in the answer choices are in squares. This is because this is a "multiple-multiple"-choice question with more than one possible correct answer choice. To get credit for this type of question, you must choose *all* of the correct choices. No partial credit is given. Multiple-multiple choice questions on the computer-based Praxis Core test require you to check the squares next to every correct choice. Here, we present choices with squares around them to indicate that more than one choice is correct.

EXAMPLE 4.10

Which of these numbers is evenly divisible by 5? Choose *all* of the correct answers.

- A 4,869,300
- B 49,273,729
- C 8,491,735
- D 90
- E 7.845,919

SOLUTION

The correct answers are A , C , and D . You must choose all three to earn credit.

Good solution: Divide 5 into each number to see if it divides evenly (without a remainder), or use your calculator to do that.

Better solution: Recognize that 5 times any number always ends in a 0 or a 5, which is true only for answers A , C , and D —a quick and easy solution.

DECIMALS

Understanding Decimals

Decimals are based on the number 10. The placeholders for numbers written in decimal form are as shown below.

1	2	3	4	5	.	6	7	8	9
ten thousands	thousands	hundreds	tens	units	decimal point	tenths	hundredths	thousandths	ten thousandths

The decimal point is the "borderline" between the whole number part of a decimal number and the decimal part of the number. Note that although there is a units column for the whole numbers, the smallest unit for decimals is tenths. You should be able to read any decimal number according to the place values of its digits. The decimal point is stated as "and."

So, placing the digits in their correct places, we can see that 4.3 is read as four and three tenths, and 2,006.73 is read as two-thousand six and seventy-three hundredths.

EXAMPLE 4.11

How would you write the decimal number for one million seventeen and nine thousandths?

(A) 1,017,000.009

(B) 1,000,017.009

(C) 1,000,017.9

(D) 1,000,000.179

(E) 117,000,000.009

SOLUTION

The correct answer is (B), 1,000,017.009.

Note that zeroes fill in for the tenths and hundredths places before writing nine thousandths.

When multiplying or dividing a decimal by 10, 100, and so on, all that needs to be done is to move the decimal point. When multiplying by 10 or a power of 10, since the number will be larger, move the decimal point in the original number to the right the same number of spaces that there are zeroes in the multiplier. Conversely, when dividing by 10 or a power of 10, since the number will be smaller, move the decimal point in the original number to the left the same number of spaces that there are zeroes in the divisor.

For example, $134.5278 \times 100 = 13452.78$ (move the decimal point two spaces to the right because there are two zeroes in 100), and $4592.401 \div 1000 = 4.592401$ (move the decimal point three spaces to the left because there are three zeroes in 1000).

Scientific Notation

Scientific notation refers to a way of writing numbers that are either too large or too small to be conveniently written as decimals. Examples are the distance of Earth from the sun, which is 93,000,000 miles (this number is rounded—see the next section), or the weight of an atomic particle, which is .000,000,000,000,000,000,000,000,006,645 kilograms (also rounded).

Numbers in scientific notation have two parts, a decimal with an absolute value from 1 to 10 (but not including 10), and a power of 10. The scientific notation for the two values in the preceding paragraph is written like this: 9.3×10^7 and 6.645×10^{-27}. Notice that in scientific notation, there is only one digit before the decimal point and that the power of 10 reflects how many places the decimal point in the original (long) number had to move to end up with only one digit before it. A negative exponent indicates that the original number is less than 1, and a positive exponent indicates that the original number is 1 or greater.

EXAMPLE 4.12

Which of these numbers is not in scientific notation?

(A) 5.15×10^8

(B) -3.16×10^{17}

(C) 6.2038×10^8

(D) 0.427×10^1

(E) 9.0×10^{-4}

SOLUTION

The correct answer is (D), 0.427×10^1.

This is not in scientific notation because the absolute value of 0.427 is not between 1 and 10. Note that answer choice (B) is in scientific notation because negative numbers are allowed, and answer choice (E) is also in scientific notation because the exponent is negative for values less than 1.

Rounding

Rounding numbers comes up especially when dealing with decimals. Rounding is what is done when you are asked for a number "to the nearest dollar," or "to the nearest hundredth." You actually do rounding without thinking of it when you see something that sells for $3.98 and you automatically say to yourself that the price is four dollars.

The rule for **rounding** is to look at the next placeholder after the one you want to round to, and if it is 5 or more, add 1 to the placeholder to the left. If it is less than 5, just drop that digit and all the others to the right. So to round $3.98 to the nearest dollar, look only at the digit to the right of the dollar digit. It is 9, which is greater than 5, so add 1 to the 3 dollars, and you get $4.00. Forget about the 8, which is in the hundredths (cents) place. It doesn't even get considered.

EXAMPLE 4.13

Round $12.49 to the nearest dollar.

(A) $13.00

(B) $12.00

(C) $12.50

(D) $12.45

(E) $1.245

SOLUTION

The answer is (B), $12.00.

You should look only at the 4, the next number after the dollar column. Four is less than 5, so just drop the 4 and everything to the right of it. Don't fall into the trap of rounding the 49 cents to 50 cents and then adding 1 to the $12 because the next column to the right is now equal to 5. Look only at the column right next to the one you are rounding. Ignore the others.

Addition and Subtraction of Decimal Numbers

Decimals are added, subtracted, multiplied, and divided similar to integers, but the decimal point must be taken into account.

When adding or subtracting decimal numbers, simply align the decimal points and fill in zeroes as needed.

EXAMPLE 4.14

Add the following decimals: $83.295 + 4.17 + 245.6 = \boxed{}$.

SOLUTION

The correct answer is 333.065.

Add these numbers on the calculator, but be sure you include the decimal point in the correct position, and the answer will come up with the decimal point placed correctly. If adding these numbers by hand, be sure to align the decimal points.

$$
\begin{array}{r}
83.295 \\
4.170 \\
+\ 245.600 \\
\hline
333.065
\end{array}
$$

Note that zeroes are filled in to help align the numbers, and the addition is the same as for whole numbers.

The same is true for subtraction, as shown in Example 4.15.

EXAMPLE 4.15

The electric usage in June at Kayla's house was 85.522 kWh, and in July it jumped to 118.76 kWh. How much more energy was used in July, when the air conditioner was running full-time?

SOLUTION

The correct answer is 33.238 kWh.

We get the answer by subtracting 85.522 from 118.76.

$$
\begin{array}{r}
118.760 \\
-\ 85.522 \\
\hline
33.238
\end{array}
$$

Notice a few things about this solution. First, the decimal points must be aligned. Second, a zero was added to 118.76 so that the two numbers had the same number of digits after the decimal point. And third, the answer has the same measurement as the original numbers (kWh, which stands for kilowatt-hours). We will talk about measurement at the end of this chapter. This subtraction can be done manually or on the calculator.

Multiplication of Decimal Numbers

Multiplication of decimals is done the same as for whole numbers. The placement of the decimal point is determined after the multiplication process. Count from the decimal point to the end of each number being multiplied. This total is the number of places to count from the end of the answer to put the decimal point.

EXAMPLE 4.16

Multiply $26.25 \times 37.5 = \boxed{}$.

    (A) 98.4375

    (B) 984.375

    (C) 9.84375

    (D) 98.4300

    (E) .984375

SOLUTION

The correct answer is (B), 984.375.

Good solution: If you multiply this out by hand, you should get:

$$
\begin{array}{r}
2\ 6.2\ 5 \quad \text{(2 decimal places)} \\
\times\ 3\ 7.5 \quad \text{(1 decimal place)} \\
\hline
1\ 3\ 1\ 2\ 5 \quad\quad\quad\quad\quad \\
1\ 8\ 3\ 7\ 5\ 0 \quad\quad\quad\quad \\
7\ 8\ 7\ 5\ 0\ 0 \quad\quad\quad\quad\quad \\
\hline
9\ 8\ 4.3\ 7\ 5 \quad \text{(3 decimal places)}
\end{array}
$$

Notice that there are $2 + 1 = 3$ total decimal places in the numbers being multiplied, so there should be three decimal places in the answer. Of course, given the option, you would do this multiplication by using a calculator; be sure to enter the decimal places in their original positions, and the decimal in the answer will automatically be in the correct position.

Better solution: Note that the numbers to be multiplied are close to 25 and 40, whose product is about 1,000, so (B) is the only logical answer.

Best solution: Use your analytical powers to notice that the answer must have three digits after the decimal point, so the only correct answer must be (B), no matter what the numerals are. Note that even if (D) were to be considered (after all, zeroes at the end of a decimal don't change the value), the answer must end in a 5 because the two multipliers end in 5's and $5 \times 5 = 25$, so the answer must end in a 5 as well.

Let's look at another example involving multiplication of decimals.

EXAMPLE 4.17

Theo has a job that pays an hourly wage of $9.75 plus commission on the sales he makes. His commission rate is .015. Last month, Theo sold $12,450.75 in goods. What was his commission?

    (A) $186.76

    (B) $187.00

    (C) $196.75

    (D) $186.77

    (E) Cannot tell from the information given.

SOLUTION

The correct answer is (A), $186.76.

To find the commission, multiply his sales times his commission rate, $12,450.75 \times 0.015$. Use the calculator or do it by hand:

$$
\begin{array}{r}
1\ 2\ 4\ 5\ 0\ .\ 7\ 5 \quad \text{(2 decimal places)} \\
\times \qquad .\ 0\ 1\ 5 \quad \text{(3 decimal places)} \\
\hline
6\ 2\ 2\ 5\ 3\ 7\ 5 \qquad\qquad \\
1\ 2\ 4\ 5\ 0\ 7\ 5\ 0 \qquad\qquad \\
0\ 0\ 0\ 0\ 0\ 0\ 0\ 0 \qquad\qquad \\
\hline
1\ 8\ 6\ .\ 7\ 6\ 1\ 2\ 5 \quad \text{(5 decimal places)}
\end{array}
$$

Since we are talking about money, this answer should be rounded to the nearest cent, and since the digit to the right of the "cents" (hundredths) digit is 1, we just drop it and all the others, and we get $186.76. Nowhere does it say anything about rounding to the nearest dollar, so choice (B) is wrong. This is not a "trick" question (relax—the Praxis Core Math test doesn't have trick questions), but it does give you more information than you need by telling you his hourly wage. That doesn't figure into Theo's commission, so answer (C) is wrong for several reasons. Answer (D) is just rounded incorrectly, and, of course, there is enough information given, so answer (E) is incorrect.

Division of Decimal Numbers

Just as for the other operations on decimals, when dividing decimals, do the division as though you were dividing whole numbers. But after the division, figure out where the decimal point should go in the answer by using the following method.

Count the number of places after the decimal point in the divisor (number doing the dividing), and starting at the existing decimal point in the dividend (number being divided into), count over that many places, and put the decimal point in the **quotient** (the answer) above that place.

EXAMPLE 4.18

Divide 96.39 by 3.5.

SOLUTION

The correct answer is 27.54.

Divide as though the problem had whole numbers: 9639 divided by 35 (for the time being, ignore the decimal points). Then, when you get the answer, figure out where the decimal point goes. The number of places after the decimal point in 3.5 is 1. Starting at the existing decimal point in 96.39, count over one place to between the 3 and the 9, and place the decimal point in the answer above it. Here that is between the 7 and 5, the numbers above the 3 and the 9. When done, the division will look like the following:

$$
\begin{array}{r}
2\ 7.5\ 4 \\
3.5\overline{)\ 9\ 6.3\ 9\ 0} \\
\underline{7\ 0} \\
2\ 6\ 3 \\
\underline{2\ 4\ 5} \\
1\ 8\ 9 \\
\underline{1\ 7\ 5} \\
1\ 4\ 0 \\
\underline{1\ 4\ 0}
\end{array}
$$

Note that we added the last zero in the dividend because adding zeroes to the right after the decimal point does not change the value of a number, and in this case, it makes the answer come out evenly. Of course, a calculator will figure out where the decimal point goes automatically.

EXAMPLE 4.19

Jane wants to give each of the kids at her daughter's party four nickels to hide for a game. There are 9 girls at the party, and Jane has $1.70 in nickels. Does she have enough nickels?

    (A) Yes, and she will have two nickels ($.10) left over.

    (B) Yes, that is exactly the right amount.

    (C) No, she needs two more nickels ($.10 more).

    (D) No, she needs ten more nickels ($.50 more).

    (E) Cannot tell from the information given.

SOLUTION

The correct answer is (C), no, she needs two more nickels ($.10 more).

Good solution: Determine how many girls can get four nickels each if the nickels add up to $1.70. Four nickels is $.20, so we divide $1.70 by $.20 to see whether we get 9 (or more):

$$.20 \overline{)1.70\,0}\quad 8.5$$

Note that we added the last zero in the dividend because adding zeroes at the end of a decimal point does not change the value of a number, and in this case, it makes the answer come out evenly. Note also that 8.5 rounded up would give us 9, but in the context of this problem, we cannot round up 8.5. When an answer involves a part of a person, such as here where we got 8.5 people, we usually round down, even if the number after the decimal point is greater than 5, because a part of a person doesn't make sense. Here we are interested only in whether the answer is ≥ 9.

Better solution: Figure out how much money Jane needs. Each of 9 girls would have four nickels, which are worth $.05 apiece, so the amount of money is $9 \times 4 \times \$.05 = \$1.80$, so Jane doesn't have enough. In fact, she needs $.10 (or two nickels) more.

Comparing Decimals

To compare numbers containing decimals, write each decimal part with the same number of digits, determined by the decimal with the largest number of digits. Again, as we saw previously, remember that any positive number is greater than any negative number. Next, compare the whole number parts of the number (the parts before the decimal points). Finally, for numbers with identical whole number parts, compare the decimals by comparing first the tenths digits, then the hundredths, and so on. Remember for negative numbers that the larger the digit, the smaller the negative number.

EXAMPLE 4.20

Arrange the following numbers from smallest to largest:

$$9.325, -8.44, 6.053, 0.2988, 0, 0.5$$

(A) $9.325 < -8.44 < 6.053 < 0.5 < 0.2988 > 0$

(B) $-8.44 < 0 < 6.053 < 0.5 < 0.2988 < 9.325$

(C) $-8.44 < 0 < 0.2988 < 0.5 < 6.053 < 9.325$

(D) $-8.44 < 0.2988 < 0.5 < 0 < 6.053 < 9.325$

(E) $9.325 < 6.053 < 0.5 < 0.2988 < 0 < -8.44$

SOLUTION

The correct answer is (C), $-8.44 < 0 < 0.2988 < 0.5 < 6.053 < 9.325$.

This answer choice has the negative number as the smallest, then the 0, which separates the negative number from the positive numbers, which are arranged according to their whole number parts. The two numbers with a 0 whole number part are arranged according to the tenths place. Note that answer choice (E) arranges the numbers from largest to smallest, the wrong order.

Now let's arrange some decimal numbers that have no whole number parts.

EXAMPLE 4.21

Arrange the following numbers from smallest to largest:

$$0.325, -0.44, 0.053, -0.2988, 0, 0.05$$

SOLUTION

The correct answer is –0.44, –0.2988, 0, 0.05, 0.053, 0.325.

In this case, we have only the decimal parts to compare since there are no whole numbers. It is easiest to do this by writing the numbers in a vertical list with the decimal points aligned (but we aren't going to add them, just compare them—it is easier to see in column form). Also, fill in zeroes after the numbers so all decimals have the same number of places, as shown below.

$$0.3250$$
$$-0.4400$$
$$0.0530$$
$$-0.2988$$
$$0.0000$$
$$0.0500$$

Since negative numbers are always smaller than positive numbers, and the example asks for smallest to largest, first group the negative numbers together and compare the tenths place. Remember that the digits in negative numbers are ordered opposite from positive numbers (see the number line). Zero goes between the negative and positive numbers. When comparing positive numbers, if any numbers have the same digit in the tenths place, compare the hundredths places, and if necessary compare the thousands places. So now we have

$$-0.4400$$
$$-0.2988$$
$$0.0000$$
$$0.0500$$
$$0.0530$$
$$0.3250$$

or, dropping the extra zeroes at the ends of the decimals, and writing the answer horizontally,

$$-0.44, -0.2988, 0, 0.05, 0.053, 0.325.$$

The next section looks at fractions, which are just another way to write decimals. To convert a decimal to a fraction, just write out the digits over the lowest placeholder. For example, the lowest placeholder for .25 is hundredths, so this is $\frac{25}{100}$ in fraction form. Often these fractions can be rewritten as simpler fractions, which will be shown next.

FRACTIONS

Understanding Fractions

Yet another number classification is **rational numbers**, which are simply all numbers that can be written as fractions, or one integer divided by another integer. Examples are $\frac{1}{4}$, $\frac{2}{3}$, $\frac{5}{1}$, $\frac{12}{5}$.

A fraction has two parts, a **numerator** (top) and a **denominator** (bottom).

$$\text{fraction} = \frac{\text{numerator}}{\text{denominator}}$$

 HINT

> As a reminder of which part of the fraction gets divided into the other part, think of the fraction $\frac{1}{4}$, which we normally call a quarter. Then think of the coin called a quarter. If you divide the bottom number (denominator) into the top (numerator), you get $4\overline{)1.00}$ with $.25$ on top, which is the value of a quarter, $.25$. If you make the mistake of dividing the top number into the bottom number, you get $1\overline{)4.00}$ with 4.00 on top, or $4, obviously wrong.

Fractions are actually division problems, in which the numerator is divided by the denominator and the answer is a decimal. If that decimal ends (the remainder becomes zero) or if that decimal repeats, it is a rational number. If the decimal equivalent doesn't end or doesn't repeat, it is not a rational number, and it is called (no surprise) an irrational number. Examples of irrational numbers include some square roots, discussed later in this chapter, and the symbol π, used with circles and discussed in the chapter on geometry.

Now let's look at the four example fractions above $\left(\frac{1}{4}, \frac{2}{3}, \frac{5}{1}, \frac{12}{5}\right)$ to see whether they are rational. We already looked at the first one, $\frac{1}{4}$, in the Hint.

Next, $\frac{2}{3} = 3\overline{)2.000}$ with 0.666 on top. This is an example of a repeating decimal; so $\frac{2}{3}$ is rational (of course it is because it is a fraction with an integer over an integer).

The fraction $\frac{5}{1} = 1$, also rational, is included here to show that all whole numbers are rational numbers because they can all be made into fractions with 1 as the denominator.

The last fraction, $\frac{12}{5} = 5 \overline{)12.0}^{\,2.4}$ is rational and also a mixed number, which means it has a whole number part and a decimal part, or a whole number part and a fraction (in this case, $2\frac{2}{5}$), as we will see next.

Improper Fractions and Mixed Numbers

Fractions come in two flavors: proper and improper. **Proper fractions** have values less than or equal to 1. **Improper fractions** have values greater than 1. The first three of the fractions we just discussed are proper fractions. We saw that we can divide the numerator into the denominator to get their decimal equivalents.

Fractions are recognized as being improper if the numerator is larger than the denominator, like $\frac{12}{5}$ above. To convert an improper fraction into a mixed number (with a whole number part and a fraction part), just divide the numerator into the denominator, as we did above, but once you get the whole number, convert the remainder into the numerator of the new fraction part of the mixed number (the denominator is the same as the original denominator, or the divisor). For example, as we showed above for $\frac{12}{5}$, when 5 is divided into 12, we get 2 as the whole number part and the remainder is $12 - 10 = 2$, which now is the new numerator of the fraction in the mixed number, so $\frac{12}{5} = 2\frac{2}{5}$. This is an important concept, so let's do a drill on this. You should be able to do these calculations in your head.

Drill: Converting Improper Fractions into Mixed Numbers

a. $\frac{79}{10}$	b. $\frac{85}{9}$	c. $\frac{23}{8}$	d. $\frac{61}{7}$	e. $\frac{43}{6}$
f. $\frac{27}{5}$	g. $\frac{18}{4}$	h. $\frac{17}{4}$	i. $\frac{9}{2}$	j. $\frac{32}{5}$

Answers on page 88.

Conversely, we can convert mixed numbers into improper fractions, which we will see can be useful when multiplying and dividing fractions. Since we divided to convert $\frac{12}{5}$ into $2\frac{2}{5}$, we use multiplication (because multiplication and division are inverses of each other, as shown later in this chapter) to convert $2\frac{2}{5}$ back into an improper fraction. Multiply the denominator and the whole number, and then add the numerator to that number for the new numerator; the denominator remains the same. So we have $2\frac{3}{5} = \frac{(5 \times 2) + 3}{5} = \frac{13}{5}$. Again, you should be able to do most conversions from mixed numbers to improper fractions in your head.

EXAMPLE 4.22

What is the simplest mixed number equivalent of $\frac{17}{4}$? Choose *all* of the correct answers.

A $4\frac{3}{4}$

B 4.25

C $4\frac{1}{17}$

D $4\frac{1}{4}$

E $3\frac{5}{4}$

SOLUTION

The correct answers are B, 4.25, and D, $4\frac{1}{4}$.

Even though 4.25 is a decimal, it still can technically be considered a mixed number if it has a whole number part and a decimal number part. However, the term "mixed number" is usually used for fractions. It was included here to alert you to look for equivalent answers. The Praxis test won't throw you a curve like this one, though—it is more straightforward and there are no trick questions. Answer choice A is incorrect because of a math error. Answer choice C is incorrect because the denominator should stay the same, it isn't changed to the numerator. Answer choice E is incorrect because it still has an improper fraction in it, and the question asked for the *simplest* mixed number. Note that more than one answer is indicated by the squares on the answer choices as well as the "Choose *all* of the correct answers" statement.

EXAMPLE 4.23

Convert $5\frac{3}{8}$ to an improper fraction. Choose *all* of the correct answers.

A $\frac{43}{8}$

B 5.375

C $\frac{86}{16}$

D $\frac{29}{8}$

E $\frac{40}{8}$

SOLUTION

The correct answers are A , $\frac{43}{8}$, and C , $\frac{86}{16}$.

There are a couple of curves being thrown here to keep you on your toes. Answer choice A is straightforward. Answer choice C is not so obvious, but it is just double $\frac{43}{8}$, so it qualifies as an improper fraction also equal to $5\frac{3}{8}$. Answer choice B , although it is equivalent to $5\frac{3}{8}$, is not an improper *fraction*, which is what the question asked. Answer choice D multiplied the denominator by the numerator and added the whole number—a jumble of the true calculation, and answer choice E forgot to add the numerator (3) in the final calculation.

Simplifying Fractions

We usually want fractions to be in their "lowest form," which means $\frac{1}{2}$ rather than its equivalents $\frac{4}{8}$ or $\frac{3}{6}$. Simplifying a fraction is based on the mathematical rule that 1 times any value doesn't change the value (that is, $6 \times 1 = 6$), and the fact that a fraction that is the same on the top and bottom is equivalent to 1, such as $\frac{5}{5} = 1$. So if you multiply the top and bottom of a fraction by the same number, the value of the fraction remains the same: $\frac{3}{4} = \frac{3}{4} \times \frac{2}{2} = \frac{3 \times 2}{4 \times 2} = \frac{6}{8}$. So $\frac{3}{4}$ and $\frac{6}{8}$ are equal.

Putting a fraction in its lowest form, called *simplifying* the fraction, involves recognizing whether there is a number that divides evenly into both numerator and denominator. (Instead of multiplying by the same numbers, as we did in the preceding paragraph, we divide.) For example, to simplify the fraction $\frac{24}{40}$, since both numerator and denominator are even numbers, they each have a factor of 2, so let's divide both top and bottom by 2: $\frac{24}{40} = \frac{24 \div 2}{40 \div 2} = \frac{12}{20}$. But wait—this still can be simplified because both numbers are even again, so we have $\frac{12}{20} = \frac{12 \div 2}{20 \div 2} = \frac{6}{10}$. This yields two more even numbers, so here we go again: $\frac{6}{10} = \frac{6 \div 2}{10 \div 2} = \frac{3}{5}$. Are we there yet? Yes, there are no more numbers that divide evenly into 3 and 5, so $\frac{24}{40}$ simplifies to $\frac{3}{5}$.

Of course, there is a better way to do this if we recognize that 8 divides evenly into 24 and 40, so $\frac{24}{40} = \frac{24 \div 8}{40 \div 8} = \frac{3}{5}$. If you don't recognize right away what number divides into both numerator and denominator evenly, you can work your way up to the answer anyway, just in more steps.

To recognize what number divides evenly into two or more numbers, called a **common factor** of the numbers, use the following facts, which you probably already know.

- 2 divides into all even numbers.

- 5 divides into all numbers that end in 0 or 5.

- 10 divides into all numbers that end in 0.

On the Praxis, it is common for a fraction answer to be a fill-in, in which the numerator and denominator are typed into boxes that appear as a fraction:

$$\frac{\boxed{}}{\boxed{}}$$

EXAMPLE 4.24

Simplify the fraction $\dfrac{360}{400} = \dfrac{\boxed{}}{\boxed{}}$.

SOLUTION

The correct solution is $\dfrac{9}{10}$.

Good solution: $\dfrac{360}{400}$ can be divided evenly by 5, or—better yet—by 10, and hopefully when you do that and get $\dfrac{36}{40}$, you'll recognize the numerator and denominator are divisible by 4 to get $\frac{360}{400} = \frac{9}{10}$. If not, dividing by 2 twice will get you to the same result.

Better solution: Recognize that 360 and 400 are both divisible by 40: $\frac{360}{400} = \frac{360 \div 40}{400 \div 40} = \frac{9}{10}$.

Multiplication of Fractions

Usually, addition and subtraction are discussed before multiplication and division, as we did for decimals. But for fractions, multiplication and division are much easier, so we'll start with them. Multiplying a fraction by a fraction is just straight-across multiplication, as we saw in the last section.

$$\frac{3}{4} \times \frac{7}{10} = \frac{3 \times 7}{4 \times 10} = \frac{21}{40}$$

Having done the multiplication, check to see whether the answer is in simplest form, and if not, do that final step. Multiplication of a fraction by a fraction is just that simple, and the multiplication can be made even more simple if you recognize that if there is a common factor for *any* numerator and *any* denominator, meaning they don't have to be in the same fraction, you can simplify along the way. For example,

$$\frac{3}{14} \times \frac{7}{9} = \frac{3 \times 7}{14 \times 9} = \frac{21}{126}$$

which we might recognize as being divisible by 3, $\frac{21}{126} = \frac{21 \div 3}{126 \div 3} = \frac{7}{42}$, which is also divisible, by 7 this time, $\frac{7}{42} = \frac{7 \div 7}{42 \div 7} = \frac{1}{6}$, so $\frac{21}{126}$ simplifies to $\frac{1}{6}$. (It would be great if you recognized right away that 21 divides into 21 and 126 evenly.)

Wouldn't it have been even better if we didn't have to divide 126 by 21? This is where recognizing a common factor in any numerator and any denominator comes in. The original problem was

$$\frac{3}{14} \times \frac{7}{9} = ?$$

The 3 divides evenly into the 9, and the 7 divides evenly into the 14, so we can do the simplification (called cancellations) before we even tackle the multiplication (the small numbers are the results of the cancellations):

$$\frac{3}{14} \times \frac{7}{9} = \frac{3^{1}}{14_{2}} \times \frac{7^{1}}{9_{3}} = \frac{1}{2} \times \frac{1}{3} = \frac{1}{6}$$

Note that you should be able to mentally do a lot of what has been written out in the explanations above.

If any of the fractions are mixed numbers, convert them to improper fractions before multiplying. For example,

$$4\frac{1}{2} \times 2\frac{2}{3} = \frac{9}{2} \times \frac{8}{3}, \text{ which after cancellations becomes}$$

$$\frac{\cancel{9}^{3}}{\cancel{2}_{1}} \times \frac{\cancel{8}^{4}}{\cancel{3}_{1}} = \frac{12}{1} = 12$$

Division of Fractions

If you understand and are comfortable with multiplication of fractions, division won't need much explanation. In fact, you only need to know what a **reciprocal** is, which is best illustrated by example. The reciprocal of 2 is $\frac{1}{2}$, the reciprocal of $\frac{2}{3}$ is $\frac{3}{2}$, and the reciprocal of $\frac{1}{5}$ is 5—"flipping over the fraction bar," so to speak.

So to divide fractions, you multiply the dividend by the reciprocal of the divisor. That's it! For example, $\frac{4}{5} \div \frac{3}{8} = \frac{4}{5} \times \frac{8}{3} = \frac{32}{15}$, which we learned can be rewritten as a mixed number, $2\frac{2}{15}$.

This calculation brings up a few points:

- To do division of fractions, you must use fractions, not mixed numbers.

- Don't be tempted to do any cancellation on the division problem—wait until it is converted to a multiplication problem. (In the case above, it looks tempting to cancel the 4 into the 8, but you can't.)

- The answers to fractional division problems often result in improper fractions, which usually must be converted to mixed numbers. Check to see what you are asked to do in the problem.

Drill: Multiplication and Division of Fractions

a. $\frac{3}{7} \div \frac{5}{6} =$

d. $3\frac{4}{7} \div \frac{5}{12} =$

b. $2\frac{1}{4} \div \frac{3}{8} =$

e. $4\frac{11}{13} \div 2\frac{11}{26} =$

c. $2\frac{2}{9} \div \frac{5}{12} =$

Answers on page 88.

Addition and Subtraction of Fractions

Addition and subtraction of fractions are more difficult than multiplication and division because all terms must have the same denominators. We didn't have to do that when we just multiplied the numerators and denominators across the fractions. When the denominators are all the same, then we can add or subtract the numerators (as the signs indicate), and keep the same denominator. As examples,

$$\frac{1}{7} + \frac{2}{7} = \frac{3}{7}$$

and $\frac{5}{8} - \frac{3}{8} = \frac{2}{8}$, which can be simplified to $\frac{1}{4}$.

To convert fractions to the same denominator, we use the same rule that if the top and bottom of any fraction are multiplied by the same number, the value of the fraction is unchanged because it is essentially being multiplied by 1. So to make the denominator of a fraction such as $\frac{1}{3}$ into a fraction with a denominator of 6, we would multiply the numerator and denominator by 2:

$$\frac{1}{3} \times \frac{2}{2} = \frac{2}{6}$$

This can be thought of as "unsimplifying" a fraction. The goal in addition and subtraction of fractions is to find the lowest common denominator (LCD), also called the least common multiple (LCM), which is the lowest number that is a multiple of all of the denominators. For denominators such as 3, 4, and 6, perhaps you see that this is 12, but for other numbers, such as 4, 5, and 6, even though they are small numbers, it is not so easy. Let's look at some examples to show how this is done.

EXAMPLE 4.25

What is the sum $\frac{1}{4} + \frac{3}{8}$?

SOLUTION

The correct answer is $\frac{5}{8}$.

In this addition problem, we need to change only the denominator of $\frac{1}{4}$ to eighths because that would make both denominators the same:

$$\frac{1}{4} + \frac{3}{8} = \left(\frac{1}{4} \times \frac{2}{2}\right) + \frac{3}{8} = \frac{2}{8} + \frac{3}{8} = \frac{5}{8}$$

Every step was written out above, but in reality you should try to do most of the work in your head if the numbers are small. But that's not so easy for a problem such as Example 4.26.

EXAMPLE 4.26

What is the sum of $\frac{1}{3} + \frac{2}{7}$?

SOLUTION

The correct answer is $\frac{13}{21}$.

There is no obvious number that 3 and 7 both divide into evenly, but the fallback is to use the product of the denominators, in this case 21, because we know each number will divide into it. Now we have to multiply each fraction by 1 in the form of a fraction with matching numerator and denominator. For $\frac{1}{3}$, since we want the denominator to be 21, we would multiply by $\frac{7}{7}$. Similarly, we would multiply $\frac{2}{7}$ by $\frac{3}{3}$. (We don't have to multiply the fractions by the same numbers since they are separate terms.) What we get is equivalent to the original problem.

$$\frac{1}{3} + \frac{2}{7} = \frac{1}{3}\left(\frac{7}{7}\right) + \frac{2}{7}\left(\frac{3}{3}\right) = \frac{7}{21} + \frac{6}{21} = \frac{7+6}{21} = \frac{13}{21}.$$

EXAMPLE 4.27

Evaluate $\frac{2}{3} + \frac{1}{2} - \frac{1}{6}$.

SOLUTION

The correct answer is 1.

We use the same principle—what is the least common denominator? In this case, it is 6, so we have

$$\frac{2}{3} + \frac{1}{2} - \frac{1}{6} = \frac{2}{3}\left(\frac{2}{2}\right) + \frac{1}{2}\left(\frac{3}{3}\right) - \frac{1}{6} = \frac{4}{6} + \frac{3}{6} - \frac{1}{6} = \frac{4+3-1}{6} = \frac{6}{6} = 1$$

This solution actually looks more complicated than it is.

EXAMPLE 4.28

Evaluate $\dfrac{4}{5} - \dfrac{3}{4} + 2\dfrac{1}{3}$.

SOLUTION

The correct answer is $2\dfrac{23}{60}$.

In figuring out how to answer this example, two questions come to mind immediately. (1) How can we easily find the lowest common denominator? (2) Do we have to convert the mixed fraction to an improper fraction?

To find the lowest common denominator if the numbers aren't as friendly as they were in Examples 4.25–4.27, write multiples of each denominator and find the lowest one that is common to all. Start with the largest number so you have to write fewer numbers. You can extend it later, if necessary, but don't do more than is necessary. For this problem, the denominators are 5, 4, and 3. Multiply each by 1, 2, 3, … until you have your common multiple. As you write the multiples of 5, stop whenever that number is a multiple of 4 and check if it is also a multiple of 3. If so, that's your LCD.

Try 5 and check whether each number that is a multiple of 5 and 4 is also a multiple of 3:

5, 10, 15, 20 (stop—no, even though this is a multiple of 4, it isn't a multiple of 3, so continue), 25, 30, 35, 40 (stop—no, even though this is a multiple of 4, it isn't a multiple of 3), 45, 50, 55, 60 (Bingo! That's it). The LCD is 60.

Actually, 60 is the product of 5, 4, and 3, so we could just as well have multiplied those three numbers. But multiplying the denominators isn't always the best way to go, especially if they are large. Also, for this example, we didn't have to write out all of the multiples of 5 because we could have done those mentally and just wrote down the ones that were also multiples of 4.

Getting back to our second question to find the answer to the example, do we have to convert the mixed number to an improper fraction? No, although we can do that, we also could just work with the fraction part and then add the 2 to the fraction answer at the end, since $2\dfrac{1}{3}$ is just 2 plus $\dfrac{1}{3}$. So let's do it that way.

$$\frac{4}{5} - \frac{3}{4} + 2\frac{1}{3} = \frac{4}{5}\left(\frac{12}{12}\right) - \frac{3}{4}\left(\frac{15}{15}\right) + \frac{1}{3}\left(\frac{20}{20}\right) + 2 = \frac{48}{60} - \frac{45}{60} + \frac{20}{60} + 2 =$$

$$\frac{48 - 45 + 20}{60} + 2 = \frac{23}{60} + 2 = 2\frac{23}{60}$$

This solution does seem like a lot of work, and it is. Most likely the fill-in fraction questions will involve simpler numbers, but the multiple-choice questions on fractions can involve larger numbers because, remember, multiple-choice problems don't always have to be solved. You just have to be able to analyze which of the answer choices is the right one. Example 4.29 is the same as Example 4.28, but now it is a multiple-choice problem. Notice that we don't have to go through all of the calculations above to get the correct answer.

EXAMPLE 4.29

Evaluate $\dfrac{4}{5} - \dfrac{3}{4} + 2\dfrac{1}{3}$.

(A) $\dfrac{23}{60}$

(B) $2\dfrac{23}{60}$

(C) $1\dfrac{23}{60}$

(D) $1\dfrac{4}{5}$

(E) $3\dfrac{23}{60}$

SOLUTION

The correct answer is (B), $2\dfrac{23}{60}$.

But here we can eliminate all of the answers except that one just by looking at the problem. We know the answer must be more than $2\dfrac{1}{3}$ since $\dfrac{4}{5} - \dfrac{3}{4}$ is a positive number and certainly less than 1, so we can eliminate all of the answer choices except (B) right away.

It's a Fact!

How do we know that $\dfrac{4}{5} - \dfrac{3}{4}$ is a positive number? It is easy to remember the following fact, and it can come in handy, especially when comparing fractions, which we discuss next.

$$\frac{1}{2} < \frac{2}{3} < \frac{3}{4} < \frac{4}{5} < \frac{5}{6} < \frac{6}{7} < \frac{7}{8} < \frac{8}{9} < \frac{9}{10}$$

Comparing Fractions

The previous fact is a help when comparing fractions, but the surefire way to compare fractions is to convert them to their decimal equivalents and then compare the decimals. Some problems may involve arranging numbers from small to large, and the numbers can be all kinds of numbers. Rely on facts that you know to do these problems, and if you have to compare a fraction to a decimal, then convert the fraction to the decimal.

EXAMPLE 4.30

Arrange the following values in order from smallest to largest:

$$\frac{2}{3}, \text{one-half}, .80, -\frac{3}{2}, -.80$$

(A) $-\frac{3}{2}, \frac{2}{3}$, one-half, .80, $-.80$

(B) $-\frac{3}{2}, -.80, \frac{2}{3}$, one-half, .80

(C) $-.80, \frac{2}{3}$, one-half, .80, $-\frac{3}{2}$

(D) $-\frac{3}{2}, -.80$, one-half, $\frac{2}{3}$, .80

(E) $-\frac{3}{2}, -.80$, one-half, .80, $\frac{2}{3}$

SOLUTION

The correct answer is (D).

Good solution:

Change every answer to decimals and check the columns to put them in order.

Better solution:

A quicker way is to put the negative numbers on the left, and since $-\frac{3}{2}$ is an improper fraction, we know that it is less than $-.80$ because it has a whole number part to it. For the positive numbers, remember the fact about fractions, $\frac{1}{2} < \frac{2}{3} < \frac{4}{5}$.

A variation on putting the numbers in order is a little less time consuming. You can be asked just to pick the smallest (or the largest) number in a group of numbers.

EXAMPLE 4.31

Which of the following fractions is larger than the others?

$$\frac{12}{13}, \frac{13}{14}, 0, \frac{165}{164}, \frac{167}{168}$$

SOLUTION

The correct answer is $\frac{165}{164}$.

This is easier than putting them all in order, and in fact, we don't even have to do any figuring here. Clearly, 0 isn't the largest, and of the remaining fractions, only one is greater than 1 because only one has a numerator greater than the denominator, and that is $\frac{165}{164}$.

NEXT, LET'S TALK ALGEBRA

Most of the math questions on the Praxis Core Math test will involve algebra, even if they aren't presented as algebra problems. The following sections on proportions and percentages are more easily done if you use algebra. In addition, algebra will help you to solve problems even if they look like just number problems or geometric figures or probability questions. You will see that a lot of the problems on the Praxis test combine all of the different math topics, so the approach in this book is also to integrate all of the topics as well.

Algebra is the topic for the next chapter, but let's discuss some basic algebra ideas here. The heart of algebra problems is finding a value for an unknown quantity, usually called x. The following subsections review some basic algebra facts that will help in solving problems in the rest of this chapter on numbers and quantity, the first of the four math topics covered on the Praxis test. After we get through this preliminary algebra stuff, we will see how it works with the number and quantity problems, and then in the next chapter we will work on other algebra topics, but hopefully by then you will be familiar with x, the unknown.

Equations

Equations simply say two quantities are equal. Think of a balance scale.

Just like the scale, to keep an equation in balance, whatever you do to one side of the equation you must do to the other. Often, this is accomplished by using inverses.

Inverses

Addition and subtraction are inverses; multiplication and division are inverses. This means that if you add and subtract the same value, nothing changes. Likewise, if you multiply and divide the same value, nothing changes. Inverses are important in solving algebra problems because if you want the value of x, you may have to use them to get the x "alone" on one side of the equation. A few examples will help to illustrate this.

$$x + 7 = 12$$

Since the 7 is added to x, we can get x alone by subtracting 7, and to keep the equation in balance, we must do this to both sides. So we have

$$x + 7 - 7 = 12 - 7$$

The 7's on the left-hand side of the equation cancel each other out, and we have

$$x = 12 - 7 = 5$$

For subtraction, the inverse is addition, so just add the same value to both sides of the equation. Therefore, to get a value for x in the equation

$$x - 14 = 1$$

we add 14 to both sides to get $x = 15$. Here, the addition of 14 to both sides of the equation was done mentally. It isn't necessary (and takes time) to write every step in uncomplicated equations. Now let's try an equation involving multiplication:

$$3x = 18$$

Here, the x is being multiplied by 3, so again to keep the equation in balance we must do the inverse operation on both sides, meaning divide both sides by 3. Then we have $\frac{3}{8}x = \frac{18}{3}$. The 3's on the left-hand side of the equation cancel each other out, so we have $x = \frac{18}{3} = 6$. Finally, let's do a division equation:

$$\frac{x}{3} = 4$$

Since x is being divided by 3, we multiply both sides by 3 to get $x = 12$. Again, we can do this multiplication mentally.

As a general rule, if there is a fraction in the equation, multiply every term by the denominator to get rid of the fraction before solving the equation. The key words here are *every term*—after all, this is an equation so you have to treat every term the same.

Translation from English to Algebra

The reason so many problems, even ones that don't seem to be algebra problems, can be solved by using basic algebra is that certain words can be translated into algebraic symbols. For example, x is the unknown that we want to find in an equation. In a problem, the words "what" and "how many" are the unknowns, so they translate into x. The English word "is" (as in "this is that," meaning "this" is the same as "that") translates into an equal sign. And the rest of the equation is built on the other words in the sentence.

The word "of," as in "$\frac{1}{2}$ of 100," means multiply. We have no trouble with translating the sentence "Two times 30 is 60": $2 \times 30 = 60$. However, if instead of a whole number "two," we have a fraction, somehow it can be harder to recognize it is the same type of sentence. But we usually don't say "$\frac{1}{2}$ times 100" (when that is really what we mean), we say "$\frac{1}{2}$ of 100." The "of" is the same as "times" in this sentence.

Let's try a few examples:

Sentence	Equation	Solution	Answer
What *is* the sum of 4 and 7?	$x = 4 + 7$	$x = 11$	11
What is $\frac{2}{3}$ *of* 60?	$x = \frac{2}{3} \times 60$	$x = \frac{2}{3} \times \frac{60}{1} = \frac{120}{3} = 40$	40
Thirty is equal to three times what?	$30 = 3x$	$3x = 30, x = \frac{30}{3} = 10$	10
What number is 7 more than 12?	$x = 12 + 7$	$x = 19$	19
What number decreased by 7 is 12?	$x - 7 = 12$	$x = 12 + 7 = 19$	19
What is the difference between 32 and 28?	$x = 32 - 28$	$x = 4$	4

The Praxis test won't be asking you to solve simple equations such as the following, but you must be able to do these quickly and accurately to get the answers to the problems that are presented. So before we go on, be sure this drill becomes easy for you.

Drill: Algebra

Solve for x:

a. $x - 80 = 50$ b. $x + 7 = 50$ c. $x - 3 = 4$ d. $5x = 4$ e. $\dfrac{x}{2} = 72$

f. $x = \dfrac{42}{2}$ g. $3x = 17$ h. $3 = x + 2$ i. $3 = x - 12$ j. $7x = -14$

Answers on page 89.

Substitution

Algebraic expressions can be evaluated by substituting values for the variables. For example, you may want to evaluate $x + 4$ when $x = 2$. Just substitute 2 for the x, and the expression equals 6. Substitution is used a lot in algebra. You don't even have to know what the expression or equation means to do substitution.

EXAMPLE 4.32

What is the value of $x^2 - xy + \dfrac{y}{2}$ when $x = 1$ and $y = 2$?

SOLUTION

The correct answer is 0.

Substitute $x = 1$ and $y = 2$ into the given expression and evaluate:

$$x^2 - xy + \frac{y}{2}$$

$$= (1)^2 - (1)(2) + \frac{2}{2}$$

$$= 1 - 2 + 1 = 0.$$

RATIOS AND PROPORTIONAL RELATIONSHIPS

A **ratio** is a way of comparing two quantities. Ratios can be expressed as fractions, as decimals, or by two numbers separated by a colon. For example, let's say the ratio of the length to the width of a bathmat is 3 feet to 2 feet. This can be written as 3:2, $\frac{3}{2}$, or even that the length is 1.5 times the width.

EXAMPLE 4.33

Bill's age is triple his son Will's age. Express the ratio of Bill's age to Will's age as a fraction.

SOLUTION

The answer is $\frac{3}{1}$, read as "3 to 1."

If the question instead asked for the ratio of Will's age to Bill's age, the answer would be $\frac{1}{3}$. It is very important to state the ratio in the correct order. It would make no sense for this case to say that the ratio of the son's age to the father's age is 3:1.

A **proportion** is the equivalence of two ratios.

If we said that Will's age is 10 years, and we know that Bill's age is triple Will's age, we can easily say that Bill is 30 years old. We can do this mentally. The proportion for this situation is

$$\frac{3}{1} = \frac{\text{Bill's age}}{10}.$$

So Bill's age is 30. Remember that "like" quantities must be in like places in a proportion. On the left-hand side of this proportion, the numbers represent Bill's age on top and Will's age on the bottom. So on the right-hand side, we should have the same: Bill's age on top and Will's age on the bottom. The proportion works out because indeed $\frac{3}{1}$ does equal $\frac{30}{10}$.

But often the numbers aren't as easy as this. In that case, we would set up a proportion, filling in all of the values we know and use the proportion to find the value we are asked to find. Luckily, algebra comes to the rescue and makes a complicated-sounding problem easy to do. By using algebra, we are told to get the unknown, x, alone on one side of the equation. After all, that is what we are trying to find—the value of x.

But it turns out that for every proportion, doing the multiplying or dividing that you have to do to get x on one side of the equation always happens to end up being something called *cross-multiplication*. If you cross-multiply, you will end up with a short equation in which x has a multiplier, so you just divide both sides of that equation by the multiplier (remember, division is the inverse of multiplication), and you get x right away.

Let's do the Bill-Will example (No. 4.33) by using cross multiplication. We are asked to find Bill's age, knowing that Will's age is 10 and Bill's age is triple that. The proportion is

$$\frac{3}{1} = \frac{x}{10}.$$

where x is Bill's age. Just like it sounds, cross multiplication means multiplying in the shape of a cross, where the two multiplications equal each other.

$\frac{3}{1} \diagdown\!\!\!\!\diagup \frac{x}{10}$, so $3 \times 10 = x \times 1$, or $x = 30$.

Now let's try a similar problem, but one that is harder to do mentally.

EXAMPLE 4.34

Mike's age today is exactly 4 times his son Ike's age. It's Mike's 34th birthday today. How old is Ike? (Choose the *best* answer.)

   (A) 8

   (B) $8\frac{1}{2}$

   (C) 9

   (D) 136

   (E) Cannot tell from the information given.

SOLUTION

The correct answer is (B), $8\frac{1}{2}$.

The proportion is

$$\frac{4}{1} = \frac{34}{x}$$

with Mike's age on the top.

This problem brings up quite a few test-taking tips worth remembering. First, the question says, "Choose the *best* answer." That is a clue that maybe two or more answers seem right, but only one is the *best*. Indeed, Ike is 8, but more precisely he is $8\frac{1}{2}$. And not 9, either. Answer choice (D) sounds silly—136 years old!! But that is what you will get if you set up the proportion upside-down, $x \times 1 = 34 \times 4 = 136$. So to repeat what has been said many times already—take the time to make sure your answer makes sense. Sometimes a preposterous number is an answer choice, and you might choose it if you don't take the time for this final step.

Let's look at another typical proportion example, in which units make a difference.

EXAMPLE 4.35

Alyson can type 75 words a minute. How many words can she type in an hour?

   (A) 3,000

   (B) 4,500

   (C) 6,000

   (D) 900

   (E) 450

SOLUTION

The answer is (B), 4,500.

The ratio that is given is $\dfrac{75 \text{ words}}{1 \text{ minute}}$. The unknown is how many words (remember, "how many" is one of the catch phrases that indicate x in algebra). So the corresponding ratio for the unknown is $\dfrac{x \text{ words}}{1 \text{ hour}}$. This brings up the most important rule in proportions: "like" things must be in like places *with like units*. So if the given information is in words per minute, the unknown ratio must also be in words per minute. Since 1 hour = 60 minutes, the proportion is

$$\frac{75}{1} = \frac{x}{60}$$

and $x = 4,500$ words per hour, or Alyson can type 4,500 words in an hour.

Notice the different placements of the x between this proportion and the one in Example 4.34. The placement of the x in the proportion can be in the numerator or denominator of the proportion. It just depends on what information is given and what is asked for. However, if you remember that "like" things must be in like places with like units and how to cross multiply, you should always get the correct answer.

Proportions aren't always given as single units (per minute, for example). Sometimes after cross-multiplying, the *x* has a coefficient (a multiplier). The solution for the unknown *x* is found by simply dividing (the inverse of multiplying) both sides of the equation by this coefficient, as stated above.

EXAMPLE 4.36

Suppose Pablo walks 2 miles in 48 minutes. If he keeps the same pace, how far can he walk in 2 hours?

    (A) 5

    (B) 2.5

    (C) .083

    (D) 5,760

    (E) Cannot tell from the information given.

SOLUTION

The correct answer is (A), 5 miles.

Set up the proportion as usual—don't change the method at all because it works for all proportions. The units for this problem are miles per minute.

$$\frac{2}{48} = \frac{x}{120}$$

Both sides of the proportion match, once we convert the 2 hours into 2(60) = 120 minutes, so the units match. Then cross-multiplication gives the following equation:

$$48x = 240$$

Divide both sides of the equation by the coefficient of *x*. On the left side of the equation, the 48's will cancel each other, so we end up with the value of *x*, the answer to the problem:

$$\frac{48x}{48} = \frac{240}{48}, \text{ or } x = 5$$

Pablo can walk 5 miles in 2 hours. Note that answer choices (B), (C), and (D) are answers if the proportion isn't matched up or the hours aren't converted to minutes. Again, don't change the method at all because it works for all proportions. By the way, answer choices (C) and (D) should be eliminated right away as being too small or too large to make sense.

EXAMPLE 4.37

Suppose a car is going 45 miles per hour. How many miles per minute is this?

(A) $1\frac{1}{3}$

(B) $\frac{3}{4}$

(C) 45

(D) $\frac{1}{4}$

(E) Need to know how far the car went.

SOLUTION

The correct answer is (B), $\frac{3}{4}$.

Good solution: Set up the conversion. As a ratio, this is $\frac{45 \text{ miles}}{1 \text{ hour}}$.

$$\frac{45 \text{ miles}}{1 \text{ hour}} \times \frac{1 \text{ hour}}{60 \text{ minutes}} = \frac{45 \text{ miles}}{60 \text{ minutes}} = \frac{3}{4} \text{ mile per minute}$$

so 45 miles per hour is the same as $\frac{3}{4}$ mile a minute. A few facts are used in this calculation. First, we did a conversion of miles to minutes by multiplying by $\frac{1 \text{ hour}}{60 \text{ minutes}}$, which equals 1 (and multiplication by 1 doesn't change a value, so it's okay). How did we know to put the hour over the 60 minutes and not the other way around? Since we are looking for miles per minute, that tells us that the minutes should go on the bottom of the conversion fraction. Also, we can cancel the "hour" in the multiplication, leaving us with miles per minute(s).

A second fact is that, just as we "canceled" the "hour" from the top and bottom of the multiplication, we used the fact that both 45 and 60 are divisible by 15, so $\frac{45}{60}$ mile per minute reduces to $\frac{3}{4}$ mile per minute.

Better solution: Realize that the car is going less than 60 mph, which is a mile a minute (this is a good proportion to know: 60 mph = 1 mile per minute), so the answer has to be less than 1, which leaves only answer choices (B) and (D), and (D) seems to be too slow.

PERCENTAGES

Percentages as Decimals

The word "percent" is made up of two parts: "per" means divide, and "cent" means 100 (think of 100 cents in a dollar). So "percent" means per 100, or to divide by 100. Therefore, changing a decimal to a percentage means dividing the decimal by 100, which in turn means moving the decimal point 2 places (for the two zeroes in 100) to the left (because we are dividing).

So 50% means .50, 3% means .03, 100% means 1, and 125% means 1.25.

Likewise, if we want to convert a decimal into a percentage, we have to multiply by 100.

So .75 = 75%, one-third = .33$\frac{1}{3}$ = 33$\frac{1}{3}$%, and 2 = 200%.

Percentage Discounts

Algebra is helpful as a tool when working with percentages. Typical percentage problems involve solving questions such as "What is 7% of 300?" or "Twenty is what percent of 200?" or "What is the price of a $25.00 sweater after a 10% discount?" Many people have trouble working with percentage problems because they cannot remember which number to divide into what number. However, translating the question into an algebra problem helps tremendously.

Let's review and add to some of the "translations" from questions into algebra. We already said that the unknown in a problem, usually represented by x, is the "what" part of the question. The verb "is" or variations of it translates into an equal sign. Let's add another translation that has to do with percentages. Wherever you see "percent," substitute the fraction $\frac{1}{100}$. And again, the word "of" indicates multiplication.

Now, let's tackle some of these percentage problems.

EXAMPLE 4.38

What is 7% of 300?

    (A) 210

    (B) 21

    (C) 42.86

    (D) 4.286

    (E) 428.6

SOLUTION

The correct answer is (B), 21.

Word-by-word, this question translates into

$$\text{What } (x) \text{ is } (=) \text{ 7\% } \left(\frac{7}{100}\right) \text{ of } (\times) \text{ 300?}$$

So, in algebra-speak, this is

$$x = \frac{7}{100} \times 300$$

The unknown, x, is already isolated on one side of the equation, so the solution is just $\frac{7}{100} \times 300 = 21$. No confusion about whether to divide or multiply by 7 or where the decimal point should go. It is plain and simple.

EXAMPLE 4.39

Twenty is what percent of 200?

    (A) 10

    (B) 20

    (C) 100

    (D) 200

    (E) .10

SOLUTION

The correct answer is (A), 10.

Good solution: Translate the sentence into algebra:

$$\text{Twenty } (20) \text{ is } (=) \text{ what percent } \left(\frac{x}{100}\right) \text{ of } (\times) \text{ 200?}$$

$$20 = \frac{x}{100} \times 200$$

We want the unknown, x, to be alone on one side of the equation, but it is multiplied by 200 and divided by 100. So we must do the inverses of those operations: first, let's divide both sides by 200.

$$\frac{20}{200} = \frac{x}{100} \times 200 \div 200 \text{ or (since the 200's on the right side cancel)}$$

$$\frac{20}{200} = \frac{x}{100}.$$

Now let's multiply both sides by 100:

$$\frac{20}{200} \times 100 = \frac{x}{100} \times 100$$

and since the 100's cancel each other out on the right side, we have

$$\frac{20}{200} \times 100 = x, \text{ or } x = 10$$

Better solution: If you recognized that $\frac{20}{200} = \frac{x}{100}$ was in the form of the proportion $\frac{1}{10} = \frac{x}{100}$, you could immediately cross-multiply to get $10x = 100$, or $x = 10$, eliminating a lot of steps along the way.

The point, again, is that translation into algebra eliminates any confusion about which number gets divided into (or multiplied by) what number in a percentage problem.

EXAMPLE 4.40

The price of a \$25.00 sweater after a 10% discount is ⬚ .

SOLUTION

The correct answer is \$22.50.

This problem, and ones like it that have to do with discounts, need a little more knowledge before applying algebra. Basically, this type of problem deals with two amounts: the original price and the sale price after the discount. Logically, the sale price equals the original price minus the discount.

So this problem translates into

$$x = \$25.00 - (.10)(\$25.00) = \$25.00 - \$2.50 = \$22.50$$

However, this is the same as 90% of \$25.00, so sometimes it is faster and easier to translate a discount percentage into what percentage will be paid. It is just 100% minus the discount percentage.

Sometimes a double discount is taken; for example, when there is an initial 25% discount but the goods don't sell, the store may offer an additional 60% discount. Don't be fooled—this is not the same as 85% off. The reason is that the 60% discount is off the price that has been reduced 25% already.

Let's look at some typical numbers. Suppose the original price of a coat is $100. In the middle of the winter, the store offers a 25% discount, so the coat is $75. But it still doesn't sell, and now it is the end of winter, so the store offers "an additional 60% off." That would be 60% off the $75 price, not the $100 original price. So the second discount ends up being $45.00, and the coat now costs $30. It's a good deal, but it isn't $15, which would be the 85% discount price. We can calculate the final price of the coat by considering the percentages to be paid, which are 40% of the 75% of the original cost of the coat, where "of" means multiply:

$$.40 \times (.75 \times \$100) = \$30$$

POWERS AND ROOTS

Powers and roots are types of inverses of each other. A **power** of a value indicates how many times that value is a factor in a multiplication of itself. Therefore, 2^8 is simply

$$2^8 = 2 \times 2 \times 2 \times 2 \times 2 \times 2 \times 2 \times 2 = 256$$

This is called 2 to the 8th power, or the 8th power of 2. Many times a power is incorrectly defined as how many times a factor is multiplied by itself, but it is clear from the above 8th power of 2 that it is the 2, and not the ×, that appears eight times. There actually are seven multiplications but eight factors.

If you multiply two numbers with the same base, add their exponents; if you divide two numbers with the same base, subtract their exponents. Thus $2^3 \times 2^5 = 2^{3+5} = 2^8$ and $3^9 \div 3^5 = 3^{9-5} = 3^4$. Count the number of factors in the write-outs of these two facts. This type of write-out will help if you get confused during a test, as well:

$$2^3 \times 2^5 = (2 \times 2 \times 2) \times (2 \times 2 \times 2 \times 2 \times 2) = 2 \times 2 \times 2 \times 2 \times 2 \times 2 \times 2 \times 2 = 2^8$$

$$3^9 \div 3^5 = \frac{3 \times 3 \times 3 \times 3 \times 3 \times 3 \times 3 \times 3 \times 3}{3 \times 3 \times 3 \times 3 \times 3} = 3 \times 3 \times 3 \times 3 = 3^4$$

A **root** is the opposite of a power. From the above, we can see that 32 is the eighth root of 2. Usually, though, we talk about square roots, which are the second root, written with the sign $\sqrt{}$, or cube roots, written with the sign $\sqrt[3]{}$. The small number is the root, and the number under the radical sign (the **radicand**) is the number whose root is being taken. Note that usually the small "2" isn't written for a square root because a radical sign without a small number is always the square root. So we can say $\sqrt{4} = 2$ because $2 \times 2 = 4$, and $\sqrt[3]{8} = 2$ because $2 \times 2 \times 2 = 8$.

You should be familiar with the squares of the integers up to 10, as well as some powers of 2 and 3 and their roots, as follows. You probably know some of them already, or you can find them by using a calculator.

Powers:						
$2^2 = 4$	$2^3 = 8$	$2^4 = 16$	$2^5 = 32$	$2^6 = 64$	$3^2 = 9$	$3^3 = 27$
$4^2 = 16$	$5^2 = 25$	$6^2 = 36$	$7^2 = 49$	$8^2 = 64$	$9^2 = 81$	$10^2 = 100$
Roots:						
$\sqrt{4} = 2$	$\sqrt[3]{8} = 2$	$\sqrt[4]{16} = 2$	$\sqrt[5]{32} = 2$	$\sqrt[6]{64} = 2$	$\sqrt{9} = 3$	$\sqrt[3]{27} = 3$
$\sqrt{16} = 4$	$\sqrt{25} = 5$	$\sqrt{36} = 6$	$\sqrt{49} = 7$	$\sqrt{64} = 8$	$\sqrt{81} = 9$	$\sqrt{100} = 10$

If you know these, you also know the powers of tens (10^2, 20^2, 30^2, etc.) because each of these is the single-digit integer multiplied by 10^2; for example, $20^2 = 2^2 \times 10^2 = 4 \times 100 = 400$. Likewise, $\sqrt{400} = 20$ because it is $\sqrt{400} = \sqrt{4 \times 100} = \sqrt{4} \times \sqrt{100} = 2 \times 10 = 20$. If you can remember these two examples of $20^2 = 400$ and $\sqrt{400} = 20$, they will remind you of the general rule that

$$\sqrt{a \times b} = \sqrt{a} \times \sqrt{b} \quad \text{and} \quad (a \times b)^2 = a^2 \times b^2, \text{ where } a \text{ and } b \text{ are any two numbers.}$$

This rule is true for the higher roots and powers, not just for square roots and squares. Be careful, though, because the rule applies only to multiplication, not to addition or subtraction. Clearly, $\sqrt{4} \neq \sqrt{1} + \sqrt{3}$, as we will see next.

IRRATIONAL, IMAGINARY, AND UNDEFINED NUMBERS

Irrational Numbers

This chapter and the Praxis Core Math test mostly use real numbers. Earlier in this chapter, we said that rational numbers are real numbers that can be represented as fractions. This includes decimals that either end or repeat. Examples are 5 (because it can be written as the fraction $\frac{5}{1}$), the decimal 2.5 (because it can be written as $\frac{5}{2}$), and the repeating decimal 0.333 . . . (because it can be written as $\frac{1}{3}$).

Some roots are rational, such as $\sqrt{4}$, $\sqrt{9}$, and $\sqrt{100}$, because they equal the rational numbers 2, 3, and 10, respectively. In fact, there is a name for such roots, which have a whole number value. These are called **perfect roots**. But what about a number such as $\sqrt{6}$ or $\sqrt{40}$? If roots are not perfect, they are called **irrational roots**. We can, of course, use the calculator to get a numerical value for such roots, but it will be a decimal that doesn't repeat. We can also get an idea of the value of irrational roots by what we know about perfect roots.

We know that the value of $\sqrt{6}$ has to be between the values of $\sqrt{5}$ and $\sqrt{7}$, but we don't know the values of either of those numbers (they are also irrational). Therefore, we should use numbers whose values we do know, which are the perfect squares closest to $\sqrt{6}$. The best we can do in estimating the value of $\sqrt{6}$ (without using the calculator) is to say it is between $\sqrt{4}$ and $\sqrt{9}$, or $\sqrt{4} < \sqrt{6} < \sqrt{9}$, or $2 < \sqrt{6} < 3$. So we can say the value of $\sqrt{6}$ is somewhere between 2 and 3. Furthermore, since 6 is closer to 4 than it is to 9, $\sqrt{6}$ is probably in the lower half of that interval, or between 2 and 2.5. This type of estimation, although not precise, is helpful in solving problems.

EXAMPLE 4.41

We will learn about right triangles in the chapter on geometry. We will find that that a triangle with sides of 2 units and 3 units has a third side of $\sqrt{13}$ units. About how long is that?

    (A) 3.00 units

    (B) 3.30 units

    (C) 3.60 units

    (D) 4.00 units

    (E) 4.60 units

SOLUTION

The correct answer is (C), 3.60 units.

We know that 13 is between the perfect squares 9 and 16. Therefore, $\sqrt{13}$ is between $\sqrt{9}$ and $\sqrt{16}$, or between 3 and 4. Since 13 is closer to 16 than 9, its square root should be closer to 4 than 3, and answer choice (C) is the correct answer.

Imaginary Numbers

We talked earlier about real numbers—essentially all of the numbers with which we are familiar: integers, fractions, and decimals. There are, however, a class of numbers that are "unreal," or *imaginary*. **Imaginary numbers** involve the square root of a negative number. Since the number under the square root sign is the product of the root multiplied by itself (for example, $\sqrt{4} = 2$, so $2 \times 2 = 4$), and since when we multiply two negative numbers, we get a positive number, there is no way we can get a real number that we can multiply by itself and get a negative number. So $\sqrt{-4}$, for example, is an impossible, or imaginary number. To take care of describing such a number, there is a new quantity, the imaginary number called $i = \sqrt{-1}$. So, as we saw in the preceding section that the square root of a product is the product of the square roots, we can say $\sqrt{-4} = \sqrt{4 \times (-1)} = \sqrt{-4} \times \sqrt{-1} = 2i$. It is important that you know of the existence and meaning of the imaginary number i.

Undefined Numbers

While we are talking about unusual number forms, we should include undefined numbers. An **undefined number** is a number that is defined as undefined. That sounds strange, but that is the case. What do you get if you divide a number by 0? First of all, how *can* you divide a number by 0? How can you take a quantity and, for example, distribute it to 0 people? You can't. So any fraction in which the denominator is 0 is undefined, and there isn't anything we can do to give it a value.

UNITS

We already have encountered units in the examples in this chapter. Basically, you should know that there are two systems of units in use in the United States: (1) the U.S. standard (or customary) system and (2) the metric system, also known as the International System of Units (SI). The metric system is used outside of the United States and in the scientific, medical, and international trade communities; the U.S. standard system is the primary system used in the United States. Although the Praxis test doesn't require that you know how to convert from one system to the other, questions on the test assume that you have a basic knowledge of both systems.

U.S. Standard System

Since the common system in use in the United States is the U.S. standard system, let's start with that.

The U.S. system is based on a British system that dates back to millennia before the United States even became a nation. The conversion numbers within the U.S. system can be unwieldy (1 mile = 5280 feet, 1 yard = 3 feet, 1 foot = 12 inches), but if you have to convert any measurements, such as from miles to yards, the Praxis test will give the conversion rate or means for you to figure it out.

Measurement is basically of three kinds:

- Length, such as inch, foot, yard, mile.

- Weight, such as ounce, pound, and ton.

- Volume, such as cubic inches, cubic feet, and cubic yards; also, teaspoons, tablespoons, cups, pints, quarts, and gallons (the latter are used for liquid measures, and also for agricultural products, such as a quart of strawberries).

Volume (the amount of space an object takes up) is technically different from capacity (the amount of space that is available), although the two terms are sometimes used interchangeably.

Metric System

The metric system is based on the number 10.

- Length is based on the meter, which is a little more than a yard.

- Weight is based on the gram, about the weight of a paper clip.

- Volume is based on the cubic meter (volume) and the liter (for liquids such as a bottle of soda, which is about a quart).

The names of these basic units are then combined with prefixes that tell how many times 10 the value is:

- milli-, meaning one-thousandth.

- centi-, meaning one hundredth.

- kilo-, meaning times one thousand.

- mega-, meaning times one million.

- giga-, meaning times one billion.

Measurements in the metric system consist of combining the prefixes with the basic units, such as centimeters, kilograms, or milliliters. Some common metric combinations and their sizes are:

- millimeter (the size of a pin head)

- centimeter (an inch = 2.54 centimeters, so it's less than four-tenths of an inch)

- kilometer (about five-eighths of a mile, but if you can't remember that, know that it is a little more than a half mile)

- cubic centimeter (about the size of a sugar cube).

- milligram (so tiny that you cannot see it; capsule pills often contain 1000 milligrams).

- kilogram (a little more than 2 pounds, the weight of a pineapple, for example).

The important thing is that you have a sense of the size of these units, such as knowing that the length of a piece of writing paper should be measured in centimeters rather than meters or kilometers. Or that the weight of a baseball is measured in grams or fractions of a kilogram, but never in metric tons. Or that your weight can be measured in kilograms. Or that a bathtub has a capacity of about 200 liters.

You probably are familiar enough with the U.S. standard system. A good way to get a sense of metric units, so that you can answer questions such as the one in Example 4.42, is to become aware of the metric units for the everyday things you use or food you eat. Almost everything sold in the United States has its metric equivalent written on the package.

EXAMPLE 4.42

The weight of a typical cell phone is in what range?

    (A) 1–2 pounds

    (B) a half ounce

    (C) 80–150 grams

    (D) 80–150 kilograms

    (E) 8 centimeters

SOLUTION

The correct answer is (C), 80–150 grams.

This is equivalent to 3 to 5 ounces, but that isn't one of the choices. This question is best answered by elimination. Answer choice (E) is eliminated right away because it is a measure of length, not weight. Answer choices (A) and (D) are way too big, and answer choice (B) is way too small, leaving only answer choice (C). If you remember that a small paperclip weighs about a gram, then 80–150 grams makes sense.

EXAMPLE 4.43

The length of a pencil can best be measured in which of the following units? (Choose *all* of the correct answers.)

    A grams

    B inches

    C gigabytes

    D centimeters

    E kilometers

SOLUTION

The correct answers are B and D.

Answer choice A is a measure of weight, not length; C is a measure of computer capacity, equal to 1 billion bytes; and E is too large for measuring a pencil (it is more than a half mile).

Practice Exercises

1. Jose has a stamp collection. He had 210 stamps, and his sister gave him 30 more. Then Jose gave 53 stamps to his friend. How many stamps does Jose have now?

   (A) 240

   (B) 187

   (C) 293

   (D) 127

   (E) 263

2. Rick has a comic book collection. He had 125 comic books, and his father gave him 98 more. How many comic books does he have in all?

   (A) 122

   (B) 123

   (C) 213

   (D) 223

   (E) 323

3. The lottery is $9,125,000. What is the value of 1 in the number 9,125,000?

   (A) 1 hundred

   (B) 1 thousand

   (C) 1 ten thousand

   (D) 1 hundred thousand

   (E) 1 million

4. Which of these numbers is equal to half a million?

   (A) $\dfrac{1}{2,000,000}$

   (B) $\dfrac{2}{1,000,000}$

   (C) 50,000

   (D) 500,000

   (E) 1,500,000

5. What percentage of 216 is 54?

    (A) 4%

    (B) 40%

    (C) 25%

    (D) 0.4%

    (E) 0.25%

6. Kevin scored 24 points in last night's basketball game, which was 40% of the final score for Team A. Their opponent, Team B, scored 70 points in the game. What was the difference in scores between the two teams? Fill in the box.

7. If Nancy drives at a steady speed of 50 miles per hour, how long will it take her to drive 20 miles?

    (A) 20 minutes

    (B) 10 minutes

    (C) 15 minutes

    (D) 30 minutes

    (E) 24 minutes

8. In which order would the numbers -8.1, $\sqrt{69}$, 8, 2π, and 0.8 appear when arranged from least to greatest?

    (A) $-8.1, 0.8, \sqrt{69}, 8, 2\pi$

    (B) $-8.1, 0.8, 2\pi, 8, \sqrt{69}$

    (C) $-8.1, \sqrt{69}, 2\pi, 0.8, 8$

    (D) $-8.1, 0.8, 8, 2\pi, \sqrt{69}$

    (E) $-8.1, 0.8, 2\pi, \sqrt{69}, 8$

9. A grant of $5,000 was given to the music department of a school for upgrades. They estimate about $3,850 will be used for new instruments and $1,000 for sheet music. If new music stands cost $15 each, how many can they buy?

    (A) 6

    (B) 8

    (C) 10

    (D) 15

    (E) 20

10. The next term in the sequence 0, 1, 1, 2, 3, 5, 8, 13, ... is

    (A) 15

    (B) 18

    (C) 20

    (D) 21

    (E) Cannot tell

11. How many prime numbers are there in the interval from 31 to 41, including the endpoints.

    (A) 1

    (B) 2

    (C) 3

    (D) 4

    (E) 37

12. Which of the following values of x satisfy the inequality $|2x - 7| \geq 11$? Choose *all* that apply.

    | A | −7 |
    | B | −2 |
    | C | 0 |
    | D | 7 |
    | E | 9 |

13. If m and n are consecutive integers, which can never be even? Choose *all* that apply.

    | A | mn |
    | B | $m + n$ |
    | C | $n(m + 1)^2$ |
    | D | $m(n - 1)^2$ |
    | E | $m^2 + n^2$ |

14. The price of a book is increased by 20%, and then the new price is discounted by 20%. Compared to the original price of the book, what is the final price?

    (A) 10% less

    (B) 4% less

    (C) Same as the original price

    (D) 4% more

    (E) 10% more

15. A speed of 3.5 miles in 1 hour and 45 minutes is the same as how many miles per hour?

    (A) 6.125

    (B) 3.5

    (C) 2.4

    (D) 2

    (E) 0.5

16. The bookstore reduced a set of books from $80 to $64. By what percentage was the set of books reduced?

    (A) 16%

    (B) 20%

    (C) 25%

    (D) 80%

    (E) 125%

17. The following numbers are listed in order from least to greatest. The value of b could be which of the following numbers? Choose *all* that apply.

$$\frac{1}{2}, \ \frac{5}{6}, \ b, \ \frac{\frac{1}{2}}{0.5}, \ \pi$$

    A $\frac{7}{8}$

    B $\sqrt{3.9}$

    C 0.9

    D $-\frac{7}{8}$

    E $\frac{3}{4}$

18. Alyce receives an allowance of $40 a month. She saves $\frac{1}{8}$ of her allowance and spends the rest. This month she is going to spend $\frac{2}{5}$ of the remainder on the amusement park. How many dollars will she spend at the amusement park? Fill in the box.

    ☐

Solutions

1. (B), 187. The arithmetic is $210 + 30 - 53 = 187$.

2. (D) 223. Adding the comic books Rick is given to those he already has yields $125 + 98 = 223$.

3. (D), 1 hundred thousand.

4. (D), 500,000. Half a million is $\frac{1}{2} \times 1,000,000 = 500,000$.

5. (C), 25%. Set this up as an equation by "translating" the words:

$$\frac{x}{100} \times 216 = 54$$

$$x = \frac{54}{216} \times 100$$

$$x = 25\%$$

6. 10 points. Kevin scored 24 points, which was 40% of Team A's score. The equation to find the team's score x is $24 = .40x$, or $x = 60$ points. Team B's score was 70 points. The difference is 10 points, so even though Kevin did a fine job, his team lost.

7. (E), 24 minutes. Since there are 60 minutes in an hour, this problem can be solved with the following proportion: $\frac{50}{60} = \frac{20}{x}$

$$50x = 1200$$
$$x = 24$$

8. (B), -8.1, 0.8, 2π, 8, $\sqrt{69}$. The two unknowns are 2π and $\sqrt{69}$. Since $\pi \approx 3.14$ (as seen in Chapter 8), $2\pi \approx 6.28$, and since $\sqrt{69} > \sqrt{64}$, it is also >8. Remember that a negative number is less than any positive number.

9. (C), 10. Of the $5,000, the department set aside $4850 for instruments and sheet music, leaving $150 for the music stands. At a cost of $15 each, they can buy $150 \div 15 = 10$ stands.

10. (D), 21. Instead of this being an arithmetic or geometric (multiplication) series, this is the well-known Fibonacci series, which adds the last two terms to get the next one. $8 + 13 = 21$.

11. (C), 3. Including 31 and 41 as primes, there is one more in the interval, and it is 37. Thus, the total is 3.

12. $\boxed{A}$, $\boxed{B}$, and $\boxed{E}$. Change the equation within the absolute value signs into two inequalities, one with a value of ≥ 11, and one with a value of ≥ -11, since $|11| = |-11| = 11$. Then, since this is an inequality, solve each equation, remembering to change the inequality sign when multiplying or dividing by a negative number. Thus,

$$|2x - 7| \geq 11 \text{ is solved by}$$

$$2x - 7 \geq 11 \qquad\qquad (2x - 7) \geq -11$$
$$2x \geq 18 \qquad\qquad 2x + 7 \geq -11$$
$$x \geq 9 \qquad\qquad 2x \geq -4$$
$$\qquad\qquad\qquad x \leq -2$$

The solution is $x \leq -2$ or $x \geq 9$, so answer choices -7, -2, and 9 are included, but 0 and 7 are not.

13. $\boxed{B}$ and $\boxed{E}$. Consecutive integers are an even number and an odd number. The question asks which answer choices can never be even, which is the same as asking which are always odd. Answer choices $\boxed{B}$ and $\boxed{E}$ are always odd because an odd integer plus an even integer always equals an odd integer. Answer choices $\boxed{A}$, $\boxed{C}$, and $\boxed{D}$ are always even because anything times an even integer is even, and each of these answer choices involves an even integer times an odd integer.

14. (B), 4% less. If the original price is x, the increased price is $1.20x$. This is then discounted by 20%, which means it is now 80% of the increased price, or $.80(1.20x) = .96x$, which is 4% less than x. Alternatively, use \$100 as a convenient number to calculate the answer: \$100 increased by 20% = \$120; 20% off is \$24; \$120 − \$24 = \$96, which is 4% less than the original price.

15. (D), 2. First, convert 1 hour and 45 minutes to 1.75 hours (45 minutes is three-fourths of an hour). The two ratios in miles per hour should be equal: $\dfrac{3.5 \text{ miles}}{1.75 \text{ hours}} = \dfrac{x \text{ miles}}{1 \text{ hour}}$, or $1.75x = 3.5$, so $x = 2$. Right away, answer choices (A) and (B) should be eliminated because they are greater than or equal to the distance for 1.75 hours. Answer choice (E) should be eliminated as being too low because at a half mile an hour, the time for 3.5 miles would have been 7 hours!

16. (B), 20%. To figure the percentage of reduction, divide the amount of reduction by the original price. Always use the original price in this type of problem, not the sale price. Use the sale price, though, to figure the amount of reduction: \$80 −\$64 = \$16. The calculation of the percentage is thus $\dfrac{16}{80} = 20\%$.

17. $\boxed{A}$, $\frac{7}{8}$, and $\boxed{C}$, 0.9. The only calculation that has to be done here is to figure out what $\frac{\frac{1}{2}}{0.5}$ equals, but since the numerator and denominator are equivalent, the value is 1. So the problem reduces to finding b if $\frac{5}{6} > b > 1$. Answer choice $\boxed{B}$ is eliminated because it is greater than 1, answer choice $\boxed{D}$ is eliminated because it is negative, and answer choice $\boxed{E}$ is eliminated because it is less than $\frac{5}{6}$. Remember the handy fact that $\frac{1}{2} < \frac{2}{3} < \frac{3}{4} < \frac{4}{5} < \frac{5}{6} < \frac{6}{7} < \frac{7}{8} < \frac{9}{10}$. Therefore, the values in answer choices $\boxed{A}$ or $\boxed{C}$ could each be values for b.

18. (C), $14. Alyce saves $\frac{1}{8}$ of her allowance, which leaves $\frac{7}{8}$ for spending. She will have $\frac{2}{5}$ of $\frac{7}{8}$ of $40 for the amusement park. Remember that "of" means multiply, so the calculation is

$\frac{2}{5} \times \frac{7}{8} \times \$40 = \$14$.

Answers to Drill: Converting Improper Fractions into Mixed Numbers
(page 53):

a. $7\frac{9}{10}$ b. $9\frac{4}{9}$ c. $2\frac{7}{8}$ d. $8\frac{5}{7}$ e. $7\frac{1}{6}$

f. $5\frac{2}{5}$ g. $4\frac{2}{4} = 4\frac{1}{2}$ h. $4\frac{1}{4}$ i. $4\frac{1}{2}$ j. $6\frac{2}{5}$

Answers to Drill: Multiplication and Division of Fractions *(page 58)*:

a. $\dfrac{3}{7} \times \dfrac{6}{5} = \dfrac{18}{35}$

b. $\dfrac{9}{4} \times \dfrac{8}{3} = \dfrac{\cancel{9}^{3}}{\cancel{4}_{1}} \times \dfrac{\cancel{8}^{2}}{\cancel{3}_{1}} = 6$

c. $\dfrac{20}{9} \times \dfrac{12}{5} = \dfrac{\cancel{20}^{4}}{\cancel{9}_{3}} \times \dfrac{\cancel{12}^{4}}{\cancel{5}_{1}} = \dfrac{16}{3} = 5\dfrac{1}{3}$

d. $\dfrac{25}{7} \times \dfrac{12}{5} = \dfrac{\cancel{25}^{5}}{7} \times \dfrac{12}{\cancel{5}_{1}} = \dfrac{60}{7} = 8\dfrac{4}{7}$

e. $\dfrac{63}{13} \div \dfrac{63}{26} = \dfrac{63}{13} \times \dfrac{26}{63} = \dfrac{\cancel{63}^{1}}{\cancel{13}_{1}} \times \dfrac{\cancel{26}^{2}}{\cancel{63}_{1}} = 2$

Answers to Drill: Algebra *(page 67):*

a. $x = 130$ b. $x = 43$ c. $x = 7$ d. $x = \dfrac{4}{5}$ e. $x = 144$

f. $x = 21$ g. $x = \dfrac{17}{3} = 5\dfrac{2}{3}$ h. $x = 1$ i. $x = 15$ j. $x = -2$

Algebra and Functions

REVIEW OF THE BASICS

You use algebra every day without realizing it. By mentally doing algebra, you come up with answers to questions such as "How many hours of parking will I get for $5.00 if the hourly rate is $1.25?" or "If I have to write a 1500-word paper, how many pages would that be if a typical typed page contains 300 words?" These are typical word problems, but you solve them without even thinking you are doing algebra.

The introduction to algebra from the preceding chapter discussed three main rules for solving an equation:

1. Whatever operation you perform on one side of the equal sign, you must perform on the other side to preserve the equality.

2. Use inverses to isolate the unknown variable on one side of the equation. Addition and subtraction are inverse operations, and multiplication and division are inverse operations.

3. To simplify a word problem, translate "what" or "how many" or similar phrases into the unknown, usually x. Use the following other translations: "of" means multiply, "is" or other forms of that verb mean equals.

Now we will discuss other algebra topics that will make solving equations easier, especially word problems. Let's start with a word problem.

EXAMPLE 5.1

Jim scored 7 baskets and 4 free throws during the basketball game. How many points did Jim score? (Each basket is worth two points and each free throw is worth one point.)

(A) 4

(B) 11

(C) 14

(D) 18

(E) 42

SOLUTION

The correct answer is (D), 18 points.

You probably figured that the baskets were worth $7 \times 2 = 14$ points, and the free throws were worth $4 \times 1 = 4$ points, so Jim scored $14 + 4 = 18$ points. You also probably figured that out faster than you read this explanation.

The question "How many points did Jim score?" can be set up algebraically as

$$x = (7 \times 2) + (4 \times 1) = 14 + 4 = 18$$

What math did you have to know to do this problem? Most important, you had to be able to *analyze* the problem, from which you figured out that you would have to add two separate events (basket points and free throw points) to get the total points.

If you set up the problem without the parentheses, which are included here to separate the points for baskets from the points for free throws, the equation might look like this: $x = 7 \times 2 + 4 \times 1$. If you didn't use the PEMDAS rule from the last chapter, you might have found the incorrect answer to Example 5.1: $7 \times 6 \times 1 = 42$.

ORDER OF OPERATIONS

The following list reviews the order of operations, which is key to evaluating mathematical expressions. Operations must be done in the following order:

1. *Parentheses:* Parentheses say "do me first." In other words, evaluate what is in the parentheses ( ) or brackets [ ] or braces { }, working from the inside out, until they are all gone.

2. *Exponents:* Evaluate any part of the expression that contains exponents next.

3. *Multiplication and Division:* Do any multiplication and/or division in order from left to right.

4. *Addition and Subtraction:* Do any addition and/or subtraction in order from left to right.

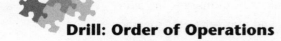

Drill: Order of Operations

a. $7 \times (3 \times 2 \div 6) + 4$	b. $(4 + 5 - 3) + 7 + 2$	c. $(10 + 2) \times (15 - 3)$
d. $(10 - 4)^2 - 6 + 5^2$	e. $3 \times (4 + 9) + (4 - 2)^3$	f. $10 + (10^2 - 10) - 10$
g. $7 + (3 + (6 - 2))^2 + 8$	h. $((6 + 2)^2 - 34)^2 + 16$	i. $4 - (3^2 - 5) + 360$

Answers on page 128.

COMBINING LIKE TERMS

A simple, but important, algebraic rule is to combine like terms. **Terms** are the parts of addition and subtraction (in other words, terms are separated by a plus sign or a minus sign). **Like terms** have exactly the same (like) letters and exponents. The coefficients can vary, and they are what you use for combining, which means adding or subtracting. (Remember that subtracting is the same as adding a negative.) For example, x and $3x$ are like terms because the letters are x to the first power. (Also remember that we usually don't write the exponent if it is 1 because anything to the first power is just itself.) When we add x and $3x$, we get $x + 3x = 4x$. If we subtract $3x$ from x, we get $x - 3x = -2x$. So we are combining the coefficients of the x's, the like terms.

EXAMPLE 5.2

Simplify the expression $7x + 3y - 2 + 6 - 2x + 4 + y$.

    (A) $9x + 8$

    (B) $5x + 4y + 8$

    (C) $5x + 4y + 4$

    (D) $9xy + 8$

    (E) $5x + 4y + 12$

SOLUTION

The correct answer is (B), $5x + 4y + 8$.

Note that the word "simplify" is used when we combine like terms. We saw the word "simplify" before when we talked about simplifying fractions. The idea is the same: to put an expression in a form that cannot be combined (or in the case of fractions, reduced) any further.

Good solution: In this example, combine the x terms, the y terms, and the numbers individually, but do not try to combine the x, y, and number terms together since they are "unlike." Use the commutative and associative laws to group the like terms:

$$7x + 3y - 2 + 6 - 2x + 4 + y =$$

$$(7x - 2x) + (3y + y) + (-2 + 6 + 4) =$$

$$5x + 4y + 8$$

Better solution: Use the approach of eliminating wrong choices first. Looking at the answer choices, eliminate choices (A) and (D) right away since they don't reflect the unknown y in the original expression. Since all three remaining choices have $5x + 4y$, look at the number terms, $-2 + 6 + 4$, which equal 8. Thus, the problem is solved in a little less time by not even finding the x term, since it is the same in all possible answer choices.

A Praxis Core Math problem that looks like simply combining like terms may involve many other areas of math, such as the distributive law, adding fractions with unlike denominators, or using PEMDAS. For example, finding the full solution for Example 5.3 can take several minutes. Keep in mind, however, that for multiple-choice questions, you can eliminate choices that are obviously incorrect and get the correct choice quicker and easier.

EXAMPLE 5.3

Simplify the expression $(8 + 7x^2 + 4x - 3) - 2(5x^2 + 2x + \dfrac{3}{4} + 8) + 5\dfrac{1}{2}$.

    (A) $3x^2 - 6$

    (B) $-3x^2 - 7$

    (C) $-3x^2 + 8x - 7$

    (D) $-3x^2 - 8x + 7$

    (E) $3x^2 - 7$

SOLUTION

The correct answer is (B), $-3x^2 - 7$.

Good solution:

$$(8 + 7x^2 + 4x - 3) - 2(5x^2 + 2x + \dfrac{3}{4} + 8) + 5\dfrac{1}{2}$$

Using PEMDAS and the distributive law, first remove the parentheses:

$$8 + 7x^2 + 4x - 3 - 10x^2 - 4x - \frac{6}{4} - 16 + 5\frac{1}{2}$$

Then, using the commutative and associative laws, rearrange the terms to group the like terms:

$$(7x^2 - 10x^2) + (4x - 4x) + (8 - 3 - \frac{6}{4} - 16 + 5\frac{1}{2})$$

$$(3x^2 + (8 - 3 - 16 - \frac{6}{4} + 5\frac{1}{2})$$

Next, combine like terms. Reduce $\frac{6}{4}$ and use the improper fraction for $5\frac{1}{2}$ to get the same denominator for the fractions.

$$-3x^2 + (-11 - \frac{3}{2} + \frac{11}{2}) =$$

$$-3x^2 - 11 + \frac{8}{2} = -3x^2 - 11 + 4 = -3x^2 - 7$$

Better solution: Instead of doing all of the math, start by figuring the coefficient of the x^2 term. Then look at the answer choices, and eliminate two of them. The two x^2 terms are $7x^2$ and $-2(5x^2)$, which combine to form $7x^2 - 10x^2 = -3x^2$. That reduces the choices to (B), (C), and (D). Next, look at the x terms, which are $4x$ and $-2(2x)$, which combine to $4x - 4x = 0$. There is no x term! So only answer choice (B) is left. You don't have to do anything with the number terms (which takes a lot of time). This technique for multiple-choice questions can be quite a time-saver.

WORKING WITH UNKNOWNS IN THE DENOMINATOR

The last chapter, on numbers and quantity, discussed fractions. To add or subtract fractions, we often need to find a common denominator. But what if the denominators have unknowns in them? The procedure is exactly the same. The common denominator is simply the product of the denominators, and we multiply each term by an expression equal to 1 (which often is the fraction formed by the common denominator divided by the common denominator).

This means that the denominator of the sum or difference we are finding may still have an unknown in the denominator, but that's okay. The only numbers we don't want in a denominator are 0 because division by 0 is undefined. We also don't want any radicals in the denominator. For that reason, whenever we have a fraction with an unknown in the denominator, we put in the restriction that the unknown cannot be a value that would make any denominator equal to zero. This is best shown by example.

EXAMPLE 5.4

Write a fraction that is equivalent to $\dfrac{3}{4x} - \dfrac{5}{7}$ ($x \neq 0$.)

SOLUTION

The correct answer is $\dfrac{21 - 20x}{28x}$.

Good solution: Since this is the difference of two fractions, we have to find a common denominator, which in this case is $4x \times 7 = 28x$. We multiply each fraction by the equivalent of 1: $\dfrac{28x}{28x}$. Both $4x$ and 7 both cancel into the $28x$. The procedure is outlined below.

$$\frac{3}{4x} - \frac{5}{7} =$$

$$\left(\frac{28x}{28x}\right)\frac{3}{4x} - \left(\frac{28x}{28x}\right)\frac{5}{7} =$$

$$\left(\frac{7}{28x}\right)\frac{3}{1} - \left(\frac{4x}{28x}\right)\frac{5}{1} =$$

$$\frac{3(7)}{28x} - \frac{5(4x)}{28x} =$$

$$\frac{21 - 20x}{28x}$$

Better solution: When there are two terms to be added or subtracted, you can go right to the last steps of the above calculation by multiplying each term by a fraction with a numerator and denominator equal to the denominator of the other term. So in this example, to find

$$\frac{3}{4x} - \frac{5}{7}$$

multiply the first term by $\dfrac{7}{7}$ ($= 1$) and the second term by $\dfrac{4x}{4x}$ (also $= 1$), to get the following step right away:

$$\left(\frac{7}{7}\right)\frac{3}{4x} - \left(\frac{4x}{4x}\right)\frac{5}{7}$$

$$\frac{21}{28x} - \frac{20x}{28x} = \frac{21 - 20x}{28x}$$

With practice, you should be able to do this mentally.

Best solution: This works only with addition and subtraction of two fractions.

Recognize that the denominator of the sum (or difference) is the product of the denominators of the two fractions, in this case $28x$. The first term of the numerator is the product of the numerator of the first term and the denominator of the second term (don't forget to take the sign of the numerator into account), and the second term of the numerator is the product of the numerator of the second term and the denominator of the first term. (This is similar to cross-multiplication discussed in the last chapter.) So you can immediately write the answer as:

$$\frac{3}{4x} - \frac{5}{7} = \frac{3(7) - 5(4x)}{28x} = \frac{21 - 20x}{28x}$$

Notice that $x \neq 0$ is written with the original expression because the denominator cannot equal 0.

EXAMPLE 5.5

What expression is equivalent to $\dfrac{3}{4x} + \dfrac{5}{y}$? $(x \neq 0, y \neq 0)$

Good solution: Here, the LCD is $4xy$. Again, we multiply top and bottom of each fraction by $4xy$, but now there is some cancellation, so we get

$$\frac{3}{4x} + \frac{5}{y} =$$

$$\left(\frac{4xy}{4xy}\right)\frac{3}{4x} + \frac{5}{y}\left(\frac{4xy}{4xy}\right) =$$

$$\frac{3y}{4xy} + \frac{20x}{4xy} =$$

$$\frac{3y + 20x}{4xy}$$

Better solution:

$$\frac{3}{4x} + \frac{5}{y} =$$

$$\left(\frac{y}{y}\right)\frac{3}{4x} + \frac{5}{y}\left(\frac{4x}{4x}\right) =$$

$$\frac{3y}{4xy} + \frac{20x}{4xy} =$$

$$\frac{3y + 20x}{4xy}$$

Best solution:

Determine that the common denominator is $4xy$, and cross multiply to find the numerator right away:

$$\frac{3}{4x} + \frac{5}{y} = \frac{3y + 20x}{4xy}$$

GRAPHING

Every equation can be graphed on a Cartesian coordinate system. This long term simply means a graph with x values and y values, such as the following.

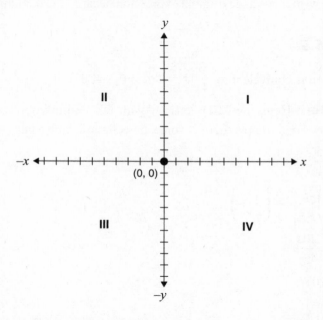

Notice that the **origin** is the intersection of the x and y axes, and that each of the axes looks like a number line, with negative x values on the left of the origin (with x value 0), just like the number line, and negative y values below the origin (with y value 0), just like a vertical thermometer. Points on the Cartesian coordinate system are plotted as (x, y). Just count the number of places for the x value, and then follow that line to the y value. Any such point is called an **ordered pair**, which gets its name because there is a specific order (x, y). The x value always goes first.

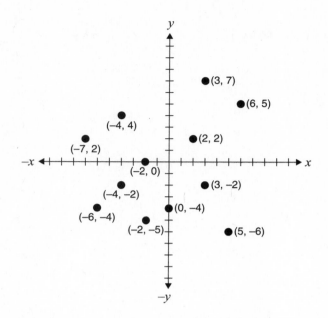

Notice that if the *x* value is positive, the point will be to the right of the *y*-axis, if *x* = 0, it will be on the *y*-axis, and if the *x* value is negative, the point will be to the left of the *y*-axis. Similarly, if the *y* value is positive, the point will be above the *x*-axis, if *y* = 0, it will be on the *x*-axis, and if the *y* value is negative, the point will be below the *x*-axis.

A line is made up of points that are connected together. In fact, there are an infinite number of points on a line. Often we are focusing on specific points on a line, maybe two or three, and not all of the points that make up the line—but they are all still there.

We must connect two points to make a specific line; three are better. Points that line up in a straight line are called collinear. The reason it is better to plot three lines is that if you made a mistake on locating either of the original two points, when you connect them you will get a line, but it might not be the correct one. But if a third point doesn't line up, that is a clue that you made a mistake somewhere.

Often, the points for a line are given in a table that gives *x* and *y* values to plot on a graph. For example, let's look at the following points, which are points on the line $y = 2x$.

x	y
1	2
2	4
3	6

And let's assume we plot the first two points on a graph as follows (one of them is incorrect, but that is precisely what we want to show here).

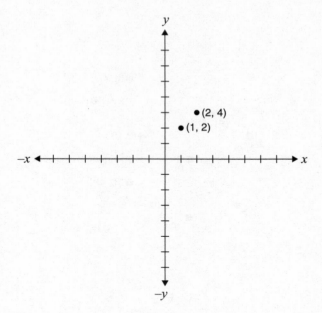

If we connect these two points, we would get a straight line. But is it the one we want? To check, we plot the third point (3, 6).

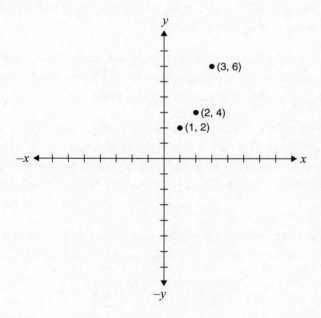

It doesn't line up with the others. Obviously there is a mistake somewhere, and sure enough, point (2, 4) was plotted as (2, 3). Once we make the correction, we see that all three points line up. And if we extend the line beyond these points, we can even find other points on the line that make the equation $y = 2x$ correct.

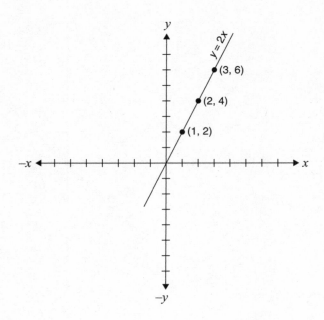

EXAMPLE 5.6

Make a table of ordered pairs for the equation $y = x$ and plot them to find the line for the equation.

SOLUTION

Since $y = x$, possible points are $(0, 0)$, $(1, 1)$, $(2, 2)$, and even the negatives, such as $(-1, -1)$, $(-2, -2)$. Any such pairs are correct for this equation. If plotted correctly, the graph will look like this:

x	y
0	0
1	1
2	2
−1	−1
−2	−2

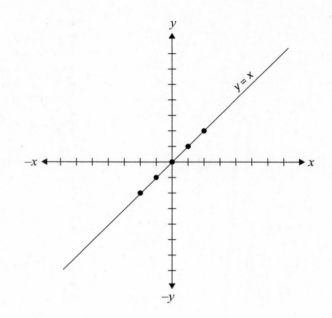

LINEAR EQUATIONS

A **linear equation** graphs as a straight line. In a linear equation. the power of the unknown variable is 1, as in x^1. Period. Not less than 1 or greater than 1—only 1. We know that $x^1 = x$. Any equation in which the exponent (power) of the unknown is different from 1 is a **nonlinear equation**. It can be a curve, a circle, even V-shaped, but it just isn't a straight line.

Straight Lines

Let's talk about straight lines. What distinguishes one straight line from another? One feature is whether the line increases or decreases from left to right. Another is how "steep" the line is, called its **slope**, defined as the change in y for each change in x, or

$$\text{slope} = m = \frac{\text{change in } y}{\text{change in } x}.$$

We called the slope m here. It could be any letter, but the usual one is m. The x and y value changes here are just the differences between any two points on a line. Just remember not to switch which point is which, since subtraction isn't commutative. In other words, to keep the points straight, we can call one point (x_1, y_1) and the other point (x_2, y_2), and then the slope will be written as

$$m = \frac{\text{change in } y}{\text{change in } x} = \frac{(y_1 - y_2)}{(x_1 - x_2)}$$

$$\text{or } m = \frac{(y_2 - y_1)}{(x_2 - x_1)}.$$

Either formula works. The important thing is that the order of points doesn't get switched and we don't have, for example $(y_2 - y_1)$ on the top and $(x_1 - x_2)$ on the bottom.

A third distinction is where this line is on a graph. Is it higher than the origin, lower than the origin, or does it go right through the origin? The placement of the line can be described by where it crosses the y-axis, as we shall see next. This is called the **y-intercept**. Note that at the y-intercept, the value of x is always 0.

Slope-Intercept Form of a Linear Equation

We actually can tell a lot about a line from its equation without even plotting the line on a graph. If the equation is written in a certain way, we can tell what the slope is and where it crosses the y-axis. There is one and only one line with precise values for these two pieces of information. The way to write this equation, which is called the **slope-intercept form**, is

$$y = mx + b,$$

where m is the slope and b is the y-intercept.

Look at the following graph to see how this works.

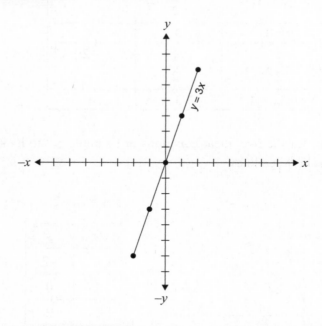

The equation is $y = 3x$. According to the slope-intercept form, $y = mx + b$, the slope $= m = 3$, and the y-intercept $= b = 0$. In other words, the graph will go up (because m is positive) 3 places in the y direction for every 1 place in the x direction, and it will cross the y-intercept at $(0, 0)$.

Now, if we look at the graph of $y = 3x$ and go from one point to another (we pick points that we can read easily on the graph), we see that for every increase of 1 for x, y increases by 3. This means the slope for $y = 3x$ is $\dfrac{\text{change in } y}{\text{change in } x} = \dfrac{3}{1} = 3$. Also, we see that the graph crosses the y-axis at the point $(0, 0)$.

EXAMPLE 5.7

Find the slope and *y*-intercept for each of the following equations without graphing.

(a) $y = 2x - 2$

(b) $y = -\frac{1}{2}x + 1$

(c) $y = 3$

(d) $y = -\frac{1}{2}x - 2$

(e) $y = 3x + 4$

SOLUTION

The answers for Example 5.7 are shown below.

Line	Equation	Slope	y-intercept
(a)	$y = 2x - 2$	2	–2
(b)	$y = -\frac{1}{2}x + 1$	$-\frac{1}{2}$	1
(c)	$y = 3$	0	3
(d)	$y = -\frac{1}{2}x - 2$	$-\frac{1}{2}$	–2
(e)	$y = 3x + 4$	3	4

Let's graph the lines for the five linear equations in Example 5.7 to look at some interesting facts about relationships between lines.

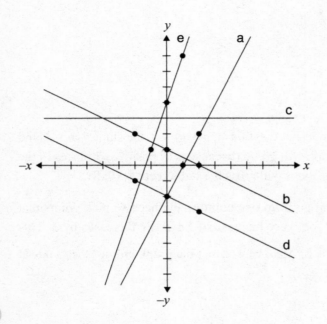

a: $y = 2x - 2$

x	y
0	–2
1	0
2	2

d: $y = -\frac{1}{2}x - 2$

x	y
0	–2
2	–3
–2	–1

b: $y = -\frac{1}{2}x + 1$

x	y
0	2
–2	2
2	0

e: $y = 3x + 4$

x	y
0	4
–1	1
1	7

c: $y = 3$

The slope of a line is given by the coefficient of x when the line is in slope-intercept form. The slope tells how steep the line is (how much y changes with respect to x) and in what direction the line lies.

Here we see that lines (a) and (e) have positive slopes, so they rise to the right. As x gets bigger, so does y. The slope of line (a) is 2 and the slope of line (e) is 3, so line (e) is steeper, which can be clearly seen on the graph.

There is no x term in the equation for line (c), so it is parallel to the x-axis. **Parallel** means the two lines (line (c) and the x-axis) will never cross. Line (c) says that no matter what x is, y will always be 3. The slope of line (c) is 0 because the change in y is 0. Incidentally, the line $x = 0$ would be parallel to the y-axis, but its slope would be "undefined," or some say it is infinity (∞); either way, it has no slope because the slope is defined as the change in y over the change in x, and since x doesn't change, that would make the denominator for the slope 0, and we cannot divide by 0.

Lines (b) and (d) have the same slope $\left(-\dfrac{1}{2}\right)$, which means exactly the same steepness, so they, too, are parallel to each other, as seen on the graph. They go down to the right, which can be seen in the graph as well as the fact that their slope in the equation is negative. The difference between lines (b) and (d) is their placement on the graph, which is determined by the y-intercept. Line (b) is above line (d) because line (b)'s y-intercept ($y = +1$) is greater than line (d)'s y-intercept ($y = -2$) (remember, any positive number is greater than any negative number).

There is one more relationship to be seen in this figure, and that is the relationship between line (a) and line (b). They are perpendicular to each other, meaning they form four equal right angles (for an explanation of the term "perpendicular," see the next chapter). This happens whenever the slopes of two lines are negative reciprocals of each other. The slope of line (a) is 2, and the slope of line (b) is $-\dfrac{1}{2}$, the negative reciprocal of 2, and the lines are therefore perpendicular. In case you were wondering, line (a) is also perpendicular to line (d) on this graph because that same relationship (slopes are negative reciprocals) exists for these two lines as well.

These facts are summarized below, and will be helpful in the next chapter, where we discuss geometry.

- The slope of a line is given by m in the slope-intercept form of the linear equation: $y = mx + b$.

- A positive slope means the line increases to the right; a negative slope means it decreases to the right.

- Two lines with the same slope are parallel to each other.

- Two lines whose slopes are negative reciprocals of each other are perpendicular.

- Any line of the form $y =$ constant, where constant here means any value (with no x), is parallel to the x-axis. Likewise, any line of the form $x =$ constant is parallel to the y-axis.

We can plot a line by substituting any x value into the equation and figuring out the y value, and finding at least three points on the line, as detailed earlier. Or we can plot the line by knowing just the slope and y-intercept. In this case, the y-intercept gives us our starting point $(0, y)$, remembering that the x value at the y-intercept is always 0. Then we use the slope to find two other points graphically.

The top number of the slope is how many spaces to go up (for a positive slope) or down (for a negative slope) from the y-intercept. The bottom number (1 if the slope is a whole number) tells how many spaces to then go to the right. That would be the second point (the first being the y-intercept). Then we can do the same thing to find a third point, using this new point as the starting point.

If we know two points on the xy-plane, we can find the equation of the line that passes through them by using what we know about slope. Remember that the definition of slope is

$$m = \frac{\text{change in } y}{\text{change in } x} = \frac{(y_1 - y_2)}{(x_1 - x_2)}$$

If we know two points we can find the slope, as we did above, and then we can use that value to find the equation of the line.

EXAMPLE 5.8

What is the equation in slope-intercept form of the line that goes through points $(1, 5)$ and $(3, -3)$?

SOLUTION

The correct answer is $y = -4x + 9$.

The sequence of steps to find the equation is to first find the slope.

$$m = \frac{(y_1 - y_2)}{(x_1 - x_2)} = \frac{5 - (-3)}{1 - 3} = \frac{8}{-2} = -4$$

Next, we put this into the same equation, using this value for m and using any point (x, y) and either one of the given points to get the equation of the line. Let's use the point $(1, 5)$:

$$m = \frac{(y - y_1)}{(x - x_1)}$$

$-4 = \dfrac{y - 5}{x - 1}$ Substitute the slope (-4) and the point $(1, 5)$

$-4(x - 1) = y - 5$ Multiply both sides of the equation by $(x - 1)$

$-4x + 4 = y - 5$ Use the distributive property

$-4x + 9 = y$ Add 5 to both sides of the equation

Therefore, the equation that contains both $(1, 5)$ and $(3, -3)$ is $y = -4x + 9$.

We can check that this is the equation by substituting the other point, $(3, -3)$, into the equation to see if it works: $-3 = -4(3) + 9$, or $-3 = -12 + 9 = -3$. It checks!

EXAMPLE 5.9

x	y
-5	-5
-3	-1
0	5
1	7
2	9

Given the above table of values, which of the following is the corresponding linear equation?

    (A) $y = 3x + 10$

    (B) $y = -2x - 15$

    (C) $y = 2x + 5$

    (D) $y = -x - 10$

    (E) $y = x$

SOLUTION

The correct answer is (C), $y = 2x + 5$.

Good solution: Take any two values from the table and find the slope. For example,

$$m = \frac{(y_1 - y_2)}{(x_1 - x_2)} = \frac{9 - 7}{2 - 1} = 2$$

Find the equation by substituting the slope, a third point, and the point (x, y) into the equation $m = \frac{(y - y_1)}{(x - x_1)}$. Let's use $(-3, -1)$ as the third point:

$$2 = \frac{(y - (-1))}{(x - (-3))} = \frac{y + 1}{x + 3}$$

Thus

$$y + 1 = 2(x + 3)$$

$$y + 1 = 2x + 6$$

$$y = 2x + 5$$

Another good solution: Another way to solve this type of problem is to substitute the values in the table into each equation choice to see whether it is true. This sounds like a lot of work, but the equations that are wrong sort themselves out rather quickly—if not by the first substitution, then certainly by the second if the equations are linear. And, of course, once the correct answer choice is found, the ones after it don't have to be checked at all.

Better solution: It isn't necessary to find the exact equation since all of the answer choices are in slope-intercept form and they all have different slopes. Just find the slope as was done before, $m = 2$, and choose the answer that has 2 as a slope.

Best solution: A much faster way is to recognize that all of the answer choices have different y-intercepts, which is the value of y when $x = 0$, and that value of the y-intercept is in the table $(0, 5)$. Then find the answer choice that has a y-intercept of 5.

Simultaneous Equations

Notice that the five lines in the graph for Example 5.7 intersected with some of the other lines. Since all of the points on a linear equation line are solutions to the equation, when two lines intersect, their point of intersection is a solution to both equations. For example, we see that lines (a) $y = 2x - 2$ and (d) $y = -\frac{1}{2}x - 2$ intersect at the point $(0, -2)$. Let's check whether that point is a solution to both equations.

For line (a):

$$y = 2x - 2$$
$$(-2) = 2(0) - 2$$
$$-2 = -2$$

For line (d):

$$y = -\frac{1}{2}x - 2$$
$$(-2) = -\frac{1}{2}(0) - 2$$
$$-2 = -2$$

Yes, indeed, $(0, -2)$ is a solution for both equations. So by graphing two equations and noting their intersection, we find the solution to both equations. Equations that share a solution are called **simultaneous equations** (because they have the same solution at the same time), or sometimes called **systems of equations**.

However, as you can see on the graph for Example 5.7, lines don't always cross at convenient, whole number points on a graph. So let's see how we can find a solution to two equations algebraically. We know that lines (a) and (e) will intersect somewhere because they are getting closer together as y decreases. The algebraic methods to find the point of intersection, or the solution to simultaneous equations, are substitution or elimination. The idea behind either one is the same: We want to combine the equations in such a way that we end up with an equation with just one of the unknowns (x or y, but not both), which we can easily solve. Remember that whatever you do to one side of an equation you must do to the other. Let's see how that works for lines (a) $y = 2x - 2$ and (e) $y = 3x + 4$.

First, the **substitution** method is just as it sounds. Both equations are equal to y, so let's just substitute one of them for y in the other equation. It makes no difference in this case which one we choose, we end up with the same equation:

$$2x - 2 = 3x + 4$$

$$-6 = x \qquad\qquad \text{Subtract } 2x \text{ and add } -4 \text{ on each side}$$

Then, knowing $x = -6$, substitute that into either of the original equations to find the corresponding value for y: $y = 2(-6) - 2 = -14$. The point of intersection, or the solution to both equations, is $(-6, -14)$. If we look at how those two lines are closing in on one another on the graph, that looks like it will work.

The **elimination** method works when all else fails. It involves adding or subtracting the two equations so that one of the unknowns (x or y) cancels out. Let's use lines (a) and (e) again, but this time we will find y by dropping out the x's.

$$y = 2x - 2$$

$$y = 3x + 4$$

To eliminate the x's by adding the two equations, we must first change the equations to equivalent equations that have x coefficients that will cancel out. If we multiply an equation by, say, 3, we must multiply every term on both sides for it to remain an equation (equal). So for line (a), we get $3(y = 2x - 2)$, or $3y = 6x - 6$. Now, if we multiply the equation for line (e) by -2, the x terms will cancel each other out when we add the two resulting equations. That multiplication results in $-2(y = 3x + 4) = -2y = -6x - 8$. Let's line up these two new equations and add them together. We can do that because we are adding equal things to both sides of the equation.

$$3y = 6x - 6$$
$$\underline{-2y = -6x - 8}$$
$$y = 0 - 14$$

Finally, substitute $y = -14$ into either *original* equation to find the value for x:

$$y = 2x - 2$$

$$-14 = 2x - 2$$

$$-6 = x \qquad\qquad \text{Add 2 to both sides and divide by 2}$$

Again, the solution for the system of equations is $(-6, -14)$.

Chances are that the Praxis Core Math test will give two simultaneous equations and multiple choices for the answer, or a situation from which to choose the two equations from multiple choices (and not have to solve the problem at all). Let's look at those types of problems:

EXAMPLE 5.10

Which of the following values are solutions to the following system of equations:

$$x + y = 3$$
$$5x + 8y = 21$$

(A) $x = -1, y = -2$

(B) $x = -1, y = 2$

(C) $x = 1, y = -2$

(D) $x = 1, y = 2$

(E) None of the above.

SOLUTION

The correct answer is (D), $x = 1, y = 2$.

Good solution: Use substitution. Rewrite the first equation to get an expression for either x or y. Let's use the expression we get for x by subtracting y from both sides of the first equation and substitute it into the second equation.

$x = -y + 3$	Rewrite the first equation
$5(-y + 3) + 8y = 21$	Substitute for x in second equation
$-5y + 15 + 8y = 21$	Use the distributive rule
$3y + 15 = 21$	Combine like terms
$3y = 6$	Subtract 15 from both sides
$y = 2$	Divide both sides by 3
$x + 2 = 3$	Substitute $y = 2$ into the original first equation
$x = 1$	Subtract 2 from both sides

So (1, 2) is the solution to both equations. A similar method also would have worked if we started with finding an expression for y (that is $y = -x + 3$) as the first step and used substitution.

Another good solution: Use elimination. For example, multiply the first equation by –5 and add the two resulting equations.

$-5(x + y = 3)$	
$-5x - 5y = -15$	Multiply the first equation by –5
$5x + 8y = 21$	Second equation
$3y = 6$	Add the two equations
$y = 2$	Divide both sides by 3
$x + 2 = 3$	Substitute $y = 2$ into the original first equation
$x = 1$	Subtract 2 from both sides

So again we find that $(1, 2)$ is the solution to both equations. A similar method would have worked if we multiplied the first equation by –8 as the first step and eliminated the y terms.

Better solution: Rather than solving the system, recognize that if this is a system of equations, the values for x and y must be true for both equations. So plug in those values from the answer choices in both equations to see which pair of values works. This sounds like a lot of work, but consider the first (simplest) of the two equations first to eliminate some answers. Right away, we can see that the only possible pair that is true for the first equation is (D), but we must also check that it is a solution to the second equation, just to be sure that we didn't make a mistake or that the answer isn't (E).

Some pairs of simultaneous equations have no solution. For example, look at lines (b), $y = -\frac{1}{2}x + 1$ and (d), $y = -\frac{1}{2}x - 2$, from Example 5.7. If we use substitution, we get $-\frac{1}{2}x + 1 = -\frac{1}{2}x - 2$, which is impossible. If we use elimination and subtract the two equations, we get $0 = -3$, again, impossible. If two equations have no solution, they never intersect, which means they are parallel, and indeed lines (b) and (d) are parallel. (See the next chapter for an explanation of parallel lines.)

In contrast, if two lines have infinite solutions, they are the same line—every point on the one line is a point on the other line. Examples would be the lines $y = 2x + 1$ and $2y = 4x + 2$, since the equation of the second line is just a multiple of the first line.

INEQUALITIES

Inequalities are represented by the following symbols introduced in the last chapter.

$<$ less than

$>$ greater than

$\leq$ less than or equal to

$\geq$ greater than or equal to

Inequalities can be combined to indicate a specific range of values. For example, $-2 \leq x < 6$, with x being a whole number, means x can be $-2, -1, 0, 1, 2, 3, 4,$ or 5.

Algebraic Inequalities

Working with inequalities is similar to working with equalities—whatever we do to one side, we must also do to the other side of the inequality, substituting the inequality sign for the equal sign. However, if we multiply or divide an inequality by a negative, the inequality sign switches direction because even though 6 is less than 8, -6 is greater than -8, as we showed in the last chapter. So to algebraically solve the following inequality for x, the steps would be

$$-2x + 6 \geq 14$$

$$-2x \geq 14 - 6 \qquad \text{Subtract 6 from both sides}$$

$$-2x \geq 8 \qquad \text{Combine like terms}$$

$$\frac{-2x}{-2} \leq \frac{8}{-2} \qquad \begin{array}{l}\text{Divide both sides by } -2\text{—notice the}\\ \text{switch in the inequality from } \geq \text{ to } \leq\end{array}$$

$$x \leq -4$$

Let's check this to see whether it works. The answer says that any number (not just whole numbers) less than or equal to -4 is our solution, so the solution can be -10, but it cannot be 0. For $x = -10$, substitute -10 for x in the original equation:

$$-2x + 6 \geq 14$$

$$-2(-10) + 6 \geq 14$$

$$20 + 6 \geq 14$$

$$26 \geq 14$$

That works, but let's also make sure $x = 0$, which is outside of our solution, doesn't work:

$$-2(0) + 6 \geq 14$$

$$0 + 6 \geq 14$$

$$6 \geq 14$$

Since this obviously doesn't work, our solution of $x \leq -4$ seems to be correct.

Graphically, this solution would look like this:

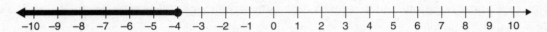

Notice that the circle at −4 is filled in. This indicates that −4 is included in the answer. If the endpoint is not included in the answer (if the inequality is < or >), the circle would be open.

Inequalities are used in problems if a limit is indicated. For example, if you have only $10 to spend at a store, your purchases (plus tax) must be ≤ $10.

EXAMPLE 5.11

Brandy is on commission and she wants to earn at least $800 in a certain amount of time. Her commission is $40 per sale. At least how many sales does she have to make to meet her goal?

(A) 20

(B) 40

(C) 50

(D) 80

(E) 200

SOLUTION

The correct answer is (A), 20.

We have to set up an inequality to find out the least number of sales that will still get Brandy the commission she needs. The inequality to use is

sales × commission ≥ $800

The symbol ≥, "greater than or equal to," translates into "at least" in plain English.

In this case, let's let sales = x, and the inequality becomes $40x \geq 800$. Dividing by 40 on both sides of the inequality, we get $x \geq 20$. Brandy must make at least 20 sales.

The graph of the answer to Example 5.11 is shown below.

Note that it is not necessary to show the negative numbers on this number line, since they don't make sense in this situation.

Graphing Linear Inequalities

To solve **linear inequalities** graphically, we follow the same procedure shown earlier in this chapter for linear equations and we plot the line as though the inequality were an equal sign. We can plot it by using a table of values, or we can put the equation in slope-intercept form and graph it by locating the y-intercept and finding points at the location indicated by the slope.

If the inequality includes the line (if the sign is $\leq$ or $\geq$), make the line solid, indicating that points on the line are included in the solution. If the inequality doesn't include the line (if the sign is $<$ or $>$), the line should be dashed to indicate it is not part of the solution.

For linear inequalities, the answer is all the points on one side of this line, which is indicated by shading the part of the graph that includes the solution points. But how do we determine whether the shading should be above or below the line? There are two quick ways to figure this out.

The following example shows the steps to find the line and which side to shade.

EXAMPLE 5.12

Show the solution to y $\leq$ 2x – 3 graphically.

Good solution: First, graph $y = 2x - 3$. One method is to make a table of values and plot at least three of the points and then draw a straight line through them. Remember that when the equation is linear, if the three points don't line up, at least one of them is incorrect, so we have to go back and check them out. The other way is to use the slope-intercept form of the equation to plot three points. Both methods were described earlier in this chapter. For this example, this line will be solid, since it is included by the $\leq$ sign.

Next, decide which side of the line to shade—it is the side that has the points that are solutions to the inequality. Pick a point, any point, on either side of the line. Plug the values of that point into the original inequality. If it is true, shade that side of the graph; if it is false, shade the other side. An easy point to pick is the origin—it is easily found, and substituting (0, 0) into the equation makes the math easy. For this graph, $y \leq 2x - 3$ becomes $0 \leq -3$, which is true, so we shade the side of the graph that has the origin in it.

Better solution: Plot the line the same way, but a faster way to determine which side to shade, if the inequality is in slope-intercept form, is to look at the inequality—if it is $<$ or $\leq$, shade below the line; if it is $>$ or $\geq$, shade above the line.

The graph for $y \leq 2x - 3$ follows.

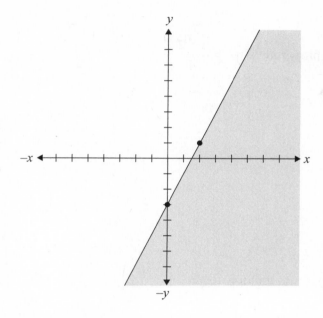

x	y
0	−3
1	−1
2	1

The Praxis Core Math test most likely will present an inequality and several graphs, and you are expected to determine which graph is the solution to the inequality.

RATIOS AND PROPORTIONS

This section starts with a review of what was covered about ratios and proportions in the previous chapter plus how to set up proportions to be solved algebraically. Previously, we set up some proportions as equal ratios and used cross multiplication to solve for the unknown quantity. This method has not changed, but now we consider proportions that involve unknowns with coefficients and as terms in a proportion.

Here is a quick list of the facts on ratios and proportions from the preceding chapter:

- A ratio is a way of comparing two quantities.

- Ratios can be expressed as fractions, decimals, or by two numbers separated by a colon.

- A proportion is the equivalence of two ratios.

- In a proportion, "like" quantities must be in like places.

- Proportions are solved by cross-multiplication and then by using algebra to find the missing part.

All of these facts are true no matter what quantities are involved in the ratio. The slope of a line is actually a ratio, $\dfrac{\text{change in } y}{\text{change in } x}$. The numerators and denominators in a ratio (or proportion) don't have to be just numbers, they can be expressions.

EXAMPLE 5.13

What is the value of x in the proportion $\dfrac{x+3}{6} = \dfrac{x-2}{4}$?

(A) 2.5

(B) 7

(C) 7.5

(D) 12

(E) 24

SOLUTION

The correct answer is (D), 12.

To solve this proportion for x, cross-multiply to get

$6(x - 2) = 4(x + 3)$	
$6x - 12 = 4x + 12$	Use the distributive law
$2x = 24$	Subtract $4x$ and add 12 on each side
$x = 12$	Divide both sides by 2

There isn't a quick way to judge which of the answer choices is correct here, so doing the math is required. Sometimes multiple-choice questions can be solved by substituting each answer into the problem, but in this case, that would involve more work and time than just solving the proportion because of the decimal answer choices. The first three answer choices are the result of not multiplying every term when using the distributive law; answer choice (E) is the result of not dividing by 2 at the end of the solution.

In this solution, we listed every step and the reasons for them, but during the test and, in fact, in real life, you should be able to do most of this problem mentally quickly and accurately without writing out every step. It takes practice, but it becomes easier the more you work with proportions as well as with algebra.

EXAMPLE 5.14

Micah wants to put a rug in a room that measures 9 feet wide by 12 feet long. He wants the dimensions of the rug to be proportional to those of the room. What is the width of the rug to the nearest tenth of a foot if its length is 10 feet?

(A) 7 feet

(B) 7.5 feet

(C) 10 feet

(D) 10.8 feet

(E) 13.3 feet

SOLUTION

The correct answer is (B), 7.5 feet.

Good solution: The dimensions of the rug must be in the same ratio as those of the room. That means setting up a proportion, where the unknown is the width of the rug.

The important thing here, as in all proportions, is to be consistent with the ratios. Here, the left side of the proportion is

$$\frac{\text{length of room}}{\text{width of room}}$$

So the right side of the proportion should be dimensions in the same pattern:

$$\frac{\text{length of rug}}{\text{width of rug}}$$

The ratio of the length to the width of a room is 12:9. The ratio of the length to the width of the rug is 10:x. Therefore the proportion is

$$\frac{12}{9} = \frac{10}{x}$$

$$12x = 90$$

$$x = \frac{90}{12} = 7.5$$

The other answer choices for this problem were the result of setting the proportion up incorrectly, perhaps with length over width on the left side and width over length on the right side.

Better solution: Look at the answer choices. Actually for this example, the last three answer choices can be eliminated because they are greater than 9, the width of the room. Eliminate answer choice (A) if you recognize that a ratio of 7:10 would be the same as 70%, and 70% of 12 is not 9 (since $.70 \times 12 = 8.4$).

FUNCTIONS

Many equations can be classified as **functions**, which defines a special relationship between input values and output values. Specifically, in a function, each input value (usually x) can have only one output value (usually y).

☞ HINT

A simple way to think of input-output is a telephone call. When you dial a specific phone number (your input), you expect one output for that number—the person you are calling. You don't expect to get the public library or your congressman or a wrong number—just the person whose number you dialed. However, the person at the other end of the line (the output for the number you called) may get calls from many people, or many inputs. In "function" words, the input has only one output, but the output can have many inputs.

The linear equations we encountered so far are all functions. A linear equation is a function because it is a line that never doubles back on itself. It just goes on in either direction. A cardiogram, a seismic readout, and the path of a baseball when it is hit are other examples of functions, so a function doesn't have to be just a straight line.

Graphically, it is easy to spot a graph that is not a function. It will have more than one y for some value of x, and maybe even many values of x. This is evident if you use the *vertical line test*, which actually can be applied visually. The vertical line test says that any vertical line can pass through the graph at only one point for that graph to qualify as a function—if it is not a function, any line parallel to the y-axis (vertical line) will cross the graph at more than one point. Graphs that are not functions, such as a circle, fail the vertical line test.

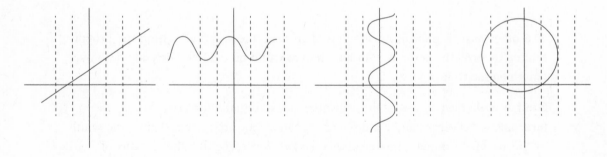

Notice that the first two graphs above pass the vertical line test, but the other two do not. Often, you can determine that a graph doesn't pass the vertical line test just by looking at the y-axis.

Working with Functions

Function notation is usually written as $f(x)$, although any letter will do. The letter within the parentheses is called the **domain**. It is the input value, and the $f(x)$, or whatever letter is used, denotes the output value, called the **range**. Actually, $f(x)$ is the same as the variable y we have been using.

☞ HINT

A handy way to remember what's called what is to notice that alphabetically, x, domain, and input each come before y, range, and output.

The function notation tells us that we can substitute anything for the quantity in the parentheses. In other words, for the function $f(x) = x^2$, we can write $f(2) = 2^2 = 4$. The substitution can even contain a variation of the input variable, so if $f(x) = x^2$, then $f(x + 4) = (x + 4)^2$. The rule is always the same: substitute the new input into the original function. Let's look at each of these cases individually.

$f(x) = x^2$ is saying that it is a function of the variable x, and it is giving the rule for what to do with any input values. So $f(2)$ is substituting 2 for x, which means we substitute 2 for x in the function, x^2. That's how we get $f(2) = 2^2 = 4$.

We do the same thing for $f(x + 4) = (x + 4)^2$. The defined function is $f(x) = x^2$, so we follow the same rule and substitute $x + 4$ for x. This seems a little peculiar because x isn't the same as $x + 4$, but if we view the x in the original function notation as just a placeholder for the domain or input to figure out what $f(x)$ (the range or output) will be, perhaps it will be easier to see.

Thus, if we have $f(x) = 5x - 3$, then

$f(1) = 5(1) - 3 = 2$

$f(4) = 5(4) - 3 = 17$

$f(b) = 5b - 3$

$f(c + 1) = 5(c + 1) - 3 = 5c + 5 - 3 = 5c + 2$

All we did in any of these was to simply replace the placeholder x with what is in the parentheses. Note how this is the same as if we asked, "If $y = 5x - 3$, what is y if $x = 1$, or $x = 4$, or $x = b$, or even $x = (c + 1)$?"

We don't have to use f all of the time, either. We can use any letter, such as $g(x) = x^2 + 2x + 4$. Then we can say $g(6) = 6^2 + 2(6) + 4 = 52$. And we don't have to use x either. What is important is that the notation means "A function of an input yields an output."

So, for example, we have $s(t) = 50t$, which is the formula for distance (s) in miles at a constant velocity of 50 mph for any time t in hours. That might seem daunting, but actually if instead we were asked, "At a speed of 50 mph, how far would a car go in 2 hours?", we would readily say 100 miles. Well, $s(2) = 50 \times 2 = 100$. It's the same thing.

So the function $f(x) = 3 - 2x + x^2$ is the same as $f(q) = 3 - 2q + q^2$, or $h(B) = 3 - 2B + B^2$, or even $w(\text{pig}) = 3 - 2\text{pig} + (\text{pig})^2$. Functional notation is just a way of telling where to put the value of the input. For any of these cases, $f(2) = h(2) = w(2) = 3 - 2(2) + 2^2 = 3$. We just substitute 2 for x, q, B, or pig.

For a relationship to qualify as a function, as was stated, every input has only one output. Each input with this matching output form an ordered pair, so a function can be seen also as a set of ordered pairs.

EXAMPLE 5.15

Write an equation for the function represented by the following ordered pairs.

x	y
−2	7
−1	4
0	1
1	−2
2	−5

SOLUTION

The correct answer is $f(x) = -3x + 1$.

Since the differences between the x values are constant, and the differences between the y values are constant, this function represents a linear equation, so let's find the slope and the y-intercept by choosing any two ordered pairs, and we can easily write the equation in slope-intercept form. For example, using (−2, 7) and (−1, 4), we can find the slope:

$$m = \frac{\text{change in } y}{\text{change in } x} = \frac{7-(4)}{-2-(-1)} = \frac{3}{-1} = -3$$

Note that we could have used any two pairs to get the slope. Since it is a linear equation, they will all give the same value of $m = -3$. The important thing when finding the slope in this way is to not mix the order up; whatever y value comes first in the formula, its x value must come first also. The y-intercept is $b = 1$ (the value of y when $x = 0$, as seen in the table).

So our equation is $y = mx + b = -3x + 1$, which, in function notation, is written as $f(x) = -3x + 1$.

Let's test this function by using $x = 2$, which we know from the table should give a value of $f(x) = -5$.

$$f(x) = -3x + 1$$

$$f(2) = -3(2) + 1 = -6 + 1 = -5$$

Combining Functions

Two or more functions can be combined, even if the function notation differs. For example, for $f(x) = 3x$ and $g(x) = 7x + 5$, just substitute to find

$$f(x) + g(x) = 3x + 7x + 5 = 10x + 5$$

$$f(x) - g(x) = 3x - (7x + 5) = 3x - 7x - 5 = -4x - 5$$

$$f(x) \times g(x) = 3x(7x + 5) = 21x^2 + 15x$$

$$f(x) \div g(x) = \frac{3x}{7x + 5}.$$ For this quotient, $g(x) \neq 0$ since division by 0 is undefined.

Composite Functions

For **composite functions** (a function of a function), the procedure is the same. Just use substitution. The typical notation for composite functions is $f(g(x))$, meaning "the function of a function." Do not confuse the notation for composite functions with the product of two functions, $f(x) \times g(x)$, which is sometimes written as $f(x)g(x)$.

If one function $f(x) = 2x + 1$ and another function $g(x) = 7x$, how would we express $f(g(x))$? Follow the same procedure as for a simple function:

$$f(g(x)) = 2(g(x)) + 1 \qquad \text{Substitute the new input into the original function } f$$

$$= 2(7x) + 1 \qquad \text{Substitute the new function } g$$

$$= 14x + 1 \qquad \text{Write in simplest terms}$$

EXAMPLE 5.16

If $f(x) = x^2 - x$, and $g(x) = 3x$, what is $f(g(x))$? Choose *all* correct answers.

- A $(3x)^2 - x$
- B $(3x)^2 - 3x$
- C $9x^2 - 3x$
- D $3x(3x - 1)$
- E $3x^2 - 3$

SOLUTION

The correct answer is choices $\boxed{B}$, $\boxed{C}$, and $\boxed{D}$.

These are all variations of the same expression. To find the answer(s), use the same steps as above, with no variation.

$$f(g(x)) = (g(x))^2 - g(x)$$
$$= (3x)^2 - 3x$$
$$= 9x^2 - 3x$$
$$= 3x(3x - 1)$$

The three solutions are equivalent expressions.

Note that $f(g(x))$ is not the same as $g(f(x))$. (This is not multiplication, and it is not commutative.) The value of $g(f(x))$ for the functions given in Example 5.16 is $g(x^2 - x) = 3(x^2 - x) = 3x^2 - 3x$. Although this looks similar to answer choice $\boxed{B}$ for Example 5.16, it is not the same because $(3x)^2 \neq 3x^2$.

Often, the values of the two functions are given in a table, which actually makes the problem easier because you don't have to do any calculations.

EXAMPLE 5.17

Given the two tables

x	f(x)
1	0
3	1
5	2
7	3

y	g(y)
−1	0
0	3
1	6
2	9

The value of $f(g(y))$ for $y = 0$ is ⬚.

SOLUTION

The correct answer is 1.

Simply find the value of $g(y)$ for $y = 0$ from the table for $g(y)$, which is 3. Then the question is actually just asking for $f(3)$, which is 1, from the table for $f(x)$. It's that simple, as long as you keep the question and table straight.

Practice Exercises

1. Find the slope of the line segment joining (2, 3) and (6, 8).

   (A) 5

   (B) 4

   (C) $\dfrac{5}{4}$

   (D) $\dfrac{4}{5}$

   (E) Not enough information given.

2. What is the distance between the point (7, 3) and (4, 3)?

   (A) (3, 0)

   (B) 3

   (C) –3

   (D) (0, 3)

   (E) Not enough information given.

3. A local Brownie troop uses the model $y = 2x - 25$ to calculate the money earned in a bake sale, where x is the number of cookies sold. If the troop sold 75 cookies, how much money did it earn?

   (A) $75

   (B) $150

   (C) $175

   (D) $25

   (E) $125

4. How is "the product of 7 and n decreased by 12" written algebraically?

   (A) $(7 + n) - 12$

   (B) $\dfrac{n}{7} - 12$

   (C) $7n - 12$

   (D) $\dfrac{7}{n} - 12$

   (E) $(7 - n)(12)$

5. If $M = \dfrac{5a}{6b}$, $b = 3a$, $b \neq 0$, what is the value of M?

   (A) $\dfrac{5}{6}$

   (B) $\dfrac{5}{18}$

   (C) $\dfrac{3}{5}$

   (D) $\dfrac{3}{18}$

   (E) $\dfrac{3}{6}$

6. Determine the value of $\dfrac{x-y}{x+y}$ if $x = 4y$. Fill in the boxes with the answer.

$$\dfrac{\boxed{}}{\boxed{}}$$

7. If $\dfrac{a}{3}$ has a value between 5 and 7, which of the following could be the value of a? Choose all that apply.

   A 13

   B 15

   C 17

   D 19

   E 21

8. In a parallel circuit in electricity, the total resistance R of resistors X and Y is given by the formula $\dfrac{1}{X} + \dfrac{1}{Y} = \dfrac{1}{R}$, where the resistance is in ohms. If $X = 12$ ohms and $Y = 6$ ohms, $R =$

   (A) 3

   (B) 4

   (C) 8

   (D) 18

   (E) 24

9. If $a = -2$ and $b = -3$, the value of $ab^2 - (ab)^2$ is

   (A) 0

   (B) −36

   (C) −54

   (D) −72

   (E) −324

10. What is the solution to the inequality $-4m + 12 \geq -20$?

   (A) $m \leq 8$

   (B) $m > 2$

   (C) $m \geq 8$

   (D) $m \leq 2$

   (E) $m < 8$

11. If $r \times t = d$, which of the following is correct?

   (A) $r = t \times d$

   (B) $r = t + d$

   (C) $r = \dfrac{t}{d}$

   (D) $r = \dfrac{d}{t}$

   (E) $r = t - d$

12. Three business partners divided the profits of the business in a ratio of 5:7:8. If the largest share was \$200,000, what was the total profit of the business?

   (A) \$100,000

   (B) \$200,000

   (C) \$250,000

   (D) \$500,000

   (E) \$1,000,000

13. Write the following sentence as the relationship between S and U using algebraic symbols.

    S is four less than T, and T is 5 more than 7 times U.

    (A) $S = -(U + 1)$

    (B) $S = 7U + 1$

    (C) $S = U + 1$

    (D) $S = 7U + 9$

    (E) $S = 7U - 1$

14. What is the value of $(5a - 5b)(3c + 3d)$ if $a - b = 6$ and $c + d = 2$? Fill in the box.

15. Once the sun went down, the temperature dropped at a steady rate. At sundown, 7:00 p.m., the temperature was 65 degrees, but by midnight, it was down to 45 degrees. What was the temperature in degrees at 10:00 p.m.? Put the number in the box.

16. What is the value of x in the equation $5(x - 2) = 2(x - 1) - 7$. Fill in the fraction boxes.

17. A straight line in the xy-plane passes through the points $(2, 2)$ and $(0, 6)$. The equation of the line in slope intercept form, $y = mx + b$ has the following values for m and b. Fill in the boxes:

    $m = \boxed{}$ $b = \boxed{}$

Solutions

1. (C), $\dfrac{5}{4}$. Slope is $\dfrac{\text{change in } y}{\text{change in } x} = \dfrac{8 - 3}{6 - 2} = \dfrac{5}{4}$.

2. (B), 3. If two points are on the same horizontal (or vertical) line, the distance between them is the vertical (or horizontal) distance. Here both points are on the line $y = 3$, so their distance is $7 - 4 = 3$. Distance is positive.

3. (E), $125. The amount of money earned, y, is found by substituting the number of cookies sold, 75, for x in the given equation: $y = 2x - 25 = 2(75) - 25 = 150 - 25 = 125$.

4. (C), $7n - 12$. The other answer choices involve the sum, difference, or quotient of 7 and n, but not the product. Note that the problem can also be read as "the product of 7 and (n decreased by 12)," which would equal $7(n - 12)$, but this other interpretation is not an answer choice.

5. (B), $\dfrac{5}{18}$. Substitute $b = 3a$ into the equation for $M = \dfrac{5a}{6b}$ to get $M = \dfrac{5a}{18a} = \dfrac{5}{18}$.

6. $\dfrac{3}{5}$. Substitute $x = 4y$ into the fraction to obtain $\dfrac{4y - y}{4y + y} = \dfrac{3y}{5y} = \dfrac{3}{5}$.

7. $\boxed{\text{C}}$, 17, and $\boxed{\text{D}}$, 19. The problem can be written as $5 < \dfrac{a}{3} < 7$. Multiplying through by 3 yields $15 < a < 21$. Answer choices $\boxed{\text{A}}$ and $\boxed{\text{E}}$ are outside of this range. Answer choice $\boxed{\text{B}}$, 15, is incorrect because the question says "between," which doesn't include the endpoints.

8. (B), 4. Substituting the variables X and Y into the formula $\dfrac{1}{X} + \dfrac{1}{Y} = \dfrac{1}{R}$ gives $\dfrac{1}{12} + \dfrac{1}{6} = \dfrac{1}{12} + \dfrac{2}{12} = \dfrac{3}{12} = \dfrac{1}{4} = \dfrac{1}{R}$; so $R = 4$.

9. (C), -54. Substitute the values for a and b into the expression $ab^2 - (ab)^2$ to get

    $(-2)(-3)^2 - ((-2)(-3))^2 = -18 - 36 = -54$.

10. (A), $m \le 8$. Solve the inequality the same way as an equality, except reverse the inequality sign if you multiply or divide by a negative number. Therefore,

    $-4m + 12 \ge -20$

    $-4m \ge -20 - 12$

    $-4m \ge -32$

    $m \le 8$

11. (D), $r = \dfrac{d}{t}$. If $r \times t = d$, divide both sides of the equation by t to get the value for r.

12. (D) \$500,000. If the ratio is 5:7:8, the division of the profits can be written as $5x$, $7x$, and $8x$. The largest share is $8x = \$200,000$, so $x = \$25,000$. Then $7x = \$175,000$ and $5x = \$125,000$, so the total profit is $\$200,000 + 175,000 + 125,000 = \$500,000$.

13. (B), $S = 7U + 1$. Write the two equations as $S = T - 4$ and $T = 7U + 5$, and combine them: $S = (7U + 5) - 4 = 7U + 1$.

14. 180. There are two ways to approach this problem. They each take about the same time. Recognize that the given values, $a - b$ and $c + d$, are factors of the original expression:

$$(5a - 5b)(3c + 3d) = 5(a - b) \times 3(c + d) = 5(6) \times 3(2) = 30 \times 6 = 180$$

Alternatively, rewrite the given equations as $a = 6 + b$ and $c = 2 - d$ and substitute them into the original expression:

$$(5a - 5b)(3c + 3d) = 5(a - b) \times 3(c + d) = [5(6 + b - b) \times 3(2 - d + d)] =$$
$$5(6) \times 3(2) = 30 \times 6 = 180$$

15. 53. The fact that the temperature dropped "at a steady rate" means that its graph is represented by a straight line. We don't have to graph it (although that method would work to get the answer here), we just have to figure out what the rate is, which would be the slope of that line. We have two points $(7, 65)$ and $(12, 45)$, so the slope is $\dfrac{\text{change in } y}{\text{change in } x}$, which is $\dfrac{65 - 45}{7 - 12} = \dfrac{20}{-5} = -4$ degrees per hour. Therefore, the temperature changed by $3(-4) = -12$ degrees. The negative sign means it dropped, so at 10:00 p.m., the temperature was $65 - 12 = 53$ degrees.

16. $\dfrac{1}{3}$.

$5(x - 2) = 2(x - 1) - 7$	
$5x - 10 = 2x - 2 - 7$	Use the distributive property
$5x - 10 = 2x - 9$	Combine like terms
$5x - 2x = -9 + 10$	Subtract $2x$ and add 10 to both sides
$3x = 1$	Combine like terms
$x = \dfrac{1}{3}$	Divide both sides by 3

17. $m = -2$, $b = 6$. Use the formula for the slope, $m = \dfrac{\text{change in } y}{\text{change in } x} = \dfrac{6 - 2}{0 - 2} = \dfrac{4}{-2} = -2$. The y-intercept, b, is the point at which $x = 0$, which is the second point, $(0, 6)$, with a y value of 6.

Answers to Drill: Order of Operations *(page 93)*:

a. $7 \times 1 + 4 = 11$	b. $6 + 7 + 2 = 15$
c. $12 \times 12 = 144$	d. $6^2 - 6 + 5^2 = 36 - 6 + 25 = 55$
e. $3 \times 13 + 2^3 = 3 \times 13 + 8 = 39 + 8 = 47$	f. $10 + 90 - 10 = 90$
g. $7 + (3 + 4)^2 + 8 = 7 + 49 + 8 = 64$	h. $(8^2 - 34)^2 + 16 = 30^2 + 16 = 916$
i. $4 - 4 + 360 = 360$	

Geometry

Geometry is defined as the area of mathematics that deals with points, lines, shapes, and space. The Praxis Core Math test focuses on shapes that we can draw on a sheet of paper (two-dimensional figures), or flat shapes such as lines, polygons, circles, and triangles, although you are also expected to be familiar with three-dimensional objects such as spheres, cubes, cylinders, and pyramids.

Every day, we see many things that have to do with geometry: tires are circles, honeycombs are hexagons (six-sided figures); the truss on a bridge is a trapezoid; and a bridge is made up of many triangles due to their rigidity.

Geometry has its own vocabulary, and learning the words that describe geometric shapes and relationships is very important. Many new terms are introduced in this chapter—and they are just the basics!

FORMING LINES AND ANGLES

Let's start with the most basic geometric object—the *point*. A true point actually has no dimensions (no length, no width, no height). So two questions come to mind: What good are points? How can we draw them if they have no dimensions?

Quick answers: Points are used for defining positions. We draw a point as a dot, which even if we use the sharpest pencil, still looks like it has a tiny length and width or maybe looks like a really small circle.

Even though a point has no dimensions, it is real, it isn't invisible, and it's really useful. We can talk about the position of a point, as we did in the last chapter when plotting ordered pairs on a graph. Points are the building blocks of all other geometric objects. So let's go on to drawing points and using them as they were meant to be used—got the point?

Lines

When we string a bunch of points together, we get a line. A line can be seen, and it has one dimension—length. By "bunch of points," we mean an infinite number. A line is made up of an infinite number of points. Between any two points on a line, there is always another point, and so on and so on.

When we talk about lines, we should be precise about what we mean.

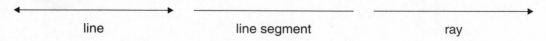

| line | line segment | ray |

A **line** goes on forever in two directions. Of course, when we draw a line, we can't draw out to outer space, so we indicate that it goes on forever by putting an arrowhead on both ends. Often, though, we are using a **line segment**, which has endpoints and a definite length. A **ray** is a special type of line—it has an endpoint on one "end" and an arrowhead on the other, indicating that it really isn't ending in that direction.

To get an idea of the infinite number of points on a line, line segment, or ray, draw a 6-inch line segment and label the endpoints A and B. Now put a mark at the halfway point, called the **midpoint** (3 inches from either end). Let's close in on point B at the end of the line. From the midpoint you just indicated, make a mark halfway to point B, then halfway again, and again, and again. Keep doing this—will you ever reach point B? No, because even though the distance to B is getting smaller and smaller, there is always a point that will be the midpoint of the remaining distance. If we were to measure these distances precisely, we never get to point B because we can always take one-half of the last distance, and the measurement quickly becomes a decimal with lots and lots of zeroes after the decimal point.

If we connect two rays at their endpoints, we form an angle. The place where the two endpoints meet is called the **vertex** of the angle.

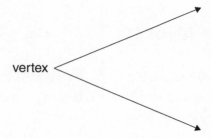

vertex

The sides of the angle, being rays, go off into space unless we put an endpoint on one or both of them. Angles are the topic of the next section in this chapter.

We can use line segments to form two-dimensional figures, with both length and width. These figures can have many sides, each one being a line segment. These line segments meet and form angles. If the figure has no open sides, it is called a **closed** figure. Imagine a closed figure with 100 equal sides. Let's open the angle between two sides and add another 100 sides there, equal to the first 100. How about doing this 100 more times? If we do this forever, the sides no longer look like line segments—in fact, the figure is close to looking like a circle, but it is a many-sided polygon. We discuss such shapes (polygons) later in this chapter.

Angles

As we said, an angle is formed by two rays connected at their endpoints. What distinguishes one angle from another is how wide open it is. The measurement of an angle is based on 360 degrees (360°), which is how many degrees there are in a circle. Indeed, if an angle has 360°, the two sides are one on top of the other and they no longer look like an angle, they look like a ray.

The Praxis test, however, is concerned mainly with angles that are less than or equal to 180°. (There is a label for an angle that is greater then 180° but less than 360°, called a **reflex angle**, but we rarely encounter it.) An angle of exactly 180° is called a **straight angle** because the rays form a straight line.

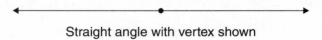

Straight angle with vertex shown

Any angle that is less than 90° is called **acute**, and any angle greater than 90° and less than 180° is called **obtuse**. An angle that equals 90° is a **right** angle. The rays of a right angle are perpendicular to each other, meaning the angle is 90°.

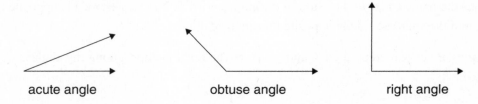

acute angle   obtuse angle   right angle

Relationships between angles mostly have to do with their measurements. **Adjacent angles** share a side. Any two angles that total 180° are called **supplementary**, and they need not be adjacent. If they are adjacent, their outer sides form a straight line. Likewise, any two angles that total 90° are called **complementary**, and they need not be adjacent. If they are adjacent, their outer sides form a right angle.

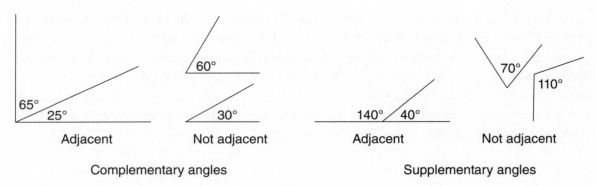

| Adjacent | Not adjacent | Adjacent | Not adjacent |

Complementary angles   Supplementary angles

As we saw in the last chapter, two lines that never meet are called **parallel lines**. If parallel lines are crossed by another line, which is called the **transversal**, eight angles are formed.

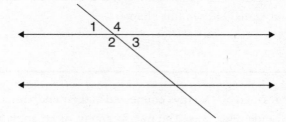

When two lines cross, the angles formed are either supplementary or they are *vertical angles*, which are the angles opposite each other, such as angles 1 and 3. Vertical angles are equal. So when two parallel lines are crossed by a transversal, we need the measure of only one of the eight angles formed to get the measures of all of them, since all of the angles are either supplementary or vertical (equal) angles. In the figure, if we know the measure of angle 1 is 50°, we can quickly and easily know the measures of all the other angles formed by the transversal—they are either 50° or 130°. Angle 2 is supplementary to angle 1 (as well as angle 3), so it is 130°, and likewise angle 4 is 130°.

TRIANGLES

Triangles are closed figures made with three line segments as the sides. They also have three angles, thus the name *triangle*. The sum of the angles is 180°. The longest side is opposite the largest angle, and the smallest side is opposite the smallest angle.

Triangles are classified by their shapes, such as the relationships among the angles.

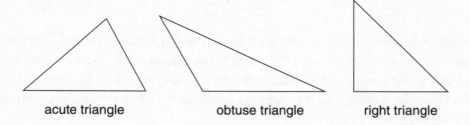

acute triangle   obtuse triangle   right triangle

A basic triangle with three acute angles is called an **acute triangle**. In an **obtuse triangle**, one angle is obtuse and the other two are acute. Since the total number of degrees in a triangle is 180°, all triangles can have at most one obtuse angle. This is because the obtuse angle, by definition, contains more than 90°, leaving less than 90° for the total degrees of the other two angles. So the other two angles must be acute angles. Similarly, a **right triangle** can have only one right angle (90°). Right triangles are so important in real life that they merit being discussed separately in the next section of this chapter.

Triangles can also be named according to the relationships among the sides.

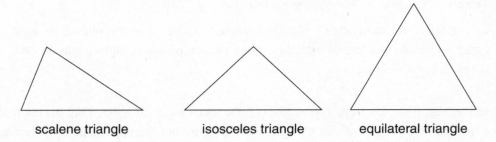

scalene triangle   isosceles triangle   equilateral triangle

A triangle with three unequal sides is called a **scalene triangle**. If a triangle has three unequal sides, then it also has three unequal angles. A special type of triangle has two equal sides. It is named an **isosceles triangle**. If a triangle has two equal sides, it also has two equal angles, called the **base angles**. The third (unequal) side is sometimes called the **base**, and it is opposite the one unequal angle. A special type of acute triangle has all sides equal and all angles equal. This is often called an **equilateral triangle** (meaning "equal sides"), but can just as well be called an **equiangular triangle** (meaning "equal angles"). Since all of the angles are equal, and we know they total 180°, we can figure that each angle is 60°.

☞ HINT

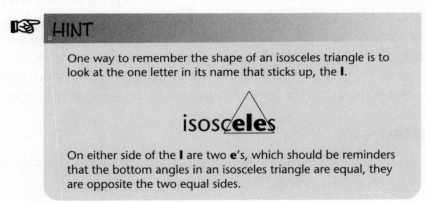

One way to remember the shape of an isosceles triangle is to look at the one letter in its name that sticks up, the **I**.

isosc**e**le**s**

On either side of the **I** are two **e**'s, which should be reminders that the bottom angles in an isosceles triangle are equal, they are opposite the two equal sides.

EXAMPLE 6.1

Which type of triangle can *only* be an acute triangle?

    (A) obtuse triangle

    (B) equilateral triangle

    (C) right triangle

    (D) scalene triangle

    (E) right triangle

SOLUTION

The correct answer is (B), equilateral triangle.

It is possible for scalene or isosceles triangles to also be acute, obtuse, or right triangles, but an equilateral triangle cannot have an obtuse or right angle. In fact, it has three 60° angles.

When forming triangles from line segments, the sides must all meet. This means that if we know the lengths of two sides of any triangle, we can figure out the upper and lower limits of the length of the third side. As an extreme example, suppose we have two line segments of lengths 8 inches and 3 inches. Our third line segment is 2 inches long. Can we make a triangle from these three line segments? The answer is no because we can't get the triangle to "close up." What if our third segment is 15 inches long? Can we make a triangle from these three line segments? The answer is also no for the same reason. The rule for this is:

> The sum of the lengths of any two sides of a triangle must be
> longer than the length of the third side.

Thus, for a triangle with two sides of 8 inches and 3 inches, if the 8-inch side is the longest side, the third side would have to be more than (8 − 3 =) 5 inches long. But it is also possible that the third (unknown) side could be the longest, and if we apply that rule again, the sum of the 8- and 3-inch sides would have to be longer than that side, so the third side would have to be shorter than (8 + 3 =) 11 inches. Therefore, we know that the third side has a length, let's call it l, such that $5 < l < 11$. It cannot equal either of these limits because the sides would all collapse on each other.

EXAMPLE 6.2

What are the length limits for the third side of a triangle with two known sides of lengths 2 inches and 4 inches?

    (A) between 2 and 6 inches

    (B) from 2 to 6 inches

    (C) from 2 to 4 inches

    (D) from 4 to 8 inches

    (E) between 4 and 8 inches

SOLUTION

The correct answer is (A), between 2 and 6 inches.

The difference of 4 and 2 gives the lower bound (> 2) and the sum of 2 and 4 gives the upper bound (< 6). The word "between" usually means not to include the numbers themselves (unless some word, such as "inclusive," indicates to include them), and the "from–to" combination means the numbers are included. That is why answer choice (A) is correct and answer choice (B) is incorrect.

RIGHT TRIANGLES

In a right triangle, since one of the angles is 90°, two of the sides are perpendicular and the other two angles are acute. Everyday examples that form right triangles are a ladder propped against a house or the shadow cast by an upright tree. In both of these cases, the ground is the third side of the triangle.

In a right triangle, the longest side, the one opposite the right angle, is called the **hypotenuse**, and the other two sides are called the **legs**. The legs aren't necessarily equal (most times they are not).

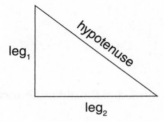

Pythagorean Theorem

One of the special things about a right triangle is that we can always figure out the exact length of a third side if all we know are the other two lengths. This isn't true for the sides of any other triangle, for which we can only tell the range, as we just did in the preceding section. Of course, for any triangle, if you know two angles, you can always find the third angle by subtracting the sum of the two angles from 180°.

To find the third side of a right triangle, we have to use the Pythagorean theorem, which is named for the Greek philosopher and mathematician Pythagoras, who lived around 500 B.C.E. and is credited with the theorem. The Pythagorean theorem states:

The square of the hypotenuse is equal to the sum of the squares of the other two sides.

The formula for this relationship is $c^2 = a^2 + b^2$, where c is the length of the hypotenuse and a and b are the lengths of the other two sides.

EXAMPLE 6.3

To get to work, Natasha drives 3 miles north and 4 miles west. If Natasha could drive to work in a straight northwest line, how many miles less would the trip be?

(A) 5 miles

(B) 4 miles

(C) 2 miles

(D) It is still the same distance.

(E) The new route is even farther.

SOLUTION

The correct answer is (C), 2 miles.

Remember to subtract the northwest distance from 7, since the question is how many miles *less* the new route would be.

First, recognize that north and west are perpendicular distances, so a right triangle is formed by the two directions Natasha presently drives. The shortcut directly to Natasha's work would be the hypotenuse. Using the Pythagorean theorem, we have $a = 3$, $b = 4$, and we have to find the hypotenuse, c, the northwest shortcut.

$$c^2 = a^2 + b^2$$

$$c^2 = 3^2 + 4^2 = 9 + 16 = 25$$

$$c = \sqrt{25} = 5 \text{ miles}$$

Since the new route would be 5 miles, and the old route was $3 + 4 = 7$ miles, the new route is 2 miles less than the old route.

Pythagorean Triples

Example 6.3 ended up with a whole number answer (5 miles) for the hypotenuse, but that's not always the case. There are, however, some whole numbers for the legs of a right triangle that will always give a whole number hypotenuse, and if you can remember them and recognize them, you will get the answers to many problems right away, without having to do the calculations for the Pythagorean theorem directly. These sets of whole numbers for the sides of a right triangle are called **Pythagorean triples**.

The easiest Pythagorean triple to remember is the one from Example 6.3. It is called the 3–4–5 triple, which means if the legs are 3 and 4, the hypotenuse will always be 5. Since all triangles of this shape are proportional, this means that any multiple of 3–4–5 works as well, such as a right triangle with sides of 6, 8, and 10, or one with sides of 9, 12, and 15. This comes in rather handy, as tests like the Praxis often use these triples a lot.

Other triples are not so easy to remember: 5–12–13 and 8–15–17, and all of the multiples of these triples. If you care to check, $5^2 + 12^2 = 13^2$ and $8^2 + 15^2 = 17^2$.

EXAMPLE 6.4

A 16-foot flagpole casts a 12-foot shadow. What is the distance from the end of the shadow to the top of the flagpole?

   (A) 12 feet

   (B) 16 feet

   (C) 20 feet

   (D) 24 feet

   (E) 28 feet

SOLUTION

The correct answer is (C), 20 feet.

Good solution: The flagpole and its shadow meet at a right angle at the foot of the flagpole. So we have a right triangle, for which the distance to be found is the hypotenuse. The legs of the triangle are 12 and 16, so the hypotenuse can be found by using the Pythagorean theorem:

$$c^2 = a^2 + b^2$$
$$= 12^2 + 16^2$$
$$= 144 + 256 = 400$$
$$c = \sqrt{400} = 20 \text{ feet}$$

Better solution: Recognize that 12 and 16 are 4 times 3 and 4 times 4, respectively, so this triangle is four times the 3–4–5 Pythagorean triple. Since the corresponding sides must be proportional, the hypotenuse must be 4 times 5, or 20 feet.

Special Right Triangles

Two additional right triangles are good to know because they are easy to remember and they will save time in finding solutions.

The first is the **30°–60°–90°** triangle. What is special about any right triangle with these angle measures is that the side across from the 30° angle is *always* half the length of the hypotenuse. That fact alone will be useful. The ratios of the sides of this special triangle are not all whole numbers, but they aren't difficult to remember: 1–2–$\sqrt{3}$, where 1 represents the side opposite the smallest angle (30°) and 2 represents the hypotenuse. Just like the Pythagorean triples, any multiples of these sides will also form a 30°–60°–90° triangle.

Be aware that any right triangle that has a ratio of 2:1 between the hypotenuse and one of the legs, or a ratio of $1 : \sqrt{3}$ for the lengths of the legs is most probably a 30°–60°–90° triangle with sides in the ratio 1–2–$\sqrt{3}$.

EXAMPLE 6.5

The hypotenuse of a right triangle is 6 and one of the sides is 3. The length of the third side is

(A) 3

(B) $3\sqrt{3}$

(C) 6

(D) $6\sqrt{3}$

(E) 1.5

SOLUTION

The correct answer is (B), $3\sqrt{3}$.

Good solution: Use the Pythagorean theorem, since this is a right triangle.

$$c^2 = a^2 + b^2$$

$$6^2 = 3^2 + b^2$$

$$b^2 = 6^2 - 3^2 = 36 - 9 = 27$$

$$b = \sqrt{27} = \sqrt{9 \times 3} = \sqrt{9} \times \sqrt{3} = 3\sqrt{3}$$

Better solution: Whenever a right triangle has a side that is half the hypotenuse, it is the special 30°–60°–90° triangle, and the sides are in the memorable ratio of 1–2–$\sqrt{3}$. If the hypotenuse is 6, then the other sides are 3 (which was given), and $3\sqrt{3}$.

EXAMPLE 6.6

The two legs of a right triangle are 4 and $4\sqrt{3}$. What is the length of the hypotenuse?

SOLUTION

The correct answer is 8.

Good solution: Use the Pythagorean theorem.

$$c^2 = 4^2 + (4\sqrt{3})^2$$

$$= 16 + (16 \times 3) = 16 + 48 = 64$$

$$c = \sqrt{64} = 8$$

Better solution: Don't even blink—the hypotenuse is 8 (twice the shortest side). The legs are obviously in the ratio $1 : \sqrt{3}$ (a major hint is $\sqrt{3}$ as to what kind of triangle this is) with a hypotenuse that is twice the shortest side.

The second special right triangle is the isosceles right triangle, a triangle that has two equal sides and a 90° angle. Because it is isosceles, the legs are equal, and the angles opposite them are also equal, at 45° each since they must total the 90° left in the triangle after the right angle is taken into account. This is a 45°–45°–90° isosceles right triangle. The ratio of the sides of this triangle is 1–1–$\sqrt{2}$, also somewhat easy to remember, with the legs being equal and the hypotenuse equal to the length of one of the legs times $\sqrt{2}$. Of course, all of the multiples of 1–1–$\sqrt{2}$ are also this type of triangle.

Be aware in this case that any right triangle problems that have either two equal legs or have a hypotenuse with a factor of $\sqrt{2}$ is probably a 45°–45°–90° isosceles right triangle with sides in the ratio 1–1–$\sqrt{2}$.

EXAMPLE 6.7

Two sides of a right triangle are 5 and 5. The length of the third side is

(A) 5

(B) $5\sqrt{3}$

(C) $5\sqrt{2}$

(D) 10

(E) 2.5

SOLUTION

The correct answer is (C), $5\sqrt{2}$.

Good solution: Since this is a right triangle, the Pythagorean theorem will give the answer.

$$c^2 = 5^2 + 5^2$$
$$= 25 + 25 = 50$$
$$c = \sqrt{50} = \sqrt{25 \times 2} = \sqrt{25} \times \sqrt{2} = 5\sqrt{2}$$

Better solution: Two equal sides on a right triangle says it is an isosceles right triangle, and therefore the sides are in the ratio 1–1–$\sqrt{2}$. Therefore, if the equal sides are 5 and 5, the third side also is a multiple of 5 and is $5\sqrt{2}$.

POLYGONS

Polygons are closed figures made with straight line segments. Closed figures have sides that begin and end at the same point without crossing over any sides.

 HINT

If you think of a figure as a cage, an animal inside it cannot escape a *closed* figure, but can move freely within every part of it.

Polygons are named for the number of sides (or angles). Polygons with all equal sides and equal angles are called **regular** polygons.

Quadrilaterals

Quadrilaterals are four-sided closed figures (*quad* means four and *lateral* means sides). Quadrilaterals have four angles that total 360°. Some common quadrilaterals are the square and the rectangle, but these are special quadrilaterals. Let's start with the basic quadrilateral and work our way up to them.

The basic quadrilateral has four sides and no special other features. We only know that the angles add up to 360°. We don't know whether there are any relationships among the sides, so we can't find, let's say, the fourth side if we know the other three. Quadrilaterals are not rigid figures like triangles, so there are few limits for the lengths of the sides.

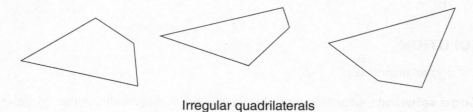

Irregular quadrilaterals

Trapezoid

Let's add a special feature to the quadrilateral and make two sides parallel (*BC // AD*). We now have a **trapezoid**. We know nothing else here, just that two sides are parallel. We don't even know whether there are any equal sides or angles. This is the basic trapezoid. If we make the two angles at the base equal, then we have an **isosceles trapezoid**, which really is the bottom part of an isosceles triangle. And not only are the base angles equal in the isosceles trapezoid, the nonparallel sides are automatically equal as well. The diagonals, which connect opposite angles, are equal in an isosceles triangle, but not in a trapezoid that isn't isosceles.

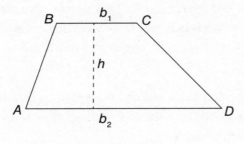

Trapezoid

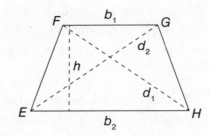

Isosceles Trapezoid
$EF = HG, \angle E = \angle H, \angle F = \angle G, d_1 = d_2$

Parallelogram

Let's add yet another special feature to the trapezoid: the parallel sides also are equal. This makes the trapezoid into a parallelogram. A **parallelogram** has two pairs of parallel sides and the opposite sides are equal. The angles across from each other are equal, and each angle is supplementary to the adjacent angle (they total 180°). The diagonals aren't equal, but they bisect each other, and either diagonal divides the parallelogram into two equal (congruent) triangles, a property we will use in the section on congruency (see Example 6.9).

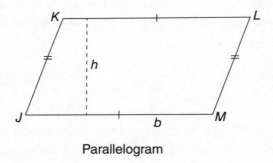

Parallelogram

Rhombus, Rectangle, and Square

We can do three things to a parallelogram to make the last three special quadrilaterals.

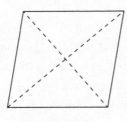

Rhombus

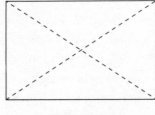

Rectangle

Square

1. Make all sides equal. That makes a **rhombus**, so a rhombus has all of the properties of a parallelogram plus all the sides are equal. An additional bonus is that the diagonals of a rhombus are perpendicular to each other.

2. Make all the angles equal. Since there are four angles and the total is 360°, that means all of the angles are right angles, and we have a **rectangle**. Thus, a rectangle has all of the properties of a parallelogram plus all angles are right angles and the diagonals are equal.

3. Combine the last two properties (making equal sides and equal angles), and we have a **square**. In fact, a square has all of the properties of the other quadrilaterals—it is a special case. A square has all of the following properties:

   • The opposite sides are parallel

   • All sides are equal

   • All angles are equal

   • The diagonals are equal, bisect each other, and are perpendicular to each other.

Other Polygons

Polygons are usually named for the number of sides they have, just like the 4-sided *quadrilateral*. Common polygons are the **pentagon** (5 sides), **hexagon** (6 sides), and **octagon** (8 sides). The total number of degrees in these larger polygons increases as the number of sides increases. Any polygon that has all equal sides and angles is called a **regular polygon**.

SIMILARITY

When we talked about special right triangles and how their ratios remained the same, we were actually talking about *similarity* between figures. Two figures are **similar** if their corresponding sides are proportional and their corresponding angles are equal. Two similar figures have the same shape but not necessarily the same size. When two figures are similar, the notation is, for example, $ABCD \sim EFGH$. That means the angles in the corresponding places are equal, $\angle A = \angle E$, $\angle B = \angle F$, $\angle C = \angle G$, and $\angle D = \angle H$, and the corresponding sides are proportional, $\dfrac{AB}{EF} = \dfrac{BC}{FG} = \dfrac{CD}{GH} = \dfrac{DA}{HE}$.

All regular polygons are similar to each other. That means a square is similar to every other square, and an equilateral triangle is similar to every other equilateral triangle. This property of similarity is not true necessarily for the other polygons, but we can say that all 30°–60°–90° triangles are similar to each other, and all isosceles right triangles, whose sides are in a ratio of 1–1–$\sqrt{2}$, as well as all triangles that we get by using multiples of Pythagorean triples. Similar figures do not necessarily have the same orientation. In addition, all circles are similar to all other circles, no matter the size.

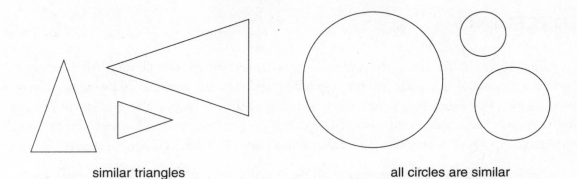

similar triangles   all circles are similar

EXAMPLE 6.8

The sides of a triangle are 10, 12, and 20. What is the length of the longest side of a similar triangle whose shortest side is 5?

 (A) 6

 (B) 2.5

 (C) 3

 (D) 10

 (E) 20

SOLUTION

The correct answer is (D), 10.

Good solution: The sides of similar polygons can be set up as proportions, keeping in mind what the corresponding sides are:

$$\frac{\text{shortest side}_1}{\text{shortest side}_2} = \frac{\text{longest side}_1}{\text{longest side}_2}$$

$$\frac{5}{10} = \frac{x}{20}$$

$$10x = 5 \times 20 = 100$$

$$x = 10$$

Better solution: Similarity means the sides are proportional. Since the shortest side of the similar triangle is half the shortest side of the given triangle, the longest side should be half the length of the longest side of the given triangle, or $\frac{1}{2} \times 20 = 10$.

CONGRUENCE

Congruence, unlike similarity, means the two figures have exactly the same size and shape. Corresponding angles are equal, and corresponding sides are also equal. If you were to place one figure on top of the other, they would match up exactly. Mirror images are an example of two congruent "things," even though their orientations are different. Orientations don't make a difference with congruent figures—only that the corresponding parts are equal. The sign for congruence is ≅.

Most questions involving congruence on the Praxis Core test have to do with congruent triangles. Two triangles are congruent if

- The three sides of one triangle equal the three corresponding sides of the other (known as SSS). If all three pairs of corresponding sides are equal, the corresponding angles are automatically equal.

- Two sides and the angle between them on one triangle are equal to the corresponding two sides and angle between them on the other triangle (known as SAS). Note that the angle has to be between the sides.

- Two angles and a side of one triangle are equal to the corresponding two angles and side of the other triangle (known as ASA if the side is between the angles, or AAS if it is not between the angles).

If the three angles of one triangle are equal to the corresponding three angles of another triangle and nothing is said about the sides, the triangles are similar, but not necessarily congruent.

EXAMPLE 6.9

How do we know that the diagonal of a parallelogram divides it into two congruent triangles? Choose *all* of the reasons that are relevant.

    A SSS

    B AAS

    C ASA

    D SAS

    E SSA

SOLUTION

The correct answers are A , B , C , and D .

The next diagram explains what is known about the triangles formed by the diagonal of a parallelogram, with the same tick marks on corresponding equal parts. Choice E isn't a reason because there is no SSA—if you know two sides and an angle of one triangle, that doesn't guarantee it will match up with another triangle with the same two sides and angle unless the angle is between the two sides (that is, SAS).

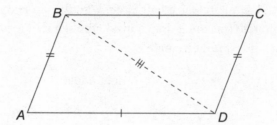

[A]: SSS works because the three pairs of corresponding sides are equal: $BC = AD$ and $AB = DC$ because they are opposite sides of the parallelogram, and $BD = DB$ because it is the same line. So $\triangle ABD \cong \triangle CDB$.

[B] and [C]: AAS and ASA work because two pairs of corresponding angles and any other side are equal: $\angle A = \angle C$ because they are opposite angles of a parallelogram; $\angle ABD = \angle CDB$ (or $\angle BDA = \angle CBD$) because sides BC and AD are parallel lines cut by a transversal (BD), making those equal angles; finally, all the pairs of corresponding sides are equal for the reason given for answer choice [A]. So there are many ways that AAS or ASA are true. So $\triangle ABD \cong \triangle CDB$.

[D]: SAS works because two pairs of corresponding sides and the angles between them are equal: $BC = AD$ and $AB = DC$ because they are opposite sides of the parallelogram, and $\angle A = \angle C$ because they are opposite angles of a parallelogram. So $\triangle ABD \cong \triangle CDB$.

CIRCLES

The definition of a *circle* requires all the points to be at a fixed distance from a certain point, called the *center* of the circle. A line that goes through the center of the circle and touches the circle in two points is called a **diameter**. The fixed distance from the center to any point on the circle is called a **radius**, and it is equal to half the diameter. All radii (plural of radius) in a circle are equal. The following figure shows some parts of a circle. Circles are usually named by their centers, so this is circle O.

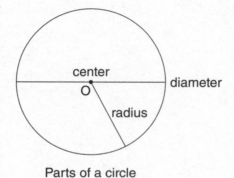

Parts of a circle

A circle contains 360°. A semicircle is a half circle with the circle diameter at its base. If a triangle is inscribed in a semicircle (meaning drawn inside the semicircle with the longest side of the triangle being the diameter), it is a right triangle.

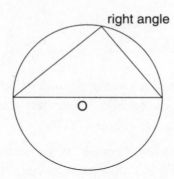

The **circumference** of a circle is the distance around the circle. The ratio of the circumference of a circle to its diameter is the same for all circles. It is a constant called **pi**, with the symbol π. Pi is an irrational number, equal to roughly 3.1416. Answers to problems concerning circles may be given in terms of π instead of multiplying it out (see Example 6.10). The equation for the circumference of a circle comes from the definition of π given above. Since π is the ratio of the circumference of a circle (C) to its diameter (d), $\pi = \dfrac{C}{d}$, we can say that

$$C = \pi d = 2\pi r$$

since the diameter is twice the radius, or $d = 2r$.

The **area of a circle** is given by

$$A = \pi r^2$$

 HINT

A good way to remember these circle formulas is by using the following mnemonic (memory aid):

Cherry pie is delicious; apple pies are too.

$C = \quad \pi \quad\quad d \quad ; \quad A = \pi \quad r^2$

EXAMPLE 6.10

What is the circumference in feet of a circle with a radius of 4 inches?

(A) $\dfrac{\pi}{12}$

(B) $\dfrac{\pi}{6}$

(C) 8π

(D) $\dfrac{2\pi}{3}$

(E) $\dfrac{4\pi}{3}$

SOLUTION

The correct answer is (D), $\dfrac{2\pi}{3}$. If the radius is 4 inches, the diameter is 8 inches, and $C = \pi d = 8\pi$ inches. However, the question is asking for the circumference in *feet*. Since there are 12 inches in a foot, use 8π inches $\times \dfrac{1 \text{ foot}}{12 \text{ inches}} = \dfrac{8\pi \text{ foot}}{12} = \dfrac{2\pi}{3}$ foot.

An **ellipse** is a two-dimensional figure that doesn't get a lot of attention compared to its "cousin," the circle. The ellipse looks like an elongated circle. To get an idea of how it looks, imagine using a knife to cut through a can that is in the shape of a cylinder. If you cut it parallel to the base, you get a circle, but if you tilt the knife, you get an ellipse, and in fact the ellipse is more elongated the more we tilt the knife.

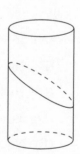

PERIMETER, AREA, AND VOLUME

Perimeter

We just discussed the circumference and area of a circle. The circumference of a circle is the same idea as the **perimeter** of a polygon—the distance around the outside. To find the perimeter of a polygon, just add all of the outside lengths. For a **composite** figure, which is a figure made up of individual shapes, add only the *outside* lengths, as can be seen in Example 6.11.

EXAMPLE 6.11

What is the perimeter of the following composite figure? The side of the square is 4 inches, and the triangle is an equilateral triangle.

(A) 15 inches

(B) 16 inches

(C) 20 inches

(D) 24 inches

(E) Not enough information is given.

SOLUTION

The correct answer is (C), 20 inches.

There are five outside segments on this figure. Each of them measures 4 inches, so the perimeter is $5 \times 4 = 20$ inches.

Even though only one dimension was given, the figure was described as a square and an equilateral triangle, so every line segment in the figure is the same length. Also, when calculating the perimeter, it does not include any lines inside the figure, only those on the outside.

EXAMPLE 6.12

What is the perimeter of the following figure, which is a semicircle with a radius of 4 inches?

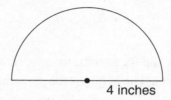

4 inches

(A) 8 π inches

(B) 4 π inches

(C) (8 π + 4) inches

(D) (4 π + 8) inches

(E) 8 inches

SOLUTION

The correct answer is (D), 4π + 8 inches.

The circular part of the perimeter is half the circumference of the circle (in inches), which was calculated in Example 6.10, or $\frac{1}{2}(8\pi) = 4\pi$. But for the perimeter, we also have to include the flat base, which is the diameter, or twice the radius, $2 \times 4 = 8$. Thus the whole perimeter is the sum, or $(4\pi + 8)$ inches.

Areas of Two-Dimensional Figures

Area is defined as the size of a surface, or the amount of space contained within the perimeter. Area is measured in square units (for example, square inches, square feet, or m², which is square meters). For quadrilaterals, area is basically length × width, or $A = l \times w$. We can also use $A = b \times h$, which stands for base × height. These measurements are the same, just different names. The tricky part of finding the area is determining what the height is.

For a square, this is easy enough. All the sides of a square are the same, so the length and width are equal. Often the side of a square is designated as s, so the area of a square is

Square $A = s \times s = s^2$

Similarly, the dimensions of a rectangle are usually given, so finding the area is straightforward.

Rectangle $A = l \times w$

Rhombuses are figured the same way as parallelograms (below), so we won't go into that here. A neat thing about a rhombus, though, is that the area also can be found by taking $\frac{1}{2}$ × (the product of the diagonals). In symbols, where d_1 and d_2 are the two diagonals,

Rhombus $\qquad\qquad A = \frac{1}{2}(d_1 \times d_2)$

When we get to parallelograms and trapezoids, though, we have to figure the height because it isn't just the length of one of the sides. The height is the *perpendicular* height between two parallel sides. It doesn't make a difference which pair of sides you use as long as the height and the corresponding sides are used. Don't mix them up. For example, in the following figure, if h is the height, the base b is either XY or WZ, but *not* XW and not YZ.

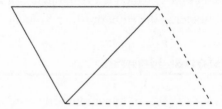

Parallelogram $\qquad\qquad A = b \times h$

Since the perpendicular height is used, if it isn't given, it can probably be found by using the Pythagorean theorem. You will have to be given enough information to find h, however.

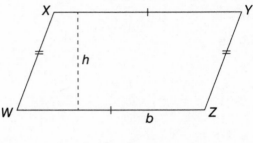

Here is where the area of a triangle comes from. If we draw a diagonal of any parallelogram, we get two identical triangles. So the area of a triangle is actually half the area of a parallelogram, but we have to remember that the height, again, is not necessarily one of the sides—it is the perpendicular from whatever side of the triangle we choose to be the base to the opposite angle.

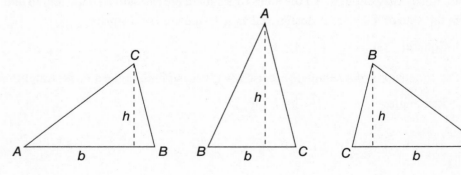

Triangle $\qquad A = \dfrac{1}{2}\, b \times h$

Right triangles are the only types of triangles that have two perpendicular sides, the legs, which makes it easier to calculate the area.

Right Triangle $\qquad A = \dfrac{1}{2}(l_1 \times l_2)$

Even though a trapezoid is the bottom part of a triangle, an additional problem comes up when finding its area. There are two unequal bases—which one do we use? The answer is that we use the average of the two (averages are discussed in the next chapter). The average is given by $\dfrac{1}{2}(b_1 + b_2)$, where b_1 and b_2 are the lengths of the two bases, and since it is addition (which is commutative), it makes no difference which bases we call b_1 or b_2.

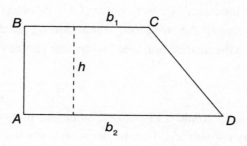

Trapezoid $\qquad A = \dfrac{1}{2}(b_1 + b_2) \times h = \dfrac{1}{2}h\,(b_1 + b_2)$

EXAMPLE 6.13

A farmer has acquired two adjacent plots of land, one in the shape of an 80-foot-by-30-foot rectangle and a smaller one that has an area half that of the rectangle. The configuration of the land is shown below. If he wants to fence in the land, what is the least amount of fencing he will need?

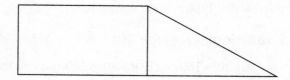

(A) 355 feet

(B) 356 feet

(C) 386 feet

(D) 400 feet

(E) Cannot tell from the information given.

SOLUTION

The answer is (B), 356 feet.

Since the four-sided plot is a rectangle, each vertex is a right angle, and the adjacent triangular plot is a right triangle. The number of feet of fencing is the perimeter, which is (starting at the bottom left corner and going clockwise), $p = 80 + 80 + 30 + 80 + x = 270 + x$, where x is the slanted length. x is also the hypotenuse of the triangle, so we use the Pythagorean theorem to compute its length.

$$x^2 = 30^2 + 80^2$$
$$x = \sqrt{900 + 6400} = \sqrt{7300} = 85.4$$

Therefore, the perimeter is 355.4 feet. The farmer will need at least 356 feet of fencing. If he uses the rounded figure of 355 feet, there will be a gap in the fence, so answer choice (A) is incorrect. Answer choice (C) is incorrect because it includes the 30-foot border between the two plots, which doesn't need fencing. The question didn't specify "to the nearest hundred," so answer choice (D) is also incorrect.

EXAMPLE 6.14

The same farmer as in Example 6.13 with the same two plots of land wants to fertilize the land. To buy enough fertilizer, he needs to know the area of the plot. The plot contains ⬚ square feet.

SOLUTION

The correct answer is 36000 square feet.

Good solution: This would be the area of the rectangle ($A = l \times w = 80 \times 30 = 2400$) plus the area of the triangle. Since this is a right triangle, the two legs can be used as the base and height, and the area is $A = \frac{1}{2} b \times h = \frac{1}{2}(80)(30) = 1200$. So the area of the plot is $2400 + 1200 = 3600$ square feet.

Another good solution: Recognize that this is a trapezoid, so the area is $A = \frac{1}{2} h(b_1 + b_2) = \frac{1}{2}(30)(80 + 160) = (15)(240) = 3600$ square feet.

Better solution: Recognize that the area of the triangular portion is half the area of the rectangle, so the answer is $A = (30 \times 80)$ plus half of (30×80), or $2400 + 1200 = 3600$ square feet.

Areas of Three-Dimensional Figures

When considering three-dimensional objects, *area* means **surface area** (SA), or the sum of the areas of all surfaces. The surface area formulas shown here will be given on the Praxis Core test if they are needed. However, take the time to see how we get them. It will help you to make sense of the formulas and what the variables are.

Rectangular Solid

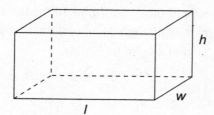

The surface area of a **rectangular solid** (the shape of a brick, also called a *right rectangular prism*) with dimensions *l*, *w*, and *h* is the sum of the areas of each of the six "faces," or rectangles. Since the six faces are actually doubles of three rectangles with areas $l \times w$, $w \times h$, and $h \times l$, the surface area is

Rectangular solid $\qquad SA = 2(lw + wh + hl)$

Cube

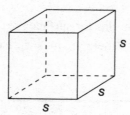

The surface area of a **cube** is similarly the sum of areas of the six faces, which are all squares, *s* units on a side, so the area of each is s^2. Thus the surface area is

Cube $\qquad\qquad SA = 6s^2$

Cylinder

The surface area of **a cylinder** with height h and radius r is the sum of the areas of circular top and bottom (each is πr^2) plus the area of the "side" (think of the label on a soup can). This side is in the form of a rectangle with height h and length equal to the circumference of the top (or bottom), so its area is $(2\pi r)h$. The surface area of a cylinder is thus

Cylinder $\qquad SA = 2\pi r^2 + 2\pi r\, h = 2\pi r(r + h)$

Sphere

A **sphere** is a three-dimensional figure for which every cross section is in the form of a circle. The only dimension for a sphere is the radius, r. The surface area of a sphere is given by

Sphere $\qquad SA = 4\pi r^2$

Any of these more complicated formulas for surface area and volume (below) will be given on the Praxis test. They are included here so there are no surprises during the test.

Volume of a Solid

Volume is used with three-dimensional figures. It is the amount of space the figure occupies, or in the case of liquids, the figure's capacity. The units for volume are cubic units (e.g., cubic inches, cm^3, which is cubic centimeters, etc.). Basically, volume is length × width × height. Since length × width has already been defined as the formula for area, volume is sometimes given by (area of the base, B) × height, where the area of the base depends on the shape of the base.

Rectangular Solid $\qquad V = l \times w \times h = B \times h$

A cube is a rectangular solid with all sides equal, usually denoted as s, so

Cube $\qquad V = s^3$

The volume of a sphere, which is the three-dimensional form of a circle, is a function of r, the radius of the sphere, defined similarly to the radius of a circle: the distance from the center to any point on the surface. The volume of a sphere is

Sphere $$V = \frac{4}{3}\pi r^3,$$

EXAMPLE 6.15

What is the volume of a 3-inch by 5-inch rectangular solid with a height of 6 inches?

    (A) 15 square inches

    (B) 15 cubic inches

    (C) 30 cubic inches

    (D) 90 square inches

    (E) 90 cubic inches

SOLUTION

The correct answer is (E), 90 cubic inches.

Good solution: The volume of a rectangular solid is $V = l \times w \times h = 3 \times 5 \times 6 = 90$. Watch out that you don't choose 90 square inches. Volume is always in cubic units.

Another good solution: Figure the base area, $B = l \times w = 3 \times 5 = 15$, and then multiply this by the height to get $V = B \times h = 15 \times 6 = 90$. The answer, since this is volume, is in cubic inches.

TRANSFORMING FIGURES IN THE CARTESIAN PLANE

Using graph paper is a good way to draw figures neatly. Graph paper also can be used to plot points for a figure. We can draw a right triangle by plotting points on either axis and connecting them. For example, the points (0, 0), (0, 3), and (4, 0) connect to make a 3–4–5 right triangle.

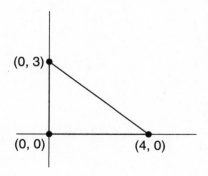

The previous chapter discussed plotting points on a Cartesian plane. Now we will discuss transforming these points and some figures in the plane. *Transformation* involves any of three movements or a combination of them.

- *translation* (moving an object left or right, up or down, but keeping the same orientation)

- *reflection* (flipping the object across a line, usually either axis)

- *rotation* (turning the object).

These mathematical transformations are useful in graphic arts, architecture, masonry, jewelry design, and many other occupations.

Translation

Translation means moving an object from one place to another. It doesn't change its size or orientation. You can think of a translation as sliding a penny across a table from one position to another without allowing it to rotate or flip over as you slide it.

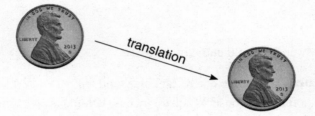

If the translation is vertical ("up" or "down"), the x-coordinate stays the same and the y-coordinate changes by the amount of the translation (+ for up and – for down). Similarly, if the translation is horizontal ("left" or "right"), the y-coordinate stays the same and the x-coordinate changes by the amount of the translation (+ for right and – for left). A translation at an angle, like the pennies, is done in two steps, horizontal and then vertical (or vice versa).

EXAMPLE 6.16

Point P (5, −3) is plotted on the coordinate grid. If point S is 4 units above point P, what are the coordinates of point S?

(A) (9, −3)

(B) (1, −3)

(C) (5, −7)

(D) (5, 1)

(E) (5, −3)

SOLUTION

The correct answer is (D), (5, 1).

Here we aren't really physically translating point P, but using what we know about translation to figure where point S would be. The translation is up (S is above point P), so we add 4 to the y-coordinate. The coordinates of S are thus (5, 1), and point S is aligned above point P.

As we saw in the chapter on numbers and quantity, distance on the number line is found by subtracting one value from the other and taking the absolute value of that difference. Distance between two points, if they are on the same horizontal or vertical line (if their x values or their y values are unchanged), is measured along the other coordinate line, just as we did on the number line.

EXAMPLE 6.17

Two points on a graph are $T(3, 5)$ and $U(3, -1)$. What is the distance between these points?

    (A) 4 units

    (B) 5 units

    (C) 6 units

    (D) 0 units

    (E) 1 unit

SOLUTION

The answer is (C), 6 units.

To find the distance between $T(3, 5)$ and $U(3, -1)$, since the x-values are the same, we just find the distance between 5 and -1:

$$|5 - (-1)| = |5 + 1| = |6| = 6.$$

It is actually how many units point T would be translated on the $x = 3$ line to get to point U.

Note that if the two points on the coordinate plane are not on the same x line or y line, the distance calculation is based on the Pythagorean theorem.

EXAMPLE 6.18

Find the distance between points $E(1, 7)$ and $F(4, 3)$.

    (A) 3 units

    (B) 4 units

    (C) 5 units

    (D) 25 units

    (E) $5\sqrt{2}$ units

SOLUTION

The correct answer is (C), 5 units.

Good solution: Sketch the two points and draw a horizontal line from one and a vertical line from the other. The orientation shown is the easiest one to work with, but the other triangles that can be formed (e.g., by drawing a horizontal line from E and a vertical line from F) also will work.

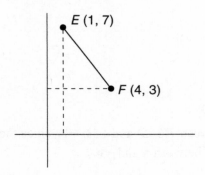

These lines will intersect at a point, let's call it G, forming right triangle EFG. Determine the coordinates of the point of intersection G. Here it is the point $(1, 3)$. The horizontal leg of triangle EFG is the distance between $(1, 3)$ and $(4, 3)$, or $GF = 3$ units. The vertical leg of triangle EFG is the distance between $(1, 3)$ and $(1, 7)$, or $GE = 4$ units. Use the Pythagorean theorem to find $EF = 5$ units.

Better solution: Draw the sketch as above, but recognize that this is a 3–4–5 right triangle, with the hypotenuse $EF = 5$ units.

The solution to Example 6.3 is similar to the approach for Example 6.18.

Sometimes the translation is actually two translations. Just do the first one, and then the second one starting from the new position.

EXAMPLE 6.19

Translate the point $(3, -5)$ down 2 units and to the right 4 units. What are the coordinates of the final translated point?

    (A) $(7, -7)$

    (B) $(3, -7)$

    (C) $(7, -5)$

    (D) $(-1, 1)$

    (E) $(-1, 3)$

SOLUTION

The correct answer is (A), $(7, -7)$.

Good solution: If the point $(3, -5)$ is translated down 2 units, subtract (because the direction is down) the number of units from the y value but leave the x value alone. So the original point now is moved to $(3, -7)$, and it is from this point that we add (because the direction is right) 4 units to the new x value, leaving the new y value alone. The final answer is $(7, -7)$.

Better solution: Do the translation in a sketch, not stopping to determine the coordinates of the results of the first translation. It's faster.

Translating points isn't very complicated. A little more complicated is translating figures, such as triangles, but we can streamline that translation as well by looking at the vertices individually instead of thinking about the whole figure. A typical Praxis Core test problem shows a figure and then asks something about new values if it were translated on the plane.

EXAMPLE 6.20

Triangle *ABC* is drawn on the coordinate plane as shown below. If the triangle were translated down 4 units, what would be the new coordinate of point *A*?

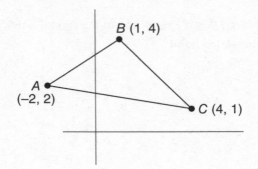

(A) (2, 2)

(B) (2, 4)

(C) (−2, −2)

(D) (4, −2)

(E) (−4, −2)

SOLUTION

The correct answer is (C), (−2, −2).

Good solution: Sketch and move the whole triangle down 4 units and read the coordinates of the new point *A*. This solution works, but it isn't so good because it takes a lot more work than necessary.

Better solution: Realize that this problem is the same as asking, "If point *A*(−2, 2) is translated down 4 units, what would be the new coordinates?" Don't let the fact that point *A* is part of a triangle throw you—it is asking only about point *A*. If we move point *A* down 4 units, we just move 4 units down for the new *y*-coordinate, and the *x*-coordinate remains the same. Four units down from 2 is −2, so the answer is (−2, −2). For this problem, it really doesn't matter where the rest of the triangle goes. It is asking only about point *A*.

Another variation of this sort of problem is to be given a choice of five graphs to determine which is the correct translation. Save time and trouble by first looking at only one point, which will probably eliminate one or two answer choices, and then look at the next point—most likely, that's all that would need to be done. Only one of the remaining choices will match those two points. The idea is that you don't have to find all three points if you are given a choice of graphs.

As mentioned above, many test-takers get confused with transformations because they look at the whole picture and it's too many points to keep straight. The tactic should be to streamline the process as much as possible, saving time and frustration. This type of thinking is shown next for reflections and rotations, notoriously confusing transformations that will now get easier.

Reflection

Reflection is just what it sounds like. If we were to place a mirror on the x- or y-axis, we would see where the reflection of a point would go. But that isn't feasible in a test setting, nor is it easy to do anyway. Reflections can be across any line, but for the Praxis test, they are usually across either the x- or y-axis.

If a point is reflected across the x-axis, we know we are going up or down, depending on where the original point was. The reflected point must be in the opposite quadrant (up or down), the x value doesn't change, and the new y value is simply the opposite of the old y-value. What do all these words mean? This explanation is longer and more complicated than actually doing a reflection problem.

EXAMPLE 6.21

Reflect the point $(4, -2)$ across the x-axis. The new coordinates are [ ].

SOLUTION

The correct answer is $(4, 2)$.

Just change the sign of the y value. The new coordinates are $(4, 2)$.

Similarly, if the reflection is across the y-axis, the opposite quadrant is left or right, the y value doesn't change, and the new x value is simply the opposite of the old x value.

EXAMPLE 6.22:

Reflect the point $(4, -2)$ (the same point) across the y-axis. What are the new coordinates?

SOLUTION

The correct answer is $(-4, -2)$.

Just change the sign of the x value. That's it.

We could have drawn the points on a grid, but it's not necessary unless we want to be extra sure of the answer. It might be easier to just mentally picture a grid that got folded on the y-axis for a reflection across the y-axis, or the x-axis for a reflection across the x-axis to see which of the two coordinates is the one for which the sign changes. The rule is: For a reflection across the x-axis, change the sign of the y-coordinate; for a reflection across the y-axis, change the sign of the x-coordinate. That's all there is to it.

What if the problem presents a triangle and wants to know how the reflected triangle will look. Again, the Praxis Core test would probably present this as multiple-choice graphs from which a selection is to be made. The same as we did for translations, break this up into pieces (actually, individual coordinates). Look at one vertex at a time, making sure the new positions have the same letter. Eliminate any graphs that don't match up. Probably only two vertices need to be checked, and maybe not even two. Don't get confused with the sides of the triangle—it's the placement of the vertices that make the difference. Usually, the correct answer choice is obvious by elimination early on.

Rotation

Rotation seems to be the toughest of the three transformations to visualize, but a simple "trick" will make it easier. Imagine a ceiling fan—don't laugh, this will work—oriented like the figure below.

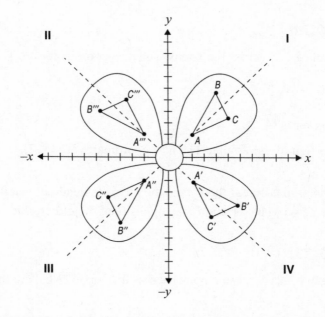

Actually the hardest part of rotations is remembering what clockwise and counterclockwise mean. **Clockwise** means what it sounds like: turning like a clock, from 1 to 2 to 3. The other way is called **counterclockwise**. Most rotation problems are clockwise.

Each quadrant is 90 degrees. Rotating a figure 90 degrees just means it will go into the next quadrant (clockwise) so, for example, from Quadrant I to Quadrant IV; 180 degrees puts the figure halfway around (clockwise or counterclockwise), for example, from Quadrant I to Quadrant III; and 270 degrees goes three-quarters of the way around, for example, from Quadrant I to Quadrant II. Rotating 270 degrees clockwise is the same as rotating 90 degrees counterclockwise, which will make visualizing simpler.

Now, back to the fan. Imagine the figure (usually a triangle or a non-regular quadrilateral) painted on one blade of the fan. When we turn the fan 90 degrees, we can readily see how the figure looks and not get confused by flipping it lengthwise or across itself. Just think of the fan blade. The point that was closest to the origin (hub of the fan) is *always* closest to the origin. It doesn't flip to the outside. And the other points keep their same positions relative to that point. When viewed from the hub, all blades look identical.

Practice Exercises

1. Which of the following statements is true concerning the intersection of perpendicular lines? Choose *all* that apply.

    A   They never intersect.

    B   They form only obtuse angles.

    C   They form right angles.

    D   They form four equal angles.

    E   Any point on either line is the same distance from the other line.

2. A line has how many dimensions?

    (A) 4

    (B) 2

    (C) 3

    (D) 1

    (E) 0

3. Angles r, s, and t are the three angles in a triangle. If $r + s = 80°$, what is the measure of t?

    (A) 80°

    (B) 100°

    (C) 120°

    (D) 280°

    (E) Cannot tell without knowing what kind of triangle it is.

4. The opposite angles of a quadrilateral are equal and the consecutive angles are supplementary. What are the measures of the four angles of the quadrilateral?

   (A) 90, 90, 90, 90

   (B) 30, 150, 30, 150

   (C) 45, 135, 45, 135

   (D) 60, 120, 60, 120

   (E) There is not enough information given.

5. If $\angle TVZ = 10x$; x could be

   (A) 3°

   (B) 6°

   (C) 9°

   (D) 16°

   (E) 20°

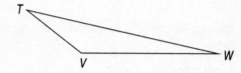

6. $y + z =$

   (A) $180° - x$

   (B) $180° - \dfrac{x}{4}$

   (C) $45° - \dfrac{x}{4}$

   (D) $90° + \dfrac{5x}{4}$

   (E) $90° - \dfrac{5x}{4}$

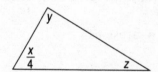

7. y (in terms of x) =

   (A) x

   (B) $x + 40°$

   (C) $140° - x$

   (D) $140° + x$

   (E) $320° - x$

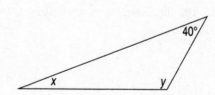

8. A cube and a rectangular solid have the same volume. If the dimensions of the rectangular solid are 1, 3, and 9, how long is one side of the cube?

    (A) 1

    (B) 3

    (C) 13

    (D) $\sqrt[3]{13}$

    (E) 27

9. A circle fits inside a square, touching all the sides of the square. If a side of the square is 6, what is the area of the circle?

    (A) 3π

    (B) 6π

    (C) 9π

    (D) $\sqrt{6\pi}$

    (E) Not enough information is given.

10. How many square inches of wrapping paper will Kara need to just cover a gift box that measures 3 inches by 5 inches by one foot?

    (A) 15 square inches

    (B) 36 square inches

    (C) 60 square inches

    (D) 111 square inches

    (E) 222 square inches

11. A rhombus is a(n) _____ parallelogram.

    (A) equiangular

    (B) equilateral

    (C) right

    (D) isosceles

    (E) none of the above

12. The area of square *C* is 36; the area of square *B* is 25.

    What is the area of square *A*?

    (A) 61

    (B) 100

    (C) 121

    (D) 900

    (E) 3721

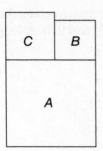

13. For right triangle *PQR*, if *PQ* = 10, *PR* = [ ].

    Fill in the box.

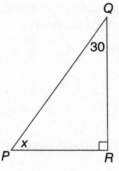

14. For the right triangle shown here, what is the value of *x*?

    (A) 10

    (B) 8

    (C) 5

    (D) 2

    (E) 1

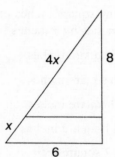

15. In the figure to the right, two parallel lines

    are crossed by a transversal. *m* − *n* =

    (A) 50°

    (B) 130°

    (C) 80°

    (D) 180°

    (E) 30°

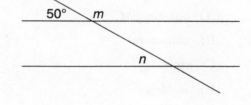

16. In the figure to the right, ∠*b* =

    (A) 45°

    (B) 60°

    (C) 90°

    (D) 105°

    (E) 135°

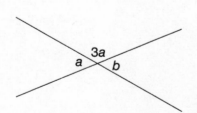

17. Two sides of a triangle are 4 and 7. If all the sides are integers, the product of the smallest possible perimeter and largest possible perimeter is

    (A) 15

    (B) 21

    (C) 40

    (D) 210

    (E) 315

18. A circle with a diameter of 12 has the same area as a square. What is the side of the square?

    (A) $\sqrt{36\pi}$

    (B) 36π

    (C) 6π

    (D) 36

    (E) 6

19. The areas of the rectangle and triangle shown are equal. If $\dfrac{LW}{4} = 20$, then $bh = $ ☐ .
    Fill in the box.

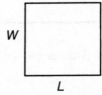

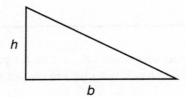

20. The perimeter of this figure, which has a right triangle–semicircle shape, is

    (A) $14 + 5\pi$

    (B) $14 + 10\pi$

    (C) $24 + 5\pi$

    (D) $24 + 10\pi$

    (E) $12 + 10\pi$

21. Two cog wheels are situated as shown in the figure. The larger cog has 36 teeth and the smaller cog has 18 teeth, so one revolution of the larger cog coincides with two revolutions of the smaller cog. If the diameter of the larger cog is 10 cm, what is the diameter of the smaller cog?

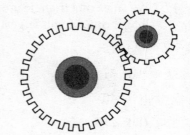

    (A) 5 cm

    (B) 7.5 cm

    (C) 2.5 cm

    (D) 10π cm

    (E) 5π cm

22. Imagine a knife cutting through a cardboard cylindrical can as shown. As angle A between the knife and the horizontal increases, the ellipse formed

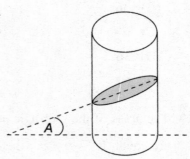

    (A) gets smaller

    (B) doesn't change

    (C) gets larger

    (D) becomes more circular

    (E) cannot tell from the information given

Solutions

1. $\boxed{C}$, $\boxed{D}$, and $\boxed{E}$ are all true. Answer choice $\boxed{A}$ is true for parallel lines. Answer choice $\boxed{B}$ is wrong because it is impossible to have two adjacent obtuse angles.

2. (D), 1. A line has only one dimension, length. It has no width, even though when we draw a representation of a line we have to give it width so we can see it. A point has no dimensions, but when we draw it, again, we have to give it a little length and width so we can see it. A plane (like a sheet of paper) has two dimensions (length and width), and space has three dimensions.

3. (B), 100°. All triangles contain a total of 180°, so if two of them total 80°, the third one must be $180° - 80° = 100°$.

4. (E), There is not enough information given. The information given is true for all parallelograms, but unless one of the angles is given, there is no way to determine the exact measures of the angles. Any of the answer choices (A)–(D) could be correct, as well as an infinite number of other measures.

5. (D), 16°. $\angle TVZ$ is obtuse, so it must be between 90° and 180°, so $90° < 10x < 180°$, and $9° < x < 18°$.

6. (B), $180° - \dfrac{x}{4}$. The angles of a triangle total $180°$. Therefore, $\dfrac{x}{4} + y + z = 180°$, and $y + z = 180° - \dfrac{x}{4}$.

7. (C), $140° - x$. The angles of a triangle total $180°$. Therefore,

    $x + y + 40° = 180°$

    $x + y = 140°$

    $y = 140° - x$.

8. (B), 3. The volume of the rectangular solid is $V = lwh = 1 \times 3 \times 9 = 27$; and the volume of a cube is s^3. Then the length of a side of the cube is $\sqrt[3]{27} = 3$.

9. (C), 9π. The diameter of the circle must be the same length as the side of the square, which is 6. So $r = 3$, and the area is $A = \pi r^2 = \pi(3^2) = 9\pi$.

10. (E), 222 square inches. The surface area of a rectangular solid (which is the shape of this gift box) is the areas of the six sides, or twice the area of the top plus twice the area of one side plus twice the area of the other side. Don't forget to change 1 foot to 12 inches. Then, the area is

    $2(12 \times 5) + 2(3 \times 12) + 2(5 \times 3)$

    $= 2(60 + 36 + 15) = 2(111) = 222$

11. (B), equilateral. A rhombus has all the properties of a parallelogram plus all four sides are equal. Its angles, however, are not equal. If they were, it would be a square.

12. (C), 121. If the area of square B is 25, then the side is 5, and if area of square C is 36, then the side is 6, so the side of square A must be $5 + 6 = 11$, and thus its area is $11^2 = 121$.

13. 5. This is a $30°$–$60°$–$90°$ triangle. One of the features of this triangle is that the side opposite the $30°$ angle is half the hypotenuse, so $PR = \dfrac{1}{2} PQ = \dfrac{1}{2}(10) = 5$.

14. (D), 2. Look at the whole triangle. The Pythagorean theorem gives:

    $(5x)^2 = 8^2 + 6^2$

    $25x^2 = 64 + 36 = 100$

    $x^2 = 4$

    $x = 2$

But a better solution is found by recognizing that this is a 6–8–10 right triangle (a multiple of the Pythagorean triple 3–4–5). Therefore, the hypotenuse is 10, so $4x + x = 10$, $5x = 10$, and $x = 2$.

15. (C), 80°. When two parallel lines are cut by a transversal, the angles formed are either equal (corresponding angles or vertical angles) or supplementary. Here, 50° and m are supplementary, so $m = 180° - 50° = 130°$. Also, 50° and n are corresponding angles, so $n = 50°$. The question asks for $m - n = 130° - 50° = 80°$.

16. (A), 45°. Two geometric rules are used here: two angles that form a straight line are supplementary, which means they total 180°, and vertical angles are equal. Therefore, $3a + a = 180°$, $4a = 180°$, and thus $a = 45°$. Since a and b are vertical angles, they are equal, so $b = 45°$.

17. (E) 315. The third side s must be between the limits of $7 - 4 < s < 7 + 4$. Since all the sides are integers, s could be any integer 4 through 10. Thus, the smallest perimeter is $4 + 4 + 7 = 15$, and the largest is $10 + 4 + 7 = 21$. The question asks for the product of these perimeters, so the correct answer is $15 \times 21 = 315$.

18. (A) $\sqrt{36\pi}$. The area of the circle with diameter 12 (radius = 6) is $A = \pi 6^2 = 36\pi$. The area of a square is $A = s^2$, so the side is the square root of the area, or $\sqrt{36\pi}$.

19. (E), 160. If $\dfrac{LW}{4} = 20$, then $LW = 80$, so the area of the rectangle and the triangle are 80. The area of the triangle is $A = \dfrac{1}{2}bh = 80$, so $bh = 160$.

20. (A), $14 + 5\pi$. The perimeter is the sum of the two sides of the triangle plus the length of the semicircle. The semicircle is half of a circle whose diameter is the hypotenuse of the right triangle. This is a 6–8–10 right triangle (a multiple of the 3–4–5 Pythagorean triple), so the hypotenuse is 10. The circumference of the whole circle is thus 10π, and the length of the semicircle is half that, or 5π. Therefore, the perimeter of the figure is $6 + 8 + 5\pi = 14 + 5\pi$.

21. (A), 5 cm. The ratio of the number of teeth on the cogwheels is the same as the ratio of their circumferences, or 2:1. Since the formula for circumference is directly related to the diameter by the equation $C = \pi D$, the diameters are also in a ratio of 2:1. Therefore, $\dfrac{C}{c} = \dfrac{2}{1} = \dfrac{D}{d} = \dfrac{10}{d}$, and thus $d = 5$.

22. (C), gets larger. When angle $A = 0°$, the cut of the knife is a circle the same size as the top (or bottom) of the can, but it elongates into an ellipse, as shown, that gets bigger as angle A increases, until at the extreme case, $A = 90°$, the cut looks like a rectangle.

Probability and Statistics

Probability and statistics are part of our everyday lives. Weather reports, election results or predictions, and even the scoring of the Praxis test are but a few of the many examples.

PROBABILITY

Probability can be confusing because of all of the jargon: mutually exclusive, independent, dependent, conditional, compound events, complementary events, and so on. Even the word "success" as it is used for probability is confusing because "success" isn't always a positive situation, as we would think. For probability, success just means that something of interest occurs. For example, if we are asked for the probability that a student will fail an exam, we would normally think of failing an exam as being unsuccessful, but here failing is treated as a "success" in probability-language. (It's better to speak of passing the exam!)

So let's just talk about probability in plain words to show that it is fairly logical if you don't get confused by the language. Of course, we'll include the vocabulary terms in the table at the end of this section, but it's more important here to understand how probability works.

Probability is simply the chance that something will occur, and it is this "something" that should be our focus. So, the probability of something happening is calculated as

$$\text{Pr(something happening)} = \frac{\text{number of ways something can happen}}{\text{number of ways something can and cannot happen}},$$

Probability is therefore a fraction (or its equivalent ratio or percentage) between 0 and 1.

At one end, a probability of 0 means that something cannot happen. Period. Since in this case the number of ways something can happen is 0, we don't even have to worry about the number of ways it can and cannot happen (the denominator) because 0 divided by anything (except another 0) is 0. An example is pigs flying. Pigs cannot fly, so the probability of a pig flying is 0.

At the other end, a probability of 1 means that something always happens. It cannot "not happen" and we have the same number at the top and bottom of the fraction, so it equals 1. Do you have to know how many ways something can happen if it always happens? No, what you have to know is that it cannot not happen, so the probability is 1, or 100% certain. A simple example is the probability that your birthday will be on the month and day you were born. It's a sure thing—there is no wiggle room. The probability is 1. Period.

All other types of probability always fall between 0 and 1. There are no negative probabilities.

But what if we are considering something that has more than one part. If we consider two parts, let's call them A and B. What is the probability that A *or* B will occur? Or what is the probability that A *and* B will occur? The following general rules will help:

"or" means add
"and" means multiply

 HINT

> To remember that "and" means multiply, think of a jar of only yellow marbles. Of course, the probability of picking a yellow marble from the jar is 1 since they all are yellow. The probability of picking two yellow marbles is likewise 1. But if we used addition for "and," we would have gotten Pr(yellow and yellow) = 1 + 1 = 2, which is impossible since all probabilities are between 0 and 1. So Pr(yellow and yellow) = 1 × 1 = 1.

Let's look at some examples and follow them to their logical conclusions. We will introduce more complicated situations as we go, but the idea is the same for all. Notice in these examples that everything must be fair. For instance, a coin must not be weighted to favor one side, and a die (singular of dice) also must not be weighted, so each side has an equal chance of being the top number.

EXAMPLE 7.1

What is the probability of tossing heads on one flip of a fair coin?

SOLUTION

The correct answer is $\frac{1}{2}$.

Since there are only 2 ways a coin can land and one of them is heads, the probability is Pr(heads) = $\frac{1}{2}$.

EXAMPLE 7.2

What is the probability of tossing a 3 on a die?

SOLUTION

The correct answer is $\frac{1}{6}$.

Since there are 6 ways the die can land and only one of them is a 3, the probability is Pr(3) = $\frac{1}{6}$.

EXAMPLE 7.3

What is the probability of tossing a 7 on the toss of a die?

SOLUTION

The correct answer is 0.

The numbers on a die are 1 through 6, so you can't toss a 7. Pr(7) = 0. It's impossible.

EXAMPLE 7.4

What is the probability of tossing a 1 through 6 on a die?

SOLUTION

The correct answer is 1.

Since the numbers must be 1 through 6, that is always going to happen, so Pr(1 through 6) = 1.

Let's look at Example 7.4 another way. The question could have been asked as in Example 7.5.

EXAMPLE 7.5

What is the probability of tossing a 1 or a 2 or a 3 or a 4 or a 5 or a 6 on a die?

SOLUTION

The correct answer is 1.

We saw in Example 7.2 that the probability of tossing a 3 is $Pr(3) = \frac{1}{6}$. That is true for the other five numbers as well. Each has a probability of $\frac{1}{6}$, and this is an "or" situation, so we *add* the probabilities: $Pr(1 \text{ or } 2 \text{ or } 3 \text{ or } 4 \text{ or } 5 \text{ or } 6) = Pr(1) + Pr(2) + Pr(3) + Pr(4) + Pr(5) + Pr(6) = \frac{1}{6} + \frac{1}{6} + \frac{1}{6} + \frac{1}{6} + \frac{1}{6} + \frac{1}{6} = 1$. This answer is included here to show that *or* means *add* works. It's much better to solve this example by thinking the way we did for Example 7.4.

EXAMPLE 7.6

What is the probability of tossing a number greater than 4 on a die?

SOLUTION

The correct answer is $\frac{1}{3}$.

A number greater than 4 would be a 5 or a 6, which means 2 of the possible tosses, so $Pr(5 \text{ or } 6) = \frac{2}{6} = \frac{1}{3}$. Or, doing it the longer way, $Pr(5 \text{ or } 6) = Pr(5) + Pr(6) = \frac{1}{6} + \frac{1}{6} = \frac{2}{6} = \frac{1}{3}$.

This is all well and good because we are talking about one toss of one die. What if we now talk about tossing two dice, or even one die twice?

EXAMPLE 7.7

What is the probability of getting two 1's on the two tosses of one die or on one toss of two dice (called "snake eyes")?

SOLUTION

The correct answer is $\frac{1}{36}$.

This is an "and" situation, so we multiply the probabilities: $Pr(1 \text{ and } 1) = Pr(1) \times Pr(1) = \frac{1}{6} \times \frac{1}{6} = \frac{1}{36}$.

EXAMPLE 7.8

What is the probability of getting a 1 and a 6, in that order, on two tosses of one die or on one toss of two dice?

SOLUTION

The correct answer is $\dfrac{1}{36}$.

$\Pr(1 \text{ and } 6) = \Pr(1) \times \Pr(6) = \dfrac{1}{6} \times \dfrac{1}{6} = \dfrac{1}{36}$.

The situation is the same for several tosses of a fair coin or a toss of several coins.

EXAMPLE 7.9

What is the probability of tossing a coin four times and getting four heads?

SOLUTION

The correct answer is $\dfrac{1}{16}$.

This is an "and" situation, so the probability of getting a head (H) and another H, and another H, and another H is $\Pr(\text{HHHH}) = \Pr(\text{H}) \times \Pr(\text{H}) \times \Pr(\text{H}) \times \Pr(\text{H}) = \dfrac{1}{2} \times \dfrac{1}{2} \times \dfrac{1}{2} \times \dfrac{1}{2} = \dfrac{1}{16}$.

Can you see that the answer would be the same if we asked for $\Pr(\text{HTTH})$ or $\Pr(\text{HHTT})$, where T is "tails"? Why is this so? In each toss, whether it is successive tosses of the same coin, or a toss of four coins, the probability of landing heads or tails doesn't have any effect on the probability of any other coin or other toss. Therefore, if you tossed a coin seven times and it came up heads each time, the probability of the eighth toss being a head is still only $\dfrac{1}{2}$. The probability of the exact string of tosses, $\Pr(\text{HHHHHHHH}) = \left(\dfrac{1}{2}\right)^{8} = \dfrac{1}{2^{8}} = \dfrac{1}{256}$, or 1 in 256.

This is true for any string of events that don't influence each other (called *independent* events). Let's look at some examples of these.

EXAMPLE 7.10

What is the probability of tossing snake eyes on four successive tosses of two dice?

SOLUTION

The correct answer is $\left(\dfrac{1}{36}\right)^4$.

We saw in Example 7.7 that the probability of one toss of snake eyes is $\dfrac{1}{36}$. If we rolled snake eyes once, does it influence the next toss? No, they are totally independent events. So the probability here is an "and" situation: Pr(snake eyes on first toss AND snake eyes on second toss AND snake eyes on third toss AND snake eyes on fourth toss) = $\dfrac{1}{36} \times \dfrac{1}{36} \times \dfrac{1}{36} \times \dfrac{1}{36} = \left(\dfrac{1}{36}\right)^4$, which is the same as 1 in 36^4 or 1 in 1,679,616.

Now let's look at a combination "or" and "and" situation. Notice that each situation presented so far just involves logic and multiplication or division. So does Example 7.11, but it needs some more thinking.

EXAMPLE 7.11

What is the probability of getting a *total* of 4 with a toss of two dice?

SOLUTION

The correct answer is $\dfrac{1}{12}$.

Watch out here. We have to first figure out how many ways we can get a total of four:

(1, 3), (3, 1), and (2, 2), or three ways. So the probability is

Pr(1 and 3 OR 3 and 1 OR 2 and 2) =

Pr(1 and 3) + Pr(3 and 1) + Pr(2 and 2) =

[Pr(1) × Pr(3)] + [Pr(3) × Pr(1)] + [Pr(2) × Pr(2)] =

$$\frac{1}{36} + \frac{1}{36} + \frac{1}{36} = \frac{3}{36} = \frac{1}{12}.$$

The challenge in the solution to Example 7.11 is figuring out all of the parts, but they are the same as the calculations in all of the preceding examples.

The reason we don't count another (2, 2) is that (2, 2) is the same whether the first or second die comes up a 2. To see how (2, 2) counts as only one possibility, whereas the combination of 1 and 3 counts as two possibilities, let's look at a chart of the 36 tosses of a die, where the vertical column is the first die and the horizontal column is the second die.

	1	2	3	4	5	6
1	(1,1)	(1,2)	(1,3)	(1,4)	(1,5)	(1,6)
2	(2,1)	(2,2)	(2,3)	(2,4)	(2,5)	(2,6)
3	(3,1)	(3,2)	(3,3)	(3,4)	(3,5)	(3,6)
4	(4,1)	(4,2)	(4,3)	(4,4)	(4,5)	(4,6)
5	(5,1)	(5,2)	(5,3)	(5,4)	(5,5)	(5,6)
6	(6,1)	(6,2)	(6,3)	(6,4)	(6,5)	(6,6)

All of the double tosses (1,1), (2,2), and so on appear only once, whereas (3,1) is considered a different toss than (1,3).

It's a Fact!

There are 36 possibilities on a toss of two dice, 6 possible numbers on the second die (or second toss of a single die) for each of the 6 numbers on the first die (or second toss of the same die).

Now, let's consider a similar situation that is a favorite on most tests: selecting socks in a drawer. This involves two assumptions. First, the socks are chosen without looking. This is similar to using a fair coin or a fair die. (Besides, if the person selecting the socks looks, then the probability would be 100% that the socks selected are the ones that are wanted.) Second, the socks are in color-matched pairs, not just tossed into the drawer when they come from the dryer, which is the usual scenario.

EXAMPLE 7.12

If Jim has 9 pairs of socks in a drawer, 2 tan, 3 brown, and 4 black, and he selects a pair without looking,

    a.   What is the probability that he picks a pair of brown socks?

    b.   What is the probability that he picks a pair of brown or tan socks?

    c.   What is the probability that he doesn't pick a pair of black socks?

SOLUTION

The correct answers are (a) $\frac{1}{3}$, (b) $\frac{5}{9}$, and (c) $\frac{5}{9}$.

a. Jim has 9 pair of socks and 3 are brown, so the probability of picking a brown pair is $\frac{3}{9} = \frac{1}{3}$.

b. This is Pr(brown or tan) = Pr(brown) + Pr(tan) = $\frac{2}{9} + \frac{3}{9} = \frac{5}{9}$.

c. This is a new type of scenario. We are asking the probability of something NOT happening. Since the probability of something not happening plus the probability of it happening equals 100%, we can say

   Pr(something not happening) = 1 – Pr(something happening)

   in which the something in this case is choosing a pair of black socks. So Pr(not black) = 1 – Pr(black) = $1 - \frac{4}{9} = \frac{5}{9}$. This answer is the same as that for part (b), the probability of picking brown or tan socks, which makes sense. If Jim doesn't pick black socks, he must pick brown or tan socks.

We now will ratchet up the probability a little more, but the logic will be similar. This is another favorite type of problem on many tests. It is similar to the socks-in-a-drawer problem, but it involves *replacement*.

EXAMPLE 7.13

Let's say we have a jar that contains 20 marbles, 3 red, 4 yellow, 6 green, and 7 blue. Further, when we pick one or more marbles from the jar, we don't look.

a. What is the probability of picking a yellow marble from the jar, putting it back in the jar, and then picking a blue marble?

b. What is the probability of picking a yellow marble from the jar, not putting it back in the jar, and then picking a blue marble?

SOLUTION

The correct answers are (a) $\frac{7}{100}$ and (b) $\frac{28}{380}$.

a. The probability is

   Pr(yellow and blue, with replacement) = Pr(yellow) × Pr(blue) =

$$\frac{4}{20} \times \frac{7}{20} = \frac{28}{400} = \frac{7}{100} = .07 = 7\%.$$

b. This scenario is different because in the second pick, there aren't 20 marbles anymore. The yellow one is missing. The method is still the same, though—only the numbers change.

Pr(yellow and blue, without replacement) = Pr(yellow) × Pr(blue) =
$$\frac{4}{20} \times \frac{7}{19} = \frac{28}{380} = 0.0737 = 7.37\%.$$

The difference between the situations in the two parts of Example 7.13 is the replacement. In part (a), with replacement, the two picks were independent. But in part (b), the probability of picking a blue marble depends on the fact that once the yellow marble was taken out, there was a greater chance of picking a blue marble.

VENN DIAGRAMS

Often, situations that involve events that overlap are best shown by using **Venn diagrams**, a sample of which is shown below.

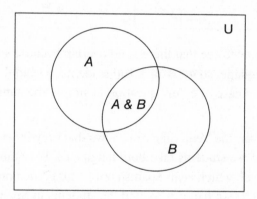

All of the space within the borders of a Venn diagram represent the universe, U, which doesn't necessarily have anything to do with outer space—it simply means the population of interest. In the space within the borders are two or more circles, each representing a specific part of the universe. For Examples 7.1 to 7.13, the circles wouldn't intersect, but we are now going to consider cases in which they do intersect.

The Venn diagram here consists of two overlapping circles, one labeled *A* and one labeled *B*. The intersection of the two circles is labeled *A* & *B*. Each section of the Venn diagram represents the items that belong to *A*, *B*, or both. The items can be anything that "overlaps." Let's consider students' language classes and look at two scenarios. Suppose students at School A can study only one foreign language. So students who have Spanish classes cannot also have French classes. School B also offers Spanish and French, but allows students to take two languages at the same time.

In the Venn diagrams shown below, School A is shown on the left, with all the students at the school being the universe. There is no overlap between the circles because no student is in both Spanish and French class. School B is shown on the right, with the universe again being all the students in the school. The two circles represent students who are taking at least one language. The portion shared by the two circles represents those students who are taking both Spanish and French. The space outside of the circles in both diagrams represents all the students who aren't taking Spanish or French at all.

EXAMPLE 7.14

The school A diagram shows that 40 students are in Spanish class and 60 are in French class. Likewise, the school B diagram shows that 40 students are in Spanish class and 60 are in French class. However, at school B, 10 students take both classes. How many students in each school are taking at least one language?

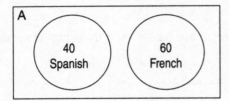
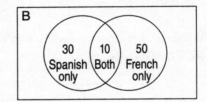

For school A, it is easy to see that there is no overlap because students are allowed to take only one language, so 40 + 60 = 100 students in school A take a French or Spanish class. In this case, the "or" question is simply the sum of the students in each language class.

For school B, however, the Venn diagram shows that only 90 students take French or Spanish. Ten of these students take both languages. We cannot count those students twice in the total, which is 30 Spanish only + 50 French only + 10 both Spanish and French = 90. If we had just totaled the students in Spanish class (30 + 10) and the students in French class (50 + 10), we would have gotten 40 + 60 = 100, which is incorrect, as we can see in the Venn diagram. We cannot count students who take both classes twice, so we must subtract the extra 10 for both classes from the total.

How this translates into probability is that with an "or" situation, if any of the events overlap, we must be careful not to count the overlap twice. The next example shows this calculation.

EXAMPLE 7.15

In a class of 30 students, 20 have dogs or cats. Thirteen have a dog, and 10 have a cat. If a student is chosen at random from the class, what is the probability that the student has a dog or cat?

SOLUTION

The correct answer is $\dfrac{20}{30}$.

Some of the students must have both pets because $13 + 10 \neq 20$. In fact, 3 of the students must have both pets. If we don't take into consideration that some students have both pets, we might incorrectly calculate Pr(dog or cat) = Pr(dog) + Pr(cat) = $\dfrac{13}{30} + \dfrac{10}{30} = \dfrac{23}{30}$, when in fact only 20 of the 30 students have a dog or cat, so the correct answer is Pr(dog or cat) = $\dfrac{20}{30}$.

Notice that the information for the answer to Example 7.15 comes directly from the first sentence of the example, without having to use Venn diagrams. But let's look at the Venn diagram for this situation to explain the discrepancy between the incorrect and correct answers.

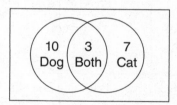

In this Venn diagram, we can see that 13 students do have dogs (the whole left circle for dogs and both) and 10 students do have cats (the whole right circle for cats and both). But we have counted the students who have both pets twice, once for dogs and once for cats. We have to subtract one of the duplicate "both" cases.

Formally, the probability for overlapping cases is given by

Pr(A or B) = Pr(A) + Pr(B) − Pr(A and B)

In fact, this calculation works for all cases, but if the two situations are mutually exclusive, meaning they do not overlap, the Pr(A and B) part equals 0.

For Example 7.15, the calculation would be

$$Pr(dog \text{ or } cat) = Pr(dog) + Pr(cat) - Pr(dog \text{ and } cat)$$

$$= \frac{13}{30} + \frac{10}{30} - \frac{3}{30} = \frac{20}{30}$$

The following table summarizes how to find probabilities, as shown in Examples 7.1 through 7.15.

Description	Example	Formula	Type of Probability
One event	Flip of a fair coin	$Pr(A) = \dfrac{\text{number of ways A can happen}}{\text{number of ways A can and cannot happen}}$	Simple probability
Event A or event B	Tossing a 5 or 6 on a die	$Pr(A \text{ or } B) = Pr(A) + Pr(B)$	Independent events
Event A and event B	Getting THHT in four tosses of a coin (or a toss of 4 coins)	$Pr(T \text{ and } H \text{ and } H \text{ and } T)$ $= Pr(T) \times Pr(H) \times Pr(H) \times Pr(T)$ T = tails; H = heads	Independent events
Events (A and B) or (C and D)	Getting a total of 4 with a toss of two dice	$Pr(A \text{ and } B \text{ OR } C \text{ and } D)$ $= Pr(A \text{ and } B) + Pr(C \text{ and } D)$ $= [Pr(A) \times Pr(B)] + [Pr(C) \times Pr(D)]$	Independent events
Pr(not A)	Probability of not choosing event A	$Pr(\text{not } A) = 1 - Pr(A)$	Simple probability
Pr(A and B) in two events, no replacement	Picking a blue marble and then a yellow marble	$Pr(A \text{ and } B) = Pr(A) \times Pr(B)$, where the denominator for event B depends on event A	Dependent events
Pr(A or B) with Pr(A and B) ≠ 0	Dealing with overlapping events	$Pr(A \text{ or } B) = Pr(A) + Pr(B) - PR(A \text{ and } B)$	Not mutually exclusive events

THE COUNTING PRINCIPLE

Statistics and probability have a lot to do with counting, and thus with the **counting principle**. An example of this principle is that if there are 2 ways for one activity to happen and 3 ways for a second activity to happen, then there are 2 × 3 = 6 ways for both to happen. A tree diagram shows how this works. Suppose a soft-serve shop has two ice cream flavors and three toppings. How many choices are there? The tree diagram shows there are 6.

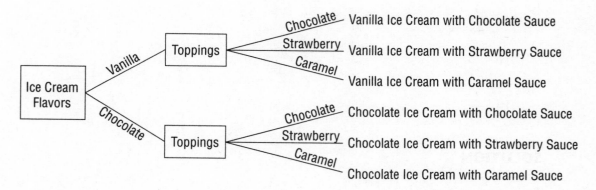

The counting principle works with any number of inputs. Even though a tree diagram for the following would be too big to show here, the principle is the same: If a restaurant offers 3 types of meat, 2 types of potato, 4 types of vegetable, and 5 different desserts, how many choices does a customer have, picking only one from each category? Surprisingly, the customer has 3 × 2 × 4 × 5 = 120 choices.

Notice that if in addition one of the choices was to not have a vegetable or dessert, thus adding 1 (none) to each of those choices, the customer would have 3 × 2 × 5 × 6 = 180 choices.

We can compute the probability that someone picked a specific type of meat, potato, vegetable, and dessert (assuming "no thank you" isn't allowed). That would be 1 × 1 × 1 × 1 = 1 choice out of 120, $\frac{1}{120}$, or .0083.

EXAMPLE 7.16

If a sandwich menu offers 6 types of meat, 4 types of cheese, and 2 types of bread (rye or white), what is the probability that someone chooses a sandwich on rye bread?

    (A) 1

    (B) $\dfrac{1}{2}$

    (C) $\dfrac{1}{48}$

    (D) $\dfrac{1}{24}$

    (E) $\dfrac{1}{10}$

SOLUTION

The correct answer is (B), $\dfrac{1}{2}$.

Good solution: The total number of choices are $6 \times 4 \times 2 = 48$. The number of choices of a sandwich on rye would be $6 \times 4 \times 1 = 24$. So the probability is 24 out of 48, $\dfrac{1}{2}$, or .50.

Better solution: This solution is much simpler if only the bread choices are taken into account. There are two bread choices, and rye is one of them: 1 out of 2, $\dfrac{1}{2}$, or .50. Analyzing a problem before proceeding can eliminate a lot of unnecessary multiplication and division.

STATISTICS

Probability is closely related to **statistics**, which involves four steps

- collecting data

- analyzing data

- presenting data

- interpreting data

In the menu selection shown in Example 7.16, we performed all of these functions, but we were dealing with a relatively small amount of data. What if the possibilities are humongous? What if we wanted to represent responses from the whole population of the United States? The answer lies in taking statistics from a representative sample of the population, as shown in the following sections.

Collecting Data

Statistics presents data from a sample taken from a specific population and states the probability that the sample results are representative of that whole population. By "population," as we already discussed with Venn diagrams, we don't necessarily mean people, we just mean the subjects of interest. For example, statistics can present data on elections as well as on money, age, and brand names, among myriad other populations.

How we pick the sample from the population is most important. The sample must be *representative* of the population of interest and *unbiased*. As a simple example, if we wanted to gather information on egg sizes from chicken farms in New Jersey, the population would be all the chicken farms in New Jersey. The sample therefore would not include any chicken farms in any other state. It would not include farms in New Jersey that didn't produce eggs. It would include only chicken farms in New Jersey, which would take care of the representative part of sampling.

In addition, the sample would not include farms in just one county in New Jersey because that would introduce a bias. Suppose the farms in the southern part of the state used a breed of chickens that produced larger eggs than the breed used in the northern part of the state? Suppose the water in the western part of the state was remarkably different from that in the eastern part, and that contributed to the size of eggs produced? To be unbiased, the sample must be drawn from the whole population with every member of the population having an equal chance of being picked for the sample. Random sampling is one way to take bias out of a sample. An example would be to take every tenth name on a relevant list from the entire population.

You could ask why not just use every member of the population in the first place. If we are talking about a small population, it is possible to do that, but for a large population, the costs and time involved in querying every member quickly become prohibitive. If the constraints on statistics (such as representative and unbiased samples) are strictly followed, the results from a sample mimic the results of the whole population.

It is important, however, that the sample be large enough to be truly representative of the whole population. If a machine can package 5-ounce bags of potato chips at the rate of 100 per minute, and the foreman of the factory wants to be sure, allowing some variation, that the bags contain close to 5 ounces of chips, a sample of 3 bags won't give as much assurance as a sample of, say, 100 bags taken at random throughout the production day. In actuality, the sample number for "quality assurance" is much larger.

EXAMPLE 7.17

For a sample to be representative of a population, the sample must be _____.
(Choose all of the correct answers.)

A	unbiased
B	random
C	chosen only from members of the population
D	of a sufficient size
E	none of the above

SOLUTION

The correct answers are A, B, C, and D.

These four choices are the conditions for a representative sample, and the sample must fulfill all of them.

EXAMPLE 7.18

Suppose we want to know how satisfied customers are with a new checkout procedure in a supermarket. Which of the following groups would be the best sample to use for such a survey?

(A) Choose every 50th name in the phonebook for the city in which the supermarket is located.

(B) Go door-to-door in the neighborhood within five blocks of the supermarket.

(C) Choose every 20th customer leaving the store throughout a day.

(D) Wait in the parking lot and ask every customer who returns a cart in a given period of time.

(E) Choose every 50th name on the supermarket's advertisement mailing list and send a survey to those people.

SOLUTION

The correct answer is (C).

The population for this exercise is "customers," so we want to sample customers. Although most answer choices seem to somehow be logical, let's first look at why the other answers aren't representative or unbiased. Answer choice (A) is wrong on several counts. It is biased toward only people who have telephones and are listed in the phonebook, so it excludes many people who no longer have landlines or choose not to be listed in the phonebook. In addition, it includes many more people than those who shop at that particular store. For the same reason, answer choice (B) is incorrect because not everyone who lives within five blocks of the store is necessarily a customer, and such a sample excludes all the people who are customers but live farther away. Answer choice (D) excludes customers who didn't drive to the store (and likely includes only the considerate ones who return their carts). Answer choice (E) includes many noncustomers who get advertisements from that store as well as many others, and it introduces the problem of how to contact these people to solicit their responses. All of these reasons for incorrect responses are just a few that come to mind.

Choosing every 20th customer leaving the store throughout a day (answer choice (C)), especially if the day is chosen at random, is correct because it is representative of the population—people who actually shop at that supermarket and use the checkout. The choice of every 20th customer makes the sample random, and the choice to do the sampling throughout the day doesn't incidentally exclude any part of the population. For example, possible biases due to time of day include senior citizens who are less likely to shop late at night, and certainly people who have a daytime job and probably don't shop during the hours of 8 a.m. to 5 p.m. So of all the answer choices, (C) is the best sample.

Analyzing Data

Once the data are collected, they must be analyzed so the results can be interpreted statistically. For raw data (the actual data points that are collected), we must first determine whether they are *categorical* (answers are categories, such as yes/no—sometimes called *qualitative*), or *quantitative* (answers are numbers—therefore, these are sometimes called *numerical*).

Categorical Data

Categorical data are often represented pictorially, such as on a pie chart or bar chart, as discussed in the next section on Presenting Data. Descriptive comparisons can be made among categories, but there can be no "average" as such. For example, if the categories are Democrat, Republican, and Other, what is the political party of the average respondent? There is no meaningful answer to that question—what we can see, however, is which category has the most respondents.

The categories in this type of data can also be ordered choices, such as "poor," "fair," "average," "good," "excellent," but the idea is still the same—the data are categories.

Quantitative Data

Quantitative data can be analyzed by standard statistical methods. Three measures give a sense of central tendency, or how the group of data tends to look, whether the data points represent age, height, hours, or another numerical value.

- The **mean**, also called the **average**, is the most popular. It is calculated by totaling all of the data points and dividing by the number of points. For example, a student who scored 45, 65, 80, and 90 on four tests would have an average of $\dfrac{45+65+80+90}{4} = 70$ on the four tests. The good grades on the last two tests are offset by the poor performance on the first two tests. Notice that the mean doesn't have to be a member of the data set. It is just the average so that the differences from the data points cancel each other out, giving it the quality of being representative of the whole data set. In this case, the four differences from the average score (70) are 25, 5, –10, and –20, which total 0.

- The **median** is the middle data point. To find the median, the data have to be arranged in order. It makes no difference if it is lowest to highest or highest to lowest. The exact middle point, which has as many data points above it as below it, is the median. For a data set with an odd number of points, it is easy to count over to find the median. For an even number of data points, two are in the middle, so the median is the average of the two. For example, for the data set 1, 2, 4, 5, 6, 9, 10, the median is 5, with three data points above it and three below it. If the data set was just 1, 2, 4, 5, 6, 9, the median would be the average of the two middle points, 4 and 5, and it would be 4.5. Therefore, the median need not be a member of the data set if the number of data points is even. Notice that the mean of the 7-number set is 5.3 ($= \dfrac{1+2+4+5+6+9+10}{7}$), so the mean and median are often not the same value.

- The **mode** is the data point with the highest frequency. This has meaning if the data points repeat values, such as in 3, 4, 5, 5, 5, 6, 7, 7, 8, 9, 9, 9, 9. The mode here is 9, with a frequency of 4 (the frequency of 5 is 3, and the frequency of 7 is 2). This value (remember to use the *value*, not its frequency) is always a member of the data set. It is less precise in describing the data set, as we can see in this data set, where 9 is not very representative of the rest of the numbers.

Another measure of qualitative data is called the **range**, which is simply the highest value minus the lowest value. The range gives information on how spread out the data are. For example, for the data set 2, 2, 15, 16, 45, the range is 43 (= 45 – 2), which is very large for a set of only five data points. This measure isn't a measure of central tendency, since it doesn't tell us anything about the data values, even what the highest and lowest points are, but just about how spread out the data are.

EXAMPLE 7.19

The freshman class at a local college is required to take a test in their first week of classes. Anyone who fails the test must have remedial work to continue taking classes in the school. We want to know how many students will need remedial work.

Several versions of the same test were given, with the following results:

Version of Test	Pass	Fail
A	200	50
B	225	25
C	210	40
D	220	30

The data presented in this table are what kind of data?

    (A) quantitative, because they involve numbers

    (B) categorical, because they involve two categories

    (C) neither quantitative nor categorical because they don't give any useful information

    (D) both quantitative and categorical, depending on the emphasis

    (E) numerical because we can say 855 students passed and 145 students failed

SOLUTION

The correct answer is (B), categorical, because the data involve two categories.

The data fall within the two categories of "pass" and "fail." The numbers are the data points, but they can be presented only as a histogram or a pie chart (see next section on Presenting Data).

EXAMPLE 7.20

This is similar to Example 7.19, except that it includes the criteria for pass/fail, which is a score of 70. We want to know how many students will need remedial work.

So the table becomes:

Version of Test	≥ 70 points	< 70 points
A	200	50
B	225	25
C	210	40
D	220	30

The data presented in this table are what kind of data?

(A) quantitative, because they involve numbers

(B) categorical, because they involve two categories

(C) neither quantitative nor categorical because they don't give any useful information

(D) both quantitative and categorical, depending on the emphasis

(E) numerical because we can say 855 students scored ≥ 70 points, and 145 students scored < 70 points

SOLUTION

The answer is still (B), categorical, because the data involve two categories.

Even though these categories have numbers (≥ 70 points and < 70 points), they are still categories, just different ways of stating pass and fail. This example is included here to show that categories may include numbers, but that doesn't make the data numerical. It is the data, not how they are sorted, that determines whether a data set is numerical or categorical. Here we don't have the individual data points, just the categories into which they fall.

EXAMPLE 7.21

This example is similar to Example 7.20, except that the data are for 20 students taking a particular test. We want to examine whether the test seems fair, based on the test scores.

The scores are:

45, 95, 69, 99, 86, 71, 68, 79, 69, 68, 87, 94, 85, 68, 91, 83, 88, 87, 88, 99

These data represent what kind of data?

(A) quantitative

(B) categorical

(C) neither quantitative nor categorical because they don't give any useful information

(D) both quantitative and categorical, depending on the emphasis

(E) qualitative

SOLUTION

The correct answer is (A), quantitative.

These are quantitative, or numerical, data. Of course, we can categorize these into scores that are 70 and above (pass), and below 70 (fail), as we did before, but now that we have the individual scores, we can say a lot more about the data, by presenting and analyzing the data points, as shown in the following sections. Notice that of the scores that indicate "failing," only one (45) is far from passing, but five of them, the 68's and 69's, are close to passing scores. That could be useful information for the college that isn't shown when the data are just put into categories. For example, if instead of the 68's and 69's, the scores were 38's and 39's. Then the college should consider that the test is perhaps biased or that their admission standards should be revised.

Presenting Data

Data can be presented in many forms. In addition to the table format, visual presentations can make data quite understandable.

Categorical Data

The table for categorical data points consists of two or more columns, and it may be sufficient for most of these data sets. For two columns, the left column usually lists the categories and the right column lists the number of responses for that category or the percentage of all responses for that category. An example of such a table would show the education levels of the chief executive officers of the 500 top U.S. companies:

Education Level	Number of CEOs
No college	15
Bachelor's degree	165
MBA	190
Law degree	50
Other higher education degree	80

The data in this table also can be presented as a **bar graph** or **bar chart**, which makes comparison of the numbers of CEOs in each different education level easier to visualize.

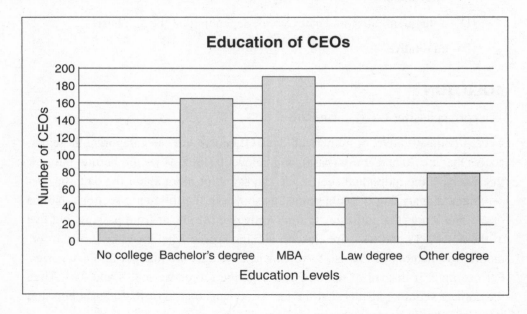

The following table revises the same data so that the number of respondents is reported as a percentage of the 500 respondents, which also makes comparison easier to see.

Education Level	Number of CEOs	Percentages
No college	15	3%
Bachelor's degree	165	33%
MBA	190	38%
Law degree	50	10%
Other higher education degree	80	16%

From percentage data such as shown in this table, we can construct another clear comparison of the education levels of the CEOs, in a **pie chart** (sometimes called a **circle graph**). Pie charts are usually constructed from percentages, even though they may report actual numbers. The pie chart below reports both actual numbers and percentages.

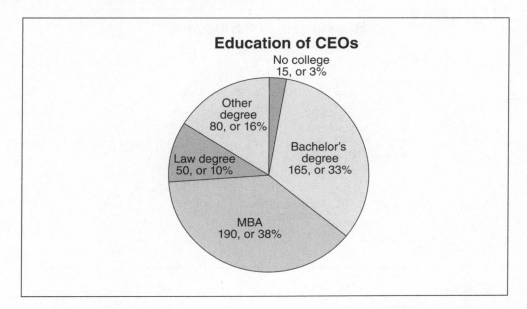

Education of CEOs

No college
15, or 3%

Other degree
80, or 16%

Law degree
50, or 10%

Bachelor's degree
165, or 33%

MBA
190, or 38%

In a pie chart, the percentages must add up to 100%. This means a pie chart is not appropriate for a survey in which people are asked to "choose all that apply" from the choices, since multiple choices for a question will add up to more than 100%. For example, if a survey asks what type of vacation people prefer, person A may choose mountains, beaches, and international; person B may choose only mountains; and person C may choose mountains and cities. The tally for this would be as follows:

Mountains	3
Beaches	1
International	1
Cities	1

This tally implies that there were six inputs, and half of them chose the mountains, when in fact there were three inputs, and they all chose the mountains. Therefore, multiple-response data cannot be shown on a pie chart.

EXAMPLE 7.22

From the following pie chart, what would be the missing numerical value if the total number of students is 500?

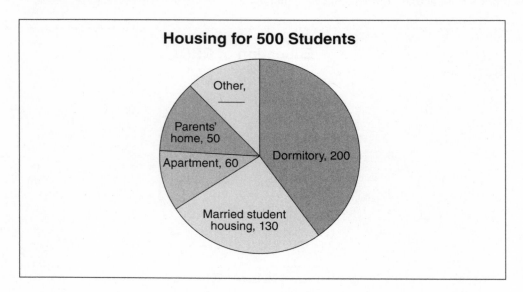

Housing for 500 Students

Other, _____

Parents' home, 50

Apartment, 60

Dormitory, 200

Married student housing, 130

(A) 50

(B) 60

(C) 70

(D) 170

(E) Cannot tell from the data given

SOLUTION

The correct answer is (B), 60.

The total of all of the sectors must equal 500, so $200 + 130 + 60 + 50 + x = 500$, or $440 + x = 500$; thus, $x = 60$.

EXAMPLE 7.23

For the data given in Example 7.22, what percentage of students live in college housing (dormitories or married student housing)?

(A) 40%

(B) 26%

(C) 66%

(D) 34%

(E) 12%

SOLUTION

The correct answer is (C) 66%.

Good solution: The percentage of the 500 students who live in dormitories is $\frac{200}{500} = 40\%$, and the percentage of students who live in married student housing is $\frac{130}{500} = 26\%$, so the total is $40\% + 26\% = 66\%$

Better solution: The number of students who live in dormitories (200) and married student housing (130) totals 330, so the percentage is $\frac{330}{500} = 66\%$.

Best solution: From the pie chart, we can see that more than half of the students live in dormitories and married student housing. The only answer that is greater than 50% is (C), 66%. No math required.

Quantitative Data

The choice of how to present quantitative data depends partly on the size of the data set. For example, if there are just a few (perhaps fewer than 12) numerical data points, each individual data point can be presented clearly. But if there are many numerical data points, it is best to group them. If we were to start with a table for individual data points, let's say 20 points, that could get very unwieldy.

For example, consider the following data points showing years of experience of 20 teachers in a particular school:

2, 2, 5, 11, 9, 7, 3, 2, 13, 18, 2, 4, 16, 14, 27, 12, 17, 21, 8, 15

A table of these values would be 17 lines long (the value 2 appears four times), but it wouldn't give us much more information than the list above. However, if we group the data in intervals, let's say, 1–5, 6–10, 11–15, 16–20, 21–25, 26–30, and 31–35 years (notice that each interval has the same number of years), the table would be only 7 lines long, which is much more readable, although it is still not ideal. A better choice for readability would be a histogram.

A **histogram** looks like a bar chart, but it has one important difference. It is continuous because each equal interval is numerical and there are no gaps between the bars. All of the bars touch each other. The histogram for the data above, grouped in five-year intervals is shown next.

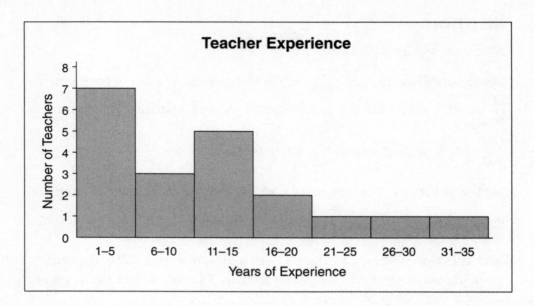

This histogram readily shows that the majority of the teachers at that school have 15 or fewer years of experience. These same data can also be shown in a **line graph** by connecting the midpoints of each bar by a line.

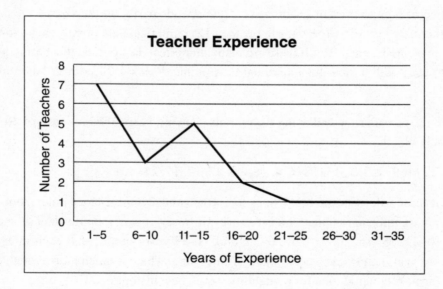

Note that for the data above, the years were reported as whole numbers. Quantitative data can be reported as fractions or decimals as well. In those cases, the intervals for the data above might be stated as 1–5.99, 6–10.99, 11–15.99, etc., or any intervals that don't overlap and are of equal size.

Another way to show data is by using **dot plots**, which is like tallying. A tally for the above data is shown on the left, and the corresponding dot plot is shown on the right. Note that the dot plot is like a tally viewed from the side.

Years of Experience

1–5	ꞁꞁꞁꞁ ꞁꞁ
6–10	ꞁꞁꞁ
11–15	ꞁꞁꞁꞁ
16–20	ꞁꞁ
21–25	ꞁ
26–30	ꞁ
31–35	ꞁ

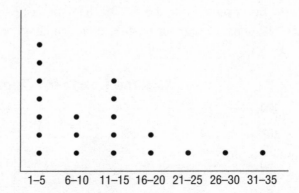

The mean and median can be calculated from a dot plot that has quantitative data, and the mode can be seen right away. If, instead of the intervals in the dot plot above, we used the middles of the intervals as their values (so we have 3, 8, 13, 18, 23, 28, and 33 as the years), we can see that the mean of the data would be calculated as

$$\text{mean} = \frac{3(7) + 8(3) + 13(5) + 18(2) + 23(1) + 28(1) + 33(1)}{20}$$

$$= \frac{230}{20} = 11.5 \text{ as the average number of years of experience.}$$

The median would be 10.5, and the mode is clearly the interval 1–5 years of experience.

Pictographs are an eye-catching way to display data. They are related to dot plots, but use icons instead of dots; in addition, each icon can represent multiples of the data. An example is shown here. Note that each ice cream cone icon represents not one, but 100 ice cream cones, and the half cone represent 50 ice cream cones.

Cafeteria Ice Cream Sales			
Sept.	🍦🍦🍦⸍	Feb.	🍦🍦
Oct.	🍦🍦	Mar.	🍦🍦
Nov.	🍦⸍	Apr.	🍦🍦
Dec.	🍦	May	🍦🍦🍦
Jan.	⸍	June	🍦🍦🍦⸍
🍦 = 100 Ice Cream Cones			

EXAMPLE 7.24

On the histogram below, the sum of the number of students in two of the columns exactly equals the number of students in which other column?

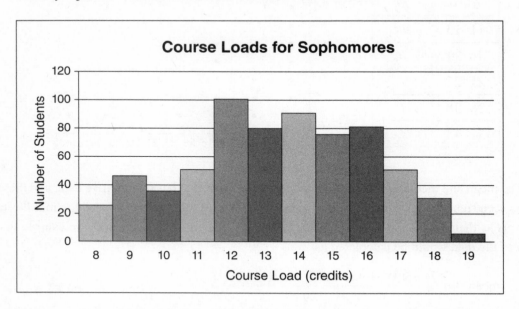

In other words, fill in the blanks for the following sentence based on the histogram. Mark all correct answers.

The number of students taking _____ and _____ credits = the number of students taking _____ credits.

> A. 11, 17, 12
>
> B. 9, 10, 13
>
> C. 12, 19, 14
>
> D. 18, 19, 10
>
> E. 12, 8, 14

SOLUTION

The correct answers are A, B, and D.

Good solution: First, realize that trying to find the combinations from the chart and then checking them against the answer choices would take a long time (there are 220 combinations!). So just check out all of the answer choices. Because more than one answer choice can be correct, you must check all five answer choices. Read the number of students from the histogram. For A, the numbers of students are 50 + 50 = 100, so that's correct. For [B], the numbers are 45 + 35 = 80, so that is also correct. Choice C gives 100 + 5 = 90, incorrect. Choice D gives 30 + 5 = 35, correct. Choice E gives 100 + 25 = 90, incorrect.

Better solution: Having realized that just checking the answers rather than finding the solution and trying to match it to an answer choice is the way to go, a further time- and energy-saving method in multiple-choice questions is to look at the choices and eliminate any that can't be correct. There are no entries with more than 100 students (the number for 12 credits), so eliminate answer choices $\boxed{C}$ and $\boxed{E}$ right away because they both have 12 credits as an addend, so their sums must be more than 100. Then you are down to checking only three answer choices.

Let's look at the line curve obtained by joining the midpoints of each column for the data shown in Example 7.24. For very large numbers of data, this line curve can be smoothed out to a frequency curve, in which the vertical axis can be numbers of students or percentage of the total of 665 sophomores in the college and the horizontal axis is the number of credits the students are taking. This curve can aid in interpreting data, discussed next.

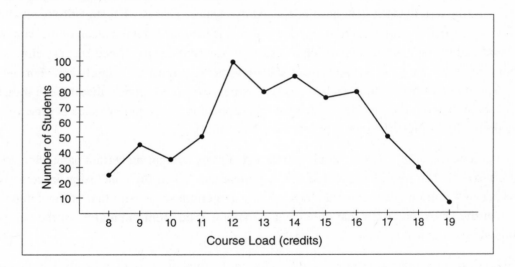

Interpreting Data

For categorical data, as already stated, there is no mean or median. Categorical data can be interpreted by using the mode, or which category had the highest count. A pie chart or bar graph of the data visually indicates the distribution of the categories.

For numerical data, the **frequency curve** is a smoothed-out line that more or less connects all points. An ideal frequency curve, called a **bell-shaped curve** for obvious reasons, is the normal curve shown below.

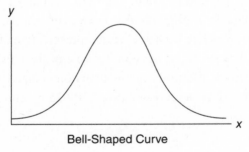

Bell-Shaped Curve

The horizontal axis shows the data (usually, but not necessarily, in intervals), and the vertical axis is the frequency of each data point. The normal curve forms the basis of statistics, and how actual data points vary from it allows statisticians to make their analyses.

An example of a situation that would have a normal curve is the toss of a fair coin, where the horizontal axis would be the number of heads. (The term "fair coin," as mentioned in the Probability section of this chapter, simply means it is equally weighted, so there is no bias for heads or tails.) The vertical axis would be the frequency of getting the number of heads in a number of trials.

For example, if you flip a coin 32 times, and write down the number of times heads came up, and then repeat the experiment a thousand times, a graph of the number of 32-flip sets that resulted in a given number of heads would look very much like a bell-shaped curve. The high point would be for exactly 16 heads, occurring (in this ideal case) in 500 of the thousand times.

Most of the data will appear near the middle of a bell curve, and the farther from the middle a data point is, the less likely it is to have happened by chance. That is what statistics is all about— basically, if a verifiable data point (one not due to error) is very far from the mean of the data, which is the middle of the bell curve, then the chances that it occurred due to chance are very slim, so that data point must be due to something, or in statistics-speak, it must be "significant." For our coin experiment, if one of the 32-flip sets had heads 31 times, we would suspect that there is something "unfair" about the coin because the chances of this happening due to pure chance is very, very low (with a probability of less than .003, or less than 3 in 1,000).

As a practical example, DNA sampling uses statistics by comparing certain parameters to what would be expected in a random sample of the population. When the conclusion in court is that there is a 1 in 4 million chance that the DNA found at a crime scene isn't that of the defendant, it means that the DNA match for that defendant is extremely far from the middle of the bell curve, determined by statistical analysis.

For analysis of quantitative data, in addition to the normal curve, which involves higher mathematics, we can look at the mean, median, or mode to get a sense of the central tendency of the data, or at the range, to get a sense of how spread out the data points are. Usually, the mean is used for simple analysis, and it works fine unless the data are skewed. **Skew** means one or a few high (or low) points pull the mean too far in one direction or another.

To illustrate how skew affects data, consider the salaries of nine bank employees, in thousands of dollars:

25   25   27   28   30   35   35   40   200

There are two modes, $25,000 and $35,000, and both are fairly representative of most of the salaries. How about the median? It is $30,000, also fairly representative of the salaries. However, the mean (average) is $49,444, which is far from being representative of the salaries of the employees, because included in the data set is the $200,000 salary of the CEO of the bank. If the CEO's salary is excluded from the data set, the mode and median don't change much (the median becomes $29,000), but the mean now becomes a representative $30,625 by eliminating the skew caused by the $200,000 salary.

Correlation

To determine whether there is a **correlation** (or association) between two variable quantities, we use **scatter plots**. These look similar to line graphs in that they have an *x*- and *y*-axis. If two variables are perfectly correlated (meaning a cause-and-effect relationship exists) the plot is a straight line. The more the line deviates from a straight line, the less the two variables are correlated. A common example of correlation is hours of study time and grades—it is a positive correlation in that as the hours of study time increase, so do grades.

Do the data points line up exactly in a straight line? No, but they are close to a straight line, called the **line of best fit**, from which the distances of the actual points above and below cancel each other out, as shown in the graph below.

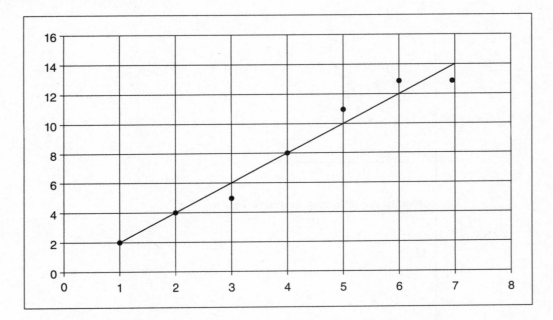

The above graph has a positive correlation. A negative correlation is still a correlation, but indicates that as one variable increases the other decreases (it looks like a line with a negative slope). An example of a negative slope is that as temperatures increase, the hardware store sells fewer space heaters. A zero correlation means there is no relationship between the two variables, and looks like a jumble of points. Correlation can vary between +1 and −1. The data shown in the graph above have a correlation of about 0.9. The data in the graphs below have correlations of about 0.5 (left) and 0 (right).

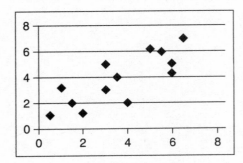
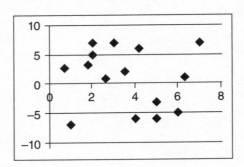

EXAMPLE 7.25

Match the correlation coefficient c to the sample correlation curves below. Fill in the closest correlation coefficient for each curve.

(A) $c = -0.8$

(B) $c = +0.8$

(C) $c = 0.3$

(D) $c = -0.3$

(E) $c = 0$

a.

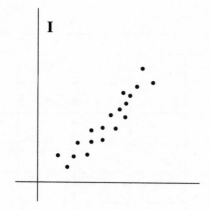

The correlation coefficient for curve I is _____.

b.

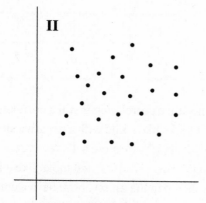

The correlation coefficient for curve II is _____.

c.

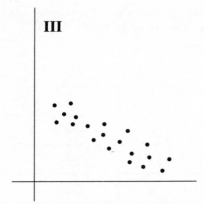

The correlation coefficient for curve III is _____.

SOLUTION

The correct answers are:

    a.   (B)

    b.   (E)

    c.   (A)

Practice Exercises

1.   What is the median of the following group of numbers?

      4, 38, 17, 5, 9, 11

  (A) 9

  (B) 10

  (C) 11

  (D) 14

  (E) There is no median.

2. What is the mode for the data shown in the pictograph, where ✉ represents the pieces of junk mail received throughout the week? Put your answer in the box.

Monday	✉	✉			
Tuesday	✉	✉	✉	✉	
Wednesday	✉	✉	✉	✉	✉
Thursday	✉	✉	✉	✉	
Friday		✉	✉		
Saturday	✉	✉			
Sunday					

✉ = Pieces of junk mail

3. A 6-sided numbered die is tossed; then a fair coin is flipped. What is the probability that a head and a number greater than 4 will come up together?

(A) $\frac{1}{12}$

(B) $\frac{1}{6}$

(C) $\frac{1}{4}$

(D) $\frac{1}{3}$

(E) $\frac{5}{12}$

4. If two intersecting circles on a Venn diagram contain the following numbers: R = 5, 6, 7, 8, 9; and S = 2, 7, 9, 10, 11, how many numbers will be in the intersection of R and S?

(A) 0

(B) 2

(C) 7

(D) 9

(E) Not enough information is given.

5. If the median of 15 numbers is 20 and each of the numbers is decreased by 2, how is the new median affected?

   (A) It is increased to 22.

   (B) It is decreased to 18.

   (C) It stays the same.

   (D) It is decreased to 10.

   (E) Cannot tell from the information given.

6. A factory produces widgets. An inspection is held randomly to inspect a sample of 200 widgets for defects. The graph below shows the results of the latest inspection. What percentage of the widgets in the 200 had at most one defective part?

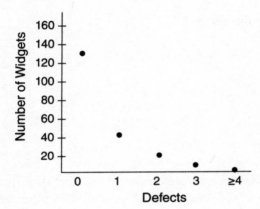

   (A) 130%

   (B) 85%

   (C) 65%

   (D) 40%

   (E) 15%

7. If someone flips a coin 10 times, what is the probability that it lands heads up all 10 times?

   (A) 2^{10}

   (B) $\left(\dfrac{1}{10}\right)^{2}$

   (C) $\left(\dfrac{1}{2}\right)^{10}$

   (D) $\dfrac{1}{2}$

   (E) $\dfrac{1}{20}$

8. The following dot plot shows the pulse rates of 25 individuals.

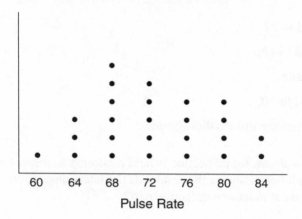

Pulse Rate

The mean pulse rate of this group is

(A) 64.2

(B) 84.3

(C) 80.4

(D) 72.5

(E) 72.0

9. The table below, from the journal *Reefkeeping*, shows that the salinity of the water at 23.0 °C and a specific gravity of 1.0210 is exactly the same as the salinity at what other pair of parameters?

Salinity (in practical salinity units, or PSU)

Specific Gravity	Temperature (°C)						
	23.0	23.5	24.0	24.5	25.0	25.5	26.0
1.0200	25.73	25.93	26.15	26.34	26.56	26.78	27.00
1.0202	26.00	26.20	26.42	26.61	26.83	27.05	27.27
1.0204	26.25	26.46	26.66	26.88	27.10	27.32	27.54
1.0206	26.51	26.73	26.93	27.15	27.37	27.59	27.81
1.0208	26.78	27.00	27.20	27.42	27.64	27.83	28.08
1.0210	27.05	27.25	27.47	27.69	27.88	28.10	28.32

(A) 23.5°C, 1.0208

(B) 24.5°C, 1.0206

(C) 25.0°C, 1.0204

(D) 25.5°C, 1.0202

(E) 26.0°C, 1.0200

Solutions

1. (B), 10. The median is the middle number when all the numbers are put in order. These numbers in order are 4, 5, 9, 11, 17, 38, and since the number of values is even, the median is the average of the two middle ones: 9 and 11. So the median here is 10. Answer choice (C) is the average of the middle values 17 and 5 when the given values aren't put in order.

2. Wednesday. The mode is the data point with the greatest frequency. It doesn't have to be a number. This indicates that the greatest number of pieces of junk mail arrived on Wednesday.

3. (B), $\frac{1}{6}$. Probability $= \frac{\text{Success}}{\text{Possibilities}}$. The probability of a 5 or 6 on a 6-sided die is $\frac{2}{6}$, and the probability for a head on a coin is $\frac{1}{2}$. These are independent events so their joint probability is their product, or $\frac{2}{6} \times \frac{1}{2} = \frac{1}{6}$.

4. (B), 2. There are exactly 2 numbers (7 and 9) that are in both circles.

5. (B), It is decreased to 18. Since all of the numbers are decreased by 2, the middle value, whatever it is, must also be decreased by 2. The old median is 20, so the new median must be 18.

6. (B), 85%. "At most one" means "zero or one." The number of parts with 0 defects is 130, and the number of parts with 1 defect is 40, so there are a total of 170 out of 200 widgets with at most one defect. The percentage is therefore $\frac{170}{200} = 85\%$. Answer choice (A) can be eliminated right away because it is more than 100%, or all widgets. Answer choices (C) through (E) present percentage when groups other than at most one are considered; for example, answer choice (C) is the answer for only 0 defects, not including the group with 1 defect.

7. (C), $\left(\frac{1}{2}\right)^{10}$. Each of the flips of the coin is independent of all the other flips, and each has a $\frac{1}{2}$ probability of landing heads up, so the probabilities are multiplied: $\frac{1}{2} \times \frac{1}{2} \times ... = \left(\frac{1}{2}\right)^{10}$.

8. (D), 72.5. The calculation, using the dots in the plot as weights for each pulse rate, is

$$\text{mean} = \frac{60(1) + 64(3) + 68(6) + 72(5) + 76(4) + 80(4) + 84(2)}{25}$$

$$= \frac{60 + 192 + 408 + 360 + 304 + 320 + 168}{25} = \frac{1812}{25} = 72.5$$

Note that the mean isn't found just by using the seven temperature values (which would give a mean of 72, answer choice (E)), but by their weighted values (numbers in the parentheses).

9. (D), 25.5°C, 1.0202. The salinity at 23.0°C and 1.0210 is shown to be 27.05. This value appears in one other place on the table, at 25.5°C and 1.0202. All other data pairs have a specific gravity that is close to 27.05, but not exactly equal to it.

PART III:
Praxis Core Reading Review

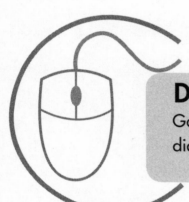

Diagnostic Test
Go to the online REA Study Center to take the diagnostic test to help focus your study.

(www.rea.com/studycenter)

OVERVIEW OF THE READING TEST

Some of the best advice you'll ever hear for succeeding on the Praxis Core Reading test may be this: Shut out the world. That's right, deal only with what's in front of you. This is because questions on this test ask you to evaluate the information contained in passages and statements, or sometimes to interpret information from charts or tables. It is paramount that you glean your answers entirely from the source material.

When you sit for the computerized Praxis Core Reading test, you will have 85 minutes to complete 56 selected-response questions. (This timing does not count the optional test tutorial, which explains test navigation and technology.) ETS uses the term "selected response" because while most items have just one correct answer, some have more than one and you won't know how many are correct.

The texts on the Praxis Core Reading test tie in with the widespread adoption of the Common Core State Standards. The test reflects the increased rigor of the Common Core standards by using more complex stimulus material. Accordingly, we can't overstate the need to read as you prepare for the test—and not just any texts but complex texts as they are outlined by the Common Core standards (see *http://www.corestandards.org/assets/Appendix_B.pdf* for a list of text exemplars).

This chapter will help you hone your critical reading and thinking skills. By brushing up on these skills, you will build your confidence for the Praxis Core Reading test.

What's so complex about the reading passages?

Even though the term "complex" as it applies to this test may at first sound daunting, it shouldn't. "Complex" means we are moving beyond superficial reading that involves skimming and scanning for discrete pieces of information in a traditional text. Instead, we are engaging in the demanding, cognitive task of reading to understand more difficult material. As M.J. Adams put it, "To grow, our students must read lots, and more specifically they must read lots of 'complex' texts—texts that offer them new language, new knowledge, and new modes of thought."

If your future students are going to be working with more demanding material, so too must you. The Reading test consists of shorter passages followed by anywhere from one to seven multiple-choice questions. In the material you will encounter, ETS is basing its selections on Common Core "text exemplars." These reading texts show complexity, quality, and range. Besides being challenging, the readings are recognized as either classic works of literary merit or significant historical/scientific texts that are noteworthy in our culture. The texts also vary over a cross-section of authors, subjects, and publication dates. The media include newspapers, journals, non-fiction books, textbooks, novels, online articles, and visual representations (art, graphs, charts, etc.).

You will encounter a sampling of this material on the Core Reading test. Since the passages and other stimuli differ, you should vary your reading rate accordingly. You also should vary your rate depending on what part of the question you are reading.

On this test you will find passages of varying lengths. Following is a simple plan of attack you can mount to make any passage manageable.

Nine Ways to Attack a Passage

1. Scan the passage and skim the questions that go with it.

2. Read the passage, but don't waste time on the details. Try to get the main idea. Use active reading strategies like annotating (use your scratch paper to write a summary word or phrase to capture the essence of each paragraph). List key words from the passage.

3. What type of stimulus is the passage or statement (e.g., fiction, nonfiction, newspaper, art, photograph, chart, etc.)?

4. Read the questions. Know what they're asking.

5. Answer each question in your own words by jotting down your answer. Then read the answer choices and see which choices agree with your answers.

6. Go back to the passage to check the line reference(s) if applicable.

7. Go back to the passage to verify your answer.

8. Use process of elimination.

9. When all else fails, guess by using your choice choice-of-the-day strategy (see Chapter 3).

Key Ideas and Details

PINPOINTING KEY IDEAS

Thirty-five percent of the Praxis Core Reading test's questions—approximately 20 items—ask examinees to identify key ideas and supporting details, and to draw inferences.

Finding the main idea of a written piece is one of the most important elements of understanding any text. Sometimes students confuse the main idea with the subject. The subject is the topic—what the passage is about. However, the main idea says why the subject matters. It narrows the topic and asserts something about it. On the Praxis Core test, you will be asked to identify a summary or paraphrase of the main idea and what flows from the text's purpose. Perhaps three or four questions will cover this. The list that follows gives you a glimpse of the kind of phrasing you might encounter. Notice that each phrase in the list bears on the main idea in some way.

 HINT

Be sure to distinguish the passage's main idea from the subject. The subject is the topic. The main idea reveals why the subject *matters*.

"Main Idea" Question Stems

- "What is the main focus of the passage?"

- "Which of the following would be the most appropriate title for the passage?"

- "Which of the following is a paraphrase of the main idea?"

- "This passage best supports the statement that…"

- "Based on the tone of the passage, the author's main purpose is to…"

- "Which of the following is the main idea of the passage?"

- "The main idea of the passage is best summed up in which statement?"

- "Based on the passage, the author would tend to agree with which of the following statements?"

- "According to the passage, a _____ is caused by _____?"

- "The main idea of the passage is to _____?"

An effective way to get at the main idea is to use a systematic method called **Topic–Point–Support, or TPS**. First, establish what the passage is about by determining the **topic**. Second, ascertain the main **point** the author's making about the topic. Third, establish what details the author offers to **support** the main point.

Let's apply TPS to the following statement by Marian Wright Edelman, president of the Children's Defense Fund. First read it. Then we'll walk through the TPS steps.

> Fifty years later, we must not give up on building a just America that ensures a level playing field for every child and person. We must not let anyone tell us that our rich nation's vaults of justice and opportunity are bankrupt. And we must not tolerate any longer any resistance to creating jobs—jobs which pay enough to escape poverty, public and private sector, and providing the education and early childhood development that every human being needs to survive and thrive. I hope we will commit ourselves on this fiftieth anniversary to building and sustaining a powerful transforming nonviolent movement to help America live up to its promises and force the will to translate America's dream into reality for all. Let's honor Dr. King and save America's future and soul by hearing, heeding, and following our greatest American prophet.
>
> (Source: *Huffington Post*, posted August 23, 2013)

The above paragraph lacks a good general statement that covers all the other sentences. To decide on the main idea, we must ask ourselves:

- *Who* or *what* is this paragraph about? (The answer is the **topic** of the paragraph.)

- What is the main **point** the author is trying to make about that topic?

- Does *all or most* of the material in the paragraph **support** this main idea?

Now let's try it with the paragraph you just read.

- *Who* or *what* is this paragraph about?

In the paragraph, the details are about education, equality, jobs, and Dr. Martin Luther King, Jr. You conclude it's about Dr. King's dream 50 years later, so that must be the topic.

- What is the main **point** the author is trying to make about that topic?

The author is saying we must not give up fighting for King's dream.

- Does *all or most* of the material in the paragraph **support** this main idea?

Yes. Every sentence is about the areas that concerned King as well as the need for America to recommit to them.

Identifying Supporting Details

On the Praxis Core Reading test, three or four questions will ask you to identify a summary or paraphrase of the supporting details of the main idea. The support can include examples, facts, and opinions. Watch for answer choices that include details not found in the passage. They are there to ensure that you read the material. Exclude those answer choices. Supporting-detail questions may ask you to show that you understand the meaning of the vocabulary used in the passage. Active reading techniques will help you stay focused on the details. Line references also are often given in these questions. The list that follows will help you understand the questions you might encounter.

Supporting-Detail Question Stems

- "According to the passage,…"

- "The passage states that [*a specific detail would be true if*] …"

- "Which of the following statements most effectively supports the validity of the author's assertion in line ___,"

- "According to the passage, which of the following statements is NOT true?"

- "In the passage, which of the following is the best meaning of the word X as it is used in line___?

- "As used in line ___, [*a term from the passage*] most nearly means . . ."

Since you can't underline or highlight on the computerized test, look for key words and phrases you may want to jot on the scratch paper. Let's practice. In the passage that follows, **three major details** support the main idea that certain factors get in the way of a good night's sleep. Read the passage and underline the key words that serve as supporting details.

Several factors can interfere with having a good night's sleep. One such factor is caffeine. To sleep well, you must avoid caffeinated beverages like coffee, tea, and soft drinks. Another cause is stress. To sleep, you need to be able to turn off your mind and relax, and sometimes this problem is relieved when a person has good exercise habits. Finally, auditory and visual distraction can interfere with sleep. If you are being distracted by the sound of a television or a street light nearby, you may not nod off. Instead, you should try to find a quiet and dark environment.

Can you identify the three major details that belong in the concept map?

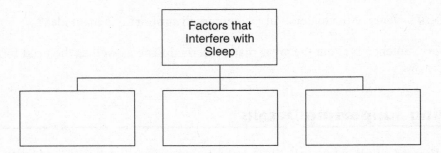

The right answer is to (1) avoid caffeine, (2) avoid stress, and (3) avoid auditory and visual distractions. However, be prepared for passages on the Praxis Core test that may not be this straightforward; in fact, you may need to infer the answer (i.e., determine what is implied by finding the supporting details and seeing how they relate to the whole).

INFERENTIAL REASONING

You make inferences by observing stated details and spotting new meanings and contexts in them. Inference questions ask you to figure out what ideas are implied by the passage and answer choices are not directly stated in the passage. The Praxis Core Reading test will ask you to perform the following tasks in inference questions:

- Read for explicit meaning and then make inferences (3–4 questions)
- Read specific details and show how they help you understand the whole (3–4 questions)
- Find distinctions the author makes (3–4 questions)
- Identify where the text leaves matters uncertain or unresolved (3–4 questions)

 HINT

If you infer that excelling on inference questions will help your test performance, you are correct. Master context clues and closely read the passages and the choices to maximize your score.

Inference involves following the clues in the text to understand the **author's attitude**, or **tone**, toward the subject. We'll delve into tone after we examine how to deal with inference questions generally. Typical inference-question stems include those listed next.

Inference-Question Stems

- "One can infer from the passage that. . . ?"

- "The passage implies that. . . ?"

- "It can be inferred that a _____ is _____?"

- "Based on the information in the passage, which of the following best describes. . . ?"

- "Based on the passage, the author's main purpose is to. . . ?"

- "Which of the following best describes the attitude of the author?"(author's attitude)

- "Based on the passage, the author would tend to agree with which of the following statements?" (author's attitude)

- "Which of the following illustrates the author's opinion of _____ x?" (author's attitude)

Follow this brief guide to approach inference questions:

1. **What's stated?** Never lose sight of what's actually contained in the passage.

2. **What do I know?** What background information do I have to make an inference?

3. **Note figurative language/allusions/emotional words.** Watch for similes (comparisons using "like/as"), metaphors (comparisons using the verb "to be"), and allusions (references to historical/cultural prior knowledge you may have).

4. **Guess**—take a stab at what the text is saying.

Let's try it with this passage from George Eliot's novel, *Middlemarch*. First, read this passage:

> If we had a keen vision and feeling of all ordinary human life, it would be like hearing the grass grow and the squirrel's heartbeat, and we should die of that roar which lies on the other side of silence. As it is, we walk about well wadded with stupidity.

1. **What's stated?** The passage describes walking through the world and experiencing nature in a heightened way.

2. **What do I know?** I know all of the words except "wadded" but from the context it sounds like "influenced by." I don't know this novel, although I know Eliot was a woman and that she wrote at the end of the 19th century. She had to pretend to be male in order to publish.

3. **Note figurative language/allusions/emotional words:** Eliot uses a simile: "like hearing the grass grow and the squirrel's heartbeat" and a metaphor "roar…on the other side of silence."

4. **Guess:** I think it says that if we could feel everything that everyone feels, it would overcome our senses in a way that would be hard to withstand. So we currently walk around living ignorantly. In other words, ignorance is bliss.

Author's Attitude Questions

It is important to mention **"author's attitude" questions**, which are a subset of inference questions. What clues can you follow in considering the author's attitude toward the subject? Is he or she positive, neutral, objective, or negative?

These questions ask you to think about the author's **purpose** and **tone**.

The **purpose** is why the author wrote the passage. It usually falls into three categories:

- **To inform:** to give information about a subject. The author provides facts or examples that will explain or teach something to readers.

    Example: Fences block visual distractions that lie beyond the confines of the garden.

- **To entertain:** to amuse and appeal to the reader's senses/imagination. Authors with this purpose set out to captivate or interest the audience.

    Example: "Long before Instagram, there was something called a photograph in a picture frame."

- **To persuade:** to convince the reader to agree with the author's view. An author with this purpose may provide facts, and the main goal is to argue or prove a point to readers.

    Example: The death penalty is deeply flawed and should be abolished.

Finding the Purpose

To uncover the author's purpose, the reader must consider the main idea, and supporting details, as well as tone. Let's try to find the author's purpose in this introductory sentence.

> Using time-outs must be encouraged as a way to discipline due to the long-term positive effects on the child.

Consider what the sentence says about time-outs and ask yourself these questions:

- Is the author going to discuss the advantages of time-outs?

- Is the author going to argue for time-outs as a means of discipline?

- Is the author going to criticize those who use other means of discipline?

Detecting the Tone

The **tone** is the author's attitude toward the subject expressed through the words and details he or she selects. To determine the author's tone, you must observe how these words and details are used.

Just as listening to someone say words can make us hear a range of feelings, a writer's tone can make us feel his or her anger, sympathy, hopefulness, sadness, respect, dislike, and so on. Understanding tone is, thus, an important part of understanding what an author has written.

Let's look at that sentence again:

Using time-outs must be encouraged as a way to discipline due to the long-term positive effects on the child.

The tone words "must" and "positive" indicate that the author favors time-outs. If this were the first sentence in a paragraph, then the phrase "long-term effects" would signal that the details are going to be organized as a list of effects.

We can conclude that the author is going to persuade the reader to use time-outs as a means of discipline.

Tone wends its way through the Core Reading test in a variety of ways. Let's look at some of the most relevant.

If you are looking for an **objective tone**, look no further than newspapers, textbooks, and professional journal articles. Those sources use an objective tone that is matter-of-fact and neutral. You also will discover explanations with details that are mostly facts. There are no feelings for or against the topic, and personal pronouns such as "I" and "you" are often avoided. The writing is formal and unbiased.

In contrast, editorials, fiction, and memoirs are usually written with a **subjective tone** by using words that describe feelings, judgments, or opinions. The details are likely to include personal experiences, thoughts, and feelings. So when we read something written in subjective tone, it is emotional and usually less formal.

Beyond these two distinctions, many words can express tone, and questions often give them in combination. Look at the chart:

Words Indicating the Author's Attitude	
absurd	silly, ridiculous
ambivalent	having mixed emotions, unsure
amused	entertained, finding humor, expressed by a smile or laugh
angry	enraged, threatening, or menacing
apathetic	lacking concern, showing little or no interest
arrogant	haughty, acting with false superiority
bitter	resentful
cheerful	happy
comic	humorous, funny
compassionate	sympathetic, having feeling for others, empathetic
complex	complicated
condescending	patronizing
critical	disapproving

Words Indicating the Author's Attitude *(continued)*	
cynical	bitterly mocking
depressed	sad, unhappy
detached	uninvolved, having no interest or feelings, objective
earnest	sincere, showing deep feeling, seriousness
formal	accepting rules, stiff, using textbook style, factual
gentle	considerate, kind, mild, soft
hard	unfeeling
incredulous	disbelieving, skeptical
indignant	angry, angered by something unjust
intense	deeply felt
intimate	personal, close, deeply associated
ironic	wry, an unexpected opposite meaning in words or events
irreverent	lacking respect or reverence
joyous	happy
malicious	spiteful, desiring harm or suffering for others
mocking	ridiculing, imitating
nostalgic	yearning for the past, homesick, wistful
objective	factual, omitting emotion or personal prejudice
optimistic	positive, believing in positive outcomes
outspoken	candid
pathetic	pitiful
pessimistic	tending to take the worst possible view of a situation
playful	fun
reticent	reserved
reverent	respectful
righteous	morally right
sarcastic	using sharp irony with the intention of inflicting pain
satiric	ridiculing by means of irony or wit
sentimental	emotional
serious	earnest, not funny
straightforward	direct, frank, honest
sympathetic	understanding
uneasy	insecure
vindictive	spiteful, unforgiving

Source: Indian River State College

Now let's practice figuring out tones as they appear in combination with each other.

This time, let's use a longer passage. Consider the following passage:

> I watched his speech. His hair was a mess, he spoke so loud that his voice became hoarse, he relied too much on his note cards, and at the very end he panicked and, what's that? Are those tears? Had he started to cry? Amid the crowd I wondered what I was doing
> *Line* here, and moreover what my intelligent, shy, twenty-year-old student was doing trying to
> *(5)* win the votes of the entire student body. Yet at the conclusion of the speech, when applause swelled collectively from the audience, I saw something rare. Perhaps it was a trick of the light, or maybe it was a professor's unique insight. In his eye, I caught a glimpse of satisfaction, maybe even delight. The clapping escalated, and then I watched him smile and take a bow. I decided to leave the auditorium then, feeling emotionally exhausted, but also having
> *(10)* an instinctive feeling that he would be okay. Better still, he would be fine without me.

Now answer this question:

What is the author's attitude?

    (A) Contemptuous disapproval

    (B) Excited interest

    (C) Neutral curiosity

    (D) Youthful nostalgia

    (E) Concern and relief

First, look at key phrases that indicate how the author feels about the subject. Then decide on an overall attitude. In this passage, you learn in Line 3 that this is a professor watching a student's campaign speech at what can be inferred to be a large public event for student government. The author's description of the audience indicates that the professor is largely disapproving, or at least cautious, of this kind of activity. But at the very end she notes that her student enjoys this experience based on his "glimpse of satisfaction." The teacher leaves the hall and notes that she thinks her student will be "okay" and even "fine without me."

So how do you find the correct attitude on this list? Start by going through your answer choices:

- "Contemptuous disapproval" (A) would be incorrect. While the professor is contemptuous and initially may have disapproved, the conclusion of the passage suggests that the teacher has come to terms with the shy student's choice to run for office, at least to some degree.

- "Excited interest" (B) is also incorrect, because she has said nothing to indicate excitement or even interest, besides maybe in the student.

- "Neutral curiosity" (C) would be wrong. The professor clearly dislikes the act of running for student council, and nothing in the passage indicates curiosity.

- "Youthful nostalgia" (D) is also irrelevant because the passage is about her watching her student now. It says nothing about the professor's memories.

- That leaves only "Concern and relief" (E), which is the correct answer. This passage actually presents two attitudes, one evolving from the other. At first, the author describes how she perceived the student's appearance and speech delivery with considerable concern. But then when she observes how well the audience accepts him as well as his reaction, she is relieved. The professor leaves the venue feeling "emotionally exhausted" but noting that the student would be fine without the teacher. The professor accepts the student's choice, but does so somewhat begrudgingly.

What are we learning? The most important thing to do with these questions is to break down your answer choices to understand the feelings they indicate. Then look at how the author describes things in the passage, checking specifically for positive and negative words, to assess the author's attitude. Try to flesh out a picture of the person speaking in the passage.

Finally, it is important to recognize that language represents and constructs how readers perceive events, people, groups, and ideas. We must recognize the positive and negative implications of language and identify how it can affect readers in different ways.

To sum up, you should always "read between the lines" for implied ideas because they are often essential for a complete understanding of what an author means.

Practice Exercises: Tone

DIRECTIONS: Select the tone reflected in each sentence from the given choices. Answers appear on page 227.

1. This place may be shabby, but since all three of my children were born while we lived here, it has a special place in my heart.

    (A) optimistic

    (B) bitter

    (C) tolerant

    (D) sentimental

    (E) humorous

2. This isn't the greatest apartment in the world, but it's not really that bad.

    (A) optimistic

    (B) bitter

    (C) tolerant

    (D) sentimental

    (E) objective

3. If only I could get a real job, I wouldn't be reduced to living in this miserable dump.

    (A) optimistic

    (B) bitter

    (C) tolerant

    (D) humorous

    (E) objective

4. This place does need some repairs, but I'm sure the landlord will be making those improvements as soon as she can.

    (A) optimistic

    (B) bitter

    (C) sentimental

    (D) humorous

    (E) objective

5. When we move away, we're planning to set the place on fire to make it better.

    (A) optimistic

    (B) tolerant

    (C) sentimental

    (D) humorous

    (E) objective

6. This apartment is our current living situation, and it provides shelter.

    (A) bitter

    (B) tolerant

    (C) sentimental

    (D) humorous

    (E) objective

DIRECTIONS: Read the following sample text by Jearl Walker. Two sets of questions follow. The first set of five questions has to do with the key ideas of the passage and can be answered by reading the passage to determine the author's intent when he wrote it. The second set of five questions has to do with details in the passage. These questions pertain to specific information and involve a more in-depth understanding of the content. The Praxis Reading test presents both types of questions. Answers appear on pages 227–228.

The rides in an amusement park not only are fun but also demonstrate principles of physics. Among them are rotational dynamics and energy conversion. I have been exploring the rides at Geauga Lake Amusement Park near Cleveland and have found that nearly every ride offers a memorable lesson.

Line
(5) To me the scariest rides at the park are the roller coasters. The Big Dipper is similar to many of the roller coasters that have thrilled passengers for most of this century. The cars are pulled by chain at the top of the highest hill along the track. Released from the chain as the front of the car begins its descent, the unpowered cars have almost no speed and only a small acceleration. As more cars get onto the downward slope the acceleration increases.
(10) It peaks when all the cars are headed downward. The peak value is the product of the acceleration generated by gravity and the sine of the slope of the track. A steeper descent generates a greater acceleration, but packing the coaster with heavier passengers does not.

When the coaster reaches the bottom of the valley and starts up the next hill, there is an instant when the cars are symmetrically distributed in the valley. The acceleration is zero.
(15) As more cars ascend the coaster begins to slow, reaching its lowest speed just as it is symmetrically positioned at the top of the hill.

A roller coaster functions by means of transfers of energy. When the chain hauls the cars to the top of the first hill, it does work on the cars, endowing them with gravitational potential energy, the energy of a body in a gravitational field with respect to the distance of
(20) the body from some reference level such as the ground. As the cars descend into the first valley, much of the stored energy is transferred into kinetic energy, the energy of motion.

Walker, Jearl. "Amusement Park Physics." *Roundabout: Readings from the Amateur Scientist in Scientific American*. New York: Scientific American, 1985. From "Amusement Park Physics: Thinking About Physics While Scared to Death (on a Falling Roller Coaster)."

Practice Exercises: Key Ideas of the Passage

1. The main idea of the passage is best stated as follows:

    (A) Amusement park rides are fun.

    (B) Rotational dynamics are easy to understand.

    (C) Roller coasters are the scariest rides at any amusement park.

    (D) Rides such as roller coasters reveal the principles of physics.

    (E) Roller coasters are pulled by chains.

2. Which of the following statements best paraphrases the main idea of the passage?

    (A) Safety is the most important factor in any roller coaster.

    (B) All forms of transportation can be studied to understand physics.

    (C) Roller coasters reveal that there are physical forces behind the fun.

    (D) Gravity equals mass plus acceleration.

    (E) Gravity equals mass times acceleration.

3. Which of the following statements can be inferred from the passage?

    (A) Small children might be barred from roller coasters because of their low body mass.

    (B) People face a greater risk of injury from an automobile than they do from a roller coaster.

    (C) The laws of physics affect the design of roller coasters.

    (D) Safety on coasters is provided by seat harnesses.

    (E) Roller coasters are the safest amusement park rides.

4. Which of the following illustrates the author's opinion of roller coasters?

    (A) Roller coasters are fun.

    (B) Rotational dynamics is easy to understand.

    (C) Roller coasters are the scariest rides at any amusement park.

    (D) Roller coasters and other rides reveal principles of physics.

    (E) Not all amusement parks have roller coasters.

5. How does Walker clarify the phenomenon of acceleration in his essay?

    (A) By allowing the reader to envision a single car coaster running on a frictionless track.

    (B) By exposing the reader to concepts of physics as they apply to a real-life example.

    (C) By allowing the reader to understand formulas of physics.

    (D) By providing the mass of the coaster and its acceleration due to gravity.

    (E) By explaining the excitement of the descent.

Practice Exercises: Details of the Passage

6. The passage best supports which of the following statements?

    (A) Ride safety needs to be a priority in roller coaster construction.

    (B) The amount of energy the coaster has depends on the potential energy created by the height of the first hill.

    (C) It makes a difference if the roller coaster is made of wood or steel.

    (D) The weight of the passengers on a roller coaster makes a difference in its acceleration.

    (E) None of these.

7. According to the passage, what makes the empowered cars increase in acceleration?

    (A) They are pulled by a chain

    (B) The peak value of the speed

    (C) As more cars get onto the downward slope, the speed escalates

    (D) The force generated by packing the coaster with heavier passengers

    (E) The lack of brakes

8. When cars are symmetrically distributed in the valley, the acceleration is

    (A) slower

    (B) faster

    (C) gravitational

    (D) zero

    (E) unaffected

9. One can infer from the passage that

    (A) the bigger the coaster's hills, the faster the roller coaster will be

    (B) roller coasters work because of the inverse relationship between the height and speed of the coaster

    (C) roller coasters create a feeling of weightlessness similar to what astronauts experience in space

    (D) loops do not exist on wooden coasters

    (E) higher roller coasters go slower

10. All of the following statements about energy transfer on a roller coaster are true EXCEPT:

    (A) Kinetic energy is converted to stored energy when the cars descend.

    (B) When the cars are hauled to the top of the hill, they have potential energy.

    (C) Stored energy is converted to kinetic energy when the cars descend the hill.

    (D) The coaster functions because of energy transfer.

    (E) Potential energy is converted to kinetic energy.

Answers to Practice Exercises: Tone *(pages 222–223)*:

1. **(D)**

    "It has a special place in my heart" expresses kindhearted emotions.

2. **(C)**

    The words "not really that bad" show that the writer accepts the situation while recognizing that it could be better.

3. **(B)**

    The writer resents a situation that forces him or her to live in a "miserable dump." He or she is unhappy and dejected.

4. **(A)**

    The writer expects the apartment to be improved soon.

5. **(D)**

    The writer jokingly claims to be planning revenge on the landlord.

6. **(E)**

    The writer does not express feelings. He or she states facts.

Answers to Practice Exercises: Key Ideas and Details *(page 224–225)*:

1. **(D)**

    While the passage does say amusement parks are fun (A), this isn't the main idea. The author never states that rotational dynamics are easy to understand (B), and although he says that roller coasters are the scariest rides in an amusement park (C), this is not the main idea of the passage. Choice (D) is the best answer.

2. **(C)**

    Choice (A) is wrong because safety isn't mentioned in the passage. (B) is too general ("all forms of transportation"), so it is incorrect. Even though choice (D) is a true statement, it isn't the main idea. Choice (C) best captures the essence of the passage, which is about roller coasters and physics.

3. **(C)**

Choice (C) is the best answer. If the slope of the hill and the acceleration of going down a hill determine the speed of a coaster, the reader can infer that roller coasters are designed with physics in mind. Body mass, risk, and seat harnesses are unrelated to the main idea of the passage.

4. **(D)**

The author does describe how roller coasters are scary, but that isn't the main opinion. Choice (D) is. The other choices are not opinions expressed by the author of this passage.

5. **(B)**

Choice (B) is the right choice. Choice (A) is incorrect because there's more than one car. A formula isn't mentioned per se, nor is information about the mass of the coaster. Choice (B) is the best answer because it reflects how scientific information about the coaster was woven into the essay.

Answers to Practice Exercises: Details of the Passage *(pages 225–226)*:

6. **(B)**

Choice (A) is incorrect. There is no mention of the issue of whether the coaster is made of wood or steel, choice (C). Choice (B) is the best choice because the passage talks about this idea.

7. **(C)**

Choice (C) is the correct answer. Choice (D) isn't true per the passage. Choice (A) is irrelevant, and choice (B) is the measure of potential energy. The passage states choice (C) directly; it is thus the choice you should have selected.

8. **(D)**

Choice (D) is correct. The answer is found in the second sentence of paragraph 3.

9. **(A)**

Choice (A) is correct. Choice (B) is wrong because it isn't an indirect relationship but rather a direct one. Choice (C) is irrelevant because it isn't mentioned in the passage, and choice (D) is factual information about loop coasters, but is also irrelevant to the passage. Choice (A) expresses the central idea of the passage in a different way and is therefore the right choice.

10. **(A)**

Choice (A) is the correct choice because the answer as it reads is backwards. Stored energy is converted to kinetic energy. This is after cars go to the top of a hill and come down; then there is energy transfer.

Craft, Structure, and Language Skills

Thirty percent of the questions on the Reading test (approximately 14–19 questions) ask students to think about craft, structure, and language skills. Specifically, examinees will be asked questions about:

- Vocabulary and how it influences tone

- Text organization using transitions

- Text organization by method of development

- Identifying how point of view and reference to an idea or text influence an author's argument

- Determining fact versus opinion

- Using context clues to identify unknown and multiple-meaning words

- Understanding figurative language and nuances in word meanings

- Understanding college- and career readiness-level words and phrases

WHAT ARE CRAFT, STRUCTURE, AND LANGUAGE SKILLS?

Craft is the skill employed in making the text. A well-crafted complex text might have multiple meanings. A good example of this is satire, wherein the author's literal message is the opposite of his or her underlying message. A complex informational text also may have a hidden purpose.

Structure is organization. It means the parts and how they are put together. Highly complex texts have multifaceted, implicit, and especially in literary texts, unconventional structures. For instance, a simpler text might organize events in chronological order, whereas a complex text such as a short story may use flashbacks, flash-forwards, and other manipulations of time and sequence. Complex informational texts are more likely to conform to the norms and conventions of a specific discipline. Highly complex graphs and charts have more concentrated information. They also can contain extra information that may be unnecessary and must be sorted out and ignored.

Language is the wording. In the reading passages, the language will often transcend literal, clear, and conversational communication. Instead, the language will often use figurative, ironic, ambiguous, purposefully misleading, archaic, or otherwise unfamiliar words and phrases as well as general academic and domain-specific vocabulary.

EIGHT KEYS TO THE READING PASSAGE QUESTIONS

Craft, structure, and language combine to make the **reading passage.** As students of the Core test, we are well-advised to pay particular attention to the following:

1. *Vocabulary and how it influences tone*—In these questions, the author chooses specific vocabulary to get across the **tone** or **attitude** he or she is trying to convey. For instance, in the play "The Importance of Being Earnest," Oscar Wilde chooses specific words such as "supercilious" and "elaborate politeness" to deliver a satirical tone. The author mocks the values of the society he depicts. Vocabulary is sometimes specific to a domain such as a scientific community. The use of words influences tone.

2. *Text organization using transitions*—Authors make their ideas clear by using **transitions.** For instance, **"addition" words** signal further ideas. These words tell you that a writer is presenting one or more ideas that continue along the same line of thought as a previous idea. Consider the chart (on the next page). It describes 10 types of transitions.

10 Types of Transitions

Cause and Effect	To Add	Time	Example	Elaboration
Accordingly	Additionally	First	After all	Actually
As a result	Equally important	Second	As an illustration	By extension
Consequently	Also	Finally	Consider	That is
Hence	And	Last	For example	In other words
It follows, then	Besides	Subsequently	For instance	To put it another way
Since	Furthermore	Simultaneously	Specifically	To put it bluntly
So	In addition	Meanwhile	To take a case in point	To put it succinctly
Then	In fact	Currently		Ultimately
Therefore	Indeed			
Thus	Moreover			
	So too			

Conclusion	Comparison	Contrast	Concession	Importance
As a result / In the final analysis	Along the same lines	Although	Although it is true that	Above all
In short / In sum	In the same way	But	Granted	Best
It follows / To summarize	Likewise	By/In contrast	I concede that	Worst
The upshot of all of this is that / Thus	Similarly	Conversely	Of course	Most importantly
Therefore / Hence		Despite the fact that	Naturally	In particular
To sum up / In a word		Even though	To be sure	
Consequently / In the end		However		
Finally / To conclude		On the contrary		
In brief		On the other hand		
On the whole		Nevertheless		
		Nonetheless		
		Regardless		
		Whereas		
		While		
		Yet		

Let's look at a reading passage that uses transitions to get from one idea to the next.

> A friendship begins when two people show interest in each other and choose to spend time together. First, the two people talk. Then, they engage in activities together and share secrets. Next, the two people declare themselves friends by introducing each other as such to other friends and relatives. Finally, the two people celebrate the relationship by remembering each other on birthdays and other occasions.

In this example, the reading moves along as a result of the transitions (*first, then, next,* and *finally*) that occur in a sequence.

3. *Text organization by method*—Writers use different **organizational approaches.** All writers draw from **rhetorical strategies** that form these approaches. We can see these writings fall into the categories of narration, description, definition, process analysis, compare and/or contrast, classification, cause and effect, and argument.

Narration means telling a story. In "An American Girlhood," when Annie Dillard writes "Some boys taught me to play football. This was a fine sport," she is telling us a story about her upbringing.

Description means showing how something looks, sounds, feels, smells, or tastes. The description is often crafted around a dominant impression. "But in the main, I feel like a brown bag of miscellany propped against a wall…A first water diamond, an empty spool, bits of broken glass, lengths of string…" (Zora Neale Hurston, "How it Feels to be Colored Me," 1928).

Definition gives specific instances of something. The definition identifies what something is or what it is not. It could be a word, term, or concept in depth. Let's consider Henry Miller's definition of writing: "Writing is not a game played according to rules. Writing is a compulsive, and delectable thing. Writing is its own reward." (Henry Miller, *Henry Miller on Writing*. New York: New Directions, 1964).

Process Analysis explains how to do something. "Pour egg yolks into a mixing bowl, add sugar, then vanilla, then beat for one minute."

Comparison and/or contrast points out similarities and/or differences. "They were two strong men, these oddly different generals, and they represented the strengths of two conflicting currents that, through them, had come into final collision." (Bruce Catton, "Grant and Lee: A Study in Contrasts." *The American Story*. Ed. Garet Garrett. Chicago: Regenery, 1955).

Classification is when the writer organizes concepts into categories and gives examples of details that fit into each category. For example, if you choose to classify different types of Apple products (e.g., iPods, iPads, and iPhones), the writing will go on to define the characteristics of each.

Cause and effect discusses why something happens or the effects of something that has happened. "Making it requires diligent effort and deferred gratification."—Barack Obama. Here, President Obama tells us the effect ("making it"), which will result from specific causes (hard work—and indulgences that are delayed).

Argument tries to persuade the reader of a position, often by refuting the opposition. "Recreational marijuana should be legalized in all 50 states" is an argument. "The ivory trade should be shut down to save the elephant from extinction" is another.

4. *Identifying how point of view and reference to an idea or text influence an author's argument*—An argument is persuasive writing in which a thesis is asserted and based on a series of claims. "If the first woman God ever made was strong enough to turn the world upside down all alone, these women together ought to be able to turn it back, and get it right side up again"—(Sojourner Truth, "Ain't I A Woman").

In most textbook writing, argument takes the form of well-developed ideas, points, or theories supported by experiments, surveys, studies, expert testimony, reasons, examples, or other evidence. Textbook arguments usually have solid support because they have been peer reviewed.

ETS stresses the importance of recognizing that the author's view may be influenced by the ideas of another text.

5. *Determining fact versus opinions, beliefs, and feelings*—A **fact** is a statement that can be proved by direct experience or objective evidence and verification. It might come to us as physical proof, the corroborated testimony of witnesses, agreed-upon observations, or the result of research or investigation.

An **opinion** is an assertion that can be supported by examples, experience, evidence, etc.

 HINT

To help draw the distinction between fact and opinion, it may help to recall that, as Daniel Patrick Moynihan liked to say, "Everyone is entitled to his own opinion, but not to his own facts."

For example:

It is understood that the children of single mothers feel rejected.

The use of the phrase "It is understood . . ." implies that what follows has been proven. But factual support is omitted, making the statement an opinion.

Here are some facts, any of which can be checked for accuracy and thus proved true:

Fact: The viperfish can live up to eight years.
(Scientific records can confirm the viperfish's maximum lifespan.)

Fact: Albert Einstein willed his violin to his grandson.
(This statement can be checked in historical publications or with Einstein's estate.)

Fact: On September 11, 2001, terrorists destroyed New York City's World Trade Center, killing nearly 2,800 people.
(This event was witnessed in person or on television by millions, and it's in records worldwide.)

Here are some opinions, which have to be judged on merit, a judgment that can vary with one's point of view:

Opinion: The viperfish is the ugliest inhabitant of the seas.
(There's no way to prove this statement because two people can look at the same creature and come to different conclusions about its appearance. "Ugly" is a **value word**, a word we use to express a judgment. Value or judgment words signal that an opinion is being expressed.)

Opinion: Einstein should have willed his violin to a museum.
(Who says? Not his grandson. This is an opinion.)

Opinion: The attack on the World Trade Center was the worst act of terrorism in the history of humankind.
(Whether something is "worst" is debatable. *Worst* is a value word.)

6. *Using context clues to identify unknown and multiple-meaning words*—**Context** is what is around the word—it can be the overall meaning of a sentence or paragraph or a word's position or function in a sentence. When you use context as a clue to the meaning of a word or phrase, you can identify the meaning of a word unknown to you. You can use the context effectively in other ways also. For instance, you can:

1. Use the tone of a passage to determine an approximate meaning of a word.

2. Use affixes and roots as clues to the meaning of a word (for instance, "belligerent," "bellicose," and "rebel" all come from the root *bel,* which means "war").

7. *Understanding figurative language and nuances in word meanings*—On the Praxis Core Reading test, you will be asked to interpret figures of speech (e.g., literary, biblical, and mythological allusions) in context; use the relationship between particular words (e.g., synonym/antonym, analogy) to better understand each word; and distinguish among the connotations (associations) of words with similar denotations (definitions), as in this group of words related denotatively: REFINED, RESPECTFUL, POLITE, DIPLOMATIC, APPROACHABLE.

You also might be asked to consider the impact of a specific word on meaning and tone. Beyond that, you may be called upon to analyze how a sentence, chapter, scene, or stanza fits into the overall structure of a text and contributes to the development of the theme, setting, or plot. What's the point of view? How is it developed? What do the similes and metaphors mean?

Consider this example:

In the short story "Araby," James Joyce writes, "The career of our play brought us through the dark muddy lanes behind the houses…to the back doors of dark dripping gardens where odours arose from the ashpits…" This sentence contains:

(A) Idiom

(B) Irony

(C) Second person

(D) Alliteration

(E) Allegory

Here, the correct answer is choice (D). Why? We see the repetition of the consonant *d* (dark—doors—dark—dripping). The inclusion of "our" makes the passage written in first person, making choice (C) incorrect. There is no way to judge if irony is in the passage, and idiomatic phrases are undetectable here. So choices (A) and (B) are out. Choice (E), allegory, can be eliminated because of the literal nature of the excerpt.

8. *Understanding college- and career-readiness-level words and phrases*—Students need to master vocabulary in academic areas, in the college application process, and also for their careers. Knowing these words will lead to greater success. For a great resource of career and college-readiness-level words and phrases, consider the app *Words to Know Before You Go* (McGraw-Hill, 2012) or go to *www.achievethecore.org* and search the phrase "which words do I teach?" The latter resource presents important words and phrases you should have mastered in high school to prepare you for college.

Practice Exercises: Craft, Structure, and Language Skills

DIRECTIONS: After reading the following passage, select the best answer to each question from among the choices given. You should determine your answer based on what is stated or implied in the passage. No prior knowledge of the topic treated in the passage is required. (Note: In this drill, each question has only one best answer. However, on the actual Praxis Core test, you will sometimes encounter questions with multiple correct answers; in such cases, you will be directed to "select *all* that apply.") Answers appear on pages 238–240.

Recognized artistic masterpieces have long commanded substantial sums at auction. But in 1987 even veteran art dealers were shocked when Vincent van Gogh's *Still Life: Vases with Fifteen Sunflowers* sold for nearly $40 million—three times the highest amount previously paid for a painting. Just as notable, it was the first "modern" work, as opposed to older "master" paintings, to hold the record. What was in this still life of a vase filled with flowers that made it worth such a fortune? Much of the answer lies in a century-long fascination with the artist himself.

Line (5)

A restless, unhappy man throughout most of his life and almost certainly a victim of mental illness, van Gogh worked unsuccessfully for an art dealer; pursued, unsuccessfully, a career as a minister, and labored, largely unsuccessfully, at painting. At his death in 1890 at the age of 37, van Gogh was a little-known artist living alone in southern France who had sold just one of his works.

(10)

Only through a series of memorial exhibitions in Europe and the United States did van Gogh's remarkable aesthetic vision begin to draw notice, and within a decade of his death, he was widely recognized as a master artist. *Starry Night,* with its whirling stars and dark skies, became one of the world's most widely admired paintings, and his self-portraits reinforced the legend of his genius, anguish, and eventual madness. But it was *Still Life: Vase with Fifteen Sunflowers* that most clearly embodied his power as an artist.

(15)

Reprinted from Greenberg, Jan, and Jordan, Sandra.
Vincent van Gogh: Portrait of an Artist. New York: Random House, 2003.

1. Which of the following is closest in meaning to "aesthetic" as it is used in Line 14 of the passage?

   (A) Dedication to beauty

   (B) Sensitivity

   (C) Virtuosity

   (D) Undervaluation

   (E) Undiscovered

2. In looking at the organization of the text, it is clear that the answer to the question, "What was in this still life of a vase filled with flowers that made it worth such a fortune?" can most definitely be found in

   (A) Paragraph 1

   (B) Paragraph 2

   (C) Paragraph 3

   (D) Paragraphs 1 and 2

   (E) Paragraphs 2 and 3

3. Overall, the author provides his opinion as to

   (A) who van Gogh was

   (B) why van Gogh's paintings command such high prices

   (C) how van Gogh's life was terrible

   (D) why van Gogh isn't as good as the artists who came before him

   (E) how van Gogh died

4. According to the passage, what makes great art?

   (A) The struggles of the artist

   (B) The life of the artist and his talent

   (C) How the public views the artist

   (D) How much people are willing to pay for it

   (E) None of the above

5. Which of the following is an opinion from the text?

   (A) Van Gogh was a little-known artist living alone in southern France.

   (B) People are fascinated by van Gogh because of his life and his works.

   (C) At auction, recognized works command substantial sums of money.

   (D) *Still Life: Vases with Fifteen Sunflowers* sold for nearly $40 million in 1987.

   (E) *Starry Night* became one of the world's most widely admired paintings.

6. All of the following statements in paragraph 2 imply the reason why the sale price for van Gogh's work is so shocking to the authors EXCEPT:

   (A) Van Gogh was a "restless, unhappy man."

   (B) Van Gogh was "a victim of mental illness."

   (C) Van Gogh worked "unsuccessfully for an art dealer."

   (D) Van Gogh resided "in southern France."

   (E) Van Gogh "sold just one of his works."

7. The structure of the passage is best described as which of the following?

   (A) The writer raises a question and answers it by analyzing the artist's life and legacy.

   (B) The writer compares the work with another work.

   (C) The writer provides an extended definition of *Still Life: Fifteen Vases with Flowers*.

   (D) The writer recognizes the earlier artistic masters who came before van Gogh.

   (E) The writer is opinionated.

8. By using context clues, determine the meaning of the word "veteran" in Line 2.

   (A) A person who has served in the military

   (B) An old experienced soldier

   (C) A novice

   (D) A person who has a lot of experience in a particular professional field

   (E) A person who is retired

9. Van Gogh worked unsuccessfully as all of the following EXCEPT:

   (A) Art dealer

   (B) Employer of servants

   (C) Minister

   (D) Painter

   (E) Socialite

10. The passage details how after his death, van Gogh was considered

    (A) self-destructive

    (B) weak

    (C) a powerful master artist

    (D) rich and famous

    (E) None of the above

Answers to Practice Exercises: Craft, Structure, and Language Skills *(page 236)*:

1.   (A)

Choice (A) is correct. Van Gogh was probably very sensitive, and may have been a virtuoso (a person with special knowledge and skill in a field). But aestheticism pertains to beauty. In this context, it describes van Gogh's dedication to beauty. The "trap" here is factually true statements that are not responsive to the question. There are no real traps on the Praxis Core test, only questions that require alertness and alacrity (promptness in response).

2.   (C)

Choice (C) is correct. Paragraph 3 indicates the great extent to which van Gogh's self-portraits burnished his legend. This descriptive detail elaborates on the passage's main idea.

3.   (B)

While the other answer choices are discussed in the passage, the main point is to explain why his paintings sell for such large sums.

4.   (B)

Choice (B) is the best answer. The struggles alone do not make great art, and while the public's feelings about the artist are influential (C), that perception of the artist's life must be coupled by the artist's talent.

5.   (B)

Choice (B) is the correct answer. Choices (A), (C), (D), and (E) are facts presented in the passage. Choice (B) is an opinion the authors express in the passage.

6.   (D)

Choice (D) is the correct answer. That van Gogh struggled individually, mentally, and professionally for his entire life makes it shocking how much money his work commanded, the authors assert. Choice (D) is a fact about van Gogh and does not influence the tone in the passage.

7.   (A)

Choice (A) is the correct answer. The writers do not compare/contrast or define at length here. While they do mention that artistic masters preceded van Gogh, the structure of the passage is described as a question raised in paragraph 1, a discussion of the artist's story (paragraph 2), and a discussion of his legacy (paragraph 3).

8.   (D)

Choice (D) is the correct answer. In this context of "veteran art dealers," the writers aren't referring to former soldiers (A) and (B). A novice (C) is the opposite of a veteran, so that choice is incorrect. Choice (D) is the definition of a veteran in this context.

9. **(B)**

Choice (B) is the correct answer. A close reading of paragraph 2 reveals that choices (A), (C), and (D) are stated in the passage. Choice (B) is not mentioned. The passage indicates that van Gogh was hardly a socialite (E), instead dying as "a little-known artist . . . living alone."

10. **(C)**

Choice (C) is correct. The answer is contained in the last five words of the passage ("his power as an artist").

Integration of Knowledge and Ideas

Integrating knowledge and ideas leads to our thinking about ideas in more complex ways. And just such critical thinking undergirds the Common Core standards and consequently the Praxis Core Reading test. As readers, we are challenged to think about how life experiences and perspectives affect ideas, how a reading can have multiple themes, and how our cultural knowledge informs our understanding of the text. "Knowing about our knowing" is sometimes referred to as **meta-cognition**. In addition, increasing our knowledge by reading and studying more deeply in one's discipline can enrich ideas. This is the basis for developing ideas when we read and learn and then challenge ourselves.

DISSECTING VISUAL-INFORMATION QUESTIONS

What else is the test asking us to do? It asks us to analyze content in diverse media and formats, including visual texts. How do we do this?

Currently, we live in a visually dominated culture. Images on cell phones, laptops, billboards, and televisions bombard us every day. Analyzing these images often requires breaking the image apart into its pieces and then trying to assemble meaning.

A **visual text** is a document or chart that communicates primarily through images or the interaction of image and text. Just as writers choose their words and organize their thoughts based on any number of ideas, the authors of visual documents think no differently. Whether assembling an advertisement, laying out a pamphlet, taking a photograph, designing a website, or painting a subject in a piece of artwork, the author seeks to ensure that the image communicates a message with a meaning or multiple meanings.

What is the process of analyzing a visual text? The following tips are intended to help you shape your understanding of any visual text that is primarily information-driven, such as a **graph, chart, table, pictograph,** or **map.**

To interpret visual texts, ask yourself:

1. What does the title tell you about the graph's purpose?

2. Check column and row headings to observe what information is being conveyed, and how.

3. With bar graphs, look at the bars, which tend to compare things that are alike. Look at the horizontal and vertical axes to see what is being compared. See the key to find out what each bar means.

4. With line graphs, what two data pieces are being compared? Such graphs typically deal with comparisons over time. Check the time span and its intervals.

5. With pie charts, you'll be looking at segments of a whole. What do the slices, or wedges, represent? Typically percentages are shown.

6. With maps and pictographs, determine what each symbol stands for and ascertain the scale being used. What is being measured or characterized?

7. What kind of evidence does the visual text provide?

8. What is the relationship between the visual text and the verbal text?

For **art reproductions, photographs, advertisements, and cartoons,** overt and covert messages are often conveyed. Further, the designer of the image may have manipulated the image by playing with visual elements. Pay attention to:

1. Color, light, and shadow

2. The number and arrangement of objects and the relationships among them

3. What is in the front and back of the image

4. The size and font/typeface

5. The message being conveyed, which is often presented with humor to drive home a point

6. The overall artistic composition

Read visual texts as critically as you read verbal texts, which means that strategies such as annotation can help. Such questions may require you to click a portion of the graphic rather than select your answer from a list. Similarly you may be asked to click on one or more sentences or words within a reading passage.

Let's try a question with two related line-graph charts.

Evaluate the statistical information in the two charts below. Then answer the question that follows.

Graph 1

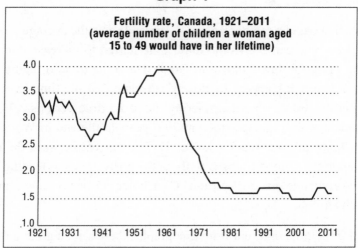

Graph 2

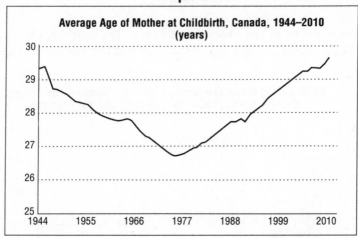

Source: Statistics Canada

Which of the following can reasonably be concluded based on information contained in the two graphs? (Select *all* that apply.)

| A | In the three decades following World War II, the average age of mothers at childbirth decreased continually. |

| B | A significant decline in the birthrate since the mid-1960s largely correlates with a rise in mothers' average age at childbirth. |

| C | The trend to delay marriage and motherhood is not uniquely a modern phenomenon. |

| D | In the wake of World War II, the Canadian birthrate steadily declined. |

| E | A steep increase in the average age of mothers at childbirth correlates with a steep decrease in birthrate. |

This is an example of one of the rare Praxis questions with more than one correct answer. Granted, you may not have faced this sort of item before, but rest assured the answers will derive entirely from the information right in front of you.

Let's explore the answers:

The chart reveals that data on mothers' ages A indeed show the average mother's age at child-birth steadily falling. As you can see from Graph 2, it started to increase during the mid-1970s. Thus, the sharp drop in the birthrate shown in Graph 1 and the trend of aging first-time mothers shown in Graph 2, B and E , appear to closely correlate, but the time lines are not the same. Indeed, the correlation is absent when considering the same time periods. Choice C is correct because first-time mothers' average age stood at 29.6 years at the end of World War II, strikingly similar to the 2010 figure of 29.5 years. Choice D is incorrect because the post-World War II actual *birthrate,* meanwhile, climbed substantially in the postwar years, leading to a baby boom in Canada. So the two correct answers are A and C . Choice D is no trick; it merely holds you to account on reading the graph.

While bar charts look quite different from line graphs, there's not a great difference in the sheer amount of information you'll need to absorb, or the time you'll need to put in to answer questions based on either. Let's examine a bar-chart question:

Evaluate the information in the chart that follows. Then answer the question, which this time—like most questions on the Praxis tests—has just one correct answer.

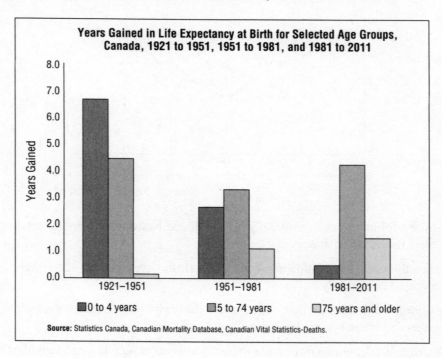

Years Gained in Life Expectancy at Birth for Selected Age Groups, Canada, 1921 to 1951, 1951 to 1981, and 1981 to 2011

Years Gained

0.0 1.0 2.0 3.0 4.0 5.0 6.0 7.0 8.0

1921–1951   1951–1981   1981–2011

■ 0 to 4 years   ■ 5 to 74 years   □ 75 years and older

Source: Statistics Canada, Canadian Mortality Database, Canadian Vital Statistics-Deaths.

According to the chart, which period contributed the most to life expectancy?

(A) 1921 to 1951

(B) 1951 to 1981

(C) 1981 to 2011

(D) There is insufficient information to answer the question.

(E) Immunizations, not age, contribute to life expectancy.

This is a straightforward question, but it still requires care. Let us explain.

Analyzing gains for each period, it is evident that declines in infant and child mortality between 1921 and 1951 accounted for the greatest gains in life expectancy at birth (A). To derive the answer, you need to inspect the bar labels and bar height. You see that for the 1921–1951 period, the tallest bar, which represents the age 0 to 4 bracket, shows the largest gains in life expectancy compared with the other Canadian population cohorts for the time period. Clearly the age 0 to 4 bracket is driving the gains, and dramatically so, but you need to add the values of all three bars to ensure this is the largest of the three period totals. During the 1921–1951 time period, of the total 11.3 years gained, we see that 6.7 years are due to reductions in infant and child death rates, about 4.5 years to the age 5 to 74 bracket, and only a month or two to the 75-year-plus bracket. Your eye may be drawn to the tallest bar, and the outsized gain seen may tip you to the answer, but it's still best to do some quick math to check yourself. (You may speculate the unusually large gain among babies and small children is attributable in large measure to childhood immunization against infectious diseases (E). Your speculation may be correct, but this factor is unseen in the graph and *exceeds the scope of the question*. You neither need to know this nor any other outside information.) From 1951 to 1981 (B), adding the values of the three bars, there was a 7.1-year gain in life expectancy. The last interval (C) saw a total life-expectancy contribution of 6.2 years. As we see, this bar graph has all the information we need to answer the question, so choice (D) is also incorrect. Choice (A) is confirmed as the one correct answer.

ETS appears to favor charts and graphs in its visual-information test bank. Still, it's worth mentioning that art, too, may appear on the test, although the wide range of potential visual-information questions may keep it from appearing on your particular version of the test. Nonetheless, understanding how to "read" artwork will help you more critically construe any text, visual or otherwise.

EVALUATING ARGUMENTS

Framing an Argument

A big key to success on the Reading test (as is also true of the Writing test) is a strong grasp of how arguments are framed. You'll be asked to "[i]dentify and evaluate an argument and specific claims in a text, including the validity of the reasoning as well as the relevance and sufficiency of the evidence."

An **argument** is just that—a disagreement between two or more viewpoints with one side trying to win the discussion. The big point the author is trying to prove is his or her **thesis**, and that thesis should be debatable, an assertion about which people could reasonably disagree. If the author's thesis is generally agreed upon or is accepted as fact, there is no need to persuade people.

Here's an example of a non-debatable thesis statement:

> Quitting smoking reduces your risk of heart disease.

This thesis is not debatable. All scientific studies agree that this is statistically the case.

Here's an example of a debatable thesis statement:

> Federal money should be set aside to educate individuals about heart disease.

This is an example of a debatable thesis because reasonable people could disagree with it. Some people might think that the public already knows about heart disease. Others might feel that we should be spending more money on other issues such as welfare-to-work programs. Still others could argue that American Heart Association, not the government, should be paying to educate the public.

The thesis needs to narrow a topic and assert something about it, which must be supported by evidence. The broader the argument, the more evidence the author will need to convince readers that his or her position is right.

Claims typically help you support the thesis. Authors can make a claim to argue their thesis by defining something, asserting that something causes something else; arguing for or against a certain solution or approach to a problem, etc. Here's an example of a claim:

> Instead of importing oil and other fossil fuels, the United States should focus on finding more ways to use renewable energy sources.

This claim would support an argument for promoting the use of electric cars to cut down on pollution.

Evidence is used to support claims, the thesis, and the entire argument. What type of evidence should be marshalled?

There are two types of evidence:

Primary evidence includes original research, such as interviews, experiments, and surveys, as well as personal experience and anecdotes.

Secondary evidence is research obtained from such sources as books, periodicals, and websites.

Judging Credibility

Regardless of the sources the author uses, they must be credible. Sources must be reliable, accurate, and trustworthy, and you can determine this by asking the following:

- Who is the author?

- How recent is the source?

- What is the author's purpose? Is there bias?

- Is it from the Internet? Be very careful in cases where an author cannot be determined. Credible websites are associated with such institutions as universities, governments, or well-known non-governmental organizations.

A well-known source for information about arguments is the Purdue University Online Writing Lab (OWL). At the website (*http://owl.english.purdue.edu*), authors Stacy Weida and Karl Stolly describe the Toulmin Method of Logic, a common and easy formula for organizing an argument based on the work of Stephen Toulmin.

The basic format for the Toulmin Method is as follows:

Claim: The overall thesis the writer will present.

Grounds: Evidence gathered to support the claim.

Warrant (also referred to as a bridge): Explanation of why or how the data supports the claim, the underlying assumption that connects the data to the claim.

Backing (also referred to as the foundation): Additional logic or reasoning that may be necessary to support the warrant.

Opposing argument/Counterclaim: A claim that negates or disagrees with the thesis/claim.

Rebuttal: Evidence that negates or disagrees with the counterclaim.

The warrant or bridge is essential to writing a good argumentative essay—the very kind of essay you'll encounter in various guises on the Reading test. If data are presented to the audience without clarifying how they support the author's thesis, the reader may not make a connection or may draw different conclusions than the thesis envisions.

Good arguments anticipate—and include—the opposing side of an argument, or counterclaim. Acknowledge what opponents say and respond to their arguments. Including rebuttals serves as an excellent debating strategy.

EXAMPLE

Claim: Gangs have caused illegal drug use and violence throughout history.

Grounds: Criminal organizations emerged during the Prohibition era. They fought against each other and against the state, causing violence and death.

Warrant: Gangs were able to protect the illegal use and abuse of alcohol during this period, leading to violence.

Counterclaim: Instead of gangs causing violence and drug abuse, the reverse is true: Drug abuse and violence cause gangs to form.

Rebuttal: While drugs and violence often lead to the formation of gangs, one should not assume that these factors cause gangs to form. Rather, the reverse may be true—that gangs and the protection they afford drug users lead to, and feed, a vicious cycle of drug abuse and violence.

Aristotle's Appeals and the Rhetorical Triangle

A good argument should be anchored in the **Rhetorical Triangle,** whose three elements— writer, audience, and context—correspond with Aristotle's three appeals.

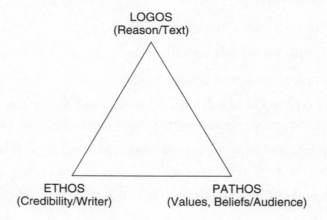

LOGOS
(Reason/Text)

ETHOS
(Credibility/Writer)

PATHOS
(Values, Beliefs/Audience)

Artistotle said a good argument includes three chief appeals:

1. **Ethos** (credibility, which is based on character, the reliability of the writer, the writer's expertise, etc.). A writer with ethos uses credible sources, cites them properly, and respects the reader by presenting opposing positions accurately.

2. **Pathos** (emotional appeal) brings the reader into the writing on an emotional level by presenting sources such as interviews and individual stories. For example, telling the story of a child whose family is poor may make for a more persuasive argument than simply discussing the national statistics on families who live below the poverty line. The personal story paints a picture of how the statistics look up close.

3. **Logos** (logic or reason, which can be inductive or deductive). **Inductive reasoning** starts with details that lead to your generalization. These facts must fairly represent the larger generalization. Conversely, **deductive reasoning** begins with a generalization and then applies it to a specific case. A starting generalization must be based on enough evidence, and the argument also should be organized logically with smooth transitions.

For an interesting video presentation on logic and reasoning in arguments, visit YouTube to view "The Fallacy Project: Examples of fallacies from advertising, politics, and popular culture."

Some common errors in reasoning that will undermine the logic of an argument include:

Bandwagon: Appealing to popular belief.

Straw man: Oversimplifying an argument.

Slippery slope: A conclusion based on the premise that if A happens, then eventually through a series of small steps, B, C . . . X, Y, Z will happen, too, thus equating A and Z. So, if Z isn't desired, A also must not be allowed to occur.

> **Example:** If we ban large SUVs because they are bad for the environment, the government will eventually ban all cars. We thus should not ban large SUVs.

Here, the author is equating banning large SUVs with banning all cars, which is not the same thing.

Hasty generalization: A conclusion based on insufficient or biased evidence, or rushing to a conclusion before getting all the facts.

> **Example:** Although it's only the first day of class, I can tell this professor is going to be boring.

The author is basing the evaluation of the entire course on one class, which is not enough evidence.

Post hoc ergo propter hoc: This conclusion assumes if 'A' occurred after 'B,' then 'B' must have caused 'A.'

> **Example:** I slept over in the hospital and now I am sick, so the hospital must have made me sick.

In this example the author assumes that if one event chronologically follows another the first event must have caused the second. But here the illness could have been caused by a number of things. There is no reason, without more evidence, to assume the hospital caused the person to be sick.

Circular argument: Restating the argument rather than proving it.

> **Example:** Oprah Winfrey is a good conversationalist because she speaks effectively.

Here, the conclusion (Winfrey is a "good conversationalist") and the evidence used to prove it ("she speaks effectively") are basically the same idea.

Either/or: A conclusion that oversimplifies the argument by reducing it to only two sides or choices.

> **Example:** We can either end this marriage or get mutual counseling.

In this example, two choices are presented as the only options, yet the author ignores a range of choices such as going on a trip, speaking to a clergy member, staying together without counseling, going for individual counseling, and so on.

Ad hominem: An attack on the character of a person rather than on the opinions or arguments.

> **Example:** Liberal ideas don't work because the people behind them are all angry left-wingers.

In this example, the author doesn't name any liberal ideas, much less evaluate those ideas. Instead, the author attacks the character of the people in the group.

Ad populum: An emotional appeal that speaks to positive (such as patriotism, religion, democracy) or negative (such as terrorism or fascism) concepts rather than real issues.

> **Example:** If you were a patriotic American, you would support the war on terrorism.

Here, the author equates being a "patriotic American" with a position on the war.

Red herring: Creating a diversion to avoid key issues.

> **Example:** The level of air pollution may be unsafe, but what will happen to all the jobs carmakers create?

Here, the writer diverts attention from pollution to job protection.

When you read, look for fallacies and avoid them when you write.

ANALYZING TWO OR MORE TEXTS

The Reading test asks you to, as ETS puts it, "[a]nalyze how two or more texts address similar topics or themes." Texts often cover the same events, but they do so differently. For example, contrast how a decision made by a government official would be described differently by the sober *New York Times* than it would be by the brash tabloid *New York Daily News,* which famously ran the headline "FORD TO NEW YORK: DROP DEAD" when President Gerald Ford refused to send federal aid to avoid bankruptcy for New York City. The same holds true for advertisements: two car insurance ads may claim that their respective plans are the cheapest and the best. Even cultures can influence the way a story gets told. For instance, the Iraq War has been described differently in the U.S. press than it has by news organizations based in the Middle East. These examples show that we need to be careful and critical readers of articles, ads, political documents, images, and even textbooks.

The Praxis Core test asks us to analyze two or more texts that address similar themes or topics and detect differing perspectives and perhaps even apply the ideas presented in one reading/visual representation to the ideas presented in another.

Knowing how to compare and contrast written texts is essential to success on the Praxis Core test. Let's remember what we learned and try to contrast two works of writing. This is the kind of activity you will most likely encounter.

Handling Paired-Passage Questions

The Praxis Core Reading test will present you with at least one question featuring two texts for side-by-side comparison and contrast. Your cue for such questions is that they'll typically appear on the computer screen alongside the passage, which will frequently have line markings to allow the questions to zero in on a given line. Such questions may also be represented with "clickable" sentences within the reading passage. Regardless, you'll want to have a sense of how to navigate within and between passages, which hinges on critical-thinking skills. Think of reading each passage as a journey, with mileposts along the way that will give you everything you need. Your job is to withstand distractor questions that may, for example, mischaracterize devices used by either author. This is done in a compare–contrast setup to check whether if you actually read the pieces. Here's how to deal with paired-passage questions.

Four Tips to Attack Paired Passages

1. Read Passage 1 and identify its genre (e.g., opinion piece, informational text, prose, etc.).

2. Read Passage 2 and note whether its genre differs from that of Passage 1.

3. Sketch out similarities and differences between the passages. How are they alike in terms of subject matter, theme, purpose, tone, etc.? How are they different in those or other ways? Where do their disagreements lie? Where do they dovetail? ("Sketch out" means to do it quickly—getting just enough of an outline to help you keep the details and the main idea clear.) This way, you'll be as well-equipped to affirm straight-ahead facts embedded in the passages as you will be to draw inferences.

4. Confirm your answers to the test questions by checking the passages.

Practice Exercises: Integration of Knowledge and Ideas

DIRECTIONS: The following two passages—the first authored by Booker T. Washington, the second penned mainly by W.E.B. DuBois—are followed by a series of questions based on their content. After reading the two passages, choose the one best answer (or, if prompted, select all the answers that apply, in which case you will be presented with check boxes). All questions should be answered based on what is *stated* or *implied* in the passages. You are not expected to have any prior knowledge of the topics covered in the passages. Note that lines are numbered continuously between the two passages. Remember to answer every question. (Answers appear on pages 256–257.)

Passage 1

Mr. President and Gentlemen of the Board of Directors and Citizens:

One-third of the population of the South is of the Negro race. No enterprise seeking the material, civil, or moral welfare of this section can disregard this element of our popula-
Line tion and reach the highest success. . . .To those of my race who depend on bettering their
(5) condition in a foreign land or who underestimate the importance of cultivating friendly relations with the Southern white man, who is their next-door neighbor, I would say: "Cast down your bucket where you are"—cast it down in making friends in every manly way of the people of all races by whom we are surrounded.

Cast it down in agriculture, mechanics, in commerce, in domestic service, and in the
(10) professions. And in this connection it is well to bear in mind that whatever other sins the South may be called to bear, when it comes to business, pure and simple, it is in the South that the Negro is given a man's chance in the commercial world, and in nothing is this Exposition more eloquent than in emphasizing this chance. Our greatest danger is that in the great leap from slavery to freedom we may overlook the fact that the masses of us are
(15) to live by the productions of our hands, and fail to keep in mind that we shall prosper in proportion as we learn to dignify and glorify common labour, and put brains and skill into the common occupations of life; shall prosper in proportion as we learn to draw the line between the superficial and the substantial, the ornamental gewgaws of life and the useful. No race can prosper till it learns that there is as much dignity in tilling a field as in writing
(20) a poem. It is at the bottom of life we must begin, and not at the top. Nor should we permit our grievances to overshadow our opportunities.

Source: Louis R. Harlan, ed., *The Booker T. Washington Papers*, Vol. 3,
(Urbana: University of Illinois Press, 1974), 583–587.

Passage 2

The members of the conference, known as the Niagara Movement, assembled in annual meeting at Buffalo, July 11th, 12th and 13th, 1905, congratulate the Negro-Americans on certain undoubted evidences of progress in the last decade, particularly the increase
(25) of intelligence, the buying of property, the checking of crime, the uplift in home life, the advance in literature and art, and the demonstration of constructive and executive ability in the conduct of great religious, economic and educational institutions.

At the same time, we believe that this class of American citizens should protest emphatically and continually against the curtailment of their political rights. We believe in man-
(30) hood suffrage; we believe that no man is so good, intelligent or wealthy as to be entrusted wholly with the welfare of his neighbor.

. . . We especially complain against the denial of equal opportunities to us in economic life; in the rural districts of the South this amounts to peonage and virtual slavery; all over the South it tends to crush labor and small business enterprises; and everywhere American
(35) prejudice, helped often by iniquitous laws, is making it more difficult for Negro-Americans to earn a decent living.

. . . We favor well-equipped trade and technical schools for the training of artisans, and the need of adequate and liberal endowment for a few institutions of higher education must be patent to sincere well-wishers of the race.

(40)   . . . The practice among employers of importing ignorant Negro-American laborers in emergencies, and then affording them neither protection nor permanent employment; and the practice of labor unions in proscribing and boycotting and oppressing thousands of their fellow-toilers, simply because they are black. These methods have accentuated and will accentuate the war of labor and capital, and they are disgraceful to both sides.

Source: "Niagara's Declaration of Principles, 1905" courtesy
of The Gilder Lehrman Center for the Study of Slavery,
Resistance, and Abolition at Yale University.

1.   Washington's attitude toward the economic system in the South is best described as which of the following?

(A) Tolerant

(B) Satiric

(C) Angry

(D) Self-Righteous

(E) Bigoted

2. As used in Lines 7 and 8, Washington's declaration, "Cast down your bucket where you are!" is most nearly paraphrased by which of the following?

   (A) Black Americans needed to depend on Southern whites.

   (B) Black Americans needed to get water.

   (C) Black Americans could benefit by compromising with and living among Southern whites.

   (D) Black Americans should pursue only intellectual activities.

   (E) Black Americans should go on strike.

3. According to Washington, the Negro should pursue work in the South in all of the following areas EXCEPT:

   (A) Domestic service

   (B) Literature and the Arts

   (C) Agriculture

   (D) Mechanics

   (E) None of the above

4. By describing in Lines 3–6 "the increase of intelligence, the buying of property, the checking of crime, the uplift in home life, the advance in literature and art, and the demonstration of constructive and executive ability in the conduct of great religious, economic, and educational institutions," DuBois is trying to show

   (A) that he could not accept these advances

   (B) that blood is thicker than water

   (C) that progress was being made by African Americans

   (D) that change would never come for black people in the Jim Crow South

   (E) that change should come from outside sources

5. DuBois is critical of the economy in the South mainly because of

   (A) the violence of black lynchings

   (B) the oppression resulting from racism and unjust laws

   (C) the rise of the Ku Klux Klan

   (D) the disenfranchisement that results from mob hostility

   (E) the Northern influence

6. Both Passage 1 and Passage 2 mention which of the following as key to economic growth among black Americans at this point in history?

   (A) Political opportunity

   (B) Segregation

   (C) The arts

   (D) Rebellion

   (E) Voting rights

7. The passages differ from each other with respect to which of the following?

   (A) The issue of educating African Americans

   (B) The issue of history

   (C) The issue of friendship

   (D) The issue of suffrage

   (E) None of the above

8. DuBois's vision of a time when African Americans could become more than sharecroppers contradicts all of the following statements attributed to Washington EXCEPT:

   (A) "No race can prosper till it learns there is as much dignity in tilling a field as in writing a poem."

   (B) "Our greatest danger is that in the great leap from slavery to freedom we may overlook the fact that the masses of us are to live by the productions of our hands"

   (C) "It is at the bottom of life we must begin, and not at the top."

   (D) "To those of my race who . . . underestimate the importance of cultivating friendly relations with the Southern white man."

   (E) "Nor should we permit our grievances to overshadow our opportunities."

9. Which statement best reveals the ideology of Booker T. Washington?

   (A) African Americans should return to Africa.

   (B) Violent resistance would remove segregation's restrictions and bring about an end to Jim Crow legislation in the South.

   (C) Working with their white brothers and sisters in vocational fields is the best way for African Americans to achieve equal opportunity.

   (D) Escaping through the Underground Railroad

   (E) None of the above

10. In these passages, DuBois and Washington find common ground in which of the following?

   (A) They differed in how they thought equality for African Americans could be achieved.

   (B) They argued for force to be used against white people.

   (C) They believed vocational education was of paramount importance for African Americans.

   (D) They believed liberal arts education was of paramount importance for African Americans.

   (E) The belief in sentiments expressed in Martin Luther King's "I Have a Dream" speech.

Answers to Practice Exercises: Integration of Knowledge and Ideas *(page 252–253)*:

Perspective on the passages and their authors

The two passages paint two distinct portraits of African Americans in the South in the years after the Civil War. In **Passage 1,** Booker T. Washington, a preeminent American educator and reformer who became the first president and principal developer of Tuskegee Normal and Industrial Institute, describes specific kinds of contributions blacks can make in the agricultural economy of the South. In **Passage 2,** W.E.B. DuBois, the leading black activist in the United States during the first half of the 20th century and a co-founder of the National Association for the Advancement of Colored People (NAACP), argues for black Americans to stand up for their rights and pursue educational goals so they can advance professionally.

1. (A)

Choice (A) is the correct answer because Passage 1 shows Booker T. Washington to be a role model of tolerance. He says that black Americans should become domestics and tradespeople to get along with Southern whites and work within their already established economy. He isn't satiric (B), angry (C), self-righteous (D), or bigoted (E), the first two traits being contrary to tolerance, and the last two being inconsistent with it, as embodied in Washington's entreaty to black Americans not to "underestimate the importance of cultivating friendly relations with the Southern white man, who is their next-door neighbor. . . ."

2. (C)

Choice (C) is the correct answer. Washington believed blacks should cast their buckets down to accept society as it is and work within it. Choice (B) is off-topic. While choice (A) may be a flow from Washington's philosophy, it does not explain his rationale. It is DuBois—not Washington—who talks about black Americans pursuing intellectual activities, so choice (D) is wrong. Choice (E) is wrong because there was no organized labor for black Americans.

3.   **(B)**

Choice (B) is correct. Washington mentions every choice—(A), (C), and (D)—except literature and the arts (B), which is DuBois's idea.

4.   **(C)**

Choice (C) is correct. In the passage, the word "progress" precedes the quoted phrase in the question stem.

5.   **(B)**

The correct answer is (B). DuBois talks about prejudice and racism. He would most likely have been critical of the ideas listed in choices (A) and (C), but these concepts are not cited in Passage 2. In Lines 29 and 30, he talks about voting rights (manhood suffrage) but not about mob violence (D).

6.   **(A)**

The correct answer is choice (A). The question asks you to find the similarities between the two passages. Segregation is negative and can't foster economic growth for blacks, so choice (B) is out. Only DuBois praises the arts, so choice (C) is incorrect. Rebellion (D) and voting rights (E) are not explained as a positive force in growing an economy, leaving choice (A) as the best answer.

7.   **(A)**

The passages do not discuss history (B), friendship (C), nor suffrage (D), but rather vocational education in a skill such as carpentry or farming (Washington's ideas) versus liberal arts education (DuBois's position).

8.   **(E)**

"Dignity in tilling a field" (A), production using one's hands (B), starting at the bottom (C), and "cultivating friendly relations with the Southern white man" (D) are all statements that contradict DuBois's sentiment that African Americans should have larger educational and professional dreams for themselves. Choice (E), however, is about grievances, so it is the outlier; it does not belong on the list with the others.

9. (C)

Choice (C) best paraphrases Washington's ideas. He never discusses African Americans returning to Africa or resisting oppression through violence or escaping through the Underground Railroad.

10. (A)

The overarching statement in choice (A) is the only viable answer. The other choices are not true.

PART IV:
Praxis Core Writing Review

Diagnostic Test

Go to the online REA Study Center to take the diagnostic test to help focus your study.

(www.rea.com/studycenter)

OVERVIEW OF THE WRITING TEST

The Praxis Core Writing test features three separately timed sections:

- 40 minutes for 40 selected-response items

- 30 minutes for the Argumentative essay

- 30 minutes for the Informative/Explanatory, or Source-based, essay

These sections are grouped under two main content category headings:

- **Content Category I:** Text Types, Purposes, and Production

- **Content Category II:** Language and Research Skills for Writing

Count on a variation in the number of selected-response questions you may see under either category. In Category I, you will find a range of 6 to 12 items with the rest of the category devoted to the two essays. In Category II, you will see 28 to 34 items. You should devote no more than one minute to each selected-response question.

You'll get additional time to run a Praxis tutorial on test navigation and tools. However, we strongly advise you to acquaint yourself with the technology platform beforehand by downloading ETS's interactive practice test, which is available at *www.ets.org/praxis.*

Scoring

The total available raw score on the Writing test is 70. But that's only part of the story. You should exercise caution in extrapolating a passing score from the raw score, especially because the scaled-score conversion varies from one version, or form, of a test to another and each state sets its own passing scores. Conversion is determined by a statistical method called equating, which enables the test maker to adjust the raw scores on subsequent test versions to make them comparable to raw scores from the first, or reference, version. Be sure to check with your teacher-credentialing agency for your state's passing-score requirements.

Meanwhile, for the sake of perspective on how to think about scoring, a multi-state standard-setting panel convened by ETS pegged passing at a 44 raw score on the Praxis Core Writing test, which scales to 162 on a 100–200 point scale. That would be about 62% correct, which may sound like a low bar. But without proper prep, it may not *feel* like a low bar on test day. We suggest you shoot for roughly 70% correct as your benchmark.

In the next two chapters, we arm you with tools you need to excel on the Writing test. Use only what you need. The section headings in this chapter and the next allow you to do this easily.

Chapter 11 features advice geared to the key distinctions between the test's two essays. We also show you how varying qualities of essays look. Chapter 12 presents cues and clues for answering the selected-response questions that measure your grasp of grammar and word usage, as well as research skills.

Question Formats

Unlike the Reading and Mathematics tests, the Praxis Core Writing test will never ask you to find more than one best answer choice for what ETS calls selected-response questions, which are multiple-choice items.

The questions test your command of usage, sentence correction, revision in context, and research skills, as follows:

- **Usage**—mechanics, grammatical/structural relationships, idiomatic expression, and word choice. Usage questions ask you to spot and fix a wide range of errors in the use of modifiers, subject/verb agreement, noun/noun agreement, pronoun/antecedent agreement, verb tense, pronoun case, pronoun number and person, and intensive pronouns. The test also assesses your ability to identify and correct faulty, or vague, pronouns and catch errors in punctuation and capitalization.

- **Sentence correction**—selecting the best way to restate a sentence by using standard written English in subject/verb agreement, pronoun/case agreement, verb tense shifts, and adjective/adverb usage, and by identifying effective paraphrasing that corrects errors in the placement of phrases and clauses.

- **Revision in context**—identifying the choice that shows how writing can be strengthened through editing and revision—looking specifically at wordiness versus conciseness, standard grammatical conventions, redundancy, jargon/technical terms, and valuable adjectives. You'll also judge style and tone.

- **Research skills**—using effective research strategies and citations, ferreting out information relevant to a research task, and assessing the credibility of sources.

 HINT

If you haven't already done so, now's the time to dog-ear your undergraduate guide to writing research papers or to bookmark the computer link to it.

Text Types, Purposes, and Production

Sixty percent of the Praxis Core Writing test falls under "Text Types, Purposes, and Production." It's important to see how coverage within this category is divided. Only a small portion of your score derives from the 6 to 12 multiple-choice items that will ask you to identify and fix sentences that need revision, a subject we cover in the next chapter. The biggest part of your score is determined by the two essays. Those essays are our next stop.

One essay is **Argumentative;** it relies on your personal knowledge and experience. The other essay is **Informative/Explanatory;** it asks you to use sources provided by ETS. You have 30 minutes to complete each essay, which puts a premium on outlining before writing. You must introduce a topic and organize and present ideas to create a unified whole.

 HINT

The short time allotted for the essays highlights the need for systematic planning so you can raise your score.

You should strive for advanced, sophisticated writing that avoids overreliance on formulaic prescriptions like the five-paragraph essay. However, you can adapt that formula by including claims (usually called assertions in rhetoric texts) that are supported logically with relevant evidence. To be sure, you need to get the structure right, but you also need to put your critical thinking on display without getting verbose.

The Praxis Core test directs examinees to develop the topic or argument artfully and thoroughly by bringing in significant facts, extended definitions, concrete details, quotations, counterclaims (when appropriate), precise language, and transitions with attention to formal academic tone as well as a demonstrated command of standard written English.

The Praxis Core essay section tests two kinds of writing. One essay asks you pick a side of an argument and support it. The other essay requires you to make an assertion, but it asks you to buttress your assertion by using information the test provides. Both essays require you to understand a prompt quickly, formulate a response, and then write an essay using examples and supporting details that reveal competency in sentence and paragraph composition. Both essay tasks invite you to weave in your own experience provided that you stay on point. The key difference in the second essay is you have two sources from which you must draw information. Both essays are scored holistically, which means the scorer reads the essay in its entirety and grades it (on a scale of 0 to 6). We'll look at each essay shortly, but first it will help to recall some valuable tips about writing for an academic audience.

16 WAYS TO IMPROVE YOUR ESSAY WRITING

As you prepare to write the two essays, here's some advice on how to invigorate them.

1. **Invoke the three C's.** Be Clear, Concise, and Correct.

2. **Favor action verbs over "to be" verbs.**

   WEAK: Frances is afraid of crocodiles.

   STRONG: Frances fears crocodiles.

3. **Make every word count.** This builds on Tip No. 2. Don't bloat your essay with extra words. If they don't pull their weight, delete them.

   WEAK: It is evident that the Midwest was being affected by high temperatures of an extreme nature last week. *(Word count = 18)*

   STRONG: Extreme heat gripped the Midwest last week. *(Word count = 7)*

4. **Write about what you know.** When you can use strong examples, your writing will be clearer and have a more confident tone.

5. **Practice.** The best way to learn to write is to write, write, and write. It's like playing the piano: The more you practice, the better you perform. Practice writing essays like those you'll need to produce for the test. Get an honest, objective appraisal from an advisor or professor.

6. **Include a beginning, a middle, and an end.** State what you are going to say in the beginning, say it, and then paraphrase what you said. You're aiming for a coherent narrative, not a repetitive one.

7. **Organize your essay mindfully.** You may want to make your strongest point first or save "the best for last" (i.e., have your final claim/assertion be the strongest one you present). You may want to organize your ideas chronologically, by similarities and differences, or by cause and effect. Base your decision on what feels right and what would

make the most sense if you were explaining it to someone in the eighth grade, which is the level at which most good newspapers are written.

8. **Expand your essay sparingly and helpfully.** On the Praxis Core Writing test, length counts but garbage does not. Don't pad your writing. Focus on expanding your ideas with examples, definitions, comparisons/contrasts, counterclaims, and so forth.

9. **Use concrete examples.** Pick the side of the issue that you can argue well, and support it vigorously. Examples may be drawn from:

   - References to historical events, literature, current events, science, art, etc. Incorporate them by saying "Recent studies have described. . . ," or "The book____ by ____ mentions that . . . ," or "According to. . . ."

   - Personal experiences (things that have happened to you or to people you know). Use them. Examples: "My father once told me that . . ." or "My experience supports this point."

10. **Adopt an appropriate point of view.** Avoid second person ("you") in formal academic essays such as these. Try to use the third person (*he, she, it, they, them*). Unless the question asks for your experiences or you are relying on them to make your case, avoid first person (*I, me, my, our, we, us*). Use concrete nouns and be precise. Avoid giving a cheesy imperative command at the end of your essay (e.g., "Stop smoking now!"). You risk leaving the reader with a bad last impression.

11. **Use the right transitions** (see the chart at the end of this list). These words and phrases help you get from idea to idea or paragraph to paragraph. Apart from helping you compose a higher-scoring essay on the Praxis Core Writing test, fluency in transitions will also help you in the usage section of the Writing test.

12. **Consider opposing arguments** (for the Argumentative Essay). The following templates from Gerald Graff and Cathy Birkenstein's book *They Say/I Say: Moves That Matter in Academic Writing* are useful here:

   - Of course, many will probably disagree with my assertion that _____.

   - Yet some readers may challenge my view that _____. Indeed, my own argument seems to ignore _____.

   - Yet is it always true that _____? Is it always the case, as I have been arguing, that _____?

   - Although I grant that _____, I still maintain that _____.

13. **Draw evidence from the source texts provided** (for the Informative/Explanatory essay). When you cite evidence, stick to the facts. Accuracy is central to your credibility with the ETS grader. Graff and Birkenstein (2006) suggest doing it like this:

   X (states, argues, asserts, explains, emphasizes, describes how)_____.
   She means that_____.

14. **Keep it tidy.** Indent your paragraphs and punctuate with care.

15. **Watch your language.** Avoid clichés, jargon, slang, and euphemisms. Clichés are expressions so common they've gone stale. Jargon is the specialized, often technical, language used by people in a particular field, profession, or social group. Slang is the informal language of conversation, text messages, and other casual social communication among friends. Euphemisms are milder words or phrases used to blunt the effect of more direct or unpleasant words or phrases. Use a formal academic tone, but don't get fancy.

16. **Proofread your work.** Don't forget this crucial step. Leave time for minor revisions and final editing—but only after you have completed a full-fledged draft of your essay.

10 Types of Transitions

Cause and Effect	To Add On	Time
Accordingly	Additionally	First, Second. . .
As a result	Equally important	Finally
Consequently	Also	Last
Hence	And	Subsequently
It follows, then	Besides	Simultaneously
So	Furthermore	Meanwhile
Then	In addition	Currently
Therefore	In fact	
Thus	Indeed	
	Moreover	
	So too	

Example	Elaboration	Conclusion
After all	Actually	As a result
As an illustration	By extension	Consequently
Consider	That is	Hence
For example	In other words	Finally
For instance	To put it another way	In a word
Specifically	Ultimately	In brief
To take a case in point		In the end
		On the whole
		To conclude
		To summarize
		In short
		In sum, then
		It follows, then
		So
		The upshot of all of this is that
		Therefore
		Thus
		To summarize

(Continued)

10 Types of Transitions (cont'd)

Comparison	Contrast	Concession	Importance
Along the same lines	Although	Admittedly	Above all
In the same way	But	Although it is true that	Best
Likewise	By/In contrast	Granted	Worst
Similarly	Conversely	Of course	Most importantly
	Despite the fact that	Naturally	In particular
	Even though	To be sure	
	However		
	On the contrary		
	On the other hand		
	Nevertheless		
	Nonetheless		
	Regardless		
	Whereas		
	Yet		

BUILDING STRONG ESSAYS

Understanding the Argumentative Essay

Think about this—when you argue with someone, what are you trying to accomplish? Usually, when you look back at an argument, you see you were trying to change someone's mind or maybe just ask the person to reevaluate or better understand an idea, issue, or problem. The same idea holds true for an argumentative essay. An **argument** is a reasoned, logical way of showing that the writer's opinion or conclusion is valid. In English class, students build arguments about what they think. They support their interpretations of issues and ideas with evidence. They look at multiple sources to support their arguments. They present their interpretations and draw conclusions to answer questions or address problems. Using data in a scientifically acceptable form, students collect and present evidence to support their claim in a logical and organized manner.

In an argument, the writer not only gives information but also presents a case with the "pros" (supporting ideas) and "cons" (opposing ideas) on a debatable issue. Because an argument must show the main thesis is valid, it needs support. That support comes from claims (topics within the paragraph) developed through sound reasoning and relevant and adequate evidence. In an argument, students often acknowledge counterclaims, an approach we'll discuss later.

On the Core Writing test, you will be asked to create an argumentative essay by drawing from personal experience, observation, or reading. As mentioned before, the other essay you will compose, the Informative/ Explanatory essay, will ask you to use two sources during the test. The Argumentative essay does not.

Understanding the Informative/Explanatory Essay

Have you been asked to explain something? Of course. Perhaps you were asked to provide information on a subject you know something about, or you had to explain a process or concept. Informational/explanatory writing is just that: You write with the goal of giving accurate information to explain something clearly and concisely.

This writing commonly addresses **types** (*What are the different types of literary devices?*) and **components** (*What are the elements of a great marketing plan?*); **size, function, or behavior** (*Why would a taser be used? How do people find employment? Why do so many Africans go hungry?*); **how things work** (*How can a bar of chocolate stop a sulfuric acid leak?*); and **why things happen** (*Why is the Human Genome Project important?*).

To write this type of essay, you should draw from what you know and from the source material ETS provides for the essay. While you can call upon your own experiences, you must not stray from the assigned topic. With practice, you will become better able to develop a thesis and a coherent essay using relevant examples, facts, and details.

You can use an array of techniques to convey your information. These techniques include **defining, describing, differentiating, comparing, contrasting, citing an anecdote** (small story from your life or elsewhere to illustrate a point), **classifying, presenting a problem and solution, discussing a cause and effect,** or **using evidence** from a source. We see this writing across the disciplines, and we also see it in instructional manuals, memos, and reports.

In the informative/explanatory essay, you will develop what you are explaining by selecting relevant facts and using precise language. You will draw from the information ETS gives you and use it to support your discussion.

In summary, arguments persuade people to change their minds about something and sometimes to change their behaviors as well. In contrast, explanations clarify because they answer questions about why or how.

The 5-20-5 System for Attacking Your Essays

You should consider three steps in setting your basic course of action as you approach your essay: Plan, Write, Revise/Edit. We call it the 5-20-5 system to illustrate the time for each step: Five minutes for planning, 20 minutes for writing, and another five on the backside for revision. Let's walk through it.

Step 1: Plan (5 minutes)

Read the prompt carefully so you know what the question asks. Take a position (AGREE, DISAGREE, or QUALIFY, which means agree in part, disagree in part, or agree but say something further.).*

---

*All templates are taken from Graff and Birkenstock, *They Say/I Say: The Moves That Matter in Academic Writing.* New York: W. W. Norton & Company, 2006.

AGREE   She argues _____, and I agree because _____.

Her argument that _____ is supported by new research showing that _____.

X is correct when he maintains _____, a point needing further emphasis.

DISAGREE   X's claim that _____ rests upon the questionable assumption _____.

However, by focusing on _____, X overlooks the deeper problem of _____.

QUALIFY   He claims that _____ and I have mixed feelings about it. On the one hand, I agree that _____. On the other hand, I insist that _____.

Although I agree with X up to a point, I cannot accept his overall conclusion that _____.

My feelings on the issue are mixed. While I support X's position that _____, I also find Y's argument about _____ equally persuasive.

In its prompts, ETS typically asks essay questions about:

- An ethical issue (e.g., differing perspectives on honesty—is it always the best way to go? What about justice? Or courage?)

- Change (Is it good or bad?)

- Roles in society (What is an individual's or government's responsibility?)

- Choices (How do you make a good decision?)

- Dualities (Taking care of others versus taking care of oneself, Success versus failure, etc.)

Brainstorm ideas. Your brainstorm could take the form of a free write (i.e., you write ideas as they come to you), a list you compose quickly (use the provided scratch paper), or a concept map.

Make a brief outline. The outline might be as simple as numbering your brainstorm list, or it could follow something like the example that follows (for an Argumentative essay):

Introduction (what you will argue, which relates directly to the prompt and contains your thesis—your statement that narrows the topic and asserts something about it).

Support:

Claim 1. _____

Support: _____

Claim 2. _____

Support: _____

Claim 3. _____

Support: _____

Counterclaims (in Argumentative essay) _____

Support: _____

Conclusion (restate your thesis in a new way; cast a note of hope at the end or describe further work that must be done in this area; end with a strong final sentence).

Step 2: Write (20 minutes)

Check your time. When you practice writing the essays, use a watch and check in to see which stage(s) slow your progress.

Step 3: Revise/Edit (5 minutes)

Proofread. Make sure your grammar, punctuation, and spelling are acceptable; that you have not repeated yourself; that your word choices are on track; and that you have effectively used transitional words and phrases.

Now let's look at a sample of each type of essay to get a sense of how the process works with a live prompt.

Argumentative Prompt

DIRECTIONS: Discuss the extent to which you agree or disagree with this opinion. Support your views with specific reasons and examples from your own experience, observations, or reading.

Read the opinion below:

> Many public schools across the United States ban students from wearing hats and hoods in school, except for medical or religious purposes. Do you agree or disagree with this policy? Plan and write an essay in which you develop your view on this issue. Support your argument with reasons and examples taken from your reading, studies, experiences, and observations.

That's the prompt. Now Let's apply the process we sketched earlier.

**Read the assignment carefully.** Do you agree or disagree with the policy to prevent students from wearing hats and hoods?

a. Agree

b. Disagree

c. Qualify—I agree in part with the policy.

Brainstorm ideas.

- Not sure of my position—I see both sides.

- It's an issue of law and justice.

- Students should have some say in what goes on at school. In college, no one cares (as far as I know).

- The policy could be tried and then revisited based on what happens.

- Maybe there's a compromise such as allowing hats and hoods to be worn in the hallways and cafeterias of schools but not in the classroom.

- Young people need to be respected and to test social boundaries to live within those boundaries.

- Wait, we live in the real world, and school is supposed to reflect that. In the real world, it's unprofessional to wear hats or hoods indoors.

- Yes, but in the real world, companies such as Amazon and Google let workers come to work in jeans and sweatshirts.

- Why do students wear hats? Some students may wear them to represent a gang, while others do it for fashion or even to cover bad hair days.

- Does the First Amendment protect students' rights to dress how they wish in school?

Make a brief outline.

Introduction: Hook the reader with a question, image, differing perspective, or quotation. Then present the debate. Thesis: Hats and hoods should be permitted in the hallways and cafeterias of schools but not in the classroom.

Claim 1: While some students may wear hats and hoods to represent a gang, the vast majority wear them for fashion or to cover bad hair days.

Support: Examples from personal experience (friends who have used hats or hoods to cover up for bad hair days, days when it's cold and students want to wear their hoods up to protect against the wind/temperature, etc.)

Claim 2: The Constitution protects a student's right to wear hats and hoods.

Support: Cite the First Amendment and explain how it is freedom of speech to dress as one wants to dress.

Claim 3: Young people need to be respected and to test social boundaries to live within those boundaries.

Support: Describe boundaries in psychology and how it is important for individuals to express themselves to mature.

Opposing arguments: We live in the real world, and school is supposed to reflect that. In the real world, it's unprofessional to wear hats or hoods. However, in the real world, companies such as Amazon and Google let workers come to work in jeans and sweatshirts. Students need to be trusted to exercise their own judgment.

Conclusion: The policy could be revisited based on what happens after it's adopted. It might be an age-appropriate issue.

Write your essay.

It would benefit our schools to allow hats and hoods in the hallways and cafeterias but not in the classrooms. Banning them restricts the student's freedom of expression. Moreover, society is changing, and students need to learn how to operate in the real world to be successful. Limiting hats and hoods in the classrooms will not only create a better learning environment, but also will help prepare students for the future.

Schools should look at why students wear hats and hoods. A stereotype portrays students who cover their heads as gang members. This is unfair. The vast majority of students wear hats and hoods to express their fashion sense. Students also wear hats and hoods to conceal a "bad hair day" or maybe even a bad haircut or color.

One benefit of allowing hats and hoods in the halls and cafeterias is to let students express their freedom of speech. The First Amendment of the U.S. Constitution says people have the right to express themselves as they choose. Opponents may claim that if the First Amendment applies in the hallways and cafeterias, it would extend to classrooms as well. However, there are limits to free speech. For instance, you cannot infringe upon the rights of others, and in this case, hats and hoods might distract other students from learning.

Another important benefit of adopting this policy in the schools would be to let students express themselves within social boundaries. In psychology, we learn that the journey from adolescence into adulthood requires young people to form their own beliefs, opinions, and attitudes that transcend the "rules" given by an "authority." Allowing freedom of expression through their attire outside of the classroom allows young people to mature within the guidelines or rules of the school. Since the policy is reasonable, it encourages students to have the "best of both worlds": They won't be distracted in the classroom by fellow students when they are trying to concentrate, and they will have the choice to express themselves and to mature outside of the classroom.

Opponents might argue that since hats and hoods are inappropriate for the workplace, allowing students to wear them in hallways and cafeterias fails to prepare them for life beyond school. However, the workplace is changing. In the real world, companies like Amazon and Google let workers come to work in jeans and sweatshirts. Work has a site-specific dress code. Some companies require suits and uniforms, but others have employees working from home in their pajamas. Students should be trusted to exercise their own judgment in deciding what they wear to school.

For several reasons, our schools should allow personal expression via fashion within the school setting. Likewise, teachers and administrators should pay less attention to how people look and put more emphasis on what they are learning. This compromise should be revisited by individual schools based on how it works in practice. It also may be an age-appropriate issue, and the policy then should reflect the age of the students.

Revise/Edit. In this example, the writer uses correct grammar and sentence structure. The writing would be strengthened if the writer paid attention to Point of View (eliminate references to "I" and "you" by putting the entire argument in third person). The second paragraph lacks relevant examples and support for the claim. Transitions are adequate.

Reviewing a Sample Argumentative Essay

(This essay demonstrates "clear competence" and would earn a score of 5.)

It would be beneficial for our schools to allow hats and hoods in the hallways and cafeterias but not in the classrooms. Banning them restricts the individual student's freedom of expression. Moreover, society is changing, and students need to learn how to operate in the real world in order to be successful. Limiting hats and hoods in the classrooms not only will create a better learning environment, but also will help prepare students for their futures.

It is important to look at why students wear hats and hoods in the first place. There is a stereotype that students who wear caps or head coverings are in gangs. This stereotype is not valid. The vast majority of students wear hats and hoods to express their individual sense of fashion. Students also wear hats and hoods to conceal a "bad hair day" or perhaps even a bad haircut or color.

One benefit of allowing hats and hoods in the halls and cafeterias is that it allows students to express their freedom of speech. Clearly, the First Amendment of the U.S. Constitution states that individuals are entitled by the government to express themselves as they choose. Some may claim that if the First Amendment applies in the hallways and cafeterias, it also applies in the classrooms. However, there are limits to free speech. For instance, one cannot infringe upon the rights of others, and in this case, hats and hoods might distract other students from learning.

Another important benefit of adopting this policy in the schools would be that it would allow students to express themselves within social boundaries. Psychology teaches us that the journey from adolescence into adulthood requires young people to form their own beliefs, opinions, and attitudes that transcend the "rules" given by an "authority." This policy of allowing freedom of expression through one's attire outside of the classroom allows a young person to grow up within the guidelines or rules of the school. Since the policy is reasonable, it encourages students to have the "best of both worlds": They won't be distracted in the classroom by fellow students when they are trying to concentrate, and they will have the choice to express themselves and mature outside of the classroom.

Critics might argue that since hats and hoods are not appropriate for the workplace, allowing students to wear them in hallways and cafeterias is not preparing them for "real life." However, the workplace is changing. Companies such as Amazon and Google let workers come to work in jeans and sweatshirts. Work really has a site-specific dress code. Some companies require suits and uniforms, but others have employees working from home often in their pajamas. Students should be trusted to exercise their own judgment, and that includes what they wear to school.

For several reasons our schools should allow personal expression within the school setting. Likewise, teachers and administrators should pay less attention to how people look and put more emphasis on learning itself. This compromise should be revisited by individual schools based on how it works in practice. It also may be an age-appropriate issue, and the policy may need to reflect the age of the students involved.

Analysis

The writer introduces a precise, thoughtful, original, and even-handed thesis. The organization is logical and includes a discussion of counterarguments, reasons, and evidence. Transitions are used well. The tone is formal and objective. The writer shows good command of the conventions of standard written English. One weakness is that paragraph 3 goes a little off course from the topic and is wordy. A new idea about pressure on students also is introduced in the conclusion, which isn't appropriate. While running on the long side at 529 words, this essay would earn a score of 5.

Now let's practice again using the Informative/Explanatory Essay. This essay will always require you to use two sources; we use only one here as a skill-building exercise.

Informative/Explanatory Prompt

DIRECTIONS: The following assignment requires you to use information from source material to discuss the most important concerns that related to a specific issue. When paraphrasing or quoting from the source, cite it by referring to the author's last name, the title, or any other clear identifier.

Some of the most successful people in the world had to lose everything to make progress. What do you think loss teaches us? What are the primary lessons that come from losing everything? Consider the poem by Elizabeth Bishop. Then, plan and write an essay that develops your view on this issue. Support your position with reasons and examples taken from the following text, your studies, and your experiences with and observations of others.

Source

"One Art" by Elizabeth Bishop

The art of losing isn't hard to master;
so many things seem filled with the intent
to be lost that their loss is no disaster.

Lose something every day. Accept the fluster
of lost door keys, the hour badly spent.
The art of losing isn't hard to master.

Then practice losing farther, losing faster:
places, and names, and where it was you meant
to travel. None of these will bring disaster.

I lost my mother's watch. And look! my last, or
next-to-last, of three loved houses went.
The art of losing isn't hard to master.

I lost two cities, lovely ones. And, vaster,
some realms I owned, two rivers, a continent.
I miss them, but it wasn't a disaster.

—Even losing you (the joking voice, a gesture
I love) I shan't have lied. It's evident
the art of losing's not too hard to master
though it may look like (*Write* it!) like disaster.

Source: Elizabeth Bishop, "One Art" from *The Complete Poems 1927–1979* (New York: Farrar, Straus and Giroux, 1983). Copyright © 1979, 1983 by Alice Helen Methfessel. Reprinted with the permission of Farrar, Straus & Giroux, LLC.

Remember our steps.

Read the prompt carefully. What do you think loss teaches us?

Loss teaches us to be strong and to make the best of what we have because life is short.

Brainstorm ideas.

• Loss makes us appreciate what we have.

• We don't lose things as much as we let them go.

• "The art of losing isn't hard to master"—in that line she says loss is part of life.

• Some people lose their memories in Alzheimer's. My great-aunt had this.

- I remember when my dad lost his wedding ring in the ocean and how mad my mom was.

- You can lose an important place in your life like high school when it's over.

- Probably the worst thing to lose is another person, which can even include yourself.

- What do these types of losses teach us? To be strong and to value each and every moment we have.

- Maybe I could organize by dividing between things, places, and people lost?

Make a brief outline. The outline might be as simple as numbering your brainstorm list, or it could follow a form like the following:

Introduction: Your hook could be the Elizabeth Bishop line, "The art of losing isn't hard to master."

Thesis: People lose things, places, other people, and themselves. It makes them stronger and more appreciative of what they have. It also forces them to let things go.

Claim 1: Sometimes we lose important items.

Support: My dad lost his wedding band in the Atlantic Ocean. Mom was mad—what did they learn?

Claim 2: Other times, we lose places because we have to move on.

Support: When I graduated high school, I had to grow up.

Claim 3: The most difficult losses we experience are those of loved ones and even of ourselves.

Support: I lost my best friend when she started hanging out with the wrong kind of people. I lost myself when I was dating Joe.

Conclusion: Sometimes when you lose something, you find something even better. You grow to become more of who you actually are.

Write your essay.

In her poem "One Art," Elizabeth Bishop explains that "the art of losing isn't hard to master." Bishop says it is easy to get good at learning how to lose things because it happens often. The poet is right. People lose things, places, other people, and even themselves. This makes them stronger and more appreciative of what they have. It also forces them to let things go.

We sometimes lose important items. My dad lost his wedding band in the Atlantic Ocean. I don't think I've seen my mother more angry and sad at the same time. But she calmed down over time and they bought a new ring. Losing the ring taught us not to wear valuables in the ocean and, more importantly, that love isn't based on material objects. Dad doesn't need a wedding band to show the world he loves Mom. He just loves her, and everyone can see that.

We also lose places because we have to move on. When I graduated high school, I lost not just the physical building but also the experiences there. I'm losing my sense of innocence and childhood. I will have to take responsibility now.

The most difficult losses we experience are those of loved ones and even of ourselves. I lost my best friend when she started hanging out with the wrong people. She was smoking pot, and I had to let her go because if I held onto her, it meant I approved of her choices and I didn't. I learned that not everything can be fixed with love. You can love someone, and they can be bad for you. In contrast, I lost myself when I was involved in an abusive relationship with my boyfriend. He would put me down and never encouraged me. By talking it over with my mom, I realized that I was better off on my own and that I could survive without him.

When we lose something, we sometimes find something better. We grow to become more of who we are.

Revise/Edit. Upon reading it to herself, the writer sees the conclusion and paragraph 3 are too short as is. She expands the essay in these two areas, and she adds a title.

Here's how it looks now. This essay shows "some competence" but is flawed and would earn a score of 3. As you read it, see where it falls short; then read the analysis that follows.

Loss

In her poem "One Art," Elizabeth Bishop explains that "the art of losing isn't hard to master." Bishop is saying that it is easy to get good at learning how to lose things because it happens all of the time. Bishop is right. People lose things, places, other people, and even themselves. This makes them stronger and more appreciative of what they have. It also forces them to let things go.

Sometimes we lose important items. For instance, my dad lost his wedding band in the Atlantic Ocean. I don't think I've seen my mother more angry and sad at the same time. As time passed, though, she calmed down and they decided to buy a new ring. It made all of us stronger. We learned not only that we shouldn't wear valuables in the ocean but also that love isn't just based on material objects. My dad doesn't need a wedding band for the world to know that he loves my mom. He just loves her, and everyone can see that.

Other times, we lose places because we have to move on. For instance, when I graduated high school, I knew I was losing not just that physical building but also all of the experiences that I had there. I'm losing my sense of innocence and childhood. I will have to take responsibility now. I know that I will have my friends but it will never be the same as when we were in school together. That experience is over.

The most difficult losses we experience are those of loved ones and even of ourselves. For instance, I lost my best friend when she started hanging out with the wrong kind of people. She was smoking pot, and I had to let her go because if I held onto her, it meant that I was approving of her choices and I wasn't. I learned that not everything can be fixed with love. You can love someone, and they can still be bad for you. In contrast, I lost myself when I was involved in an abusive relationship. My partner would put me down and never encouraged me. By talking it over with my mom, I realized that I was better off on my own and that I could survive without that kind of a relationship.

When you lose something, you sometimes find something better. You grow to become more of who you are. Don't be afraid of loss. It will strengthen you!

Analysis

The writer of this piece introduces a formulaic thesis. The organization is clear and uses examples to develop ideas. Transitions are used reasonably well, but the tone is informal. The writer shows some familiarity with the conventions of standard written English, but errs in verb conjugation. Paragraph 3 has a switch in verb tense from past to present to future. In paragraph 4, the writer fails to use the past conditional to denote a past situation or action that never happened, as seen in this phrase: "...I had to let her go because if I held onto her, it meant that I was approving of her choices and I wasn't." (The writer should have said, "... if I *had* held onto her, it *would have* meant that I was approving of her choices *even though I wasn't*.")

Other shortcomings include quoting Bishop's poem directly only once in the essay. Furthermore, the writer fails to cite the line from the poem. Proper citation is a prime factor in earning a good score. (In fact, failure to cite or otherwise acknowledge sources when paraphrasing or quoting automatically caps your score at a meager 2. So "cite as you write" should be your mantra.) The phrase "For instance" is repeated too often in the text. The conclusion can be linked back to the hook. The essay also abruptly switches to second person at the end. Also abrupt is the imperative last sentence, which signals a big shift in point of view inconsistent with the rest of the essay. Finally, titles are not necessary, and this one is vague. This middling essay would earn a score of 3.

Language and Research Skills

This chapter covers what you can expect on the selected-response section of the Praxis Core Writing test. The questions in this section will assess your grasp of grammar and usage, along with research skills. Forty* multiple-choice questions ask you to show your command of standard written English.

The selected-response, or multiple-choice, questions are divided into four sections: Usage, Sentence Correction, Revision in Context, and Research Skills.

USAGE

In English, words and sentences are put together to convey meaning. Grammar is the system of rules we follow to do that. However, within grammar, ways of speaking and writing can vary and may indicate cultural background, education level, geographic region, and even social status. These conventions are known as **usage**. Usage shows socially preferred ways for language to be communicated.

To understand usage, you need to lay the foundation with **mechanics.** This is the nuts and bolts of writing, and includes punctuation and capitalization. After mechanics we'll get into grammatical/structural relationships, the glue that allows sentences and paragraphs to cohere and that allows you to communicate your ideas. Next we'll cover idiomatic language, which poses unique challenges because it can't be explained based on either grammatical rules or its constituent parts. Finally, we'll talk about diction, or word choice.

---

*This number may vary according to how many unscored (pretest) questions appear on the test form you're given. You won't know which questions aren't scored.

Each section ends with a short series of practice exercises to reinforce your review, one skill at a time.

In a mechanics question, you will be given a sentence with four underlined parts, and you will have to decide whether the sentence is correct (in which case, you should indicate "no error") or if part of it has an error in **punctuation** or **capitalization**.

Capitalization

While emails, social media posts, and smartphone texts may make it seem otherwise, when a word is capitalized, it should be for a good reason. There are standard uses for capital letters.

 HINT

In general, you should capitalize:

- All proper nouns
- The first word of a sentence
- The first word of a direct quotation

Here are some specific tips on when and what to capitalize.

Names of ships, aircraft, spacecraft, and trains:

Airbus A380	Sputnik II
DC-10	USS North Carolina
Apollo 13	SS United States
Mariner IV	Eurail

Names of deities:

Allah	Jehovah
Buddha	Jupiter
God	Shiva
Holy Ghost	Venus

Geological periods:

Cambrian Period	Ice Age
Cenozoic Era	Pleistocene Epoch

Names of astronomical bodies:

Big Dipper	Milky Way
Halley's Comet	North Star
Mercury	Ursa Major

Personifications:

Reliable Nature brought her promised Spring.

Bring on Melancholy in his sad night.

The restless smartphone roused me from my slumber.

Historical periods:

Age of Louis XIV	Reign of Terror
Christian Era	Roaring Twenties
Great Depression	Renaissance
Great Recession	World War I
Middle Ages	

Organizations, associations, and institutions:

Common Market	National Trust for Historic Preservation
European Space Agency	New York Philharmonic
Franklin Glen High School	North Atlantic Treaty Organization
Girl Scouts	North Carolina Tar Heels
Kiwanis Club	Smithsonian Institution
League of Women Voters	Unitarian Church
Library of Congress	University of Miami

Government and judicial groups:

Arkansas Supreme Court	Sausalito City Council
Census Bureau	Senate Committee on Foreign Affairs
House of Representatives	United States Court of Appeal
Parliament	U.S. Department of State
Peace Corps	

A general term that accompanies a specific name is capitalized only if it follows the specific name. If it stands alone or comes before the specific name, it is put in lowercase:

Washington State	the state of Washington
Prime Minister Harper	the prime minister of Canada
President Obama	the president of the United States
Golden Gate Park	the park
Cooper River Bridge	the bridge
Pope Francis	the pope
Queen Elizabeth II	the queen of England
Mojave Desert	the desert
Monroe Doctrine	the United States' doctrine of expansion
Mississippi River	the river
Easter Day	the day
Treaty of Versailles	the treaty
Merriam-Webster's Dictionary	the dictionary

Use a capital letter to start a sentence:

Our car would not start.

When will you leave? I need to know right away.

Never!

Let me in! Please!

When a sentence appears within a sentence, start it with a capital letter:

We had only one concern: When would we eat?

My sister said, "I'll find the Monopoly game."

He answered, "We can only stay a few minutes."

The most important words of titles are capitalized. Those words not capitalized are conjunctions (*and*, *or*, *but*) and short prepositions (*of*, *on*, *by*, *for*). The first and last word of a title must always be capitalized:

A Man for All Seasons	"Cello Sonata in G Minor"
Crime and Punishment	"Let Me In"
Of Mice and Men	"Ode to Billy Joe"
Rise of the West	"Rubaiyat of Omar Khayyam"
Strange Life of Ivan Osokin	"All in the Family"

Capitalize newspaper and magazine names:

U.S. News & World Report	The New York Times
National Geographic	The Washington Post
San Jose Mercury News	

Capitalize broadcasting operations:

ABC News	KNX Newsradio
Cable News Network	NBC Sports
CBC Television	WBOP

Do *not* capitalize the seasons:

spring	autumn
winter	summer

Do *not* capitalize compass directions unless you're naming a region:

west	east
north	south

Capitalize regions:

Finger Lakes Wine Country

Eastern Europe

San Francisco Bay Area

But: the south of France

Downeast

the western edge of town

the West

Capitalize specific military units:

U.S. Army

German Navy

7th Fleet

1st Infantry Division

Capitalize political groups and philosophies:

Democratic Party

Socialist Party

Green Party

Whig Party

Know-Nothing Party

Federalist Party

Marxist

Existentialism

Republican Party

Transcendentalism

Also **capitalize political-party nicknames**

Grand Old Party (abbreviated *GOP*)

But **do not capitalize systems of government or individual adherents to a philosophy:**

agnostic

democracy

communism

fascist

socialist (a person who believes in socialism but is not necessarily a member of the Socialist Party)

Summary: Things to Capitalize*

- The first word of a sentence
- The first word in a sentence that is a direct quote (e.g., He said, "**T**he sky is blue.")
- The first word following a colon if there's a complete sentence after the colon (e.g., Suzi's early arrival at the airport did not matter: **T**he plane was still late).
- Proper nouns (names of relatives; e.g., I received a check from **A**unt Mary and my other aunt. She spoke to **F**ather but not to her mother.)
- Countries (e.g., **B**razil, **S**outh **A**frica)
- Team names and political parties (e.g., **N**ew **Y**ork **M**ets, the **R**epublicans)
- Titles (in government; of books, articles, songs)
- Historical periods (e.g., the **E**nlightenment)
- Gods, deities, holy figures, holy books
- Regions (e.g., **N**ortheast, **S**outhern **H**emisphere, **M**icronesia)
- Names of planets (e.g., **S**aturn)
- Brand and trade names (e.g., **P**roctor **S**ilex, **P**raxis tests)
- Salutations (e.g., "**D**ear Julio")
- Acronyms and Abbreviations (e.g., **FBI**, Navy **SEAL**)

_____

* Adapted from *http://www.towson.edu/ows/capitalization_rules.htm*

Practice Exercises: Capitalization

DIRECTIONS: Choose the response option that correctly uses capitalization. The underscored portions show you where errors may exist. If there is no error, select choice (D). Answers appear on pages 368–369.

1. Mexico is the southernmost country in <u>North America</u>. It borders the United States on the north; it is bordered on the <u>south</u> by Belize and Guatemala.

    (A) north America . . . South

    (B) North America . . . South

    (C) North america . . . south

    (D) No error

2. Until 1989, Tom Landry was the only <u>coach</u> the National <u>football</u> League's Dallas <u>cowboys</u> ever had.

   (A) Until 1989, Tom Landry was the only Coach the national Football League's Dallas cowboys ever had.

   (B) Until 1989, Tom Landry was the only coach the National Football League's Dallas Cowboys ever had.

   (C) Until 1989, Tom Landry was the only Coach the National Football league's Dallas Cowboys ever had.

   (D) No error

3. The Northern <u>Hemisphere</u> is the half of the <u>earth</u> that lies north of the <u>Equator</u>.

   (A) Northern hemisphere . . . earth . . . equator

   (B) Northern hemisphere . . . Earth . . . Equator

   (C) Northern Hemisphere . . . earth . . . equator

   (D) No error

4. My favorite works by Ernest Hemingway are "<u>The Snows of Kilimanjaro</u>," <u>*The Sun Also Rises,*</u> and <u>*For Whom the Bell Tolls*</u>.

   (A) My favorite works by Ernest Hemingway are "The Snows of Kilimanjaro," *The Sun Also Rises,* and *For Whom The Bell Tolls.*

   (B) My favorite works by Ernest Hemingway are "The Snows of Kilimanjaro," *The Sun also Rises,* and *For whom the Bell Tolls.*

   (C) My favorite works by Ernest Hemingway are "the Snows of Kilimanjaro," *the Sun also Rises,* and *for Whom the Bell Tolls*

   (D) No error

5. Aphrodite (<u>Venus</u> in <u>Roman Mythology</u>) was the <u>Greek</u> goddess of love.

   (A) Venus in Roman mythology . . . greek

   (B) venus in roman mythology . . . Greek

   (C) Venus in Roman mythology . . . Greek

   (D) No error

6. The <u>Torah</u> is considered by <u>Jews</u> to be the holy word.

   (A) torah . . . jews

   (B) torah . . . Jews

   (C) Torah . . . jews

   (D) No error

7. The <u>freshman</u> curriculum at the <u>Community College</u> includes <u>English</u>, a foreign language, <u>Algebra I</u>, and <u>History</u>.

    (A) The freshman curriculum at the community college includes english, a foreign language, Algebra I, and history.

    (B) The freshman curriculum at the community college includes English, a foreign language, Algebra I, and history.

    (C) The Freshman curriculum at the Community College includes English, a foreign language, Algebra I, and History.

    (D) No error.

8. At the <u>spring</u> graduation ceremonies, the university awarded more than 2,000 <u>bachelor's</u> degrees.

    (A) Spring . . . Bachelor's

    (B) spring . . . Bachelor's

    (C) Spring . . . bachelor's

    (D) No error

9. The fall of the <u>Berlin wall</u> was an important symbol of the collapse of <u>Communism</u>.

    (A) berlin Wall . . . communism

    (B) Berlin Wall . . . communism

    (C) berlin wall . . . Communism

    (D) No error

10. <u>National Geographic</u> reported that NASA's <u>curiosity</u> rover team revealed what the <u>magazine</u> termed "surprising spikes in methane gas."

    (A) National Geographic . . . *Curiosity* . . . *magazine*

    (B) National Geographic . . . *Curiosity* . . . *Magazine*

    (C) National geographic . . . *curiosity* . . . *magazine*

    (D) No error

Punctuation

Commas

Commas should be placed according to standard rules of punctuation for purpose, clarity, and effect.

Here's a guide to the proper use of commas.

In a series:

When more than one adjective describes a noun, use a comma to separate and emphasize each adjective. The comma takes the place of the word "and" in the series.

> the long, dark passageway
>
> another confusing, sleepless night
>
> an elaborate, complex, brilliant plan
>
> the old, grey, crumpled hat

 HINT

Some adjective–noun combinations are treated as one word. In these cases, the adjective in front of the adjective–noun combination needs no comma. How do you know when you're dealing with such a thing? There's a simple rule: If you were to insert the word "and" between the adjective-noun combination, it would not make sense.

Consider these examples:

- a stately oak tree
- an exceptional wine glass
- her worst report card

The comma is used to separate words, phrases, and whole ideas (clauses); it takes the place of "and" when used this way.

Examples:

> an apple, a pear, a fig, and a banana
>
> a lovely lady, an elegant dress, and many admirers
>
> She lowered the shade, closed the curtain, turned off the light, and went to bed.

The only question that exists about the use of commas in a series is whether one should be used before the final item. The utility of the serial, or Oxford, comma is debated. Be sure to use it, however, when its omission could result in confusion.

INCORRECT: He got on his horse, tracked a rabbit, an elk and a deer and rode on to Canton.

CORRECT: He got on his horse, tracked a rabbit, an elk, and a deer, and rode on to Canton.

With a long introductory phrase:

Usually if a phrase of more than five or six words or a dependent clause precedes the subject at the beginning of a sentence, a comma is used to set it off.

After last night's fiasco at the club, she couldn't bear the thought of looking at him again.

Whenever I try to talk about politics, my son leaves the room.

Provided you stay mum, they will never guess who you are.

It is usually not necessary to use a comma with a short sentence (with an introductory phrase of less than four words).

Examples:

In January she will go to Switzerland.

After I rest I'll feel better.

During the day no one is home.

If an introductory phrase includes a verb form that is being used as another part of speech (a *verbal*), it must be followed by a comma.

INCORRECT: When eating Mary never looked up from her plate.

CORRECT: When eating, Mary never looked up from her plate.

INCORRECT: Because of her desire to follow her faith in James wavered.

CORRECT: Because of her desire to follow, her faith in James wavered.

INCORRECT: Having decided to leave Mary James wrote her a letter.

CORRECT: Having decided to leave Mary, James wrote her a letter.

To separate sentences with two main ideas:

To understand this use of the comma, you need to be able to recognize compound sentences. When a sentence contains more than two subjects and verbs (clauses), and the two clauses are joined by a conjunction (*and, but, or, nor, for, yet*), use a comma before the conjunction to show that another clause is coming.

Examples:

I thought I knew the poem by heart, but he showed me three lines I had forgotten.

Are we really interested in helping the children, or are we more concerned with protecting our good names?

He is supposed to leave tomorrow, but he is not ready to go.

Jim knows you are disappointed, and he has known it for a long time.

If the two parts of the sentence are short and closely related, it is not necessary to use a comma.

Examples:

He threw the ball and the dog ran after it.

Jane played the piano and Michael danced.

Be careful not to confuse a sentence that has a compound verb and a single subject with a compound sentence. If the subject is the same for both verbs and not included again in the second clause, there is no need for a comma.

INCORRECT: Charles sent some flowers, and wrote a long letter explaining why he had not been able to attend.

CORRECT: Charles sent some flowers and wrote a long letter explaining why he had not been able to attend.

INCORRECT: Last Thursday we went to the concert with Julia, and afterwards dined at an old Italian restaurant.

CORRECT: Last Thursday we went to the concert with Julia and afterwards dined at an old Italian restaurant.

INCORRECT: For the third time, the teacher explained that the literacy level for high school students was much lower than it had been in previous years, and, this time, wrote the statistics on the board for everyone to see.

CORRECT: For the third time, the teacher explained that the literacy level for high school students was much lower than it had been in previous years and this time wrote the statistics on the board for everyone to see.

In general, words and phrases that stop the flow of the sentence or are unnecessary for the main idea are set off by commas.

Abbreviations after names:

Did you invite John Paul, Jr., and his sister?

Martha Harris, Ph.D., will be the speaker tonight.

Interjections (an exclamation without added grammatical connection):

Oh, I'm so glad to see you.

I tried so hard, alas, to do it.

Hey, let me out of here.

Direct address:

Roy, won't you open the door for the dog?

I can't understand, Mother, what you are trying to say.

May I ask, Mr. President, why you called us together?

Hey, lady, watch out for that car!

Tag questions:

You're really hungry, aren't you?

Jerry looks like his father, doesn't he?

Geographical names and addresses:

The concert will take place in Medina, Ohio, on August 12.

Transitional words and phrases:

On the other hand, I hope he gets better.

In addition, the phone rang constantly this afternoon.

I'm, nevertheless, going to the beach on Sunday.

You'll find, therefore, that no one is more loyal than I am.

Parenthetical words and phrases:

We know, *of course*, that this is the only thing to do.

In fact, I planted corn last summer.

The Trudeau affair was, *to put it mildly*, a shock.

He may have had a shaky start as a military strategist, but Winston Churchill, *there is little doubt,* became a great statesman.

Unusual word order:

The dress, new and crisp, hung in the closet.

Intently, she stared out the window.

With nonrestrictive elements:

Parts of a sentence that modify other parts are sometimes essential to the meaning of the sentence and sometimes not. When a modifying word or group of words is not vital to the meaning of the sentence, it is *nonessential*, and is set off by commas. Since it does not restrict the meaning of the words it modifies, it is called "nonrestrictive."

Modifiers that are *essential* to the meaning of the sentence are called "restrictive" and are not set off by commas.

ESSENTIAL:	The girl *who wrote the story* is my sister.
NONESSENTIAL:	My sister, *the girl who wrote the story*, has always loved to write.
ESSENTIAL:	The farmstand featuring pasture-raised lamb is open late on Thursdays. (This example tells readers which of two or more farmstands the writer means.)
NONESSENTIAL:	The farmstand, featuring pasture-raised lamb, is open late on Thursdays. (In this example, the phrase set off by commas merely adds information about a particular farmstand, a fact that would be known from the context.)
ESSENTIAL:	The cup *that is on the piano* is the one I want.
NONESSENTIAL:	The cup, *which my brother gave me last year*, is on the piano.
ESSENTIAL:	The people *who arrived late* were not seated.
NONESSENTIAL:	George, *who arrived late*, was not seated.

To set off direct quotations:

Most direct quotes or quoted materials are set off from the rest of the sentence by commas.

"Please read your part more loudly," the director insisted.

"I won't know what to do," said Michael, "if you leave me."

The teacher said sternly, "I will not dismiss this class until I have silence."

Who was it who said, "Do not ask for whom the bell tolls; it tolls for thee"?

 HINT

In U.S. English, commas always go inside the closing quotation mark, even if the comma is not part of the material being quoted. For example: "I can assure you that what you will observe is a vast wasteland," Newton Minow said of television programming in 1961.

Be careful not to set off indirect quotes or quotes that are used as subjects or complements, as shown here:

"To be or not to be" is the famous beginning of a soliloquy in Shakespeare's *Hamlet*. (subject)

She said she would never come back. (indirect quote)

In 1961, Newton Minow asserted that television was largely devoid of enterprising programming. (indirect quote)

Back then my favorite poem was "Evangeline." (complement)

To set off contrasting elements:

Her intelligence, not her beauty, got her the job.

Your plan will take you a little farther from, rather than closer to, your destination.

It was a reasonable, though not appealing, idea.

He wanted glory, but found happiness instead.

In dates:

Both forms of the date are acceptable.

She will arrive on December 6, 2018. (U.S. style is month, day, year.)

He left on 5 August 2010. (European style is day month year with no commas.)

In January 2010, he handed in his resignation.

On October 22, 1992, Frank and Julie were married.

Usually, when a **subordinate clause** is at the end of a sentence, no comma is necessary preceding the clause. However, when a subordinate clause introduces a sentence, a comma should be used after the clause. Some common **subordinating conjunctions** are:

after	so that
as	though
as if	till
although	unless
because	until
before	when
even though	whenever
if	while
inasmuch as	

Usually, a comma follows the conjunctive adverb. Note also that a period can be used to separate two sentences joined by a conjunctive adverb.

Some common conjunctive adverbs are:

accordingly	however	next	perhaps
besides	indeed	nonetheless	still
consequently	in fact	now	therefore
finally	moreover	on the other hand	
furthermore	nevertheless	otherwise	

Then is also used as a conjunctive adverb, but it is not usually followed by a comma.

Semicolons

Sometimes a mark stronger than a comma is needed. It becomes a job for the **semicolon,** which is notably helpful when the members of the list are actually groups within groups, requiring the separation of a series of items that have internal commas, as in the trio of "Susan, Ramon and Joan" cited in the following example. Once the semicolons are added, we can properly see Susan, Ramon, and Joan as a unit, or group, of friends, family members, team members, campers, etc.

INCORRECT: We planned the trip with Mary and Harold, Susan, Ramon, and Joan, Gregory and Jesse and Charles.

CORRECT: We planned the trip with Mary and Harold; Susan, Ramon, and Joan; Gregory and Jesse; and Charles.

There's much more to say about the semicolon; it's both a fascinating and troublesome piece of punctuation. But once you understand its purpose in life, it can help you write better essays and score higher on the Praxis Core's usage questions.

Questions testing semicolon usage require you to be able to distinguish between the semicolon and the comma, and the semicolon and the colon. This review section covers the basic uses of the semicolon: to separate independent clauses not joined by a coordinating conjunction, to separate independent clauses separated by a conjunctive adverb, and to separate items in a series with internal commas. It is important to be consistent; if you use a semicolon between *any* of the items in the series, you must use semicolons to separate *all* of the items in the series.

Use a semicolon . . .

> *. . . to separate independent clauses that are not joined by a coordinating conjunction . . .*
>
> I understand how to use commas; the semicolon I have not yet mastered.

> *. . . to separate two independent clauses connected by a conjunctive adverb . . .*
>
> He took great care with his work; *therefore*, he was very successful.

> *. . . to combine two independent clauses connected by a coordinating conjunction if either or both of the clauses contain other internal punctuation . . .*
>
> Some maintain that success in college requires intelligence, industry, and perseverance; others, fewer in number, assert that only personality is important.

> *. . . to separate items in a series when each item has internal punctuation . . .*
>
> I bought an old, dilapidated chair; an antique table, which was in beautiful condition; and a new, ugly, blue and white rug.
>
> Call our customer service line for assistance: Arizona, 1-800-555-6020; New Mexico, 1-800-555-5050; California, 1-800-555-3140; or Nevada, 1-800-555-3214.

Do *not* use a semicolon . . .

> *. . . to separate a dependent and an independent clause . . .*
>
> **INCORRECT:** You should not make such statements; even though they are correct.
>
> **CORRECT:** You should not make such statements even though they are correct.

... to substitute for a comma:

Here's an example in which the semicolon, when improperly used, stops the sentence dead in its tracks.

INCORRECT: My roommate also likes sports; particularly football, basketball, and baseball.

CORRECT: My roommate also likes sports, particularly football, basketball, and baseball.

Do *not* use a semicolon to set off other types of phrases or clauses from a sentence:

INCORRECT: Being of a cynical mind; I should ask for a recount of the ballots.

CORRECT: Being of a cynical mind, I should ask for a recount of the ballots.

INCORRECT: The next meeting of the club has been postponed two weeks; inasmuch as both the president and vice-president are out of town.

CORRECT: The next meeting of the club has been postponed two weeks, inasmuch as both the president and vice-president are out of town.

☞ HINT

The semicolon is not a terminal mark of punctuation; therefore, it should not be followed by a capital letter unless the first word in the second clause ordinarily requires capitalization.

Colons

Colon-usage questions test your knowledge of the colon preceding a list, restatement, or explanation. These questions also require you to be able to distinguish between the colon and the period, the colon and the comma, and the colon and the semicolon.

While it is true that a colon is used to herald a list, care must be taken to ensure that a complete sentence precedes the colon. The colon signals the reader that a list, explanation, or restatement of the preceding will follow. Think of it as an arrow indicating that something else is to follow.

Critically, unlike the semicolon and the period, the colon is not a terminal mark. Look at the following examples:

The Constitution provides for a separation of powers among the three branches of government.

Notice the different impact each of these forms of punctuation (period, semicolon, comma, and colon) makes in this sentence.

government. The period signals a new sentence.

government; The semicolon signals an interrelated sentence.

government, The comma signals a coordinating conjunction followed by another independent clause.

government: The colon signals a list.

Now see the colon at work, introducing a list of the three branches of American government.

Example: The Constitution provides for a separation of powers among the three branches of government: executive, legislative, and judicial.

Ensuring that a complete sentence precedes a colon means following some rules.

Use the colon . . .

. . . to introduce a list (one item may constitute a list) . . .

I hate this one course: English.

Three plays by William Shakespeare will be presented in repertory this summer at the University of Michigan: *Hamlet*, *Macbeth*, and *Othello*.

. . . to introduce a list preceded by "as follows" or "the following" . . .

The reasons she cited for her success are as follows: integrity, honesty, industry, and a pleasant disposition.

. . . to separate two independent clauses, when the second clause is a restatement or explanation of the first . . .

All of my high school teachers said one thing in particular: college is going to be difficult.

. . . to introduce a word or word group that is a restatement, explanation, or summary of the first sentence . . .

These two things he loved: tofu and chickpeas.

. . . to introduce a formal appositive . . .

I am positive there is one appeal that you can't overlook: money.

. . . to separate an appositive phrase or clause from a sentence . . .

INCORRECT: His immediate aim in life is centered on two things; becoming an engineer and learning to fly an airplane.

CORRECT: His immediate aim in life is centered on two things: becoming an engineer and learning to fly an airplane.

☞ HINT

Although the first sentence in the pair of examples above is punctuated correctly, the use of the semicolon provides a miscue, suggesting that the second clause is merely an extension, not an explanation, of the first clause. The colon provides a better clue to where the reader is headed.

WEAK: The first week of camping was wonderful; we lived in cabins instead of tents.

BETTER: The first week of camping was wonderful: We lived in cabins instead of tents.

. . . to separate the introductory words from a quotation that follows, if the quotation is formal, long, or contained in its own paragraph . . .

The actor then stated: "I would rather be able to adequately play the part of Hamlet than to perform a miraculous operation, deliver a great lecture, or build a magnificent skyscraper."

The colon should be used only after statements that are grammatically complete.

Do *not* use a colon after a verb:

INCORRECT: My favorite holidays are: Christmas, the Fourth of July, and Halloween.

CORRECT: My favorite holidays are Christmas, the Fourth of July, and Halloween.

Do *not* use a colon after a preposition:

INCORRECT: I enjoy different ethnic foods such as: Greek, Chinese, and Italian.

CORRECT: I enjoy different ethnic foods such as Greek, Chinese, and Italian.

Do *not* use a colon interchangeably with the dash:

INCORRECT: Mathematics, German, English: These gave me the greatest difficulty of all my studies.

CORRECT: Mathematics, German, English—these gave me the greatest difficulty of all my studies.

Information preceding the colon should be a complete sentence regardless of the explanatory information following the clause.

Do *not* use the colon before the words "for example," "namely," "that is," or "for instance," even though these words may be introducing a list.

> **INCORRECT:** We agreed to adopt Pedro's idea: namely, to throw the boss a surprise party.

> **INCORRECT:** There are a number of well-known American women writers: for example, Nikki Giovanni, Phillis Wheatley, Emily Dickinson, and Maya Angelou.

Apostrophes

Apostrophe questions on the Praxis Core test require you to know when an apostrophe has been used appropriately to make a noun possessive, not plural. Remember the following rules when considering how to show possession.

Add *'s* to singular nouns and indefinite pronouns:

Tiffany's flowers	at the owner's expense
a dog's bark	today's paper
everybody's computer	

Add *'s* to singular nouns ending in *s*, unless this distorts the pronunciation:

Delores's paper	for righteousness' sake
the boss's pen	Dr. Evans's office **OR** Dr. Evans' office

Add *an apostrophe* to plural nouns ending in *s* or *es*:

two cents' worth	thirteen years' experience
ladies' night	two weeks' pay

Add *'s* to plural nouns not ending in s:

men's room

children's toys

Add *'s* to the last word in compound words or groups:

brother-in-law's car

someone else's paper

Add *'s* to the last name when indicating joint ownership or possession:

Joe and Edna's home

Julie and Kathy's party

women and children's clinic

Add *'s* to both names if you intend to show individual possession by each person:

Joe's and Edna's trucks (indicates trucks owned separately)

Julie's and Kathy's pies (indicates separately baked pies)

Ted's and Jane's marriage vows (indicates separate vows to two other people, not each other)

Although it is often used to show possession, the apostrophe is not used to show all forms of possession.

Possessive pronouns change their forms *without* the addition of an apostrophe:

her, his, hers

your, yours

their, theirs

it, its

Use the possessive form of a noun preceding a gerund:

His driving annoys me.

My bowling a strike irked him.

Do you mind our stopping by?

We appreciate your coming.

Add *'s* to words as words and initials to show that they are plural:

no if's, and's, or but's

the do's and don't's of dating

three A's

Add *s* to numbers, symbols, and abbreviations to show that they are plural:

TVs

PCs

the 1800s

the returning POWs

Quotation Marks and Italics

The Praxis Core test assesses your knowledge of the proper use of quotation marks with other marks of punctuation, with titles, and with dialogue. The test also asks you to demonstrate the correct use of italics and underlining with titles and words used as sample words (for example, the word *is* is a common verb).

The most common use of double quotation marks (") is to set off quoted words, phrases, and sentences.

"If everybody minded their own business," said the Duchess in a hoarse growl, "the world would go round a great deal faster than it does."
"Then you would say what you mean," the March Hare went on.

"I do," Alice hastily replied: "at least—at least I mean what I say—that's the same thing, you know."

—from Lewis Carroll's *Alice in Wonderland*

Single quotation marks are used to set off quoted material within a quote.

> "Shall I bring 'Rime of the Ancient Mariner' along with us?" she asked her brother.
>
> Mrs. Green said, "The doctor told me, 'Go to bed as soon as you get home!'"
>
> "If she said that to me," Katherine insisted, "I would tell her, 'I never intend to speak to you again! Goodbye, Susan!'"

When writing dialogue, begin a new paragraph each time the speaker changes.

> "Do you know what time it is?" asked Jane.
>
> "Can't you see I'm busy?" snapped Mary.
>
> "It's easy to see that you're in a bad mood today!" replied Jane.

Use quotation marks to enclose words used as words (sometimes italics are used for this purpose).

> "Judgment" has always been a difficult word for me to spell.
>
> Do you know what "abstruse" means?
>
> "Horse and buggy" and "bread and butter" can be used either as adjectives or as nouns.

If **slang** is used within more formal writing, the slang words or phrases should be set off with quotation marks.

> Harrison's decision to leave the conference and to "stick his neck out" by flying to Jamaica was applauded by the rest of the conference attendees.

When words are meant to have an unusual or specific significance to the reader, for instance irony or humor, they are sometimes placed in quotation marks.

> For years, women were not allowed to buy real estate in order to "protect" them from unscrupulous dealers.
>
> The "conversation" resulted in one black eye and a broken nose.

To set off titles of TV shows, poems, stories, and book chapters, use quotation marks. (Book, motion picture, newspaper, and magazine titles are underlined when handwritten and italicized when published.)

> The article "Moving South in the Southern Rain," by Jergen Smith in the *Southern News*, attracted the attention of our editor.
>
> The assignment is "Childhood Development," Chapter 18 of *Human Behavior*.
>
> My favorite essay by Montaigne is "On Silence."
>
> "Happy Days" led the TV ratings for years, didn't it?
>
> You will find Keats's "Ode on a Grecian Urn" in Chapter 8 in Cody's *A Selection from the Great English Poets* (Chicago: A.C. McClurg & Company, 1905).

Errors to avoid with quotation marks . . .

Remember that quotation marks always come in pairs. Do not make the mistake of using only one set and forgetting about the corresponding pair. If you open quotes, you also have to close them.

> **INCORRECT:** "You'll never convince me to move to the city, said Thurman. I consider it an insane asylum."

> **CORRECT:** "You'll never convince me to move to the city," said Thurman. "I consider it an insane asylum."

> **INCORRECT:** "Idleness and pride tax with a heavier hand than kings and parliaments," Benjamin Franklin is supposed to have said. If we can get rid of the former, we may easily bear the latter."

> **CORRECT:** "Idleness and pride tax with a heavier hand than kings and parliaments," Benjamin Franklin is supposed to have said. "If we can get rid of the former, we may easily bear the latter."

When a quote consists of several sentences, do not put the quotation marks at the beginning and end of each sentence; put them at the beginning and end of the entire quotation.

> **INCORRECT:** "It was during his student days in Bonn that Beethoven fastened upon Schiller's poem." "The heady sense of liberation in the verses must have appealed to him." "They appealed to every German."—John Burke

> **CORRECT:** "It was during his student days in Bonn that Beethoven fastened upon Schiller's poem. The heady sense of liberation in the verses must have appealed to him. They appealed to every German."—John Burke

Instead of setting off a long quote with quotation marks, if it is longer than five or six lines you may want to indent and single space it. If you do indent, do not use quotation marks.

In his *First Inaugural Address*, Abraham Lincoln appeals to the war-torn American people:

> We are not enemies, but friends. We must not be enemies. Though passion may have strained, it must not break, our bonds of affection. The mystic chords of memory, stretching from every battlefield and patriot grave to every living heart and hearthstone all over this broad land, will yet swell the chorus of the Union when again touched, as surely they will be, by the better angels of our nature.

Be careful not to use quotation marks with indirect quotations.

INCORRECT: Mary wondered "if she would get over it."

CORRECT: Mary wondered if she would get over it.

INCORRECT: The nurse asked "how long it had been since we had visited the doctor's office."

CORRECT: The nurse asked how long it had been since we had visited the doctor's office.

When you quote several paragraphs, it is not sufficient to place quotation marks at the beginning and end of the entire quote. Place quotation marks at the *beginning of each paragraph,* but only at the *end of the last paragraph.* Here is an abbreviated quotation for an example:

"Here begins an odyssey through the world of classical mythology, starting with the creation of the world . . .

"It is true that themes similar to the classical may be found in any corpus of mythology . . . Even technology is not immune to the influence of Greece and Rome . . .

"We need hardly mention the extent to which painters and sculptors . . . have used and adapted classical mythology to illustrate the past, to reveal the human body, to express romantic or antiromantic ideals, or to symbolize any particular point of view."

Remember that in American English, commas and periods are *always* placed inside the quotation marks even if they are not actually part of the quote.

INCORRECT: "Life always gets colder near the summit", Nietzsche is purported to have said, "—the cold increases, responsibility grows".

CORRECT: "Life always gets colder near the summit," Nietzsche is purported to have said, "—the cold increases, responsibility grows."

INCORRECT: "Get down here right away", John cried. "You'll miss the sunset if you don't."

CORRECT: "Get down here right away," John cried. "You'll miss the sunset if you don't."

INCORRECT: "If my dog could talk", Mary mused, "I'll bet he would say, 'Take me for a walk right this minute'".

CORRECT: "If my dog could talk," Mary mused, "I'll bet he would say, 'Take me for a walk right this minute.'"

Other marks of punctuation, such as question marks, exclamation points, colons, and semicolons, go inside the quotation marks if they are part of the quoted material. If they are not part of the quotation, however, they go outside the quotation marks. Be careful to distinguish between the guidelines for the comma and period and those for other marks of punctuation.

INCORRECT:	"I'll always love you"! he exclaimed happily.
CORRECT:	"I'll always love you!" he exclaimed happily.
INCORRECT:	Did you hear her say, "He'll be there early?"
CORRECT:	Did you hear her say, "He'll be there early"?
INCORRECT:	She called down the stairs, "When are you going"?
CORRECT:	She called down the stairs, "When are you going?"
INCORRECT:	"Let me out"! he cried. "Don't you have any pity"?
CORRECT:	"Let me out!" he cried. "Don't you have any pity?"

Use only one mark of punctuation at the end of a sentence ending with a quotation mark.

INCORRECT:	She thought out loud, "Will I ever finish this paper in time for that class?".
CORRECT:	She thought out loud, "Will I ever finish this paper in time for that class?"
INCORRECT:	"Not the same thing a bit!", said the Hatter. "Why, you might just as well say that 'I see what I eat' is the same thing as 'I eat what I see'!".
CORRECT:	"Not the same thing a bit!" said the Hatter. "Why, you might just as well say that 'I see what I eat' is the same thing as 'I eat what I see'!"

Dashes and Parentheses

Rounding out the basic punctuation marks are **dashes** and **parentheses**, which provide a way to set off words, phrases, and clauses that are not part of the main clause but provide additional information. Because they are interruptive, they should be used sparingly in your Praxis Core essays.

Basic Rules of Punctuation

	Use 1	Use 2	Use 3	Use 4
Commas	**Separate items in a series** Example: I had a book, a crayon, and a pencil.	**After an introductory phrase or clause** Example: In the beginning, there was a great storm.	**Before coordinating conjunctions (FANBOYS):** *for, and, nor, but, or, yet, so*) **to combine independent clauses** Example: Sarah is good at soccer, but she's even better at lacrosse.	**To set off non-essential phrases and clauses** Example: Bill, the oldest member of the group, lives in Madison.
Semicolons	**To combine two independent clauses in a sentence** Example: I like ice cream; mint chip is my favorite flavor.	**To separate items when the things you are listing contain commas** Example: The menu includes an appetizer choice of soup or salad; an entrée choice of sautéed flounder, grilled quail in BBQ sauce, or fennel-braised pork belly; and, for dessert, white chocolate pomegranate cake, raspberry or lemon sorbet, or blackberry cobbler.		
Colons	**To introduce a list, definition, or brief explanation** This is what you'll see at the library: books, shelves, and librarians.			
Dashes	**To indicate a break in thought** I left my soda in the fridge—no, actually it's in the hot car.	**To call attention to supplementary information** At 12 noon—when Salvatore is just starting his workday—most people are preparing to eat lunch.		
Apostrophes	**In a contraction** I don't have work today.	**In the possessive form of a noun** Bill's suitcase is still at the airport.		

Practice Exercises: Punctuation

DIRECTIONS: Choose the response option that punctuates the underscored portion of the sentence correctly. If there is no error, select choice (D). Answers appear on pages 370–371.

1. Indianola, <u>Mississippi, where B.B. King and my father grew up,</u> has a population of about 11,000 people.

    (A) Mississippi where, B.B. King and my father grew up,

    (B) Mississippi where B.B. King and my father grew up,

    (C) Mississippi; where B.B. King and my father grew up,

    (D) No change is necessary.

2. John Steinbeck's best known novel, *The Grapes of Wrath*, is the story of the <u>Joads an Oklahoma family</u> who were driven from their dustbowl farm and forced to become migrant workers in California.

    (A) Joads, an Oklahoma family

    (B) Joads, an Oklahoma family,

    (C) Joads; an Oklahoma family

    (D) No change is necessary.

3. All students who are interested in student teaching next <u>semester, must submit an application to the Teacher Education Office.</u>

    (A) semester must submit an application to the Teacher Education Office.

    (B) semester, must submit an application, to the Teacher Education Office.

    (C) semester: must submit an application to the Teacher Education Office.

    (D) No change is necessary.

4. Whenever you travel by <u>car, or plane, you</u> must wear a seatbelt.

    (A) car or plane you

    (B) car, or plane you

    (C) car or plane, you

    (D) No change is necessary.

5. Wearing a seatbelt is not just a good <u>idea, it's</u> the law.

   (A) idea; it's

   (B) idea it's

   (C) idea. It's

   (D) No change is necessary.

6. Senators and representatives can be reelected <u>indefinitely; a</u> president can serve only two terms.

   (A) indefinitely but a

   (B) indefinitely, a

   (C) indefinitely a

   (D) No change is necessary.

7. Students must pay a penalty for overdue library <u>books, however, there</u> is a grace period.

   (A) books; however, there

   (B) books however, there

   (C) books: however, there

   (D) No change is necessary.

8. Among the states that seceded from the Union to join the Confederacy in 1860–1861 <u>were:</u> Mississippi, Florida, and Alabama.

   (A) were

   (B) were;

   (C) were.

   (D) No change is necessary.

9. The art exhibit displayed works by many famous <u>artists such as:</u> Dali, Picasso, and Michelangelo.

   (A) artists such as;

   (B) artists such as

   (C) artists. Such as

   (D) No change is necessary.

10. The National Shakespeare Company will perform the <u>following plays</u>: *Othello, Macbeth, Hamlet,* and *As You Like It.*

    (A) the following plays,

    (B) the following plays;

    (C) the following plays

    (D) No change is necessary.

PARTS OF SPEECH: A REFRESHER

Now we arrive at a discussion of **grammatical/structural relationships.** In this category, Praxis Core questions are based upon whether a sentence is written in correct standard written English. Does the sentence follow the rules of grammar? Let's break that down.

The Core Writing test does not require that you know such grammatical terms as **gerund, subject complement,** or **dependent clause,** although familiarity with the terms is a plus. However, you will be asked to identify what correct written language looks like when it comes to grammar and structure. Following is a refresher on parts of speech so you can brush up your grammar.

Adjectives and Adverbs

Correct Usage

Adjectives are words that modify nouns or pronouns by defining, describing, limiting, or qualifying those nouns or pronouns.

Adverbs are words that modify verbs, adjectives, or other adverbs and that express such ideas as time, place, manner, cause, and degree. Use adjectives as subject complements with linking verbs; use adverbs with action verbs.

> The old man's speech was *eloquent.* (Adjective)
>
> Mr. Brown speaks *eloquently.* (Adverb)
>
> Please be *careful.* (Adjective)
>
> Please drive *carefully.* (Adverb)

Good or well

Good is an adjective; its use as an adverb is colloquial and nonstandard.

> **INCORRECT:** He plays *good.*
>
> **CORRECT:** He looks *good* for an octogenarian.
>
> The quiche tastes very *good.*

Well may be either an adverb or an adjective. As an adjective, *well* means "in good health."

> **CORRECT:** He plays *well*. (Adverb)
>
> My mother is not *well*. (Adjective)

Bad or badly

Bad is an adjective used after sense verbs such as *look*, *smell*, *taste*, *feel*, or *sound*, or after linking verbs (*is, am, are, was, were*).

> **INCORRECT:** I feel *badly* about the delay.
>
> **CORRECT:** I feel *bad* about the delay.

Badly is an adverb used after all other verbs.

> **INCORRECT:** It doesn't hurt very *bad*.
>
> **CORRECT:** It doesn't hurt very *badly*.

Real or really

Real is an adjective; its use as an adverb is colloquial and nonstandard. It means "genuine."

> **INCORRECT:** He writes *real* well.
>
> **CORRECT:** This is *real* leather.

Really is an adverb meaning "very."

> **INCORRECT:** This is *really* a diamond.
>
> **CORRECT:** Have a *really* nice day.
>
> This is *real* amethyst. (Adjective)
>
> This is *really* difficult. (Adverb)
>
> This is a *real* crisis. (Adjective)
>
> This is *really* important. (Adverb)

Sort of and kind of

Sort of and *kind of* are often misused in written English by writers who actually mean *rather* or *somewhat*.

> **INCORRECT:** Jan was *kind of* saddened by the results of the test.
>
> **CORRECT:** Jan was *somewhat* saddened by the results of the test.

Faulty Comparisons

Sentences containing a **faulty comparison** often sound correct because their problem is not one of grammar but of logic. Read these sentences closely to make sure that like things are being compared, that the comparisons are complete, and that the comparisons are logical.

When comparing two persons or things, use the **comparative**, not the **superlative** form, of an adjective or an adverb. Use the superlative form for comparison of more than two persons or things. Use *any*, *other*, or *else* when comparing one thing or person with a group of which it or he or she is a part.

Most one- and two-syllable words form their comparative and superlative degrees with *-er* and *-est* suffixes, respectively. Adjectives and adverbs of more than two syllables form their comparative and superlative degrees with the addition of *more* and *most*.

Positive–Comparative–Superlative

good – better – best	lonely – lonelier – loneliest
old – older – oldest	talented – more talented – most talented
friendly – friendlier – friendliest	beautiful – more beautiful – most beautiful

A double comparison occurs when the degree of the modifier is changed incorrectly by adding both *-er* and *more* or *-est* and *most* to the adjective or adverb.

INCORRECT: He is the *most nicest* brother.

CORRECT: He is the *nicest* brother.

INCORRECT: She is the *more meaner* of the sisters.

CORRECT: She is the *meaner* sister.

Illogical comparisons occur when there is an implied comparison between two things that are not actually being compared or that cannot be logically compared.

INCORRECT: The interest at a loan company is higher *than* a bank.

CORRECT: The interest at a loan company is higher *than* that *at* a bank.

OR

The interest at a loan company is higher *than at* a bank.

Ambiguous comparisons occur when elliptical words (those omitted) create for the reader more than one interpretation of the sentence.

INCORRECT: I like Mary better than you. (than you *what*?)

CORRECT: I like Mary better than I like you.

OR

I like Mary better than you do.

Incomplete comparisons occur when the basis of the comparison (the two categories being compared) is not explicitly stated.

INCORRECT: Skywriting is *more* spectacular.

CORRECT: Skywriting is *more* spectacular *than* billboard advertising.

Do not omit the words *other, any,* or *else* when comparing one thing or person with a group of which it or he or she is a part.

INCORRECT: Joan writes better *than any* student in her class.

CORRECT: Joan writes better *than any other* student in her class.

Do not omit the second *as* of *as . . . as* when making a point of equal or superior comparison.

INCORRECT: The University of West Florida is *as large* or larger than the University of North Florida.

CORRECT: The University of West Florida is *as large as* or larger than the University of North Florida.

Do not omit the first category of the comparison, even if the two categories are the same.

INCORRECT: This is one of the best, if not the best, hospital in the country.

CORRECT: This is one of the best hospitals in the country, if not the best.

The problem with the incorrect sentence is that *one of the best* requires the plural word *hospitals,* not *hospital.*

Adjectives and Adverbs: Telling Them Apart

	Definition	Example
Adjectives	describe nouns	He enjoyed the gorgeous day. (*Gorgeous* is an adjective modifying the noun *day*.)
Adverbs	describe verbs	The musician played flawlessly. (*Flawlessly* is an adverb modifying the verb *played*.)

Commonly Confused Modifiers

Good (adj.)	Julie felt **good** about the meeting.
Fewer (adj.)—used to describe plural nouns	The world has **fewer** polar bears as a result of global warming.
Bad (adj.)	I felt **bad** as a result of my cold. ("bad" modifies "I")
Well (adv.)	Tracy performed **well** on the Praxis test.
Less (adj.)— used to describe singular nouns	The city has **less** crime.
Badly (adv.)	I threw **badly** in football practice. ("badly" modifies "threw")

Practice Exercises: Adjectives and Adverbs

DIRECTIONS: Choose the correct option based on errors in modifiers that may exist in the underscored portions of each sentence. If there is no error, select choice (D). Answers appear on pages 371–372.

1. Although the band performed <u>badly</u>, I feel <u>real bad</u> about missing the concert.

    (A) badly . . . real badly

    (B) bad . . . badly

    (C) badly . . . very bad

    (D) No change is necessary.

2. These reports are <u>relative simple</u> to prepare.

    (A) relatively simple

    (B) relative simply

    (C) relatively simply

    (D) No change is necessary.

3. He did <u>very well</u> on the test although his writing skills are not <u>good</u>.

    (A) real well . . . good

    (B) very good . . . good

    (C) good . . . great

    (D) No change is necessary.

4.   Shake the medicine bottle <u>good</u> before you open it.

   (A) very good

   (B) real good

   (C) well

   (D) No change is necessary.

5.   Though she speaks <u>fluently</u>, she writes <u>poorly</u> because she doesn't observe <u>closely</u> or think <u>clear</u>.

   (A) fluently . . . poorly . . . closely . . . clearly

   (B) fluent . . . poor . . . close . . . clear

   (C) fluently . . . poor . . . closely . . . clear

   (D) No change is necessary.

DIRECTIONS: Select the sentence that most clearly and effectively states the idea and has no structural errors.

6.   (A) Los Angeles is larger than any city in California.

   (B) Los Angeles is larger than all the cities in California.

   (C) Los Angeles is larger than any other city in California.

7.   (A) Art history is as interesting as, if not more interesting than, music appreciation.

   (B) Art history is as interesting, if not more interesting than, music appreciation.

   (C) Art history is as interesting as, if not more interesting, music appreciation.

8.   (A) The baseball team here is as good as any other university.

   (B) The baseball team here is as good as all the other universities.

   (C) The baseball team here is as good as any other university's.

9.   (A) I like him better than you.

   (B) I like him better than I like you.

   (C) I like him better.

10. (A) You are the most stingiest person I know.

   (B) You are the more stingiest person I know.

   (C) You are the stingiest person I know

Nouns (Agreement)

A **noun** refers to a person, place, thing, event, substance, quality, quantity, or idea.

The **dog** sat on the **rug**.

Please hand in your **paper** by the **end** of the **week**.

John Adams was the second **president** of the **United States of America**.

Nouns have to agree in number—start with plural, end with plural; start with singular, end with singular. But be careful. Take this example:

Catherine and Sue are planning to move to Hawaii in order to become a beach bum.

Two people, *Catherine and Sue*, can't become **one** beach bum so we revise the sentence as follows:

Catherine and Sue are planning to move to Hawaii in order to become **beach bums.**

Another commonly tested feature of nouns on the Praxis Core test is **countability**. Look at the following sentences:

I have many feelings.

To mature is to transcend much failure.

Both sentences are correct. *Feelings* are something one can count; they are discrete entities like rocks. *Failure*, however, cannot be counted; *failure* is an abstract state of being, like *sorrow*, *liberty*, *hatred, love*, and *happiness*. Concrete entities can be **noncountable** as well: *air* and *water*, to name two.

Practice Exercises: Nouns

DIRECTIONS: Identify the noun that serves as the subject in the sentence. Answers appear on pages 372–374.

1.   The Thai restaurant accepts only cash.

     (A) Thai

     (B) Restaurant

     (C) Accepts

     (D) Cash

2. The lawnmower in the yard is annoying me.

    (A) Lawnmower

    (B) Yard

    (C) Annoying

    (D) Me

3. Tomatoes taste terrible with salt.

    (A) Tomatoes

    (B) Taste

    (C) Terrible

    (D) Salt

4. Soccer fans love the World Cup.

    (A) Soccer

    (B) Fans

    (C) Love

    (D) World

5. At the park, the mothers were drinking coffee.

    (A) At

    (B) Park

    (C) The

    (D) Mothers

DIRECTIONS: For Questions 6–10, identify the proper noun in each pair of lettered choices.

6. Many couples go to Hawaii for a vacation.

    (A) Hawaii

    (B) couples

7. Along the shore of the Chesapeake Bay is the nation's first civilian aeronautics research laboratory, established in 1917.

    (A) Chesapeake Bay

    (B) aeronautics research laboratory

8. Tell Aunt Liz to leave me some stuffing.

   (A) Aunt Liz

   (B) Me

9. The Arctic Circle sees 24 hours of continuous sunlight once a year.

   (A) sunlight

   (B) Arctic Circle

10. Before penning the Declaration of Independence, America's Founding Fathers looked for a precedent and found it in the Magna Carta.

    (A) Declaration of Independence

    (B) America's

    (C) Founding Fathers

    (D) Magna Carta

    (E) All of the above

Pronoun Case

Pronoun case questions test your knowledge of the use of **nominative** and **objective** case pronouns:

Nominative Case	Objective Case
I	me
he	him
she	her
we	us
they	them
who	whom

Let's answer the most frequently asked grammar questions, which are also the ones most likely to show up on the Praxis Core Writing test:

- When to use *I* and when to use *me*

- When to use *who* and when to use *whom*.

Some writers avoid *whom* altogether, mistakenly thinking it sounds stuffy, and instead of distinguishing between *I* and *me*, many writers incorrectly use *myself* (which is actually a **reflexive pronoun,** e.g., "I saw myself in the mirror." See Pronoun–Antecedent Agreement).

Use the nominative case (subject pronouns) . . .

> *. . . for the subject of a sentence:*
>
> *We* students studied until early morning for the final.
>
> Rafael and *I* "burned the midnight oil," too.

> *. . . for pronouns in apposition to (having the same meaning as) the subject:*
>
> Only two students, Alex and *I*, were asked to report on the meeting.

> *. . . for the predicate nominative/subject complement:*
>
> The actors nominated for the award were *she* and *I*.

> *. . . for the subject of an elliptical clause:*
>
> Molly is more experienced than *he*.

> *. . . for the subject of a subordinate clause:*
>
> Robert is the driver *who* reported the accident.

Use the objective case (object pronouns) . . .

> *. . . for the direct object of a sentence:*
>
> Mary invited *us* to her party.

> *. . . for the object of a preposition:*
>
> The books that were torn belonged to *her*.
>
> Just between you and *me*, I'm bored in class.

> *. . . for the indirect object of a sentence:*
>
> Walter gave a dozen red roses to *her*.

> *. . . for the appositive of a direct object:*
>
> The committee elected two delegates, Barbara and *me*.

> *. . . for the object of an infinitive:*
>
> The young boy wanted to help *us* paint the fence.

> *. . . for the object of a gerund:*
>
> Enlisting *him* was surprisingly easy.

. . . for the object of a past participle:

Having called the other students and *us*, the school secretary went home for the day.

. . . for a pronoun that precedes an infinitive (the subject of an infinitive):

The supervisor told *him* to work late.

. . . for the complement of an infinitive with an expressed subject:

The fans thought the best player to be *him*.

. . . for the object of an elliptical clause:

Bill tackled Joe harder than *me*.

. . . for the object of a verb in apposition:

Charles invited two extra people, Carmen and *me*, to the party.

When a conjunction connects two pronouns or a pronoun and a noun, mentally remove the "and" and the other pronoun or noun to determine what the correct pronoun form should be:

Mom gave Tom and *myself* a piece of cake.

Mom gave Tom and *I* a piece of cake

Mom gave Tom and *me* a piece of cake.

The correct pronoun is now revealed:

Mom gave *me* a piece of cake.

The only pronouns that are acceptable after *between* and other prepositions are: *me, her, him, them,* and *whom.* When deciding between *who* and *whom,* try substituting *he* for *who* and *him* for *whom.* Then follow these easy transformation steps:

1. Isolate the *who* clause or the *whom* clause:

    whom we can trust

2. Invert the word order, if necessary. Place the words in the clause in the natural order of an English sentence, subject followed by the verb:

    we can trust whom

3. Read the final form with the *he* or *him* inserted:

    We can trust whom (him).

When a pronoun follows a **comparative conjunction** such as *than* or *as*, complete the **elliptical construction** to help you determine which pronoun is correct.

She has more credit hours than me [do].

She has more credit hours than I [do].

Pronoun–Antecedent Agreement

These kinds of questions test your knowledge of using an appropriate pronoun to agree with its antecedent in number (singular or plural form) and gender (masculine, feminine, or neuter). An **antecedent** is a noun or pronoun to which another noun or pronoun refers.

Here are the two basic rules for pronoun reference–antecedent agreement:

1. Every pronoun must have a conspicuous antecedent.

2. Every pronoun must agree with its antecedent in number, gender, and person.

When an antecedent is one of ambiguous gender such as *student*, *singer*, *artist*, *person*, and *citizen*, use *his* or *her*. However, depending on the use and frequency, this may sound stilted. Some careful writers change the antecedent to a plural noun to avoid using the sexist, singular masculine pronoun *his*:

INCORRECT: Everyone hopes that he will win the lottery.

CORRECT: Most people hope that they will win the lottery.

Ordinarily, the relative pronoun *who* is used to refer to people, *which* to refer to things and places, *where* to refer to places, and *that* to refer to places or things. The distinction between *that* and *which* is a grammatical distinction (see the section on Word Choice).

Many writers prefer to use *that* to refer to collective nouns.

EXAMPLE: A family *that* traces its lineage is usually proud of its roots.

Many writers, especially students, are not sure when to use the reflexive case pronoun (which ends in -self) and when to use the possessive case pronoun. The rules governing the usage of the reflexive case and the possessive case are quite simple. Let's check them.

Use the possessive case . . .

. . . before a noun in a sentence . . .

Our friend moved during the semester break.

My dog has fleas, but *her* dog doesn't.

. . . before a gerund in a sentence . . .

Her running helps to relieve stress.

His driving terrified her.

. . . as a noun in a sentence . . .

Mine was the last test graded that day.

. . . to indicate possession . . .

Karen never allows anyone else to drive *her* car.

Brad thought the book was *his,* but it was someone else's.

Use the reflexive case . . .

. . . as a direct object to rename the subject . . .

I kicked *myself.*

. . . as an indirect object to rename the subject . . .

Henry bought *himself* a tie.

. . . as an object of a prepositional phrase . . .

Tom and Lillie baked the pie for *themselves.*

. . . as a predicate pronoun:

She hasn't been *herself* lately.

Do *not* use the reflexive in place of the nominative pronoun:

INCORRECT: Both Randy and *myself* plan to go.

CORRECT: Both Randy and *I* plan to go.

INCORRECT: *Yourself* will take on the challenges of college.

CORRECT: *You* will take on the challenges of college.

INCORRECT: Either James or *yourself* will paint the mural.

CORRECT: Either James or *you* will paint the mural.

Watch out for careless use of the pronoun form:

INCORRECT: George *hisself* told me it was true.

CORRECT: George *himself* told me it was true.

INCORRECT:	They washed the car *theirselves*.	
CORRECT:	They washed the car *themselves*.	

Notice that reflexive pronouns are not set off by commas:

INCORRECT:	Mary, *herself*, gave him the diploma.
CORRECT:	Mary *herself* gave him the diploma.
INCORRECT:	I will do it, *myself*.
CORRECT:	I will do it *myself*.

Pronoun Reference

Pronoun reference questions require you to determine whether the antecedent is in plain sight in the sentence or whether it is remote, implied, ambiguous, or vague—none of which contributes to clear writing. Make sure that every italicized pronoun has a conspicuous antecedent and that one pronoun substitutes only for another noun or pronoun, not for an idea or a sentence.

Pronoun Agreement

Person	Number	Subjective	Objective	Possessive
First	Singular	I	Me	My, mine
Second	Singular	You	You	Your, yours
Third	Singular	He	Him	His
	Singular	She	Her	Her
	Singular	It	It	Its
Third	Plural	They	Them	Their, theirs

Pronoun-reference problems occur . . .

. . . when a pronoun refers to either of two antecedents . . .

INCORRECT:	Joanna told Arlene that *she* needed a new hairstyle.
CORRECT:	Joanna told Arlene, "I need a new hairstyle."

. . . when a pronoun refers to a remote antecedent . . .

INCORRECT:	A strange car followed us closely, and *he* kept blinking his lights at us.
CORRECT:	A strange car followed us closely, and its driver kept blinking his lights at us.

. . . when "this," " that," and "which" refer to the general idea of the preceding clause or sentence rather than the preceding word . . .

INCORRECT:	The students could not understand the pronoun reference handout, which annoyed them very much.
CORRECT:	The students could not understand the pronoun reference handout, a fact which annoyed them very much.

OR

The students were annoyed because they could not understand the pronoun reference handout.

. . . when a pronoun refers to an unexpressed but implied noun . . .

INCORRECT:	My husband wants me to knit a blanket, but I'm not interested in it.
CORRECT:	My husband wants me to knit a blanket, but I'm not interested in knitting.

. . . when "it" is used as something other than an expletive to postpone a subject . . .

INCORRECT:	It says in today's paper that the newest shipment of cars from Detroit seems to include outright imitations of European models.
CORRECT:	Today's paper says that the newest shipment of cars from Detroit seems to include outright imitations of European models.
INCORRECT:	The football game was canceled because it was bad weather.
CORRECT:	The football game was canceled because the weather was bad.

. . . when "they" or "it" is used to refer to something or someone indefinitely, and there is no definite antecedent . . .

INCORRECT:	At the job placement office, they told me to stop wearing ripped jeans to my interviews.
CORRECT:	At the job placement office, I was told to stop wearing ripped jeans to my interviews.

. . . when the pronoun does not agree with its antecedent in number, gender, or person . . .

INCORRECT:	Any graduate student, if they are interested, may attend the lecture.
CORRECT:	Any graduate student, if he or she is interested, may attend the lecture.

OR

All graduate students, if they are interested, may attend the lecture. (This example avoids the awkward "he or she" reference by shifting the subject to its plural form and using the plural form of the verb.)

INCORRECT:	Many Americans are concerned that the overuse of slang and colloquialisms is corrupting the language.
CORRECT:	Many Americans are concerned that the overuse of slang and colloquialisms is corrupting their language.
INCORRECT:	The Board of Regents will not make a decision about a tuition increase until their March meeting.
CORRECT:	The Board of Regents will not make a decision about a tuition increase until its March meeting.

. . . when a noun or pronoun has no expressed antecedent . . .

INCORRECT:	In the president's address to union members, he promised no more taxes.
CORRECT:	In his address to union members, the president promised no more taxes.

☞ HINT

Don't leave pronouns ambiguous. As we see here, the fix is often simple.

Example: In the directions, they say to screw in the lamp base first. (Who are "they"?)

Revision: The directions say that the lamp base should be screwed in first.

Practice Exercises: Pronouns

DIRECTIONS: Determine whether there is an error in the underscored portion of the sentence. If so, select the proper revision according to requirements of standard written English. If there is no error, choose (D). Answers appear on pages 374–375.

1. My friend and <u>myself</u> bought tickets for *Cats*.

   (A) I

   (B) me

   (C) us

   (D) No change is necessary.

2. Alcohol and tobacco are harmful to <u>whomever</u> consumes them.

   (A) whom

   (B) who

   (C) whoever

   (D) No change is necessary.

3. Everyone is wondering <u>whom</u> her successor will be.

   (A) who

   (B) whose

   (C) who'll

   (D) No change is necessary.

4. Rosa Lee's parents discovered that it was <u>her who</u> wrecked the family car.

   (A) she who

   (B) she whom

   (C) her whom

   (D) No change is necessary.

5. A student <u>who</u> wishes to protest <u>his or her</u> grades must file a formal grievance in the dean's office.

   (A) that . . . their

   (B) which . . . his

   (C) whom . . . their

   (D) No change is necessary.

6. One of the best things about working for this company is that <u>they pay</u> big bonuses.

   (A) it pays

   (B) they always pay

   (C) they paid

   (D) No change is necessary.

7. Every car owner should be sure that <u>their</u> automobile insurance is adequate.

    (A) your

    (B) his or her

    (C) its

    (D) No change is necessary.

8. My mother wants me to become an engineer, but I'm not interested in <u>it</u>.

    (A) this

    (B) engineering

    (C) that

    (D) No change is necessary.

9. Since I had not paid my electric bill, <u>they</u> sent me a delinquent notice.

    (A) the power company

    (B) he

    (C) it

    (D) No change is necessary.

10. Margaret seldom wrote to her sister <u>when she</u> was away at college.

    (A) , who

    (B) when her

    (C) when her sister

    (D) No change is necessary.

Verb Forms

This section covers the principal parts of some irregular verbs including troublesome verbs such as *lie* and *lay*. The use of regular verbs such as *look* and *receive* poses no real problem to most writers because the past and past participle forms end in *-ed*; it is the irregular forms that pose the most serious problems—for example, *seen*, *written*, and *begun*.

Before we discuss verbs, let's recap how they need to agree with their subjects. Subjects and verbs agree in person ("I am" is first person versus "They are," which is third person) and in number ("She takes the train" versus "They take the train"). In this case, a singular subject "she" takes a singular verb and a plural subject "they" takes a plural verb). Collective nouns (e.g., a group, team, family) are singular.

Different Forms of Verb Tenses

	Simple	Progressive	Why used
Present	I live	I am living	Actions in the present; habitual actions, things that are always true
Past	I lived	I was living	Actions that took place in the past and are done
Future	I will live	I will be living	Actions that will happen in the future
Present Perfect	I have lived	I have been living	Actions that started in the past and continue in the present
Past Perfect	I had lived	I had been living	Actions that were completed before other past actions
Future Perfect	I will have lived	I will have been living	Future actions that will take place before other future actions

Nevertheless, there are irregular verbs that have different forms and "break the rules." For instance, the verb "to be" is irregular since the present is "I am" while the past isn't "I amed" but rather "I was." If English is not your first language, you will have to look up these irregular verb forms and stay alert to them as you read. (What you read matters: Make time for periodicals of superior editorial merit.)

Like pronouns, verbs must agree with their subjects in person ("I am going to Rome") *and* in number ("Sam takes the bus" versus "The employees take the bus").

Verb Tenses

Tense sequence indicates a logical time sequence.

Use present tense . . .

> *. . . in statements of universal truth . . .*
>
> I learned that the sun *is* 93 million miles from Earth.

> *. . . in statements about the contents of literature and other published works . . .*
>
> In this book, Sandy *becomes* a nun and *writes* a book on psychology.

Use past tense . . .

> *. . . in statements concerning writing or publication of a book . . .*
>
> He *wrote* his first book in 1949, and it *was* published in 1952.

Use present perfect tense . . .

> *. . . for an action that began in the past but continues into the future . . .*
>
> I have *lived* here all my life.

Use past perfect tense

> *. . . for an earlier action that is mentioned in a later action . . .*
>
> Cindy ate the apple that she *had picked.*
>
> (First she picked it, then she ate it.)

Use future perfect tense . . .

> *. . . for an action that will have been completed at a specific future time . . .*
>
> By May, I *shall have graduated.*

Use a present participle . . .

> *. . . for an action that occurs at the same time as the verb . . .*
>
> *Speeding* down the interstate, I saw a trooper's flashing lights.

Use a perfect participle . . .

> *. . . for an action that occurred before the main verb . . .*
>
> *Having read* the directions, I started the test.

Use the subjunctive mood . . .

> *. . . to express a wish or state a condition contrary to fact . . .*
>
> *If it were not raining,* we could have a picnic.

> *. . . in "that" clauses after verbs like "request," "recommend," "suggest," "ask," "require," and "insist," and after such expressions as "it is important" and "it is necessary" . . .*
>
> It is necessary that all papers *be* submitted on time.

Subject–Verb Agreement

Agreement is the grammatical correspondence between the subject and the verb of a sentence: *I do; we do; they do; he, she, it does*.

English verbs have six basic tenses, although it's estimated that just three (present simple, past simple, and present perfect) account for 80% of the verb tense use in academic writing.

Study these rules governing subject-verb agreement:

A verb must agree with its subject, not with any additive phrase in the sentence such as a prepositional or verbal phrase. Ignore such phrases when deciding which verb form to use.

> Your *copy* of the rules *is* on the desk.

> Ms. Craig's *record* of community service and outstanding teaching *qualifies* her for a promotion.

In an inverted sentence beginning with a prepositional phrase, the verb still agrees with its subject.

> At the end of the summer *come* the best *sales*.

> Under the house *are* some old Mason *jars*.

Prepositional phrases beginning with compound prepositions such as *along with, together with, in addition to*, and *as well as* should be ignored when deciding which verb form to use because they do not affect subject-verb agreement.

> *Gladys Knight*, as well as the Pips, *is* riding the midnight train to Georgia.

A verb must agree with its subject, not its subject complement.

> *Taxes are* a problem.

> A *problem is* taxes.

When a sentence begins with an expletive such as *there, here*, or *it*, the verb agrees with the subject, not the expletive.

> Surely, there *are* several *alumni* who would be interested in forming a group.

> There *are* 50 *students* in my English class.

> There *is* a horrifying *study* on child abuse in *Psychology Today*.

Indefinite pronouns such as *each, either, one, everyone, everybody*, and *everything* are singular.

> *Somebody* in Detroit *loves* me.

> *Does either* [one] of you have a pencil?

> *Neither* of my brothers *has* a car.

Indefinite pronouns such as *several, few, both*, and *many* are plural.

> *Both* of my sorority sisters *have* decided to live off campus.

> *Few seek* the enlightenment of transcendental meditation.

Indefinite pronouns such as *all, some, most*, and *none* may be singular or plural depending on their referents.

> *Some* of the food *is* cold.

> *Some* of the vegetables *are* cold.

> I can think of some retorts, but *none* seem appropriate.

> *None* of the children *is* as sweet as Sally.

Fractions such as *one-half* and *one-third* may be singular or plural depending on the referent.

> *Half* of the mail *has* been delivered.

> *Half* of the letters *have* been read.

Subjects joined by *and* take a plural verb unless the subjects are thought to be one item or unit.

> *Jim* and *Tammy were* televangelists.

> *Earth, Wind, and Fire is* my favorite group.

In cases when the subjects are joined by *or, nor, either . . . or*, or *neither . . . nor*, the verb must agree with the subject closer to it.

> Either the teacher or the *students are* responsible.

> Neither the students nor the *teacher is* responsible.

Relative pronouns that refer to plural antecedents, such as *who, which*, or *that*, require plural verbs. However, when the relative pronoun refers to a singular subject, the pronoun takes a singular verb.

> She is one of the girls *who cheer* on Friday nights.

> She is the only cheerleader *who has* a broken leg.

Subjects preceded by *every, each*, and *many a* are singular.

> *Every* man, woman, and child *was* given a life preserver.

> *Each* undergraduate *is* required to pass a proficiency exam.

> *Many a* tear *has* to fall before one matures.

A collective noun, such as *audience, faculty, jury*, etc., requires a singular verb when the group is regarded as a whole, and a plural verb when the members of the group are regarded as individuals.

> The *jury has* made its decision.

> The *faculty are* preparing their grade rosters.

Subjects preceded by *the number of* or *the percentage of* are singular, while subjects preceded by *a number of* or *a percentage of* are plural.

> *The number of vacationers* in Florida *increases* every year.

> *A number of vacationers are* young couples.

Titles of books, companies, name brands, and groups are singular or plural depending on their meaning.

> *Great Expectations is* my favorite novel.

> The Rolling Stones *are* performing in the Superdome.

Certain nouns of Latin and Greek origin have unusual singular and plural forms.

Singular	Plural
criterion	criteria
alumnus	alumni
datum	data
medium	media

> The *data are* available for inspection.

> The only *criterion* for membership *is* a high GPA.

Some nouns—for example, *deer, shrimp,* and *sheep*—have the same spellings for both their singular and plural forms. In these cases, the meaning of the sentence determines whether they are singular or plural.

> *Deer are* beautiful animals.

> The spotted *deer is* licking the sugar cube.

Some nouns—for example, *scissors, jeans,* and *eyeglasses*—have plural forms but no singular counterparts. Many such nouns have two parts joined as one thing. These nouns almost always take plural verbs.

> The *scissors are* on the table.

> My new *jeans fit* me like a glove.

Words used as examples, not as grammatical parts of the sentence, require singular verbs.

> *Can't is* the contraction for "cannot."

> *Cats is* the plural form of "cat."

Mathematical expressions of subtraction and division require singular verbs, while expressions of addition and multiplication take either singular or plural verbs.

Ten *divided* by two *is* five.

Five *times* two *is/are* ten.

OR

Five *times* two *equal/equals* ten.

Nouns expressing time, distance, weight, and measurement are singular when they refer to a unit and plural when they refer to separate items.

Fifty yards is a short distance.

Ten years have passed since I finished college.

Expressions of quantity are usually plural.

Nine out of ten dentists *recommend* that their patients floss.

Some nouns ending in *-ics*, such as *economics* and *ethics*, take singular verbs when they refer to principles or a field of study; however, when they refer to individual practices, they usually take plural verbs.

Ethics is being taught in the spring.

His unusual business *ethics are* what got him into trouble.

Some nouns like *measles, news*, and *calculus* appear to be plural but are actually singular in number. These nouns require singular verbs.

Measles is a very contagious disease.

The *news* from Sudan is grim.

Calculus requires great skill in algebra.

A verbal noun (infinitive or gerund) serving as a subject is treated as singular, even if the object of the verbal phrase is plural.

Hiding your mistakes *does* not make them go away.

To run five miles *is* my goal.

A noun phrase or clause acting as the subject of a sentence requires a singular verb.

What I need is to be loved.

Whether there is any connection between them is unknown.

Clauses beginning with *what* may be singular or plural depending on the meaning, that is, whether *what* means "the thing" or "the things."

What I want for Christmas is a new motorcycle.

What matters are Clinton's ideas.

A plural subject followed by a singular appositive requires a plural verb; similarly, a singular subject followed by a plural appositive requires a singular verb.

When the girls throw a party, *they* each bring a *gift*.

The *board*, all ten members, *is* meeting today.

Practice Exercises: Verbs

DIRECTIONS: Choose the response option that correctly uses the verbs in each sentence. Answers appear on pages 375–377.

1. If you <u>had been concerned</u> about Marilyn, you <u>would have went</u> to greater lengths to ensure her safety.

    (A) had been concern . . . would have gone

    (B) was concerned . . . would have gone

    (C) had been concerned . . . would have gone

    (D) No change is necessary.

2. Susan <u>laid</u> in bed too long and missed her class.

    (A) lays

    (B) lay

    (C) lied

    (D) No change is necessary.

3. The Great Wall of China <u>is</u> 1,500 miles long; it <u>was built</u> in the third century B.C.E.

    (A) was . . . was built

    (B) is . . . is built

    (C) has been . . . was built

    (D) No change is necessary.

4. Joe stated that the class <u>began</u> at 10:30 a.m.

    (A) begins

    (B) had begun

    (C) was beginning

    (D) No change is necessary.

5. The ceiling of the Sistine Chapel <u>was</u> painted by Michelangelo; it <u>depicted</u> scenes from the Creation in the Old Testament.

    (A) was . . . depicts

    (B) is . . . depicts

    (C) has been . . . depicting

    (D) No change is necessary.

6. After Christmas <u>comes</u> the best sales.

    (A) has come

    (B) come

    (C) is coming

    (D) No change is necessary.

7. The bakery's specialty <u>are</u> wedding cakes.

    (A) is

    (B) were

    (C) be

    (D) No change is necessary.

8. Every man, woman, and child <u>were given</u> a life preserver.

    (A) have been given

    (B) had gave

    (C) was given

    (D) No change is necessary.

9. Hiding your mistakes <u>don't</u> make them go away.

    (A) doesn't

    (B) do not

    (C) have not

    (D) No change is necessary.

10. The board of directors <u>has declared</u> a dividend.

    (A) have declared

    (B) has been declared

    (C) had declared

    (D) No change is necessary.

SENTENCE STRUCTURE SKILLS

To be adept at writing a solid sentence, you need to know what it takes to build one. Let's start with a chart that delineates the distinction between a phrase, a clause, and a sentence.

Phrase versus Clause versus Sentence

Phrase	Just a group of words—it lacks both a subject and a verb.
	Example: Looking up at the sky
Clause (dependent versus independent)	A group of words that has a subject and a verb
	Example: Because the tomatoes were fresh (dependent clause; needs something to complete it)
	We went to the store. (independent clause—has a subject and verb)
Sentence	An independent clause with a subject and a verb that is punctuated correctly and expresses a complete thought.
	Example: The room was cold because the heat was turned off.

Subordination, Coordination, and Predication

Suppose, for the sake of clarity, you wanted to combine the information in these two sentences to create one statement:

I studied a foreign language. I found English quite easy.

How you decide to combine this information should be determined by the relationship you'd like to show between the two facts. *I studied a foreign language, and I found English quite easy* seems rather illogical.

The **coordination** of the two ideas (connecting them with the coordinating conjunction *and*) is ineffective. Using **subordination** instead (connecting the sentences with a subordinating conjunction) clearly shows the degree of relative importance between the expressed ideas:

After I studied a foreign language, I found English quite easy.

When using a conjunction, be sure that the sentence parts you are joining are in agreement.

INCORRECT: She loved him dearly but not his dog.

CORRECT: She loved him dearly but she did not love his dog.

A common mistake that is made is to forget that each member of the pair must be followed by the same kind of construction.

INCORRECT: Town officials complimented the firefighters for their bravery and they thanked them for their being kind.

CORRECT: Town officials complimented the firefighters for their bravery and thanked them for their kindness.

While refers to time and should not be used as a substitute for *although*, *and*, or *but*.

INCORRECT: While I'm usually interested in Fellini movies, I'd rather not go tonight.

CORRECT: Although I'm usually interested in Fellini movies, I'd rather not go tonight.

Where refers to place and should not be used as a substitute for *that*.

INCORRECT: We read in the paper where scientists are making great strides in DNA research.

CORRECT: We read in the paper that scientists are making great strides in DNA research.

After words like *reason* and *explanation,* use *that*, not *because*.

INCORRECT: His explanation for his tardiness was because his alarm did not go off.

CORRECT: His explanation for his tardiness was that his alarm did not go off.

There are seven types of adverbial clauses, so called because such clauses function as adverbs. A subordinating conjunction connects a dependent clause to a main clause. In the following sentence, a famous quotation from Edward R. Murrow, the conjunction "when" signals the subordinate clause:

"No cash register ever rings when a mind is changed."

Below is a guide to common conjunctions used in adverbial clauses.

Common adverbial (subordinating) conjunctions

Contrast clauses	although, though, even though
Reason clauses	because, as
Place clauses	where, wherever, everywhere
Purpose clauses	so that, so, because + want
Result clauses	so that, so . . . that, such . . . that
Time clauses	when, before, after, since, while, as, as soon as, by the time, until
Conditional clauses	if, unless, provided (that), as long as

Practice Exercises: Sentence Structure Skills

DIRECTIONS: Choose the sentence that expresses the thought most clearly. The correct answer should have no error in structure when considered in terms of carefully written English. Answers appear on pages 377–378.

1. (A) Many gases are invisible, odorless, and they have no taste.

   (B) Many gases are invisible, odorless, and have no taste.

   (C) Many gases are invisible, odorless, and tasteless.

2. (A) Everyone agreed that she had neither the voice or the skill to be a speaker.

   (B) Everyone agreed that she had neither the voice nor the skill to be a speaker.

   (C) Everyone agreed that she had either the voice nor the skill to be a speaker.

3. (A) The mayor will be remembered because he kept his campaign promises and because of his refusal to accept political favors.

   (B) The mayor will be remembered because he kept his campaign promises and refused to accept political favors.

   (C) The mayor will be remembered because of his refusal to accept political favors and he kept his campaign promises.

4. (A) While taking a shower, the doorbell rang.

   (B) While I was taking a shower, the doorbell rang.

   (C) While taking a shower, someone rang the doorbell.

5. (A) He swung the bat, while the runner stole second base.

   (B) The runner stole second base while he swung the bat.

   (C) While he was swinging the bat, the runner stole second base.

DIRECTIONS: Choose the correct response option that corrects the error in the underscored portion of the sentence. If there is no error, select (D).

6. Nothing grows as well in Mississippi as <u>cotton. Cotton</u> being the state's principal crop.

   (A) cotton, cotton

   (B) cotton; cotton

   (C) cotton cotton

   (D) No error

7. It was a heartrending <u>movie there</u> wasn't a dry eye in the house.

   (A) movie but there

   (B) movie; there

   (C) movie. Yet

   (D) No error

8. Traffic was stalled for three miles on the <u>bridge. Because</u> repairs were being made.

   (A) bridge because

   (B) bridge; because

   (C) bridge, because

   (D) No error

9. The ability to write complete sentences comes with <u>practice writing</u> run-on sentences seems to occur naturally.

   (A) practice, writing

   (B) practice. Writing

   (C) practice and

   (D) No error

10. Even though she had taken French classes, she could not understand native French <u>speakers they</u> all spoke too fast.

   (A) speakers, they

   (B) speakers. They

   (C) speaking

   (D) No error

MISPLACED AND DANGLING MODIFIERS

A **misplaced modifier** is one that is in the wrong place in the sentence. Misplaced modifiers come in all forms—words, phrases, and clauses. Sentences containing misplaced modifiers are often very comical: *Mom made me eat the spinach instead of my brother*. Misplaced modifiers, such as the one in the previous sentence, are usually too far away from the word or words they modify. This sentence should read: *Mom made me, instead of my brother, eat the spinach*.

Modifiers like *only*, *nearly*, and *almost* should be placed next to the word they modify and not in front of some other word, especially a verb, that they are not intended to modify.

A modifier is misplaced if it appears to modify the wrong part of the sentence or if we cannot be certain what part of the sentence the writer intended it to modify. To correct a misplaced modifier, move the modifier next to the word it describes.

> **INCORRECT:** She served hamburgers to the men on paper plates.
>
> **CORRECT:** She served hamburgers on paper plates to the men.

Split infinitives also result in misplaced modifiers. Infinitives consist of the marker *to* plus the plain form of the verb. The two parts of the infinitive make up a grammatical unit that should not be split. Splitting an infinitive is placing an adverb between the *to* and the verb.

> **INCORRECT:** The weather service expects temperatures to not rise.
>
> **CORRECT:** The weather service expects temperatures not to rise.

Sometimes a split infinitive may be natural and preferable, even though it may still bother some readers.

> **Example:** Several U.S. industries expect to more than triple their use of robots within the next decade.

A squinting modifier may refer to either a preceding or a following word, leaving the reader uncertain about what it is intended to modify. Correct a squinting modifier by moving it next to the word it is intended to modify.

> **INCORRECT:** Snipers who fired on the soldiers often escaped capture.
>
> **CORRECT:** Snipers who often fired on the soldiers escaped capture.
>
> **OR**
>
> Snipers who fired on the soldiers escaped capture often.

A **dangling modifier** is a modifier or verb in search of a subject: the modifying phrase (usually an *-ing* word group but sometimes an *-ed* or *-en* word group, or a *to + a verb* word group—participle phrase, or infinitive phrase, respectively) either appears to modify the wrong word or has nothing to modify. It is literally dangling at the beginning or the end of a sentence. The sentences often look and sound correct: *To be a student government officer, your grades must be above average.* (However, the verbal modifier has nothing to describe. Who is *to be a student government officer*? Your grades?)

Praxis Core questions assessing your command of dangling modifiers require you to determine whether a modifier has a **headword** (a word or phrase it can modify) or is dangling at the beginning or the end of the sentence.

 HINT

> To avoid misplaced and dangling modifiers, place words as close as possible to what they describe. The hilarity that can ensue from putting the modifiers in exactly the wrong place was not lost on comedian Groucho Marx, who joked, "The other day, I shot an elephant in my pajamas. How he got in my pajamas, I'll never know."

To correct a dangling modifier, reword the sentence by either: (1) changing the modifying phrase to a clause with a subject, or (2) changing the subject of the sentence to the word that should be modified. The following are examples of a dangling infinitive and a dangling participle:

INCORRECT: Shortly after leaving home, the accident occurred.
(Who is leaving home, the accident?)

CORRECT: Shortly after we left home, the accident occurred.

INCORRECT: To get up on time and not be late for school, a great effort was needed.
("To get up" needs a subject.)

CORRECT: To get up on time and not be late for school, I made a great effort.

Practice Exercises: Misplaced/Dangling Modifiers

DIRECTIONS: Choose the sentence in which modifiers are used correctly according to the requirements of standard written English. Answers appear on pages 378–380.

1. (A) Entering the turnpike at Interchange 14, we noticed that traffic was heavy.

   (B) Entering the turnpike at Interchange 14, traffic looked heavy.

2. (A) While writing the paper, the cell phone rang.

   (B) While I was writing the paper, the cell phone rang.

3. (A) The girls look beautiful to the adults in their holiday dresses.

   (B) The girls in their holiday dresses look beautiful to the adults.

4. (A) Sam took down from the door an old photograph of a musician.

   (B) Fastened to the door, Sam took down an old photograph of a musician.

5. (A) The teacher sat reading a book having lunch.

   (B) While reading a book, the teacher had lunch.

6.　(A)　The salesperson sold the BMW to the buyer with leather seats.

　　(B)　The salesperson sold the BMW with leather seats to the buyer.

7.　(A)　Hungry and thirsty from the run, Adam made the restaurant his destination.

　　(B)　Hungry and thirsty from the run, the restaurant became Adam's destination.

8.　(A)　Noah drove the truck into a wall that he borrowed from his dad.

　　(B)　Noah drove the truck that he borrowed from his dad into a wall.

9.　(A)　After slurping a Tang drink on *Friendship 7,* General Foods saw sales soar.

　　(B)　After slurping a Tang drink on *Friendship 7,* astronaut John Glenn caused General Foods' sales to soar.

10.　(A)　Having walked up and down the dairy aisle three times, the brand of grapefruit juice I wanted wasn't there.

　　(B)　Having walked up and down the dairy aisle three times, I realized the store didn't have the brand of grapefruit juice I wanted.

COORDINATING/SUBORDINATING CONJUNCTIONS

Coordinating conjunctions join sentences, phrases, and words that are equally important. Coordinating conjunctions are used with a comma to connect two independent clauses.

Example: Jill looked in the window, but she didn't see her mother.

In this example, the coordinating conjunction, *but,* is used to join clauses that could stand on their own.

FANBOYS—which stands for *For, And, Nor, But, Or, Yet, So*—is a good acronym to help you remember coordinating conjunctions. *And, but,* and *or* are the most commonly used conjunctions.

Example: The cat drank the milk and left the kitchen.

Here, the conjunction *and* coordinates two parts ("drank the milk" and "left the kitchen"). Since the second part is a verb phrase (and not an independent clause), no comma is necessary before the word "and."

Subordinating conjunctions "work for" or "are subordinate to" the main part of the sentence and show a relationship between words. Example: "Because it was sunny, I couldn't see the road." On its own, the phrase "Because it was sunny" is a fragment. It depends on or is subordinate to another part of the sentence. The subordinate conjunction is the word *because,* but there are many others. Common ones include *before, after, as, although, if, while, unless, since,* and *though.*

Practice Exercises: Coordinating and Subordinating Conjunctions

DIRECTIONS: Identify whether the sentence contains a coordinating or a subordinating conjunction. Answers appear on pages 380–381.

1. The nurse went to work when evening fell.

2. Mr. Manchello told me to finish the test before I went outside.

3. Jennifer can sing or dance.

4. I am not going to the movies unless Michael comes.

5. I read the magazine, but I forgot to put it back.

6. I am feeling better as each day passes.

7. He went to the store and came home.

8. Catherine is sick because she ate too much candy.

9. Randy loves his son and his daughter.

10. The traffic was backed up because there was an accident.

FRAGMENTS

A fragment is an incomplete construction that may or may not have a subject and a verb. Fragments are rampant in electronic messaging and social media, and can also be found both in celebrated novels and masterly marketing copy. For example, Italian health supplements company

Bioenergy Nutrition, in a bid to promote the benefits of low cholesterol, ran a print ad in recent years that read: "Bad cholesterol. Sometimes, horrifying." Which only goes to prove, once you know the rules of English grammar, you can break them, and do so to good effect. But the Praxis Core Writing test has declared fragments faulty. The test wants you to show you know the rules of standard written English; this is construed as leaving no room for fragments.

Here, then, is advice on how to identify and ensure you don't get tripped up by fragments.

First, realize that a fragment is a group of words masquerading as a sentence. Not all fragments appear as separate sentences, however. Often, fragments are separated by semicolons.

INCORRECT: Traffic was stalled for ten miles on the freeway. Because repairs were being made on potholes.

CORRECT: Traffic was stalled for ten miles on the freeway because repairs were being made on potholes.

INCORRECT: It was a funny story; one that I had never heard before.

CORRECT: It was a funny story, one that I had never heard before.

Four Types of Fragments

1. **Subordinate conjunction fragments** begin with subordinate conjunctions (also known as dependent words) like *unless, before, when, because, as*. They are often corrected by joining the fragment to the sentence that comes before or after it.

   Example with fragment: I won't eat cake. Unless you do.

   Corrected: I won't eat cake unless you do.

2. **Gerund, or –ing, fragments.** To correct one of these fragments, connect it to the sentence it goes with or write a new sentence.

   Example with fragment: Playing with their phones. The teenagers didn't even talk to each other.

   Corrected: Playing with their phones, the teenagers didn't even talk to each other.

3. **Added detail fragments** begin with words such as *like, also, with, without* and *for example*. To correct the fragment, connect it to the sentence it goes with or write a new sentence (with a subject and a verb).

   Example with fragment: I like horses. For example, Secretariat.

   Corrected: I like horses. For example, I like reading about the thoroughbred Secretariat.

4. **Missing-subject fragments** are just as they sound (no subject—just a verb phrase). To correct, connect it elsewhere or add a subject.

   Example with fragment: I read the golf magazine. While listening to the radio.

   Corrected: I read the golf magazine while listening to the radio.

Practice Exercises: Sentence Fragments

DIRECTIONS: Read each pair of response options. Identify the fragment. Answers appear on pages 381–382.

1. (A) My mother called my name.

    (B) Before I even got to my car.

2. (A) The tornado upended the homes.

    (B) That were on Springfield Avenue.

3. (A) Unless the rain falls soon.

    (B) The crops will die.

4. (A) Tatyana stayed in the library all morning.

    (B) Reading a book.

5. (A) I like bagels.

    (B) With cream cheese.

6. (A) The woman petted the dog.

    (B) Then led him back to his crate.

7. (A) Bill and Ted have similar hobbies.

    (B) For instance, woodworking.

8. (A) To brighten up the office.

    (B) We painted the walls a nice beige.

9. (A) This gym is often crowded.

    (B) Especially on Wednesday and Friday mornings.

10. (A) At the supermarket, Rosita found a phone on the ground.

    (B) And put it in her purse.

RUN-ONS, COMMA SPLICES, AND FUSED SENTENCES

A compound sentence that's not punctuated correctly may produce a run-on, comma splice, or fused sentence. Such a sentence need not be a long sentence; in fact, a run-on may be two short sentences disguised as one, as we see here:

Dry ice does not melt it evaporates.

A run-on results when the writer fuses or runs together two separate sentences without any correct mark of punctuation separating them.

INCORRECT: Knowing how to use a dictionary is no problem each dictionary has a section in the front of the book telling how to use it.

CORRECT: Knowing how to use a dictionary is no problem. Each dictionary has a section in the front of the book telling how to use it.

Even if one or both of the fused sentences contains internal punctuation, the sentence is still a run-on.

INCORRECT: Bob bought dress shoes, a suit, and a nice shirt he needed them for his sister's wedding.

CORRECT: Bob bought dress shoes, a suit, and a nice shirt. He needed them for his sister's wedding.

A comma splice is the unjustifiable use of only a comma to combine what really is two separate sentences.

INCORRECT: One common error in writing is incorrect spelling, the other is the occasional use of faulty diction.

CORRECT: One common error in writing is incorrect spelling; the other is the occasional use of faulty diction.

Both run-on sentences and comma splices may be corrected in one of the following ways:

RUN-ON: Neal won the award he had the highest score.

COMMA SPLICE: Neal won the award, he had the highest score.

Separate the sentences with a period:

Neal won the award. He had the highest score.

Separate the sentences with a comma and a coordinating conjunction *(and, but, or, nor, for, yet, so)*:

Neal won the award, for he had the highest score.

Separate the sentences with a semicolon:

Neal won the award; he had the highest score.

Separate the sentences with a subordinating conjunction such as *although*, *because*, *if*:

Neal won the award because he had the highest score.

Practice Exercises: Run-Ons/Fused Sentences and Comma Splices

DIRECTIONS: Indicate if each of the following is a run-on sentence, a comma splice, or neither. Answers appear on pages 382–383.

1.   The front cover of the book is a radiant image of autumn leaves, it may be autumn's ending.

2.   This haunting memoir of a surgeon is best read as his story and not as a war chronicle.

3.   Large parts of the book are not about war, however the war that rages inside the author continues throughout the book and gives the reader glimpses of wisdom gained during his remarkable journey of life amidst death.

4.   The book came from journal writings that the author kept throughout his travels.

5.   The book proceeds chronologically each chapter is named for the location of the trauma.

6.   The brutality of people against people is somberly portrayed in this book be prepared for an eloquent narrative of suffering and dislocation.

7.   At one point, he returns to Africa but finds himself depressed.

8.   He is a medical humanitarian serving on the front lines of pain and suffering.

9.   I loved this book it was the best book I ever read.

10.   When you read this book, please remember the compassion of the doctor who is depicted.

CORRELATIVE CONJUNCTIONS

Correlative Conjunctions are words that appear in pairs and connect two equal grammatical items with *either/or*, *neither/nor*, *both/and*, *not only/but also*, *so/as*, and *whether/or*. The phrases create idiomatic language, which is why some of these pairs are listed in that section as well.

Examples:

You should **either** go to the mall **or** go to the movies.

Today, it was **not only** warm **but also** cool.

Practice Exercises: Correlative Conjunctions

DIRECTIONS: Read each sentence below. Fill in the blanks with the correct correlative conjunctions (*either/or*) or (*neither/nor*). If there is more than one set of responses, indicate all that apply. *Example: She _____ wants to play cards _____ leave. Answer: She <u>either</u> wants to play <u>or</u> leave.* Answers appear on pages 384–385.

1. We _____ are going to the park _____ are going home.

2. At night _____ the cats _____ the dogs jump on the bed.

3. John will _____ start today _____ start tomorrow.

4. He should___study for the exam___finish his homework.

DIRECTIONS: For exercises 5–10, choose the correct pair of correlative conjunctions from the choices given.

5. _____Sue_____Sam like to go hiking.

    (A) Whether . . . or

    (B) Both...and

    (C) So . . . as

    (D) Neither . . . nor

6. Fran needs to decide _____ she wants to go to the movies _____ to the zoo today.

   (A) whether...or

   (B) either...or

   (C) neither...nor

   (D) not only...but also

7. "Well," said Ron, "_____ you start shoveling _____ you are grounded."

   (A) whether . . . or

   (B) either . . . or

   (C) neither . . . nor

   (D) not only . . . but also

8. _____ it is raining _____ snowing, you are expected to attend the ceremony.

   (A) Whether . . . or

   (B) Either . . . or

   (C) Neither . . . nor

   (D) Not only . . . but also

9. _____ the secretary _____ the maintenance person wanted to admit there was a problem with the phones.

   (A) Whether . . . or

   (B) Neither . . . nor

   (C) Either . . . or

   (D) Not only . . . but also

10. My uncle can____ read_____write. He is illiterate.

   (A) Whether . . . or

   (B) Neither . . . .nor

   (C) Either . . . or

   (D) Not only . . . but also

PARALLELISM

Parallel structure is used to express matching ideas. It refers to the **grammatical balance** of a series of any of the following:

Phrases:

The squirrel ran *along the fence*, *up the tree*, and *into his burrow* with a mouthful of acorns.

Adjectives:

The job market is flooded with *very* talented, *highly* motivated, and *well-educated* young people.

Nouns:

You will need a *notebook*, a *pencil*, and a *dictionary* for the test.

Clauses:

The children were told to decide *which toy they would keep* and *which toy they would give away*.

Verbs:

The farmer *plowed*, *planted*, and *harvested* his corn in record time.

Verbals:

Reading, *writing*, and *calculating* are fundamental skills that all of us should possess.

Correlative conjunctions:

Either *you will do your homework* or *you will fail*.

Repetition of structural signals: (e.g., articles, auxiliaries, prepositions, and conjunctions)

INCORRECT: I have quit my job, enrolled in school, and am looking for a reliable babysitter.

CORRECT: I have quit my job, have enrolled in school, and am looking for a reliable babysitter.

Note: Repetition of prepositions is considered formal and is not necessary.

> You can travel by car, by plane, or by train; it's all up to you.

OR

> You can travel by car, plane, or train; it's all up to you.

When a sentence contains items in a series, check for both punctuation and sentence balance. When you check for punctuation, make sure the commas are used correctly. When you check for parallelism, make sure that the conjunctions connect similar grammatical constructions, such as all adjectives or all clauses.

Practice Exercises: Parallelism

DIRECTIONS: Select the underlined portion of the sentence in which an error in parallel structure exists. If there is no error, select (E). Answers appear on pages 385–386.

1. When I get home from school, I review my notes, read the next day's assignment, and
           (A)   (B)   (C)

    is studying for any upcoming tests. No error.
        (D)   (E)

2. In spite of the rain, I am still playing tennis, walking home, and I will stay positive. No error.
      (A)   (B)   (C)   (D)   (E)

3. The dropout rate among high school students is increasing because of lack of opportunity,
             (A)   (B)

    gang involvement, and teen pregnancy. No error.
        (C)   (D)   (E)

4. Peanut butter and jelly is my favorite lunch on Fridays. No error.
      (A)   (B)   (C) (D)   (E)

5. My mom expects us to be patient, to obey, and kind. No error.
                 (A)   (B) (C) (D)   (E)

6. It is easier to sleep late than getting up early. No error.
        (A)   (B)   (C)   (D)   (E)

7. I add <u>sugar</u> <u>not only</u> <u>to coffee</u> but also <u>spaghetti</u>. <u>No error</u>.
      (A)   (B)   (C)   (D)   (E)

8. The <u>sun is up</u>, the <u>sky is blue</u>, <u>and</u> <u>it's beautiful</u>. <u>No error</u>.
        (A)   (B)   (C)   (D)   (E)

9. <u>Every morning</u>, <u>I</u> have to <u>take a shower</u> and <u>eating my breakfast</u>. <u>No error</u>.
       (A)   (B)   (C)   (D)   (E)

10. The president vowed to <u>cut taxes</u>, <u>reduce spending</u>, <u>and</u> <u>fight crime</u>. <u>No error</u>.
                (A)   (B)   (C)   (D)   (E)

Idiomatic Expressions

Idioms are words we use every day that sound right in a sentence. They're inherently tough to deal with because you have to know what they mean apart from the dictionary definitions the individual words within them may have. For instance, "a fresh pair of eyes" means bringing in, say, an editor who hasn't looked at the text yet—hence, a fresh perspective. It doesn't literally mean a fresh pair of eyes! If I ask you to be my editor, you might say, "I'm all ears." This means you're listening carefully. If you admire a reporter, you may say he or she has a "nose for news" for "sniffing out" good information. Non-native speakers of English in particular need to pay attention to idiomatic phases because they can be confusing. The following chart shows only a few common idioms (many of which contain correlative conjunctions). Especially if English is your second language, we encourage you to consult a book about idioms, or to look online for exercises in this area. Always pay attention to how language sounds, particularly to which words work alongside which prepositions.

Some Common Idiomatic Phrases

Either/Or	Either Michael or John will drive.
Neither/Nor	The table is neither heavy nor smooth.
As/as	That dress is as pretty as the one you are wearing.
Not only/but also	In college, you must take not only Freshman Seminar but also English Composition.
Characteristic of	The architecture is characteristic of the Victorian Era.
Different from	He is different from his sister.
Sympathize with	I can sympathize with you.
Guilty of	They are guilty of leaving the scene of the crime.

Practice Exercises: Idioms

DIRECTIONS: Select the underlined portion of the sentence in which an idiomatic error exists. Answers appear on pages 386–387.

1. The <u>behavior</u> we saw displayed was <u>characteristic</u> <u>with</u> his <u>disability</u>. <u>No error.</u>
        (A)   (B)   (C)   (D)   (E)

2. I can <u>sympathize</u> <u>with</u> the <u>woman</u> who spoke. <u>No error.</u>
    (A)   (B)   (C)   (D)   (E)

3. I <u>can't</u> believe <u>how</u> prices are <u>going</u> <u>off</u> each year. <u>No error.</u>
      (A)   (B)   (C) (D)   (E)

4. She <u>seems</u> mean <u>at</u> times, but <u>for sure</u> she is a good <u>person</u>. <u>No error.</u>
        (A)   (B)   (C)   (D)   (E)

5. <u>Over and over</u>, <u>Mary</u> <u>enjoys</u> driving <u>to</u> the beach. <u>No error.</u>
        (A)   (B) (C)   (D)   (E)

6. <u>The girl</u> did not go <u>to the mall</u> <u>than</u> to the <u>ice skating rink</u>. <u>No error.</u>
    (A)   (B)   (C)   (D)   (E)

7. In <u>America</u>, it is <u>widely accepted</u> that <u>young people</u> <u>coming from poverty</u> are in trouble. <u>No error.</u>
        (A)   (B)   (C)   (D)   (E)

8. <u>Psychologists</u> have accepted that <u>negative words or attitudes</u> <u>on teachers</u> can make students
           (A)   (B)   (C)

    feel <u>discouraged</u>. <u>No error.</u>
        (D)   (E)

9. <u>Dan</u>, who was paralyzed <u>from the waist down, has found</u> that <u>people</u> <u>freak out</u> in his presence.
    (A)   (B)   (C)   (D)

    <u>No error.</u>
     (E)

10. Vitiligo is a <u>condition</u> that causes <u>skin</u> to lose <u>its</u> pigment. <u>No error.</u>
          (A)   (B)   (C)   (D)   (E)

Word Choice

Word choice, or **diction,** means finding words that capture the meaning you want to express. When a teacher writes a comment such as "awkward," "vague," or "wordy" on your draft, the teacher is asking you to work on diction. In this area, you might find redundancy as well as words often confused or used incorrectly.

Some areas to consider:

- **Connotative and Denotative Meanings:** The denotative meaning of a word is its literal, dictionary definition. What the word denotes is what it "means." The connotative meaning of the word is a meaning apart from what the word literally means. What the word connotes is what is what it "suggests." A writer should choose a word based on the tone and context of the sentence; words should contain the appropriate connotation while still conveying the correct denotation. For example, a gift might be described as "cheap," but the negative connotation of "cheap" is something of little or no value. The word "inexpensive" has a more positive connotation, even though "cheap" is a synonym for "inexpensive." Questions about diction require you to decide which words and phrases are appropriate for the tone and context of a sentence.

- **Slang** is informal writing that is inappropriate in formal academic writing.

    Example: "It was my bad" versus "It was my fault." **(Slang versus formal)**

- **Clichés** are worn phrases that should be avoided because they are overused.

    Example: I loved him from the bottom of my heart.

This phrase has been used so much that it has lost its freshness.

Commonly Confused Words

The following is a list of commonly confused words. These words can confuse a writer because they sound alike or are nearly alike in sound or spelling. Sound-alikes are called **homophones.**

ACCEPT to receive

She <u>accepts</u> defeat well.

EXCEPT to take or leave out

Please take all the shoes off the shelf <u>except</u> for the red ones.

AFFECT verb, to influence

Lack of sleep <u>affects</u> the quality of your life.

EFFECT noun, result,

> The effect of falling oil prices was equivalent to a large tax cut for the middle class.

ALLUSION an indirect reference

> The professor made an allusion to John Donne's work.

ILLUSION a false perception of reality

> They thought they saw an oasis, a common illusion in the desert.

ASCENT climb

> The airplane's ascent made my ears pop.

ASSENT agreement

> The task force recommended special zoning for a riverfront stadium and the mayor assented.

BREATH noun, air inhaled or exhaled

> You could see his breath in the cold air.

BREATHE verb, to inhale or exhale

> If you don't breathe, you will die.

CAPITAL seat of government. Also financial resources.

> The capital of Virginia is Richmond.

> The company had enough capital to build the new plant.

CAPITOL the actual building in which the legislative body meets

> The governor announced his plan in a speech given at the capitol today.

COMPLEMENT noun, something that completes; verb, to complete

> A red wine complements a meat entrée.

COMPLIMENT noun, praise; verb, to praise

> The professor complimented Sue on her essay.

CONSCIENCE sense of right and wrong

> The boy's conscience kept him from lying.

CONSCIOUS awake, aware

> He was conscious when the ambulance arrived.

ELICIT to draw or bring out

The professor elicited the correct response from the student.

ILLICIT illegal

The gang leader was arrested for his illicit activities.

ITS of or belonging to it

The puppy will cry as soon as its owner walks out of the room.

IT'S contraction for *it is*

It's a gorgeous day today.

LEAD noun, a type of metal; verb, to guide

Is that pipe made of lead?

LED verb, past tense of the verb "to lead"

She led the them over the mountain.

LIE to lie down (a person or animal). *Hint: people can tell lies*, which means they can *lie* or fib.

I feel sick, so I'm going to lie down for a while.

(also lying, lay, has/have lain—The dog has lain in the shade all day; yesterday, the dog lay there for twelve hours.)

LAY to put an object down.

Lay down that gun.

(also laying, laid, has/have laid—e.g., Pappy laid the shotgun on the ground).

LOSE verb, to misplace or not win

With keyless entry, you can't lose any keys, but you can still lose the key fob.

LOOSE adjective, to not be tight; verb (rarely used)—to release

The sweater was perfect except for one loose thread.

The dog was never set loose from his leash.

PASSED verb, past tense of "to pass," to have moved

The tornado passed through the city quickly, but it caused great damage.

PAST belonging to a former time or place

Who was the past president of this organization?

PRECEDE to come before

Studying <u>precedes</u> graduation.

PROCEED to go forward

He <u>proceeded</u> to pass back the essays.

PRINCIPAL adjective, most important; noun, a person who has authority

The <u>principal</u> element in the job is hard work.

The <u>principal</u> announces the school news each morning.

PRINCIPLE a general or fundamental truth

The course was based on the <u>principles</u> of ethics.

SIGHT vision

If the Praxis test is out of <u>sight</u>, it will be out of mind.

SITE position or place

The new housing complex was built on the <u>site</u> of a cemetery.

CITE to quote or document

I <u>cited</u> five ideas from the same author in my paper.

THAN use with comparisons

I would rather go out to eat <u>than</u> stay in.

THEN at that time, or next

I studied for my exam for three hours, and <u>then</u> I went to bed.

THEIR possessive form of they

<u>Their</u> house is at the end of the street.

THERE indicates location (hint: think of "here and there")

<u>There</u> goes my chance of dating him.

THEY'RE contraction for "they are"

<u>They're</u> in Australia for the summer.

WHO pronoun, referring to a person or persons

I wondered how Sam, <u>who</u> is so convivial, could be alone at the table.

WHICH pronoun, replacing a singular or plural thing(s); not used to refer to people

I wonder how Pluto, <u>which</u> used to be a full-fledged planet, got demoted.

THAT used to refer to things or a group or class of people; used to introduce a restrictive relative clause

<u>That</u>'s a cat—furry and finicky.

The book that I put on the table is gone.

Wrong Word Use

Wrong word use means choosing awkward, confusing, or overly formal words that are poor choices. If you wish to write with clarity and grace, you must be willing to spend some time thinking about the words you use as well as their sounds, rhythms, and connotations. Avoid words that are either too pretentious or too colloquial, and beware of jargon. Try to use language that is vivid and precise; a sentence that relies on vague and abstract language will be difficult to understand.

- **Misused words**—the word doesn't mean what the writer intends.

    Example: The Japanese were a *monotonous* culture until the Europeans arrived.

    Revision: The Japanese were a *homogenous* culture until the Europeans arrived.

- **Jargon or technical terms** make readers work unnecessarily hard. Don't throw words around to "sound smart."

    Example: The dialectical interface between Protestants and anti-disestablishment Catholics offers an important algorithm for future deontological thought.

    Revision: The dialogue between Protestant and Catholic thinkers is important for the future.

- **Loaded language.** Loaded words play upon the reader's emotions, affecting the meaning of the words around them and thus the reaction that may be elicited from the reader. Consider a 1979 study led by Elizabeth Loftus that found that when defendants were asked how fast they were going when they "smashed into" (rather than "hit") the other car, their reported speed was higher.

Practice Exercises: Word Choice

DIRECTIONS: Choose the better sentence. Answers appear on pages 387–388.

1. (A) He was airing our all of our dirty laundry to the neighbors.

    (B) He was telling all of our private matters to the neighbors.

2.   (A)   The provost blew her stack when she heard I was leaving.

     (B)   The provost was very angry when she heard I was leaving.

3.   (A)   The record was one of my favorites.

     (B)   The record was an oldie but goodie.

4.   (A)   The movie was a dud.

     (B)   The movie was a disappointment.

5.   (A)   During the police interview, Bill looked relaxed, but inside he was shaking like a leaf.

     (B)   During the police interview, Bill looked relaxed, but inside he was scared.

6.   (A)   I am going for the job of stock clerk that you told about in the paper.

     (B)   I am going for the stock clerk job you advertised in the paper.

7.   (A)   I think I would be great at the job because of my expertise.

     (B)   My contributions would be extraordinarily amazing because I have stupendous experience.

8.   (A)   The oasis appeared as an allusion.

     (B)   The oasis appeared as an illusion.

9.   (A)   A livid man walked into the supermarket.

     (B)   A man with an angry expression walked into the supermarket

10. (A)   I also helped in my father's store.

     (B)   I also hindered in my father's store.

Sentence Correction

Sentence-correction questions on the Praxis Core test do just what it sounds like: They ask you to correct mistakes in sentence structure. There will usually be a sentence with some portion underlined. Your task is to determine the best replacement. Maybe the sentence with needs to be reworded or corrected because of grammar. Or maybe it is OK, and you then choose the answer worded exactly as it is in the question, which on the Praxis Core means selecting the first choice. We've already looked at some of the problems you'll be grappling with in these sentences. They include grammatical concerns (subjects and verbs, pronouns, verb tenses/shift, adjectives/adverbs) as well as problems with structural elements (modifiers, coordinating conjunctions, fragment/run-ons, parallelism). Consider reviewing these closely to be sure you're on top of your grammar game. Your surefootedness on such questions, which are arranged in a way you may not see every day, will pay off on test day.

Pronoun Cases and Pronoun Agreement

A pronoun stands for a noun (even though, at times, it may actually refer back to another pronoun). What it refers to is called the antecedent. This is where things can get tricky.

As a rule, pronouns must agree with their antecedents.

Jorge was early because **he** drove as opposed to taking the train.

Use the objective case when a pronoun is the object of a verb or preposition.

I called **her** on the phone, *not* I called she on the phone.

Use relative pronouns "who" and "whom" (not "that") when referring to people.

The man **who** is standing by the desk is my uncle.

The woman with **whom** I am speaking is a teacher.

Use relative pronouns "which" and "that" when referring to inanimate objects.

The restaurant, **which** has a balcony, is my first choice for the rehearsal dinner.

 HINT

Common (easily fixed) errors can lead to ambiguity.

Mike doesn't like the music that they play. (Who are "they"?)

Sarah and Cathy went to the movies in her car. (Whose car? Sarah's or Cathy's?)

A Guide to Pronoun Cases

Pronouns as Subjects	Pronouns as Objects	Pronouns that Show Possession
I	Me	My, Mine
You	You	Your, Yours
He	Him	His
She	Her	Her, Hers
It	It	Its
We	Us	Our, Ours
They	Them	Their, Theirs
Who	Whom	Whose

Subject–Verb Agreement

Like pronouns, verbs must agree with their subjects in person.

I am going to Rome.

They must also agree in number.

"Sam takes the train" versus "The employees take the train."

Subjects and verbs agree in person ("I am" is first person versus "They are," which is third person) and in number ("She takes the train" versus "They take the train"). In this case, a singular subject "she" takes a singular verb, while a plural subject "they" takes a plural verb). Collective nouns (e.g., a group, team, family, board of directors) are singular.

Verb Tense Shifts

Verb Tense Shifts are another area of concern when correcting sentences. Here's a chart of different forms of verb tenses in English.

Common Regular and Irregular Verbs

Simple Form	Past Tense	Past Participle
help	helped	helped
review	reviewed	reviewed
hear	heard	heard
bet	bet	bet
choose	chose	chosen
draw	drew	drawn
drink	drank	drunk
see	saw	seen

Nevertheless, irregular verbs have different forms that must be learned. For instance, the verb "to be" is irregular since the present is "I am" while the past isn't "I amed" but rather "I was." If English is your second language, you will have to look up and memorize these irregular verb forms.

Adjectives and Adverbs

Adjectives describe nouns, whereas adverbs describe verbs.

He enjoyed the beautiful day. ("Beautiful" is an adjective modifying the noun "day.")

The musician played flawlessly. ("Flawlessly" is an adverb modifying the verb "played.")

Commonly Confused Modifiers

Good (adj)/Well (adv)	Julie felt good about the meeting.	Tracy performed well on the Praxis Core tests.
Fewer (adj describing plural noun)/Less (adj describing singular nouns)	The world has fewer fish species because of overfishing.	The city has less crime.
Bad (adj)/Badly (adv)	I felt bad as a result of my cold. (*bad* modifies *I*)	I performed badly on the exam. (*badly* modifies *performed*)

Let's take a look at another sentence-correction question. Can you find the error here, if there is one?

The <u>lawyer</u> looked <u>doubtfully</u> after the <u>jury</u> <u>returned</u> to the room. <u>No change.</u>
  (A)   (B)   (C) (D)   (E)

The correct answer is (B). The sentence needs an adjective form, "doubtful," as opposed to the adverb form given here. The reason is that "looked" is a linking verb, which is usually followed by an adjective. Adjectives (not adverbs) modify nouns with the exception of linking verbs (e.g., *appear, become, feel, look, sound, taste, remain*), so the adverb form isn't acceptable.

For sentence-correction questions, you may also have to identify effective paraphrases. In an **effective paraphrase**, a writer puts the original passage in his or her own words and uses approximately the same length as the original. The way to do it is to read the original to discover its meaning, substitute your own words for those of the source passage, and then rewrite the passage. You may need to rearrange your sentences so that they read logically and smoothly. Be open to reordering or restructuring the ideas to improve concision, coherence, and style.

Let's do an exercise that combines a mixture of sentence corrections. Remember to focus on standard written English, word choice, syntax, and punctuation. Errors in all those areas could end up on the Praxis Core test.

Practice Exercises: Sentence Correction

DIRECTIONS: In each of the following sentences, some part of the sentence or the full sentence is underscored. Choice (A) always repeats the underscored part. If you think the underscored portion is correct as it stands, select choice (A). Otherwise, select the response option that corrects the underlined portion in accordance with standard written English. Answers appear on pages 388–390.

1. Walking into the woods, I suddenly realized that my steps <u>impeded by rocks.</u>

    (A) impeded by rocks.

    (B) impeded as a result of rocks.

    (C) were being impeded by rocks.

    (D) was impeding by rocks.

    (E) was going to be impeding by rocks.

2. Bill, after many text messages <u>who took up most of his night</u>, answered my question about the meeting.

    (A) who took up most of his night

    (B) whom took up most of his night

    (C) that took up most of his night

    (D) and took up most of his night

    (E) can take up most of his night

3. As we stood in line at the amusement park, we heard a child who was <u>neither a baby or a toddler</u> crying.

    (A) neither a baby or a toddler

    (B) neither a baby nor a toddler

    (C) whether a baby so a toddler

    (D) neither a baby or that of toddler

    (E) None of these.

4.   The teacher, after passing out papers, explained that the grades were given as a result of <u>many close readings and analyzing using a rubric</u>.

   (A)   many close readings and analyzing using a rubric

   (B)   close readings and analytical using a rubric

   (C)   close readings and analysis using a rubric.

   (D)   many close readings and many analysis using a rubric.

   (E)   None of the above.

5.   After the death of Friedrich Nietzsche's grandmother, the family moved into their own house, <u>now a museum and study center</u>.

   (A)   now a museum and study center.

   (B)   now a museum that is also used as a study center

   (C)   now museum and study center.

   (D)   which is not a museum and study center.

   (E)   None of the above.

6.   Wolves with their cold eyes <u>terrifies</u> most people.

   (A)   terrifies

   (B)   terrified

   (C)   terrify

   (D)   will terrifies

   (E)   frightens

7.   Danielle enjoys walnuts, pistachios, and almonds, but <u>they</u> are her favorite.

   (A)   they

   (B)   whose

   (C)   that

   (D)   pistachios

   (E)   those

8.   As I put on my glasses, the phone <u>rings</u>.

   (A)   rings

   (B)   had rung

   (C)   ringed

   (D)   ringing

   (E)   rang

9. It is hard to do what's best for you, <u>even if</u> it involves breaking someone's heart.

    (A) even if

    (B) even though

    (C) even still

    (D) even then

    (E) both (A) and (B) are correct

10. The gazelle <u>that the tiger attacked</u> was clearly ailing.

    (A) that the tiger attacked

    (B) , which the tiger attacked,

    (C) who came under attack by the tiger

    (D) which the tiger attacked

    (E) whose attack by the tiger

REVISION IN CONTEXT

The third type of test question you will encounter will be **revision-in-context questions**. You will have to recognize the choice that shows how writing can be strengthened through editing/revision. These questions will contain errors, and you will be asked to revise (translated as "look again" for changes in organization) and edit (look closely and fix grammatical and mechanical areas).

Some areas to consider are **wordiness** (and its opposite, **conciseness**), **redundancy, vague pronouns, choppy language** (lacking transitions), **jargon,** and **interesting adjectives.**

Wordiness/Conciseness

Wordiness/Conciseness: Effective writing is concise. Wordiness undermines clarity by cluttering sentences with unnecessary words.

Wordiness questions test your ability to detect redundancies, circumlocution (failure to get to the point) and padding (with unfastened synonyms, extra adjectives, etc.). Wordiness questions require you to choose sentences that use as few words as possible to convey the message clearly, economically, and effectively. Here are some examples. Notice the difference in the impact between the first and second sentences in the following pairs:

Wordy: The medical exam that he gave me was entirely complete.

Better: The medical exam he gave me was complete.

Wordy: Larry asked his friend John, who was a good, old friend, if he would join him and go along with him to see the foreign film made in Japan.

Better: Larry asked his friend John if he would join him in seeing the Japanese film.

Wordy: I was absolutely, totally happy with the present that my parents gave to me at 7 a.m. on the morning of my birthday.

Better: I was happy with the present my parents gave me on the morning of my birthday.

Redundancy

In his book *The Elements of Style*, William Strunk explains, "Vigorous writing is concise. A sentence should contain no unnecessary words, a paragraph no unnecessary sentences, for the same reason that a drawing should have no unnecessary lines and a machine no unnecessary parts. This requires not that the writer make all his sentences short, or that he avoid all detail and treat his subjects only in outline, but that every word tell." When you write, avoid saying things twice (*12 midnight* as opposed to *midnight, exactly the same* as opposed to *the same, the end result* as opposed to *the result*) and be ready to pare down your writing to make it simpler and less wordy.

> **Example:** Next month is important. It will be filled with important events. The important actions I take will have an impact on my future.

The writer repeats ideas and word choices ("important"), which weakens the writing. You might encounter **vague pronouns** in a question and be asked to revise for greater clarity. Likewise, you might read a question that has **choppy language** and be asked to revise it. Consider this passage, which models both:

> **Example:** It was weird. You should see it.

Consider this deceptively simple example. What is "it," and who is "you"? The pronouns are vague. When you listen to these two sentences aloud, you also can hear that they are short and that the words sound awkward.

Interesting adjectives turn ordinary sentences into engaging, more precise prose.

Compare the following two sentences:

"The good fans cheered loudly."

versus

"The loyal fans cheered loudly."

In this context, "loyal" is a better adjective because it is more descriptive. "Good" is too vague and makes the writing flat. Using descriptive words should be a goal of revision.

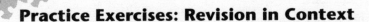

Practice Exercises: Revision in Context

DIRECTIONS: Read each sentence and determine whether the underscored portion contains an error in grammar or usage. If none of the revisions improve the sentence as it stands, select choice (A), which repeats the underscored part. Answers appear on pages 390–391.

1. Janie <u>went ahead and made a decision</u> to leave him.

    (A) went ahead and made a decision

    (B) went ahead and decided

    (C) decided

    (D) wanted

2. The fly was <u>dead as a doornail</u>, so I deposited it with a tissue into the garbage can.

    (A) dead as a doornail

    (B) deader than a doornail

    (C) dead

    (D) None of these

3. <u>Daily meditation every day is important.</u>

    (A) Daily meditation every day is important.

    (B) Daily meditation is important.

    (C) Daily meditation every day.

    (D) Daily meditation every day of my life is important.

4. Louise <u>went nuts</u> when she heard our rabbi was leaving.

    (A) went nuts

    (B) died out

    (C) flipped out

    (D) became upset

5. I left his jacket and had to return <u>back again</u> to the restaurant where I left it.

    (A) back again

    (B) Delete the underlined phrase

    (C) Replace underlined phrase with "once again"

    (D) None of these

6.   <u>I assembled the afghan hooking it back together.</u>

   (A) I assembled the afghan hooking it back together.

   (B) I built the afghan hooking it back together.

   (C) I connected the afghan hooking it back together.

   (D) I reassembled the afghan by hooking it back together.

7.   The television show I saw was <u>a loser</u>.

   (A) loser

   (B) disappointing

   (C) lame

   (D) carefree

8.   <u>In this day and age</u> my parents still read the newspaper.

   (A) In this day and age

   (B) Today,

   (C) Yesterday,

   (D) Even still in this day and age,

9.   The noisy students are <u>loud and</u> ruining my day.

   (A) loud and

   (B) loud mouths

   (C) loudly

   (D) eliminate the underlined phrase

10. The cashier <u>at the pharmacy</u> is also a teacher at the vocational school.

   (A) at the pharmacy

   (B) eliminate the underlined phrase

   (C) at the pharmacy and my friend

   (D) with her roommate

RESEARCH SKILLS

With research skills having been integrated into the Common Core State Standards, you'll be assessed on these skills on the Praxis Core Writing test.

You will be asked to recognize effective research strategies, identify the parts of a citation, find information that is relevant to a research task, and assess the credibility of sources. To that end, this section should help prepare you for those questions.

In considering effective research strategies, the following chart may help. During the actual research, of course, these categories overlap. Thus, research is often recursive.

Effective Research Strategies

Narrow the Topic	Writers must narrow the topic and determine what they will assert, given the parameters of the assignment. If it's a five-page paper, writing about "Native American Culture" is probably a bad idea since that topic is broad. However, a topic such as the Native American internment camp Bosque Redondo would be more manageable.
Gather Source Material	Find primary and secondary sources from the physical library, library databases, and the Internet. There are even more sources for sources—interviews, films, surveys (if you are doing an empirical study).
Evaluate Sources	Can you trust what you are reading? Check whether the source is connected with a reputable organization such as UNICEF or a government agency. Books in the library and articles in a library database have been vetted, meaning other scholars have read and approved their contents. With the Internet, consider the source. Is this a website from University of Pennsylvania or schooldude.com? Look at the URL for suffixes such as *.gov*, *.org*, and *.edu* (as opposed to *.com*, wherein the author has commercial interests). Always question the validity of sources. Is there no author? That might be a flag. Is it a group as an author? If so, it's important to know if the group is reputable. Check to see whether a source cites other sources (with in-text citations and a reference list at the end of what was written).
Read and Take Notes	After you gather your sources, read critically. Annotate in the margins, outline the article, etc. Use active reading strategies. When you take notes, record the full bibliographic entry so that you know where the source originates and you won't plagiarize. Remember that there are three ways to use the source in your paper: (A) Summary note (where you summarize the whole source quickly and condense it into the fewest words possible.) (B) Paraphrase (such as where you rewrite the passage in your own words) (C) Quoting (where you maintain the authenticity of your author by re-presenting the exact words in the text) All three of these notes need to be cited. Rule of thumb: If it isn't your idea, even if you put it in your own words, you need to cite it. Cite as you write, as they say.
Write	After you organize your notes, you need to write a draft. You will undoubtedly revise and have newer versions of your text, but the first step is to start. It also helps to work from an outline.

(Continued)

Effective Research Strategies (cont'd)

Refine Your Thesis	As you write and research, you might find you need to revisit your initial topic. You need to determine what you are arguing and to make sure that the ideas are well-organized.
Revise	Look again—what can be added, deleted, moved, or changed? Which paragraphs lack support or transitions? Do your claims (smaller arguments) line up with the larger problem/argument you present in the introduction? Does your thesis need to be refined? Do you have a coherent central argument?
Edit	Proofread for sentence-level errors in spelling, grammar, and mechanics. The editing phase is also when you make sure your research paper is formatted correctly (using MLA, APA, Chicago, etc.).

Answers to Practice Exercises: Capitalization *(page 285)*:

1.   (D)

"North America" is a proper noun and "south," as used here, is a cardinal point, or direction.

2.   (B)

"National Football League," a proper noun, is capitalized as is "Dallas Cowboys," the name of an NFL team. As for "coach," it should remain lowercased because it's used as a job description. However, if a person is called Coach in place of his or her name, then anytime the word "coach" stands in for that name it should be capped. If, for example, you were reading a transcript of an interview with Landry in which the interviewer addressed him as "Coach," it would capitalized. It would also be capped in "Coach Landry."

3.   (C)

"Northern Hemisphere," a geographic location, is capped, but "equator," the imaginary line that divides the earth into two hemispheres, should be lowercased. But: *Equatorial Current*.

4.   (D)

This follows the standard guidelines for capitalization in titles, in this case involving a short story and two novels.

5.   (C)

Names of deities should always be capitalized, as should terms describing a culture. "Mythology" need not be capped because it is a common noun. Proper adjectives ("Roman," "Greek") also should be capitalized.

6.   (D)

The sentence correctly capitalizes "Torah" and "Jews." The names of religious groups and religious scripture should be capitalized.

7.   (B)

The name of a specific course ("Algebra I") must be capitalized. "English" should be capped because it's a language. The common noun "freshman" is not capitalized. The generic "community college" is also not capitalized, but if it is part of a name, such as Sundance Community College, it is.

8.   (D)

Seasons should not be capitalized unless they're part of a named place or event (e.g., 25th Annual Highland Park Spring Street Fair). Academic degrees are capitalized only when the full name of the degree is used (e.g., Bachelor of Science or Juris Doctor), not for general reference (e.g., bachelor's, master's, or doctoral degree).

9.   (B)

Because it is a landmark, "Berlin Wall" is capped; however, you should not capitalize systems of government or adherents to a philosophy, so "communism" should be lowercase.

10.   (A)

"National Geographic" is the name of a magazine and thus should be capitalized. "Curiosity" is the name of a space vehicle, which, as a proper noun, merits capitalization. The common term "magazine" is not capitalized.

Answers to Practice Exercises: Punctuation *(page 306)*:

1. **(D)**

    Nonrestrictive clauses, like other nonrestrictive elements, should be set off from the rest of the sentence with commas. This includes state names that follow a city name.

2. **(B)**

    Placing commas around the phrase "an Oklahoma family" is appropriate when two non-restrictive appositive phrases modify the noun. In this case, two phrases modify the noun "Joads":

    *   "an Oklahoma family," and

    *   "who were driven from their dustbowl farm and forced to become migrant workers in California."

3. **(A)**

    No commas are necessary in this sentence. Choices (B) and (C) provide superfluous punctuation.

4. **(C)**

    There is no pause between two items separated by a coordinating conjunction—in this case, "or." Thus, there should not be a comma after "car."

5. **(A)**

    Use a semicolon to separate two independent clauses/sentences that are not joined by a coordinating conjunction. This is especially effective when the ideas in the sentences are strongly inter-related.

6. **(D)**

    Use a semicolon to separate two sentences not joined by a coordinating conjunction.

7. **(A)**

    Use a semicolon to separate two sentences joined by a conjunctive adverb.

8. (A)

Do not use a colon after a verb or a preposition. Remember that a complete sentence must precede a colon.

9. (B)

Do not use a colon after a preposition, and do not use a colon to separate a preposition from its objects.

10. (D)

Use a colon preceding a list that is introduced by words such as "the following" and "as follows."

Answers to Practice Exercises: Adjectives and Adverbs *(page 312)*:

1. (C)

"Bad" is an adjective, while "badly" is an adverb. "Real" is an adjective meaning *genuine* (e.g., a *real* problem, *real* leather). To qualify an adverb of degree to express how bad, how excited, how boring, and so forth, use *very*.

2. (A)

Use an adverb as a qualifier for an adjective. Ask yourself, *How* simple? *Relatively* simple.

3. (D)

"Good" is an adjective; "well" can be either an adjective or adverb. As adjective, "well" refers to one's state of health; it means "not ill."

4. (C)

All the other choices use "good" incorrectly as an adverb. Because "shake" is an action verb, it needs an adverb, not an adjective.

5. (A)

The verbs "speaks," "writes," "observe," and "think" all require adverbs as modifiers.

6.   (C)

The comparisons drawn in choices (A) and (B) are illogical, as these sentences suggest that Los Angeles is not, in fact, in California because it is misconstrued as larger than any city in California. The sentence needs "other" as a determiner to distinguish Los Angeles from other cities in the same state.

7.   (A)

Take care not to omit the second "as" in the correlative pair "as . . . as" when making a point of equal or superior comparison, as in choice (B). Choice (C) omits "than" from the phrase "if not more interesting [than]."

8.   (C)

Choice (A) illogically compares "baseball team" to a "university." Choice (B) illogically compares "baseball team" to "all other universities." In contrast, choice (C) offers a valid, logical comparison because the comparison is clearly made strictly from among other collegiate teams.

9.   (B)

Choices (A) and (C) are ambiguous; because these sentences are elliptical (implied words are left out), the reader is left without sufficient context.

10.   (C)

Choice (A) creates redundancy with the use of "most" with "stingiest." Choice (B) incorrectly combines the comparative word "more" with the superlative form "stingiest."

Answers to Practice Exercises: Nouns *(page 314)*:

1.   (B)

Choice (A) (Thai) is a noun but it is functioning as an adjective modifying the main subject of the sentence, choice (B). Choice (C) is a verb. Choice (D) is a noun, but it functions as a direct object here.

2.   (A)

The correct answer is (A). Choice (B) is a noun that is the object of a clause that defines the subject. Choice (C) is a verb form, and choice (D) is a direct object.

3. **(A)**

Choice (B) is a linking verb that links the main noun or subject *tomatoes* with the adverb *terrible* (how the tomatoes taste).

4. **(B)**

Choice (A) describes a noun, but it isn't the subject of the sentence (it is an adjective in this case). Choice (C) is a verb, and Choice (D) is also a noun in adjective form.

5. **(D)**

The sentence is about mothers—they were drinking the coffee. Choice (A) is a preposition introducing an adverbial phrase, so it's wrong. Although choice (B) is a noun, it is the object of a prepositional phrase and isn't the subject. Finally, choice (C) is incorrect because it is an article.

6. **(A)**

Since Hawaii is a proper noun, it is capitalized.

7. **(A)**

Chesapeake Bay is a specific named body of water. Choice (B) cannot be the answer because the research lab is not named.

8. **(A)**

Aunt Liz is a specific person. So it is the proper noun.

9. **(B)**

The Arctic Circle designates a specific geographic area, so it is a proper noun. "Sunlight" is a common noun.

10. **(E)**

The correct answer is "All of the above" for the following reasons: "Declaration of Independence" (A), because it's the name of a document; "America's" (B), because it is the possessive form of the proper noun for a nation's name; "Founding Fathers" (C), because the phrase names a specific group of people; and "Magna Carta" (D), again because it's the name of a document.

Answers to Practice Exercises: Pronouns *(page 323):*

1. **(A)**

    The correct answer is choice (A). Do not use the reflexive pronoun "myself" as a substitute for "I."

2. **(C)**

    Choice (C) is the correct answer. In the revised clause ("whoever consumes them"), whoever is the subject. Whomever is the objective case pronoun and should be used only as the object of a sentence, never as the subject. By way of a usage note, let's concede that even when the objective whomever would be strictly correct, the use of whoever may be tolerated as a casualism. However, on the Praxis Core test, as a rule, the closer you adhere to standard written English's formalisms, the better your score will be.

3. **(A)**

    Choice (A) is the correct answer. You should use the nominative case pronoun "who" as the subject complement of the verb "to be."

4. **(A)**

    Choice (A) is the correct answer. In this sentence, you should use the nominative case/subject pronouns "she" and "who" as the subject complement of the verb "wrecked."

5. **(D)**

    Choice (D) is the correct answer. "Student" is an indefinite, genderless noun that requires a singular personal pronoun. While "his" is a singular personal pronoun, a genderless noun includes both the masculine and feminine forms and requires "his" or "her" as the singular personal pronoun. This sentence would avoid the "his or her" problem by using plurals: "Students who wish to protest their grades. . . ."

6. **(A)**

    Choice (A) is the correct answer. The antecedent "company" is singular, requiring the singular pronoun "it," not the plural "they."

7.   (B)

Choice (B) is the correct answer. Choice (A) contains a shift in person, or point of view: "Your" is a second-person pronoun, while "his" and "her" are third-person pronouns. The original sentence uses the third-person plural pronoun "their" to refer to the singular antecedent "every car owner." Choice (B) correctly provides the masculine and feminine forms "his or her" required by the indefinite, gender-neutral "every car owner." Again, change to plural to avoid "her or her": "All car owners . . . their. . . ."

8.   (B)

Choice (B) is the correct answer. The implied antecedent is "engineering." Choices (A) and (C) each contain a pronoun with no antecedent. Neither "it" nor "this" is a suitable substitution for "engineer."

9.   (A)

Choice (A) is correct. The pronoun "they" in the sentence you're given has no conspicuous antecedent. Since the doer of the action is unknown (and therefore genderless), choice (B), "he," is not the correct answer. Choice (C) cannot be correct because "it" has no logical antecedent.

10.   (C)

Choice (C) is the correct answer. The sentence is ambiguous for two reasons: (i) the pronoun "she" has two possible antecedents, and (ii) it's unknown whether it is Margaret or her sister who is away at college.

Answers to Practice Exercises: Verbs *(page 332)*:

1.   (C)

Choice (C) is the correct answer. The past participle form of each verb is required because of the auxiliaries (helping verbs) "had been" (concerned) and "would have" (gone).

2.   (B)

Choice (B) is the correct answer. The forms of the irregular verb meaning "to rest" are "lie" (rest), "lies" (rests), "lay" (rested), and "has lain" (has rested). The forms of the verb meaning "to put" are "lay" (put), "lays" (puts), "laying" (putting), "laid" (put), and "have laid" (have put).

3.   **(D)**

Choice (D) is the correct answer. The present tense is used for universal truths and the past tense for historical truths.

4.   **(A)**

Choice (A) is correct. The present tense is used for customary events. Choice (B), "had begun," is the past perfect form, which would be used only if the sentence needed to convey an action that had been completed in the past before another action. Choice (C), "was beginning," would be used only if the sentence needed to indicate that the class's normal start time was not as stated (10:30 a.m.).

5.   **(A)**

Choice (A) is the correct answer. The past tense, which is marked by the verb alone (without any auxiliary), is used for historical statements (i.e., an action that has been completed). The present tense, also marked by the verb alone, is used to describe extant artworks.

6.   **(B)**

Choice (B) is the correct answer. The subject of the sentence is the plural noun "sales," not the singular noun "Christmas," which is the object of the prepositional phrase.

7.   **(A)**

Choice (A) is the correct answer. The subject, "specialty," is singular.

8.   **(C)**

Choice (C) is the correct answer. Subjects preceded by "every" are considered singular and therefore require a singular verb form.

9.   **(A)**

Choice (A) is the correct answer. The subject of the sentence is the gerund "hiding," not "your mistakes," which is the direct object of the action expressed in the gerund. "Hiding" is singular; therefore, the singular verb form "doesn't" should be used.

10. (D)

Choice (D) is correct. Though the form of the subject, "board of directors," may look plural, it's actually singular, based on the status of "board" as a collective noun.

Answers to Practice Exercises: Sentence Structure Skills *(page 336)*:

1. (C)

Choice (C) is the correct answer. Each response option contains items in a series. In choices (A) and (B), the word group after the conjunction is not an adjective like the first items in the series. Choice (C) provides the parallel adjectival construction.

2. (B)

Choice (B) is the correct answer. Choices (A) and (C) combine conjunctions incorrectly.

3. (B)

Choice (B) is the correct answer. Choices (A) and (C) appear to be parallel because the conjunction "and" connects two word groups that both happen to start with "because." But the structure on both sides of the conjunction is very different. "Because he kept his campaign promises" is a clause; "because of his refusal to accept political favors" is a prepositional phrase. Choice (B) nicely connects two dependent clauses.

4. (B)

Choice (B) is the correct answer. Choices (A) and (C) contain the elliptical clause "While . . . taking a shower." It appears that the missing subject in the elliptical clause is the same as that in the independent clause—that is, the "doorbell" in choice (A) and "someone" in choice (C). Neither of these is a logical subject for the verbal "taking a shower." Choice (B), uniquely, removes the elliptical clause and provides a logical subject.

5. (A)

Choice (A) is the correct answer. Ask yourself, Who swung the bat? Choices (B) and (C) both imply it's the runner who swung. Only choice (A) makes it clear that as he swung the bat, someone else (i.e., "the runner") stole a base.

6. (A)

Choice (A) is correct. The punctuation in the original sentence and in choice (B) creates a fragment. "Cotton being the state's principal crop" is not an independent thought because it lacks a complete verb; "being" is not a complete verb.

7. (B)

The correct answer is (B). The keys to understanding this revision are to understand the meaning of "heartrending" and to know now to properly use a colon, which works well as an alternative to two separate sentences when two ideas are closely related.

8. (A)

Choice (A) is the correct answer. The dependent clause "because repairs were being made" in choices (B) and (C) is punctuated as if it were a sentence. This results in a fragment.

9. (B)

Choice (B) is the correct answer. Choices (A) and (C) do not separate the complete ideas in the independent clauses with the correct punctuation.

10. (B)

Choice (B) is correct. Choices (A) and (C) do not separate the independent clauses with the proper punctuation.

Answers to Practice Exercises: Misplaced/Dangling Modifiers *(page 339)*:

1. (A)

The correct answer is (A). Because of the misplaced modifier, the second sentence leaves it unclear (and unsaid) who or what saw that the traffic was heavy. "We" were merging onto the roadway and thus it was "we" who noticed, so "we" needs to be in the sentence.

2. (B)

The correct answer is (B). Since there is a dangling modifier in the first sentence, grammatically it appears that the cellphone was writing the paper. Choice (B) makes it clear that "I" was writing.

3.   **(B)**

The correct answer is (B). The intended meaning is that the girls who are wearing holiday dresses look beautiful to the adults. The misplaced modifier in the first sentence suggests that the adults are wearing the holiday dresses.

4.   **(A)**

The correct answer is (A). Because of a dangling modifier, choice (B) literally says that Sam was attached to the door. The intended meaning, shown in choice (A), is that the old photograph was fastened to the door.

5.   **(B)**

The correct answer is (B). The intended meaning is that the teacher ate his or her lunch while reading a book. The misplaced modifier in the first sentence implies that the teacher sat reading a book while the book ate lunch.

6.   **(B)**

The correct answer is (B). The misplaced phrase "with leather seats" is modifying the wrong noun, "the buyer," in choice (A), making it incorrect. The phrase should be next to the noun it is supposed to modify, as in choice (B).

7.   **(A)**

The correct answer is (A). Because of the dangling modifier, choice (B) suggests that the restaurant was hungry and thirsty from the run, not Adam.

8.   **(B)**

The correct answer is choice (B). Choice (A) implies that that Noah borrowed a wall from his dad, which is not the intended meaning of the sentence.

9.   **(B)**

The correct answer is choice (B). The modifier here is the gerund "After slurping a Tang drink," which logically can only be attributed to a person, in this case the astronaut John Glenn.

10. **(B)**

The correct answer is choice (B). From the way the sentence is constructed in choice (A), it sounds as if the juice brand was walking. Choice (B) corrects the dangling modifier and makes the sentence clearer by placing the subject, "I," next to its modifier.

Answers to Practice Exercises: Coordinating and Subordinating Conjunctions (*page 341*):

1. **Subordinating**

   The correct answer is subordinating ("when").

2. **Subordinating**

   The correct answer is subordinating ("before").

3. **Coordinating**

   The correct answer is coordinating ("or").

4. **Subordinating**

   The correct answer is subordinating ("unless").

5. **Coordinating**

   The correct answer is coordinating ("but").

6. **Subordinating**

   The correct answer is subordinating ("as").

7. **Coordinating**

   The correct answer is coordinating ("and").

8. **Subordinating**

   The correct answer is subordinating ("because").

9. **Coordinating**

The correct answer is coordinating ("and").

10. **Subordinating**

The correct answer is subordinating ("because").

Answers to Practice Exercises: Sentence Fragments *(page 343)*:

1. **(B)**

Choice (B) is a subordinate clause fragment because *before* is a subordinate word. One way to correct this fragment would be to link it to the sentence that comes before it. For instance, "My mother called my name before I even got to my car."

2. **(B)**

"That were on Springfield Avenue" is a subordinate clause fragment. To correct the fragment, link it to the sentence that comes before it: "A tornado upended the homes on Springfield Avenue."

3. **(A)**

"Unless the rain falls soon" is a subordinate clause fragment that can be corrected by adding a comma and joining it to the sentence that follows: "Unless the rain falls soon, the crops will die."

4. **(B)**

Choice (B) is a verb phrase, which does not constitute a complete sentence. To correct it, try this: "Reading a book, Tatyana stayed in the library all morning."

5. **(B)**

Choice (B) is an added detail, and, in fact, this type of fragment is a called an "added detail fragment." To correct it, connect it with the sentence after it to make a complete sentence: "I like bagels with cream cheese."

6.   (B)

Choice (B) is a fragment because it lacks a subject. To correct it, connect it to the sentence before or create a new sentence by adding a subject: "The woman petted the dog and then led him back to his crate."

7.   (B)

In choice (B), "For instance," indicates that a detail is going to be added, but what follows is just a noun with no verb. To correct it, connect it to the other sentence or create a new sentence by adding a verb: "Bill and Ted have similar hobbies. For instance, they both like woodworking."

8.   (A)

Choice (A) is a fragment because it is a prepositional phrase, and it doesn't have a subject and verb. The way to fix it is to follow it with a comma and link it to the sentence that follows, yielding: "To brighten up the office, we painted the walls a nice beige."

9.   (B)

Choice (B) is an added detail and does not have a complete subject/verb. To solve this problem, link it to the sentence that precedes it: "This gym is often crowded, especially on Wednesday and Friday mornings."

10.   (B)

Choice (B) is missing a subject to make it a complete sentence. To resolve the fragment, you could rewrite the sentence and add a subject: "She put it in her purse."

Answers to Practice Exercises: Run-Ons/Fused Sentences and Comma Splices (page 345):

1.   Comma splice

Two subjects and two verbs are incorrectly punctuated in that they are joined by a comma, creating a comma splice.

2.   Neither

There is a subject (memoir) and a verb (is). It is a complete thought.

3.   **Comma splice**

The independent clause at the beginning is incorrectly punctuated with the second independent clause. correct punctuation would involve a semicolon after the word *war* and a comma after *however*.

4.   **Neither**

This is a complete sentence with a subject (book) and a verb (came).

5.   **Run-on**

There should be a period after the word *chronologically* and a capital *E* for *each* to make two sentences.

6.   **Run-on**

There is a natural break after to word "book." A solution would be to make two sentences, to put a semicolon there, or to use a comma and a contractions ("book, so be prepared . . . ").

7.   **Neither**

This sentence can stand on its own as an independent clause (i.e., a complete sentence).

8.   **Neither**

This sentence is complete.

9.   **Run-on**

There is a subject and verb ("I loved") joined with another subject and verb ("it was") without the proper punctuation. To correct the problem, the writer could use a semi-colon ("I loved this book; it was the best book I ever read,"), insert a coordinating conjunction ("I loved this book, and it was the best book I ever read,") or transform the run-on into two sentences ("I loved this book. It was the best book I ever read.")

10. **Neither**

This is a complete sentence that can stand on its own as an independent clause.

Answers to Practice Exercises: Correlative Conjunctions *(page 346)*:

1. **either/or**

2. **either/or**

3. **either/or**

4. **either/or** OR **neither/nor.**

   Both answers work in this case.

5. **(B)**

   We know this is the correct choice because the verb "like" is in plural form. Choice (D) asks for a singular verb ("likes"). The other choices do not make sense.

6. **(A)**

   It is the only choice that makes sense.

7. **(B)**

   "Either" indicates that two ideas are linked together. In this case, the ideas are being compared.

8. **(A)**

   The correlative pair whether . . . or establishes a choice between "raining" and "snowing."

9. **(B)**

   This sentence calls for a pair of correlatives (neither . . . nor) to negate both parts of the statement.

10. (B)

This choice is the only one that negates the ability to read and write, which is the definition of illiteracy.

Answers to Practice Exercises: Parallelism *(page 349)*:

1. (D)

For the sentence to be balanced and have parallel structure, it needs to use present-tense verb phrases.

2. (D)

To have parallelism, all the verbs need to be in gerund, or -ing, form. Although (D) is an independent clause (subject and verb), it is not in balance with the rest of the sentence and has to be changed.

3. (E)

This sentence has no error in parallelism since the noun phrases in the series are consistent. Therefore, the correct answer is (E), no error.

4. (E)

There is no error in parallelism.

5. (D)

To match the other verbs in the series, "kind" should be in infinitive verb form ("to be kind").

6. (C)

To "match" or form a parallel balance, look at "to sleep late" and think about how you need a verb phrase that also starts with "to." Therefore, the correct answer is (C), and the required revision of "getting up" would instead use the phrase "to get up."

7. (D)

The words that follow "but also" must be in the same form as the words that follow "not only." To match the phrase "to coffee," we need "to spaghetti" for the sentence to be parallel. Thus, the correct answer is (D).

8. (D)

To be parallel to "is up," and "is blue," we need "it is beautiful," not the contraction "it's."

9. (D)

Choice (D) is the right response because for parallelism, "eating" must be in the same form as "take."

10. (E)

There is no error in this sentence because of the parallel distribution of infinitive verb forms. As a result, choice (E) should be selected.

Answers to Practice Exercises: Idioms (page 351):

1. (C)

The idiomatic phrase we often hear is that something is "characteristic of" something else.

2. (E)

There is no idiomatic error.

3. (D)

Gas prices don't "go off"—they would "go up" or "go down."

4. (C)

"For sure" is a colloquial phrase, and a better choice might be "in truth," "in reality," etc.

5.   (A)

Choices like "Every now and then," or "Occasionally" would work better than choice (A).

6.   (C)

The phrase "than to" is not idiomatically correct. We would say "but to."

7.   (E)

There is no error.

8.   (C)

The correct colloquial phrase would be "from teachers."

9.   (D)

Choice (D) is correct because "freak out" is slang.

10. (E)

There is no error.

Answers to Practice Exercises: Word Choice *(page 356)*:

1.   (B)

Choice (B) is correct because "airing our dirty laundry" is a cliché.

2.   (A)

Choice (A) is the better choice because "blew her stack" is a cliché.

3.   (B)

Choice (B) is the better answer since "an oldie but goodie" is a cliché inappropriate for formal writing.

4. **(B)**

Choice (B) is the better choice. "Dud" is slang.

5. **(B)**

Choice (B) is the better response. "Shaking like a leaf" is a cliché.

6. **(B)**

Choice (B) is the better choice.

7. **(A)**

Choice (B) is full of jargon ("extraordinarily amazing" and "stupendous").

8. **(B)**

"Allusion" and "illusion" are commonly confused with each other. They sound nearly the same but have different meanings.

9. **(B)**

The subject used in (A) is an example of loaded language, which you should avoid in formal academic writing.

10. **(A)**

Choice (B) misuses the verb "hinder," which is the opposite of "help").

Answers to Practice Exercises: Sentence Correction *(page 361)*:

1. **(C)**

Choices (A), (D), and (E) have incorrect verb tenses because past perfect is called for here. Choice (B) is wordy.

2.   (C)

The pronoun "that" is needed. "Who" cannot be used to make reference to text messages because they are things, not people. Choice (B) is also incorrect because it refers to a person, and the conjunction "and" is not appropriate here. Choice (E) uses the wrong verb and tense.

3.   (B)

Since the correlative conjunctions "neither/nor" come together as a pair, we can eliminate choice (A), which has the mismatched "neither/or,"and choice (D), with "neither/that." Choice (C), with "whether/so," does not make sense. The correct answer is (B).

4.   (C)

The underlined portion does not have parallel structure since "readings" is a noun and "analyzing" is used as a verb.

5.   (A)

Choice (B) is wordy; choice (C) is missing words; and choice (D) changes the intended meaning of the sentence.

6.   (C)

In this sentence, the subject and verb do not agree. To correct the situation, the plural subject (wolves) must be conjugated with the plural form of the verb (terrify).

7.   (D)

The faulty pronoun reference leaves us wondering which of the three nuts are truly Danielle's favorite. None of the other choices replaces the ambiguity with a clear antecedent.

8.   (E)

In terms of verb tense consistency, the verb "ring" needs to be conjugated in the past tense in order to agree with the initial verb "put."

9. **(A)**

"Even though" is used to describe a condition that is currently true, whereas "even if" introduces a hypothetical condition. In this sentence, breaking a heart is hypothetical. Therefore, (A) is correct.

10. **(A)**

"That" is used to signal a restrictive clause. "That" phrases are integral to the meaning of the sentence; non-restrictive "which" phrases are not. Thus, because the clause dispenses a critical piece of information—that the gazelle became the prey of the tiger—(A) is the correct answer. If the sentence were written differently, with a clause indicating an incidental piece of information (e.g., mentioning that the gazelle lived on the southern edge of the preserve), a non-restrictive clause would have been used. For example: "The gazelle, which lived on the southern edge of the preserve, was clearly ailing."

Answers to Practice Exercises: Revision in Context *(page 365)*:

1. **(C)**

The underlined phrase is too wordy and repeats itself. Choice (C) is simple and gets to the point without losing the intention of meaning, as choice (D) does but misses the intent. Choice (B) is still redundant.

2. **(C)**

"Dead as a doornail" is a cliché, and "dead" is all the sentence needs.

3. **(B)**

Choices (A) and (D) are redundant. Choice (C) is a sentence fragment.

4. **(D)**

Choice (D) is correct because it's formal, not slang.

5. **(B)**

"Back again" is redundant. Replacing it with "once again" is still too wordy. Deleting "back again" simplifies the sentence and still communicates the intended meaning.

6. (D)

"Assembled," "built," and "connected" are incorrect word choices. Choice (D) conveys the message clearly and adds the preposition "by" for greater fluency.

7. (B)

Choice (D) changes the meaning, and choices (A) and (C) are slang.

8. (B)

Choices (A) and (D) are too wordy. Choice (C) does not make sense since the verb in the sentence is in the present tense. Choice (B) communicates the meaning quickly and efficiently.

9. (D)

"Noisy" already communicates that they are loud, so the underlined phrase is redundant and can be eliminated. Choices (B) and (C) continue to repeat the idea of "loud", and (B) is also slang. The best choice is (D).

10. (A)

Eliminating the phrase diminishes the meaning of the sentence, choice (C) is too wordy, and choice (D) does not make sense.

PART V:
Praxis Core Practice Test Battery

Praxis Core Mathematics Practice Test 1

Also available at the online REA Study Center *(www.rea.com/studycenter)*

The Praxis Core Mathematics (5732) test is computer-based, so we strongly recommend that you take our online practice tests to simulate test-day conditions and to receive these added benefits:

- **Timed testing conditions**—Gauge how much time you can spend on each question.

- **Automatic scoring**—Find out how you did on the test, instantly.

- **On-screen detailed explanations of answers**—Learn not just the correct answer but also why the other answers are wrong.

- **Diagnostic score reports**—Pinpoint where you're strongest and where you need to focus your study.

Praxis Core Mathematics
Practice Test 1 Answer Sheet

1. Ⓐ Ⓑ Ⓒ Ⓓ Ⓔ

2. ☐

3. Ⓐ Ⓑ Ⓒ Ⓓ Ⓔ

4. ☐

5. Ⓐ Ⓑ Ⓒ Ⓓ Ⓔ

6. ⊟

7. Ⓐ Ⓑ Ⓒ Ⓓ Ⓔ

8. Ⓐ Ⓑ Ⓒ Ⓓ Ⓔ

9. Ⓐ Ⓑ Ⓒ Ⓓ Ⓔ

10. Ⓐ Ⓑ Ⓒ Ⓓ Ⓔ

11. Ⓐ Ⓑ Ⓒ Ⓓ Ⓔ

12. Ⓐ Ⓑ Ⓒ Ⓓ Ⓔ

13. Ⓐ Ⓑ Ⓒ Ⓓ Ⓔ

14. Ⓐ Ⓑ Ⓒ Ⓓ Ⓔ

15. Ⓐ Ⓑ Ⓒ Ⓓ Ⓔ

16. Ⓐ Ⓑ Ⓒ Ⓓ Ⓔ

17. Ⓐ Ⓑ Ⓒ Ⓓ Ⓔ

18. Ⓐ Ⓑ Ⓒ Ⓓ Ⓔ

19. Ⓐ Ⓑ Ⓒ Ⓓ Ⓔ

20. Ⓐ Ⓑ Ⓒ Ⓓ Ⓔ

21. Ⓐ Ⓑ Ⓒ Ⓓ Ⓔ

22. Ⓐ Ⓑ Ⓒ Ⓓ Ⓔ

23. ☐

24. Ⓐ Ⓑ Ⓒ Ⓓ Ⓔ

25. Ⓐ Ⓑ Ⓒ Ⓓ Ⓔ

26. Ⓐ Ⓑ Ⓒ Ⓓ Ⓔ

27. Ⓐ Ⓑ Ⓒ Ⓓ Ⓔ

28. Ⓐ Ⓑ Ⓒ Ⓓ Ⓔ

29. Ⓐ Ⓑ Ⓒ Ⓓ Ⓔ

30. Ⓐ Ⓑ Ⓒ Ⓓ Ⓔ

31. Ⓐ Ⓑ Ⓒ Ⓓ Ⓔ

32. Ⓐ Ⓑ Ⓒ Ⓓ Ⓔ

33. ☐ ☐

34. Ⓐ Ⓑ Ⓒ Ⓓ Ⓔ

35. Ⓐ Ⓑ Ⓒ Ⓓ Ⓔ

36. Ⓐ Ⓑ Ⓒ Ⓓ Ⓔ

37. Ⓐ Ⓑ Ⓒ Ⓓ Ⓔ

38. Ⓐ Ⓑ Ⓒ Ⓓ Ⓔ

39. Ⓐ Ⓑ Ⓒ Ⓓ Ⓔ

40. Ⓐ Ⓑ Ⓒ Ⓓ Ⓔ

41. Ⓐ Ⓑ Ⓒ Ⓓ Ⓔ

42. Ⓐ Ⓑ Ⓒ Ⓓ Ⓔ

43. Ⓐ Ⓑ Ⓒ Ⓓ Ⓔ

44. Ⓐ Ⓑ Ⓒ Ⓓ Ⓔ

45. Ⓐ Ⓑ Ⓒ Ⓓ Ⓔ

46. Ⓐ Ⓑ Ⓒ Ⓓ Ⓔ

47. Ⓐ Ⓑ Ⓒ Ⓓ Ⓔ

48. Ⓐ Ⓑ Ⓒ Ⓓ Ⓔ

49. Ⓐ Ⓑ Ⓒ Ⓓ Ⓔ

50. Ⓐ Ⓑ Ⓒ Ⓓ Ⓔ

51. Ⓐ Ⓑ Ⓒ Ⓓ Ⓔ

52. Ⓐ Ⓑ Ⓒ Ⓓ Ⓔ

53. Ⓐ Ⓑ Ⓒ Ⓓ Ⓔ

54. Ⓐ Ⓑ Ⓒ Ⓓ Ⓔ

55. Ⓐ Ⓑ Ⓒ Ⓓ Ⓔ

56. Ⓐ Ⓑ Ⓒ Ⓓ Ⓔ

Praxis Core
Mathematics Practice Test 1

Time: 85 minutes for 56 selected-response items

Directions: Answer each question by providing the correct response or responses. Most items on this test require you to provide the one best answer. However, some questions require you to select one or more answers, in which case you will be directed to respond with all answers that apply. Such response options are shown with squares around the letter choices to distinguish them from the questions with only one answer choice. Some questions are numeric-entry, requiring you to fill in a box or boxes with the correct answer.

To our readers: This printed practice test is designed to simulate as closely as possible the computerized Praxis Core Math test (5732). On test day and on REA's online version of this practice test, you will answer each question by either clicking on the correct response or inserting your answer into designated numeric-entry boxes. An on-screen calculator is available for the actual computerized Praxis Core Math test and at the REA Study Center.

1. If two triangles are congruent, $\triangle ABC \cong \triangle DEF$, the measure of $\angle A = 70°$ and the measure of $\angle D = (4x)°$, what is the value of x?

   (A) 35

   (B) 14

   (C) 17.5

   (D) 7

   (E) Cannot be determined from the information given.

2. If you have a lunch choice of 5 sandwiches, 4 desserts, and 3 drinks, and you can have one of each, you could choose from how many different meals? Fill in the box.

3. What is the value of $x - y$ if $x = y + b$?

   (A) b

   (B) $b - x$

   (C) $x + b$

   (D) $\dfrac{x}{b}$

   (E) $\dfrac{y}{b}$

4. In a study of the correlation of diastolic blood pressure and serum cholesterol, the following dot plot shows the values of diastolic blood pressure following exercise for 20 individuals. What is the mode?

    Put your answer in the box.

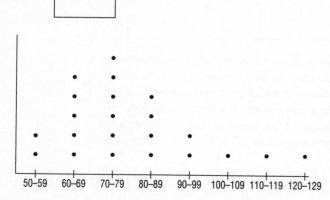

    Diastolic Blood Pressure (mm Hg)

5. If the area of a square is p, what is the diagonal in terms of p?

    (A) $p\sqrt{2}$

    (B) $\sqrt{p}$

    (C) $\sqrt{2p}$

    (D) $2\sqrt{p}$

    (E) $\dfrac{p\sqrt{2}}{2}$

6. Of a litter of 8 lab puppies, 3 are black, 1 is yellow, and 4 are chocolate. What fraction of the puppies are yellow?

    Enter the fraction using the two boxes.

7. What is the solution to the following system of equations?

    $$2x + 4y = 10$$
    $$y = 2x - 5$$

    (A) $x = 1, y = 3$

    (B) $x = 3, y = 1$

    (C) $x = 2, y = 2$

    (D) $x = 3, y = 0$

    (E) $x = 2, y = 1$

8. A coin is flipped once and a cube with numbers 1 through 6 on each side is rolled. What is the probability that the coin will show heads and the cube will show a number greater than 1?

    (A) $\dfrac{1}{2}$

    (B) $\dfrac{5}{6}$

    (C) $\dfrac{5}{12}$

    (D) $\dfrac{8}{6}$

    (E) $\dfrac{1}{12}$

9. A 60-foot ribbon is cut into 6-foot pieces. The number of cuts is

    (A) 9

    (B) 10

    (C) 11

    (D) 12

    (E) 24

10. The value of $\sqrt{52}$ lies between which two integers?

    (A) 7 and 8

    (B) 5 and 6

    (C) 6 and 7

    (D) 4 and 5

    (E) 51 and 53

11. Which of the following graphs of distance versus time reflects this scenario:

    At 8:00 a.m., Mike drove his car to the mechanic, a half mile from home, and waited in the next-door coffee shop for an hour until the oil was changed. He then got back into the car, drove 2 miles to the library and dropped his books at the front desk. When he returned to the car, he saw that it was leaking oil, so he went back to the mechanic, who was able to fix the problem in 15 minutes, after which Mike drove home.

(A)
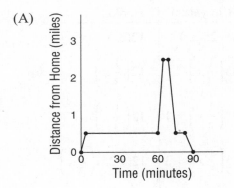

(B)
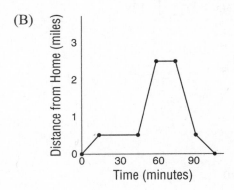

(C)
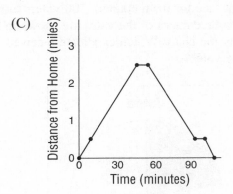

(D)
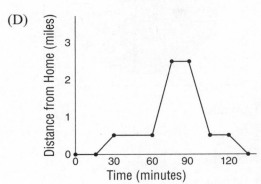

(E)
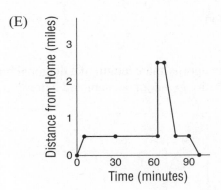

12. In a tight race for town council, 700 voters turned out. The percentages of the votes are shown in the following pie chart. Which candidate received exactly 126 votes?

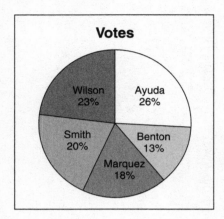

Votes

Wilson 23%
Ayuda 26%
Smith 20%
Benton 13%
Marquez 18%

(A) Ayuda

(B) Benton

(C) Smith

(D) Marquez

(E) Wilson

13. What is the approximate length of a diagonal brace to add stability to a door, as depicted below?

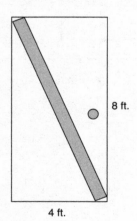

8 ft.

4 ft.

(A) 10.5 feet

(B) 10 feet

(C) 9.5 feet

(D) 9 feet

(E) 8.5 feet

14. The postage in country X is 50 cents for the first ounce and 22 cents for each additional ounce. Postage for a half-pound letter mailed in country X costs how many cents? (1 pound = 16 ounces)

(A) 204

(B) 226

(C) 248

(D) 270

(E) 292

15. Angelica is making drapes. The window is x feet wide. The width of the fabric Angelica buys must be a factor of .25 more than the width of the window to have enough to make pleats in the drapes, and then she must add another 3 feet for the vertical hems. Angelica also needs 12 hooks for every yard along the window to hang the drapes. Which of these equation pairs is the correct one to calculate the amount of fabric and number of hooks?

	Fabric (in yards)	Hooks
(A)	$3x + .25(3x)$	$12(3x)$
(B)	$1.25\left(\frac{1}{3}x\right)$	$12\left(\frac{1}{3}x\right)$
(C)	$1.25\left(\frac{1}{3}x\right) + 1$	$12\left(\frac{1}{3}x\right)$
(D)	$1.25\left(\frac{1}{3}x\right) + 3$	$12(1.25)\left(\frac{1}{3}x\right)$
(E)	$1.25(x + 3)$	$12x$

16. $\dfrac{41^2 + 41}{41} =$

(A) 41

(B) 42

(C) 82

(D) 1640

(E) 1681

    (A) 5

    (B) 6

    (C) 10

    (D) 11

    (E) 13

17. Evaluate $\dfrac{a+b}{2}+c$ when $a = 4$, $b = 6$, and $c = 1$.

    (A) 5

    (B) 6

    (C) 10

    (D) 11

    (E) 13

18. In the first six basketball games this season, Jamal scored 22, 14, 12, 16, 20, and 15 points. What is the difference between the mean and median of his scores?

    (A) 1

    (B) 0

    (C) 16.5

    (D) 15.5

    (E) None of the above

19. The speed of light is 186,000 miles per second. The distance from Earth to the moon is 239,000 miles. How long would it take for light to travel from Earth to the moon if there were no interfering forces?

    (A) 1.28 seconds

    (B) 12.8 seconds

    (C) 1.28×10^3 seconds

    (D) 1.28×10^4 seconds

    (E) 1.28×10^5 seconds

20. If brakes are applied to a car traveling 60 mph, the formula for braking distance is

$$s = -\frac{v^2}{2\mu a}$$

    where

    s is braking distance in feet (assuming no collision)

    v is the velocity of the car, which is 60 mph = 88 feet per second (fps)

    μ is the coefficient of friction of the tires, let's say 0.75 (an average value)

    a is the deceleration due to the brakes of the car, or −15 fps per second (an average value)

    Approximately how far will the car travel before it stops?

    (A) 344 feet

    (B) 160 feet

    (C) 133 feet

    (D) 88 feet

    (E) 4 feet

21. A box contains two types of cookies, chocolate chip and macadamia nut. There are 5 times as many chocolate chip as macadamia nut cookies. If the box contains two dozen cookies, how many are macadamia nut cookies?

    (A) 4

    (B) 6

    (C) 12

    (D) 18

    (E) 20

22. Choose the fraction to place in the blank to make the following list of fractions decrease from left to right.

$$\frac{6}{7}, \frac{3}{4}, \underline{\quad}, 0, -\frac{3}{4}$$

(A) $-\frac{6}{7}$

(B) 0

(C) $\frac{2}{3}$

(D) $\frac{3}{2}$

(E) $-\frac{4}{5}$

23. In the following figure, lines g and h are parallel. If $\angle y = \angle x + 80$ degrees, what is the value of x in degrees? Fill in the box.

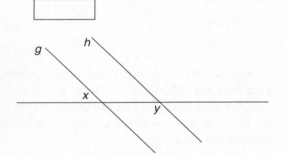

24. Wilma has 3 pairs of red socks, 6 pairs of white socks, and 5 pairs of blue socks in her dresser drawer. If she randomly selects one pair of socks, what is the probability that she will select a white pair?

(A) $\frac{1}{7}$

(B) $\frac{3}{5}$

(C) $\frac{3}{7}$

(D) $\frac{6}{5}$

(E) $\frac{5}{14}$

25. For right triangle ABC, AB is the hypotenuse and $\angle A = 30°$, what is the measure of $\angle B$ in degrees?

(A) 30°

(B) 60°

(C) 90°

(D) 150°

(E) 45°

26. $\sqrt{6561}$ is exactly

(A) 81

(B) 83

(C) 89

(D) 91

(E) 99

27. If y is four less than the square root of x, then which of the following is the expression for x?

    (A) $4 + y^2$

    (B) $4 - y^2$

    (C) $y^2 - 4$

    (D) $(4 - y)^2$

    (E) $(4 + y)^2$

28. What is the value of $2^2 \times 2^3$?

    (A) 16

    (B) 32

    (C) 4^5

    (D) 12

    (E) 64

29. A line with the same slope and y-intercept as the line $y = \dfrac{2}{3}x - 2$ is

    (A) $2x + 3y = -6$

    (B) $2x + 3y = 6$

    (C) $2x - 3y = 6$

    (D) $-2x - 3y = 6$

    (E) $-2x + 3y = 6$

30. What is the length of the missing side in a right triangle in which the two legs are 8 and 15?

    (A) 7

    (B) 12

    (C) 13

    (D) 17

    (E) 23

31. Which number is in the hundredths place when 274.936 is divided by 100?

    (A) 2

    (B) 7

    (C) 4

    (D) 9

    (E) 3

32. If $\dfrac{x-8}{y+3} = 0$, , then

    (A) $x = 0, y \neq 0$

    (B) $x = 8, y = -3$

    (C) $x = 8, y \neq -3$

    (D) $x \neq 8, y \neq -3$

    (E) $x \neq 8, y \neq 3$

33. What is the mean and median of the first nine natural numbers? Fill in the boxes.

    mean = ☐

    median = ☐

34. The area of this figure, which is a triangle-semicircle shape is

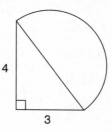

    (A) $6 + \dfrac{25\pi}{2}$

    (B) $6 + 25\pi$

    (C) $6 + 5\pi$

    (D) $12 + \dfrac{25\pi}{2}$

    (E) $12 + 25\pi$

35. If $\dfrac{m}{n} = \dfrac{2}{3}$, which of the following statements cannot be true?

   (A) $\dfrac{2m}{3n} = \dfrac{4}{6}$

   (B) $\dfrac{m+n}{n} = \dfrac{5}{3}$

   (C) $\dfrac{(n-m)}{n} = \dfrac{1}{3}$

   (D) $\dfrac{n^2}{m^2} = \dfrac{9}{4}$

   (E) $\dfrac{(m-n)}{n} = \dfrac{1}{3}$

36. The expression $18 - 6x$ is the equivalent of which of the following expressions?

   (A) $6 - 3(2x - 1) + 9$

   (B) $6 - 3(2x + 1) + 9$

   (C) $6 + 3(2x - 1) + 9$

   (D) $6 - 3(-2x + 1) + 9$

   (E) $6 - 3(2x - 1) + 9x$

37. Which chart best displays the information given in the table?

Store Location	Units Sold
Strip Mall	430,000
Second Street	250,000
River Mall	350,000
Center City	450,000

(A)

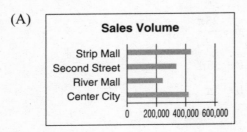

(B)

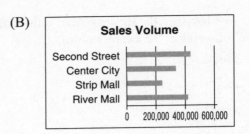

(C)

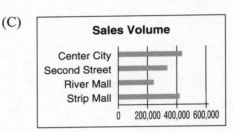

(D)

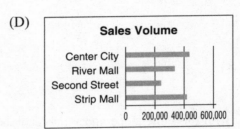

(E) None of the charts shown.

38. If the diagonal of a square is 10, its area is

   (A) 25

   (B) 50

   (C) 75

   (D) 100

   (E) 200

39. Which of the following are irrational numbers? Select all that apply.

   A $\sqrt{19}$

   B $4.\overline{35}$

   C 7.6

   D $\dfrac{81}{5}$

   E π

40. If m books cost $4 and n books cost $6, the mean cost is

   (A) $\dfrac{24mn}{m+n}$

   (B) $4m + \dfrac{6n}{mn}$

   (C) $\dfrac{4m+6n}{m+n}$

   (D) $\dfrac{4m+6n}{10}$

   (E) $\dfrac{4m-6n}{m-n}$

41. If $0 < x < 5$, which of the following statements about x^2 must be true?

   (A) $0 < x^2 < 5$

   (B) $0 < x^2 < 25$

   (C) $0 \le x^2 \le 25$

   (D) $x^2 \le 25$

   (E) All of the above.

42. If $\dfrac{1}{3} A = B$, what is the value of $\dfrac{1}{6} A$ in terms of B?

   (A) $18B$

   (B) $2B$

   (C) $\dfrac{1}{2}B$

   (D) $\dfrac{2}{3}B$

   (E) $\dfrac{B}{20}$

43. The graph below is a partial graph of the number of tickets sold to a premiere showing of a movie versus the revenue taken in. What is the cost of a ticket to the movie?

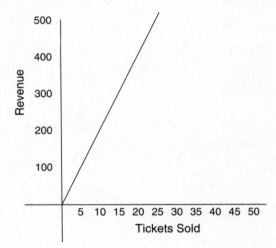

   (A) $5.00

   (B) $10.00

   (C) $15.00

   (D) $20.00

   (E) $50.00

44. A fair coin is flipped four times. What is the probability that heads will appear on each of the four flips?

   (A) $\dfrac{1}{16}$

   (B) $\dfrac{1}{8}$

   (C) $\dfrac{1}{4}$

   (D) $\dfrac{1}{2}$

   (E) $\dfrac{4}{2}$

45. The measure of the largest angle in triangle *EFG* is

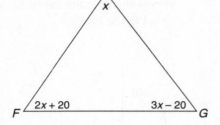

    (A) 30°

    (B) 50°

    (C) 70°

    (D) 80°

    (E) 90°

46. A $60 radio is discounted 25%, then another 10%. What is the final cost if the sales tax is 4%?

    (A) $41.06

    (B) $42.12

    (C) $43.18

    (D) $44.24

    (E) $45.30

47. If $\sqrt{x-3} = 5$, what is the value of x?

    (A) 8

    (B) 2

    (C) 22

    (D) 28

    (E) 64

48. A total of 35 students take at least French or Russian. If 25 take Russian and 10 take both languages, how many students take only French?

    (A) 5

    (B) 10

    (C) 15

    (D) 20

    (E) 25

49. Which of the following lengths is sufficient information to find the area of a circle?

    (A) radius

    (B) diameter

    (C) circumference

    (D) any of the above

    (E) none of the above

50. How many nonnegative integers x are there such that $x^4 < 1,000$?

    (A) 2

    (B) 3

    (C) 4

    (D) 5

    (E) more than 5

51. Which of the following could be the graph for a project with a fixed compensation: the more hours spent on the project, the less the hourly rate?

    (A)

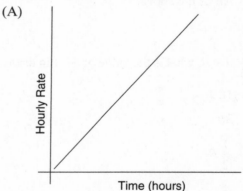

    (B)

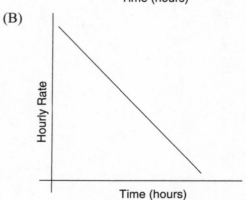

(C)

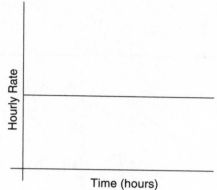

Time (hours)

(D)

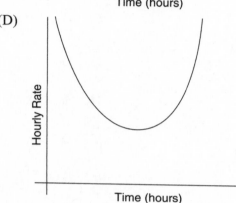

Time (hours)

(E)

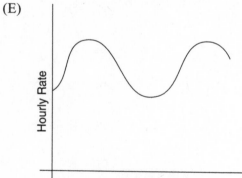

Time (hours)

52. If M = all even numbers greater than 10 and N = all prime numbers, what numbers are in both M and N?

(A) 11, 13, 15, . . .

(B) 12, 14, 16, . . .

(C) all prime numbers

(D) no numbers

(E) all numbers

53. What is the perimeter, in inches, of a square that has an area of 36 square inches?

(A) 6

(B) 12

(C) 24

(D) 30

(E) 36

54. Which number is in the hundreds place when 456.283 is multiplied by 100?

(A) 4

(B) 5

(C) 6

(D) 2

(E) 8

55. The ratio of the number of boys to the number of girls in the Forensics Club is 9 to 4. If the total number of students in the Forensics club is 39, how many girls are in the club?

(A) 4

(B) 9

(C) 12

(D) 27

(E) 39

56. If $3x + 6 > 15$, the value of x can be which of the following values? Choose all that apply.

A | 1

B | 2

C | 3

D | 4

E | 5

Praxis Core Mathematics
Practice Test 1 Answer Key

1.	C	20.	A	39.	A, E	
2.	60	21.	A	40.	C	
3.	A	22.	C	41.	B	
4.	70–79	23.	50	42.	C	
5.	C	24.	C	43.	D	
6.	$\frac{1}{8}$	25.	B	44.	A	
7.	B	26.	A	45.	D	
8.	C	27.	E	46.	B	
9.	A	28.	B	47.	D	
10.	A	29.	C	48.	B	
11.	A	30.	D	49.	D	
12.	D	31.	C	50.	E	
13.	D	32.	C	51.	B	
14.	A	33.	Mean = 5; median 5	52.	D	
15.	C	34.	A	53.	C	
16.	B	35.	E	54.	C	
17.	B	36.	A	55.	C	
18.	A	37.	D	56.	D, E	
19.	A	38.	B			

1. **(C)**, 17.5

If two triangles are congruent, their corresponding angles are equal. Since angles A and D are in corresponding places in the description, $\triangle ABC \cong \triangle DEF$, they must be equal. So $70 = 4x$, or $x = 17.5$. It is not necessary to have a reference figure for this problem.

2. 60

According to the Counting Principle, the number is the product of the choices:

$$5 \times 4 \times 3 = 60.$$

3. **(A)**, b

Subtract y from both sides of the equation $x = y + b$ to get $x - y = b$.

4. 70–79

The box plot clearly shows that the most data points are in the 70–79 column.

5. **(C)** $\sqrt{2p}$

Since the area of the square is p, each side is $s = \sqrt{p}$. From the Pythagorean theorem, the diagonal is then

$$d^2 = (\sqrt{p})^2 + (\sqrt{p})^2 = p + p = 2p$$
$$d = \sqrt{2p}$$

6. $\dfrac{1}{8}$

The fraction is given by

$$\frac{\text{part}}{\text{whole}} = \frac{\text{number of yellow puppies}}{\text{total number of puppies}} = \frac{1}{8}.$$

7. **(B)**, $x = 3, y = 1$

Systems of equations, also called simultaneous equations, can be solved by using substitution or elimination.

Substitution: Substitute the value of y from the second equation into the first equation to get:

$$2x + 4(2x - 5) = 10$$
$$2x + 8x - 20 = 10$$
$$10x = 30$$
$$x = 3$$

Look at the answer choices before continuing because this result eliminates three of the five choices right away. Only answer choices (B) and (D) have $x = 3$, so just substitute $x = 3$ and the y values into both of the original equations, and only $y = 1$ is true for both.

Elimination: Rewrite the two equations so the x, y, and number values align, and then add or subtract to get rid of one of the variables. These equations become

$$2x + 4y = 10$$
$$2x - y = 5$$

Subtract the bottom equation from the top to get $5y = 5$, or $y = 1$. Similar to the above, the answer choices reduce to two, (B) and (E), and only the values in (B) make both original equations true. Note that with both methods, once one of the variables is found, ignore the answer choices that don't have that value and check only the remaining ones.

8. **(C)**, $\frac{5}{12}$

The two events are independent of each other, so the probability of both (or "and") is the product of their probabilities. The probability of head is $\frac{1}{2}$. There are 5 numbers greater than 1 on the cube, so the probability of showing a number greater than 1 is $\frac{5}{6}$. Therefore, the probability of both events happening is $\frac{1}{2} \times \frac{5}{6} = \frac{5}{12}$.

9. **(A)**, 9

This is a logic problem. You need only 9 cuts to get 10 pieces. If you make 10 cuts, you get 11 pieces.

10. **(A)**, 7 and 8

To find an approximation of the square root of an irrational (nonperfect) number, determine the perfect squares above and below the radicand, which would be 49 and 64. Since $49 < 52 < 64$, the square roots of these numbers also have the same relationship: $7 < \sqrt{52} < 8$.

11. **Graph (A)**

Note that whenever Mike stopped, his distance was constant (horizontal line) for that period of time. The other graphs are incorrect for various reasons: Graph (B) doesn't have him waiting for 10 minutes for the repair to his car, graph (C) doesn't have him waiting 2 hours for the oil change, graph (D) has Mike waiting 15 minutes before he leaves the house, and then doesn't have the proper relative waiting times, and graph (E) has Mike going from the mechanic to the library in no time at all.

12. **(D)**, Marquez

To determine how many votes each candidate received, multiply 700 by the percentage. To cut down on calculations, do $700 \times 20\%$ first because it is easiest to calculate. That equals 140 votes, so only answer choices (B) and (D) are possible because they are less than 140.

13. **(D)**, 9 feet

Approximate the brace with the diagonal and use the Pythagorean formula.

$$c^2 = a^2 + b^2$$

$$c^2 = 16 + 64 = 80$$

$$c \approx 9$$

14. **(A)**, 204

Since 1 pound = 16 ounces, a half pound = 8 ounces. The first ounce cost 50 cents, and the remaining 7 ounces cost 22 cents each, so the calculation is $50 + 7(22) = 204$ cents.

15. **(C)**

$\frac{1}{3}x + .25\left(\frac{1}{3}x\right) + 1$ yards and $12\left(\frac{1}{3}x\right)$ hooks.

Convert feet to yards, so the window is $\left(\frac{1}{3}x\right)$ yards wide. Since the instructions for the hooks are less complicated than for the fabric, look at the hooks first and eliminate all of the wrong answer choices. Angelica needs 12 hooks for every yard of window, the number of hooks is $12\left(\frac{1}{3}x\right)$, which eliminates all the answer choices except (B) and (C). Notice that these two answer choices differ only by the +1 term in answer choice (C). Since Angelica needs an extra 3 feet (= 1 yard) for the vertical hems, the correct answer is (C).

16. (B), 42

This problem looks more difficult than it is. Factor the numerator of the fraction and then cancel common factors in the numerator and denominator:

$$\frac{41^2 + 41}{41} = \frac{41(41+1)}{41}$$
$$= 41 + 1 = 42$$

17. (B), 6

Substitute the values into the expression: $\frac{4+6}{2} + 1 = \frac{10}{2} + 1 = 5 + 1 = 6$.

18. (A), 1

The mean is $\frac{\text{sum of items}}{\text{number of items}} = \frac{99}{6} = 16.5$. The median is the average of the two middle numbers, 15 and 16, or 15.5. The difference is $16.5 - 15.5 = 1$.

19. (A), 1.28 seconds

The ratios should be equal:

$$\frac{186,000 \text{ miles}}{1 \text{ second}} = \frac{239,000 \text{ miles}}{x \text{ seconds}}$$

$$186,000x = 239,000$$

$$x = 1.28 \text{ seconds}$$

20. (A), 344 feet

That means the car will travel more than the length of a football field before it stops! Just substitute the given values for their variables. The other answer choices were due to faulty calculations, either using 60 mph instead of 88 fps (all units must match in the calculation), or forgetting to square v, or both.

21. (A), 4

First, determine how many cookies. Two dozen equals 24. If x is the number of macadamia nut cookies, then $5x$ is the number of chocolate chip cookies, so

$$x + 5x = 24$$

$$6x = 24$$

$$x = 4$$

22. (C), $\frac{2}{3}$

This can be done easily by elimination. Since the numbers are getting smaller, the answer must be > 0, so answer choices (A), (B), and (E) are eliminated. Answer choice (D) is eliminated because it is an improper fraction, and thus is greater than 1.

23. 50

When two parallel lines (notice that they don't have to be horizontal) are crossed by a transversal, the angles formed are either equal, or they are supplementary, which means they total 180 degrees. The two simultaneous equations for this problem are $x + y = 180$ and $y = x + 80$, which can be solved by either substitution or elimination:

Substitution	Elimination
$x + y = 180$	$x + y = 180$
$x + (x + 80) = 180$	$x - y = -80$
$2x = 100$	$2x = 100$
$x = 50$	$x = 50$

24. **(C)**, $\dfrac{3}{7}$

The total number of pairs of socks in the drawer is $3+6+5=14$. Of these, 6 pairs are white socks, so the probability of picking a white pair is $\dfrac{\text{number of white socks}}{\text{total number of socks}}$ $=\dfrac{6}{14}=\dfrac{3}{7}$.

25. **(B)**, 60

The angles of a triangle add up to $180°$. The other two angles are $\angle A = 30°$ and $\angle C = 90°$. So $\angle B = 180 - (30 + 90) = 180 - 120 = 60$.

26. **(A)**, 81

Since we know that $\sqrt{6400} = 80$ and the radicand ends in 1, the answer must be (A) 81 or (C) 89. The number is closer to 6400 than 8100, so it must be (A). Alternatively, multiply each answer choice by itself until it equals 6561.

27. **(E)**, $(4 + y)^2$

The algebraic translation of this problem is

$$y = \sqrt{x} - 4$$

Add 4 to each side $\qquad 4 + y = \sqrt{x}$

Square both sides $\qquad (4 + y)^2 = x$

28. **(B)**, 32

When the bases are the same in multiplication, simply add the exponents, so $2^2 \times 2^3 = 2^{2+3} = 2^5 = 32$. Or just use $4 \times 8 = 32$. Note that answer choice (C) is incorrect because the bases shouldn't be multiplied.

29. **(C)**, $2x - 3y = 6$

Two lines with the same slope and y-intercept must actually be the same line. Rewrite the given equation by multiplying all terms by 3 to get $3y = 2x - 6$. Then put this equation in general form ($Ax + By = C$), which is the form of the answer choices: $2x - 3y = 6$.

30. **(D)**, 17

This answer can be obtained by using the Pythagorean theorem:

$$c^2 = 8^2 + 15^2$$
$$64 + 225 = 289$$
$$c = 17$$

If you recognize this as a Pythagorean triple, you have the answer right away without the arithmetic. This problem can also be solved by elimination. Since the two legs of the right triangle are given, the third side is the hypotenuse, so it has to be longer than 15, the longest leg, which eliminates answer choices (A), (B), and (C). Answer choice (E) is eliminated because it is the sum of the two legs, and therefore too long to be the third side of the triangle.

31. **(C)**, 4

When dividing a decimal by a power of 10, move the decimal point to the left as many places as the power of 10 (or, alternatively, as many places as there are zeroes in the power of 10). Here, $100 = 10^2$, so move the decimal point two places, and the number becomes 2.74936 with the 4 in the hundredths place.

32. **(C)**, $x = 8, y \neq -3$

For a fraction to equal 0, its numerator must equal 0, but its denominator must not equal 0 because division by 0 is undefined. Therefore, $x - 8 = 0$, and $y + 3 \neq 0$, which yields $x = 8, y \neq -3$.

33. **5; 5.**

Mean$= \dfrac{\text{sum of items}}{\text{number of items}} = \dfrac{1+2+3+4+5+6+7+8+9}{9} = \dfrac{45}{9} = 5$; median $= 5$. Remember that the natural numbers do not include 0, negatives, decimals, or fractions.

34. **(A)**, $6 + \dfrac{25\pi}{2}$

The area of the figure is the area of the triangle plus the area of the semicircle, which is half of the circle with a diameter equal to the hypotenuse of the triangle. The triangle is a 3–4–5 right triangle, so the hypotenuse is 5. For the triangle part, the area is $\dfrac{1}{2}(3)(4) = 6$. For the semicircle part, the area is $\dfrac{1}{2}(\pi)(5^2) = \dfrac{25\pi}{2}$. So the area of the figure is $6 + \dfrac{25\pi}{2}$.

35. **(E)**, $\dfrac{(m-n)}{n} = \dfrac{1}{3}$

If the proportion $\dfrac{m}{n} = \dfrac{2}{3}$ is true, then any numbers with that ratio can be used to check the answers. Let's use the easiest, $m = 2, n = 3$. Then answer choices (A)–(D) are all true, but $\dfrac{(m-n)}{n} = \dfrac{2-3}{3} = -\dfrac{1}{3}$, so answer choice (E) cannot be true. If instead of 2 and 3, we chose $m = 4, n = 6$, all of the answers would be the same, except the answers would have to be reduced, so it's simpler to choose the lowest numbers with the given ratio.

36. **(A)**, $6 - 3(2x - 1) + 9$

You can simplify every answer choice until you get the correct one, or you can do the same but eliminate some first. Since the numerical term is more complicated, let's check the coefficient of x and eliminate any for which it isn't –6. Thus, we eliminate answer choices (C), (D), and (E) before doing any further calculations.

37. **Chart (D)**

From the table, the greatest sales volume is in Center City, and the least is in the Second Street store, which eliminates the other choices. Check the remaining two store locations in Chart (D) to be sure that the correct answer isn't answer choice (E).

38. **(B)**, 50

Use the Pythagorean theorem to find the side of the square. The diagonal divides the square into two isosceles right triangles, so

$10^2 = s^2 + s^2$

$10^2 = 2s^2$

$s^2 = \dfrac{100}{2} = 50$

Alternatively, the area of a rhombus is one-half the product of the diagonals, and a square is just a rhombus with equal angles, so $A = \left(\dfrac{1}{2}\right) d \times d = \dfrac{1}{2}(10 \times 10) = 50$.

39. $\boxed{A}$, $\sqrt{19}$, and $\boxed{E}$, π

Answer choices $\boxed{B}$, $\boxed{C}$, and $\boxed{D}$ are either terminating or repeating decimals or a fraction, respectively, and therefore are all rational.

40. (C), $\dfrac{4m+6n}{m+n}$

$$\text{Mean} = \frac{\text{Total cost of books}}{\text{Total number of books}} = \frac{4m+6n}{m+n}.$$

41. (B), $0 < x^2 < 25$

Since x is not negative, just square the inequality: $0^2 < x^2 < 5^2$, or $0 < x^2 < 25$.

42. (C), $\dfrac{1}{2}B$

Recognize that $\dfrac{1}{6} = \dfrac{1}{2} \times \dfrac{1}{3}$ to do this problem quickly, because when you multiply the left side of the equation by $\dfrac{1}{2}$, you have to multiply the right side by $\dfrac{1}{2}$ as well. Alternatively, rewrite the equation as $A = 3B$ and divide both sides by 6. Answer choices (A) and (B) can be eliminated right away because the answer obviously has to be less than B.

43. (D), $20.00

Read any point off the graph. For example, (5, 100), (10, 200), and (20, 400) are easily read from the graph. Then calculate the cost per ticket by reducing any of those ratios, such as $\dfrac{\$100}{5 \text{ tickets}} = \dfrac{\$20}{1 \text{ ticket}}$.

44. (A), $\dfrac{1}{16}$

Each flip is an independent event since any prior flips do not affect the present flip. The probability of heads is $\dfrac{1}{2}$, so the probability of four heads is $\dfrac{1}{2} \times \dfrac{1}{2} \times \dfrac{1}{2} \times \dfrac{1}{2} = \dfrac{1}{16}$.

45. (D), 80°

The total of all the angles in a triangle is 180, so

$$x + (2x + 20) + (3x - 20) = 180$$
$$6x = 180$$
$$x = 30$$

The other two angles are $2x + 20 = 80$ and $3x - 20 = 70$. The largest angle is 80°.

46. (B), $42.12

The first discount of 25% brings the cost of the radio down to $(.75)(\$60) = \$45$. The second discount of 10% makes the cost of the radio $(.90)(\$45) = \$40.50$. The tax on the radio is $(.04)(\$40.50) = \$1.62$. So the final cost of the radio, including tax, is $\$40.50 + \$1.62 = \$42.12$.

47. (D), 28

Square both sides:
$$\sqrt{x-3} = 5$$
$$x - 3 = 25$$
$$x = 25 + 3 = 28$$

48. (B), 10

Using Venn diagrams, we see that the number of students who take Russian (25) includes the 10 who take both languages, so the number who take only French is $35 - 25 = 10$.

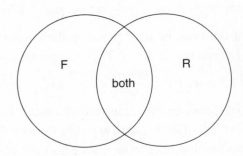

Alternatively, using the "or" logic, the students taking French or Russian is the number taking French plus the number taking Russian, but since both of these include those students taking both languages, we must subtract one of the counts of students taking both languages. So if N(F) is the number of students who take French, N(R) is the number of students who take Russian, and N(both) is the number of students who take both languages, then, since these numbers are *not* mutually exclusive (which means they *can* happen at the same time),

$$N(F) + N(R) - N(both) = N(F \text{ or } R)$$
$$N(F) + 25 - 10 = 35$$
$$N(F) = 20$$

But N(F) = 20 also includes those students who take both languages, N(both) = 10, so the number of students who take *only* French is 20 − 10 = 10.

49. (D), any of the above

The formula for the area of a circle is $A = \pi r^2$, where r is the radius. The diameter is just double the radius, so that will be sufficient. The circumference is $C = 2\pi r$, so that is also sufficient for finding the radius, since the value of π is known (3.14).

50. (E), more than 5

There are actually six, found by taking the integers to the fourth power (or squaring their squares). They are 1, 2, 3, 4, 5, and 0. Don't forget the 0!

51. (B).

This question is actually asking whether graph (A) or graph (B) could be the answer, since the last two graphs aren't linear and graph (C) shows no change. Since one variable is increasing while the other is decreasing, the slope must be negative, which is the case for graph (B).

52. (D), no numbers

M and N have no elements in common. No even numbers >2 can be prime numbers because they are all divisible by 2.

53. (C), 24

If the square has an area of 36 square inches, each side must be $\sqrt{36} = 6$ inches. The perimeter of a square is 4 × (a side) = 4 × 6 = 24.

54. (C), 6

When multiplying a decimal by a power of 10, move the decimal point to the right as many places as the power of 10 (or, alternatively, as many places as there are zeroes in the power of 10). Here, $100 = 10^2$, so move the decimal point two places, and the number becomes 45628.3 with the 6 in the hundreds place.

55. (C), 12

The ratio in this problem is 9 to 4, and we have the total, so we can represent the two groups as $9x$ and $4x$, which are still in the given ratio of 9 to 4. Then the problem becomes

$$9x + 4x = 39, \text{ so } 13x = 39, \text{ and } x = 3.$$

But that is not the answer to the question, which is how many girls are in the club. There are $4x$ girls, so that makes $4(3) = 12$ girls. Whenever a problem presents a ratio and a total, you can represent the groups as two x quantities with the same ratio. Just remember to multiply by the ratio number once you have solved for x.

56. $\boxed{\text{D}}$, 4, and $\boxed{\text{E}}$, 5

Solve the inequality: $3x + 6 > 15$, so $3x > 9$ and $x > 3$. The only answer choices that are greater than 3 are 4 and 5. Answer choice $\boxed{\text{C}}$ isn't correct because the inequality isn't ≥, so 3 is excluded.

Praxis Core Mathematics Practice Test 2

Praxis Core Mathematics
Practice Test 2 Answer Sheet

1. Ⓐ Ⓑ Ⓒ Ⓓ Ⓔ
2. Ⓐ Ⓑ Ⓒ Ⓓ Ⓔ
3. Ⓐ Ⓑ Ⓒ Ⓓ Ⓔ
4. Ⓐ Ⓑ Ⓒ Ⓓ Ⓔ
5. Ⓐ Ⓑ Ⓒ Ⓓ Ⓔ
6. Ⓐ Ⓑ Ⓒ Ⓓ Ⓔ
7. Ⓐ Ⓑ Ⓒ Ⓓ Ⓔ
8. Ⓐ Ⓑ Ⓒ Ⓓ Ⓔ
9. Ⓐ Ⓑ Ⓒ Ⓓ Ⓔ
10. Ⓐ Ⓑ Ⓒ Ⓓ Ⓔ
11. Ⓐ Ⓑ Ⓒ Ⓓ Ⓔ
12. Ⓐ Ⓑ Ⓒ Ⓓ Ⓔ
13. Ⓐ Ⓑ Ⓒ Ⓓ Ⓔ
14. Ⓐ Ⓑ Ⓒ Ⓓ Ⓔ
15. Ⓐ Ⓑ Ⓒ Ⓓ Ⓔ
16. Ⓐ Ⓑ Ⓒ Ⓓ Ⓔ
17. Ⓐ Ⓑ Ⓒ Ⓓ Ⓔ
18. Ⓐ Ⓑ Ⓒ Ⓓ Ⓔ
19. Ⓐ Ⓑ Ⓒ Ⓓ Ⓔ

20. Ⓐ Ⓑ Ⓒ Ⓓ Ⓔ
21. Ⓐ Ⓑ Ⓒ Ⓓ Ⓔ
22. Ⓐ Ⓑ Ⓒ Ⓓ Ⓔ
23. Ⓐ Ⓑ Ⓒ Ⓓ Ⓔ
24. ▭
25. Ⓐ Ⓑ Ⓒ Ⓓ Ⓔ
26. Ⓐ Ⓑ Ⓒ Ⓓ Ⓔ
27. Ⓐ Ⓑ Ⓒ Ⓓ Ⓔ
28. Ⓐ Ⓑ Ⓒ Ⓓ Ⓔ
29. Ⓐ Ⓑ Ⓒ Ⓓ Ⓔ
30. Ⓐ Ⓑ Ⓒ Ⓓ Ⓔ
31. Ⓐ Ⓑ Ⓒ Ⓓ Ⓔ
32. ▭/▭
33. Ⓐ Ⓑ Ⓒ Ⓓ Ⓔ
34. Ⓐ Ⓑ Ⓒ Ⓓ Ⓔ
35. Ⓐ Ⓑ Ⓒ Ⓓ Ⓔ
36. ▭
37. Ⓐ Ⓑ Ⓒ Ⓓ Ⓔ
38. Ⓐ Ⓑ Ⓒ Ⓓ Ⓔ

39. Ⓐ Ⓑ Ⓒ Ⓓ Ⓔ
40. Ⓐ Ⓑ Ⓒ Ⓓ Ⓔ
41. Ⓐ Ⓑ Ⓒ Ⓓ Ⓔ
42. Ⓐ Ⓑ Ⓒ Ⓓ Ⓔ
43. Ⓐ Ⓑ Ⓒ Ⓓ Ⓔ
44. Ⓐ Ⓑ Ⓒ Ⓓ Ⓔ
45. Ⓐ Ⓑ Ⓒ Ⓓ Ⓔ
46. Ⓐ Ⓑ Ⓒ Ⓓ Ⓔ
47. Ⓐ Ⓑ Ⓒ Ⓓ Ⓔ
48. Ⓐ Ⓑ Ⓒ Ⓓ Ⓔ
49. Ⓐ Ⓑ Ⓒ Ⓓ Ⓔ
50. Ⓐ Ⓑ Ⓒ Ⓓ Ⓔ
51. Ⓐ Ⓑ Ⓒ Ⓓ Ⓔ
52. Ⓐ Ⓑ Ⓒ Ⓓ Ⓔ
53. Ⓐ Ⓑ Ⓒ Ⓓ Ⓔ
54. Ⓐ Ⓑ Ⓒ Ⓓ Ⓔ
55. ▭
56. Ⓐ Ⓑ Ⓒ Ⓓ Ⓔ

Praxis Core
Mathematics Practice Test 2

Time: 85 minutes for 56 selected-response items

> **Directions:** Answer each question by providing the correct response or responses. Most items on this test require you to provide the one best answer. However, some questions require you to select one or more answers, in which case you will be directed to respond with all answers that apply. Such response options are shown with squares around the letter choices to distinguish them from the questions with only one answer choice. Some questions are numeric-entry, requiring you to fill in a box or boxes with the correct answer.

To our readers: This printed practice test is designed to simulate as closely as possible the computerized Praxis Core Math test (5732). On test day and on REA's online version of this practice test, you will answer each question by either clicking on the correct response or inserting your answer into designated numeric-entry boxes. An on-screen calculator is available for the actual computerized Praxis Core Math test and at the REA Study Center.

1. About 6,234,000 schoolchildren wear eyeglasses. What is the value of 4 in the number 6,234,000?

   (A) 4 hundreds

   (B) 4 thousands

   (C) 4 ten thousands

   (D) 4 hundred thousands

   (E) 4 million

2. Another way to show 200% of a number is to: (Select *all* that apply.)

   A multiply the number by 200.

   B add the number to itself.

   C multiply the number by 2.

   D double the number.

   E divide the number by 500.

3. If $\frac{1}{3}n + 3 = 7$, what is the value of n?

   (A) 18

   (B) 12

   (C) 6

   (D) 4

   (E) $\frac{4}{3}$

4. A salesperson gets a $10 commission on all sales, plus a $200 per week salary. If she made 40 sales in a week, what would be her earnings?

   (A) $210

   (B) $240

   (C) $440

   (D) $500

   (E) $600

5. The figure below shows a linear relation. What would be the value of y when $x = 60$?

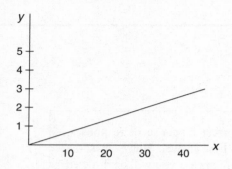

(A) 3

(B) 4

(C) 5

(D) 6

(E) 7

6. If triangle EFG as shown in the xy-plane is shifted 2 units to the right and 4 units down, the new coordinates of vertex G are:

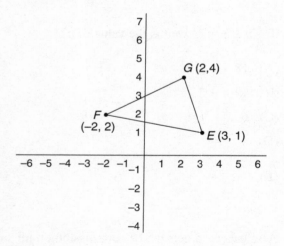

(A) (4, 0)

(B) (5, –3)

(C) (0, –2)

(D) (0, 0)

(E) (6, 2)

7. Alyssa has a bowl of mixed nuts on her coffee table. The bowl contains 15 pecans, 18 almonds, 12 Brazil nuts, and 25 cashews. What is the probability that a nut selected at random will *not* be a pecan?

(A) $\dfrac{15}{70}$

(B) $\dfrac{55}{70}$

(C) $\dfrac{18}{70}$

(D) $\dfrac{12}{70}$

(E) $\dfrac{25}{70}$

8. Trevor made a display for his science fair project. He spent $1.25 on a poster board and $3.40 on a package of construction paper. He gave the clerk a $5.00 bill. How much change did he receive?

(A) $1.60

(B) $0.35

(C) $3.75

(D) $4.65

(E) $0.45

9. A chemist needs to add 3 parts of chemical A and 4 parts of chemical B into a solution. When she adds 600 grams of chemical A into the solution, how many grams of chemical B must she add?

(A) 400

(B) 600

(C) 700

(D) 800

(E) 1400

10. The foot of a 25-foot ladder is 15 feet from a wall. If the ladder is pushed until its foot is only 7 feet from the wall, how much farther up the wall is the ladder pushed?

    (A) 4 feet

    (B) 8 feet

    (C) 12 feet

    (D) 20 feet

    (E) 24 feet

11. What is the relationship of the graphs of the following two equations?

    $$y = 2x + 4$$
    $$2y = -x + 6$$

    (A) They are parallel lines.

    (B) They are perpendicular lines.

    (C) They are two versions of the same line, so their graphs are coincident.

    (D) The graphs of the equations will intersect twice.

    (E) The graphs of the equations will never intersect.

12. Starting from the point $(4, -6)$, and using a slope of 2, as x increases, what would be the next point that contains integer values for x and y?

    (A) $(6, -5)$

    (B) $(5, -4)$

    (C) $(6, -6)$

    (D) $(4, -5)$

    (E) $(6, -4)$

13. A function $f(x)$ is said to be one-to-one if, in addition to $f(x)$ being a function of x, x is a function of $f(x)$. Which of the following sets of points could represent a one-to-one function?

    (A) $(1, 2), (2, 3), (3, 3), (4, 4)$

    (B) $(1, 2), (1, 3), (1, 4), (1, 5)$

    (C) $(1, 1), (2, 2), (3, 3), (4, 4)$

    (D) $(-1, 1), (1, 1), (-2, 2), (2, 2)$

    (E) $(1, 1), (1, -1), (2, 2), (-2, 2)$

14. For which of the following groups of numbers is the range equal to 8?

    (A) 2, 4, 5, 6, 6, 7, 8, 9

    (B) 3, 3, 3, 3, 4, 4, 7, 14

    (C) 4, 5, 8, 8, 10, 10, 10, 12

    (D) 5, 7, 9, 10, 12, 14, 17

    (E) 1, 2, 3, 4, 5, 6, 7, 8

15. Which of the following fractions is the greatest?

    (A) $\dfrac{1}{2}$

    (B) $\dfrac{4}{5}$

    (C) $\dfrac{9}{10}$

    (D) $\dfrac{9}{8}$

    (E) $\dfrac{999}{1000}$

16. If the scale on a map indicates that 2 inches is equivalent to m miles, express the measure on the map for $m + 10$ miles.

    (A) $2(m + 10)$

    (B) $\dfrac{2(m+10)}{m}$

    (C) $\dfrac{2(m+10)}{2m}$

    (D) $\dfrac{(m+10)}{2m}$

    (E) $\dfrac{2m}{m+10}$

17. Donna works at an office supply store. She earns a wage of \$350/week plus an incentive commission of \$50 for each computer she sells (not including notebooks). She needs to earn \$425 this week to pay off a debt. What is the minimum number of computers that she must sell to meet this minimum?

    (A) 1

    (B) 1.5

    (C) 2

    (D) 2.5

    (E) 3

18. If $\dfrac{6}{x} = 2$ and $\dfrac{12}{y} = 24$, then $\dfrac{3x+1}{y+2} =$

    (A) $\dfrac{5}{2}$

    (B) 3

    (C) $\dfrac{7}{2}$

    (D) 4

    (E) 6

19. In the following diagram of two parallel lines, if $m\angle 6 = 48°$ and $m\angle 3 = (6x)°$, what is the value of x?

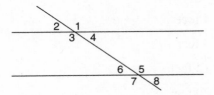

    (A) 8

    (B) 16

    (C) 12

    (D) 24

    (E) 22

20. According to the chart below, which is based on a public opinion survey of 200 people, which age group(s) had the most respondents?

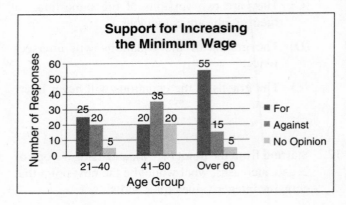

    (A) 21–40 age group

    (B) 41–60 age group

    (C) Over 60 age group

    (D) Both the 41–60 age group and over 60 age group

    (E) Cannot tell from the information given.

21. Which of the following calculations is smallest?

    (A) half of 350,000

    (B) 50% × 350,000

    (C) 35% of 500,000

    (D) $\frac{1}{3}$ of 500,000

    (E) 3.5% of 5,000,000

22. In a group of 60 children, the number of boys is twice the number of girls. The pair of equations that best describes this is

    (A) $b = 2g; b + g = 60$

    (B) $b = -2g; b + g = 60$

    (C) $b = 2g; b + 2g = 60$

    (D) $b = -2g; 2b + g = 60$

    (E) $2b = g; b + g = 60.$

23. A taxi ride cost $2.00 for the first quarter mile and 40 cents for each additional quarter of a mile. How much does a 3-mile trip cost?

    (A) $6.80

    (B) $6.40

    (C) $6.00

    (D) $5.60

    (E) $4.80

24. Jim's grade at the end of the semester is the average of his four exam scores. His first three exam scores were 75, 85, and 90. Jim must score at least how many points on his last exam to get an average grade of at least 85?

25. The figure shown is a square with an equilateral triangle on top of it, $AE = 20$. The perimeter of $ABCDE$ is

    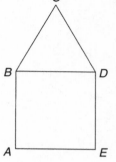

    (A) 50

    (B) 100

    (C) 120

    (D) 160

    (E) 200

26. What is true about the mode of the following group of numbers?

    6, 6, 7, 9, 12, 12, 14, 15, 15

    (A) There is no mode.

    (B) The mode is 6.

    (C) The mode is 12.

    (D) The mode is 2.

    (E) There are three modes.

27. A holiday sale on a sweater offers a 40% discount, followed by a 30% discount, followed by a 50% discount. The final price is what percent of the original price?

    (A) 6%

    (B) 12%

    (C) 21%

    (D) 42%

    (E) 60%

28. Simplify the complex fraction $\frac{\frac{1}{3}+\frac{1}{4}}{6}$.

   (A) $\frac{7}{2}$

   (B) $\frac{6}{7}$

   (C) $\frac{12}{7}$

   (D) $\frac{7}{72}$

   (E) $\frac{1}{6}$

29. Which sequence of steps will solve the equation $4x - 6 = 2x - 2$?

   (A) Add −6 to both sides of the equation, subtract $2x$ from both sides, and divide both sides by 2.

   (B) Add 6 to both sides of the equation, subtract $-2x$ from both sides, and divide both sides by 2.

   (C) Add 6 to both sides of the equation, subtract $2x$ from both sides, and divide both sides by 2.

   (D) Add 6 to both sides of the equation, subtract $2x$ from both sides, and divide both sides by 4.

   (E) Add −6 to both sides of the equation, subtract $-2x$ from both sides, and divide both sides by 2.

30. The sum $\frac{4}{5a}+\frac{3}{b}$ equals which of the following expressions ($a, b \neq 0$)?

   (A) $\frac{7}{5ab}$

   (B) $\frac{35}{ab}$

   (C) $\frac{7}{5a+b}$

   (D) $\frac{4b+15a}{5ab}$

   (E) $\frac{4b+15a}{5a+b}$

31. Triangle ABC in the figure below is translated into the first quadrant so point B is now at coordinates (4, 6). What are the new translated coordinates of point A?

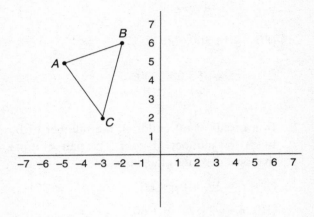

   (A) (5, 1)

   (B) (1, 5)

   (C) (2, 3)

   (D) (3, 3)

   (E) (5, 5)

32. A wheel of fortune at a carnival has 12 equally spaced segments. Eleven of these have a prize of a trinket worth 50 cents, and the twelfth segment has a prize of $1,000. Assuming the wheel is honest, after it has been spun 100 times, each time with a trinket as a prize, what is the probability that it will end up on the $1,000 prize on the 101st turn? Fill in the spaces for the fraction.

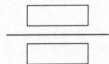

33. What is the value of $\frac{2^7}{2^3}$?

   (A) 16

   (B) 32

   (C) 1^4

   (D) 12

   (E) 64

34. Which of the following numbers is divisible by 2, 5, and 9?

    (A) 457,920

    (B) 457,921

    (C) 457,930

    (D) 457,949

    (E) 457,945

35. Makena will be x years old in 5 years. How old was she last year?

    (A) $x + 5$

    (B) $1 - x - 5$

    (C) $x + 6$

    (D) $x - 6$

    (E) $5x$

36. Kevin scored 24 points in last night's basketball game, which was 40% of the final score for Team A. Their opponent, Team B, scored 70 points in the game. What was the point difference in scores between the two teams? Fill in the box.

    [ ]

37. The graph below shows the number of miles Stacey rode her bike in a 90-mile race in 30-minute intervals. How many miles did she travel between 2:00 p.m. and 2:30 p.m.?

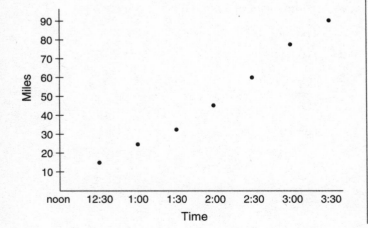

(A) 13 miles

(B) 15 miles

(C) 18 miles

(D) 45 miles

(E) 60 miles

38. In the figure below, two parallel lines are crossed by a transversal. Therefore, $x + y =$

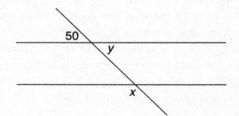

(A) 50

(B) 130

(C) 80

(D) 180

(E) 30

39. A box contains four colors of crayons: 6 blue, 5 green, 5 yellow, and some red crayons. If the probability that a red crayon is picked at random from the box is 1:3, how many total crayons are there in the box?

    (A) 5

    (B) 8

    (C) 16

    (D) 24

    (E) 30

40. What is the value of $\sqrt{3600}$?

    (A) 1800

    (B) 180

    (C) 600

    (D) 60

    (E) 6

41. Tatanya has been watching a $100 jacket in the store window display, hoping it would go on sale. On Monday, the store had a 35%-off sale on everything. When Tatanya went to the store on Friday to buy the jacket, there was a further reduction of 10% on all outerwear. How much did Tatanya save by waiting until Friday rather than buying the jacket on Monday?

    (A) $41.50

    (B) $35.00

    (C) $10.00

    (D) $6.50

    (E) $3.50

42. Which of the following is an equation that shows y as a function of x? (Choose all that apply.)

    A $x^2 + y^2 = 100$

    B $x + y = 10^2$

    C $y = x^2 + 1$

    D $y > 2x + 3$

    E $y = 6$

43. Which equation expresses the relationship between the points in the following table?

x	y
0	−4
2	0
4	4
6	8
8	12

    (A) $y = x - 4$

    (B) $y = x + 4$

    (C) $y = 2x - 4$

    (D) $y = 2x + 4$

    (E) $2y = 2x - 4$

44. Which of the following statements about the circle with center O is false? Choose all that apply.

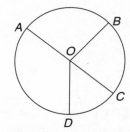

    A OB and OA have the same length.

    B The length of OD is half the length of AC.

    C $BO + OC = OD + OA$

    D The measure of angle DOC equals the measure of angle BOC.

    E Line AOC is equal in length to the sum of lines BO and OD.

45. If the mean of s and −8 is 6, then $s =$

    (A) 4

    (B) 10

    (C) 20

    (D) −20

    (E) 0

46. Which symbol belongs in the space comparing the two fractions, $\frac{1}{6}$ ____ $\frac{4}{7}$?

    (A) <

    (B) >

    (C) =

    (D) ≤

    (E) ≥

47. The perimeter of a small rectangular garden is 24 feet and its area is 20 square feet. The length of the shorter side is

    (A) 2 feet

    (B) 4 feet

    (C) 6 feet

    (D) 8 feet

    (E) 10 feet

48. What is (are) the value(s) of n in the equation $|n| + 3 = 7$?

    (A) 4

    (B) both 4 and –4

    (C) –4

    (D) 10 or –10

    (E) 10

49. In the figure shown, $L_1 \parallel AB$. What is the measure of $\angle y$?

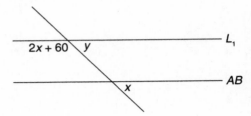

    (A) 40°

    (B) 60°

    (C) 70°

    (D) 80°

    (E) Can't be determined from the information given.

50. On the graph of the equation $y = \frac{-2}{3}x + 6$, what is the value of the y-intercept?

    (A) 6

    (B) $-\frac{2}{3}$

    (C) $5\frac{2}{3}$

    (D) –9

    (E) There is no y-intercept.

51. What is the mean of the numbers 18, 5, 34, 87, and 99?

    (A) 32

    (B) 42.4

    (C) 34

    (D) 48.6

    (E) 46.8

52. What is the value of x in the equation $\frac{3}{2}x + 2 = 8$?

   (A) $\frac{4}{3}$

   (B) 4

   (C) 6

   (D) 8

   (E) 9

53. $\angle n - \angle m =$

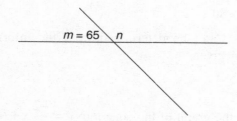

   (A) 30°

   (B) 50°

   (C) 65°

   (D) 90°

   (E) 180°

54. Arrange the sides of triangle ABC in order, largest to smallest.

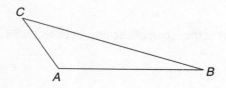

   (A) $a > b > c$

   (B) $a > c > b$

   (C) $b > a > c$

   (D) $b > c > a$

   (E) $c > a > b$

55. The following dot plot shows the pulse rates of 25 individuals. What is the median pulse rate? Put your answer in the box.

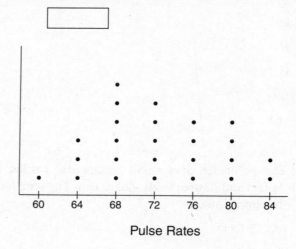

Pulse Rates

56. A jar has 7 red balls and 3 orange balls. Two balls are drawn, one at a time, without replacement. What is the probability of selecting two red balls?

   (A) $\frac{7}{15}$

   (B) $\frac{13}{19}$

   (C) $\frac{13}{90}$

   (D) $\frac{21}{50}$

   (E) $\frac{123}{90}$

Praxis Core Mathematics
Practice Test 2 Answer Key

1.	B	20.	D	39.	D
2.	B, C, D	21.	D	40.	D
3.	B	22.	A	41.	D
4.	E	23.	B	42.	B, C, E
5.	B	24.	90	43.	C
6.	A	25.	B	44.	D
7.	B	26.	E	45.	C
8.	B	27.	C	46.	A
9.	D	28.	D	47.	A
10.	A	29.	C	48.	B
11.	B	30.	D	49.	A
12.	B	31.	B	50.	A
13.	C	32.	$\frac{1}{12}$	51.	D
14.	C	33.	A	52.	B
15.	D	34.	A	53.	B
16.	B	35.	D	54.	B
17.	C	36.	10	55.	72
18.	D	37.	B	56.	A
19.	E	38.	D		

1.   **(B)**, 4 thousands

2.   B , C , D

When converting a percentage to a decimal, divide the percentage by 100, so 200% is the same as multiplying by 2. Therefore, because adding a number to itself B and doubling a number D are the same as multiplying by 2 C , all three of those answers are equivalent. The other two answer choices are not equivalent to multiplying by 2, so they are eliminated.

3.   **(B)**, 12

Multiply all terms in the equation by 3 to get $n + 9 = 21$, so $n = 12$. The other answer choices reflect answers if not all the terms in the equation were multiplied by 3. Since the first three answer choices are all multiples of 3, substituting the answer choices in the original equation works well here also.

4.   **(E)**, $600

Add $10 × 40 = $400 for commissions to her base salary of $200 to get $600.

5.   **(B)**, 4

From the graph, the slope of the line is $\frac{\text{change in } y}{\text{change in } x} = \frac{1}{15}$, and the y-intercept is 0. Therefore, the equation of the line is $y = \frac{1}{15}x$. So when $x = 60$, $y = \frac{60}{15} = 4$.

6.   **(A)**, (4, 0)

For any problem in which a triangle is translated (moved without rotation or "flipping,") but the question is about just one of the vertices, look only at that vertex. So this problem is actually asking, "If point G at (2, 4) is moved 2 units to the right and 4 units down, where will it be?" This way is much less complicated than looking at the whole triangle. If point G is moved 2 units to the right, it will be at (4, 4), and if it then is moved 4 units down, it will be at (4, 0). The other answer choices were for points E and F or for movements of G that were in the wrong directions.

7.   **(B)**, $\frac{55}{70}$

This problem can be solved by adding up the probabilities for all of the types of nuts except pecans, but a faster and easier solution to problems asking for the probability of *not A* is to figure the probability of A and then subtract it from 1. So the probability it is a pecan is $\frac{15}{70}$, and $1 - \frac{15}{70} = \frac{55}{70}$. The other answer choices are the probabilities of the other nut types.

8.   **(B)**, $0.35

Trevor's purchase was $1.25 + $3.40 = $4.65. The change from a $5.00 bill is thus $5.00 − $4.65 = $0.35.

9.   **(D)**, 800 grams

This is a ratio problem; set up as: $\frac{3 \text{ parts}}{4 \text{ parts}} = \frac{600}{B}$, which cross-multiplies to $3B = 2400$, or 800 grams of chemical B.

10. **(A)**, 4 feet

The ladder, wall, and ground form right triangles with the 25-foot ladder being the hypotenuse in both cases. Originally, the ladder is 20 feet up the wall because the ladder forms a Pythagorean triple (four times the 3–4–5 triangle). When the ladder is pushed closer to the wall, the hypotenuse is still 25, one leg (the one on the ground) is now 7, and the third leg (the height of the ladder on the wall) is found by using the Pythagorean theorem:

$$25^2 = 7^2 + h^2$$
$$h^2 = 625 - 49$$
$$h^2 = 576$$
$$h = \sqrt{576} = 24$$

Since the new height of the ladder on the wall is 24 feet, the ladder is $24 - 20 = 4$ feet farther up the wall, which is what the problem is asking.

Alternatively, this problem can be solved by observation. The answer choices have to be added to the original 20-foot height, but the height up the wall cannot be more than 25 feet, the length of the ladder, which is the hypotenuse and thus the longest side of the triangle that is formed. All of the answer choices, when added to 20, will give heights that are greater than 25 feet, so (A) is the only possible answer.

11. **(B)**, they are perpendicular lines

If the second equation is written in slope-intercept form, as the first equation is, it would be $y = -\frac{1}{2}x + 3$. Thus, the slopes (coefficients of x) are negative reciprocals of each other, which is the criterion for perpendicular lines. Thus, answer choices (A) and (E), which say the same thing, are incorrect; answer choice (C) is incorrect because these have two different slope-intercept equations; and answer choice (D) is incorrect because these are both linear equations, so they intersect at most once (in this case, once, at right angles).

12. **(B)**, (5, –4)

A slope of 2 means that for every change of +1 for x, there is a change of +2 for y. Add 1 to the x value and 2 to the y value to get (5, –4). This problem could also be solved by sketching a graph, but it's faster to think it through first.

13. **(C)** (1, 1), (2, 2), (3, 3), (4, 4)

For an (x, y) relation to be one-to-one, every x value must have a distinct y value and every y value must have a distinct x value. Therefore, no x or y values can repeat. This is true only for answer choice (C).

14. **(C)**, 4, 5, 8, 8, 10, 10, 10, 12

The range is the highest value minus the lowest value, or $12 - 4 = 8$. All of the answer choices are arranged in numerical order, and no other one has a range of 8.

15. **(D)**, $\frac{9}{8}$

All of the other answer choices are fractions with values less than 1 because their numerators are less than their denominators. Answer choice (D) has a value more than 1 because its numerator is more than its denominator. You don't even have to evaluate any of the fractions.

16. **(B)**, $\frac{2(m+10)}{m}$

The ratio for the map is $\frac{2 \text{ inches}}{m \text{ miles}}$, and that ratio should hold for all map readings and miles. Therefore,

$$\frac{2 \text{ inches}}{m \text{ miles}} = \frac{x \text{ inches}}{(m+10) \text{ miles}}, \text{ or } \frac{2}{m} = \frac{x}{(m+10)}.$$

Cross-multiply to get $\qquad xm = 2(m + 10)$

$$x = \frac{2(m+10)}{m}$$

17. **(C)**, 2

This solution is most easily found by substituting the answer choices into the inequality $350 + 50x \geq 425$. First of all, eliminate answer choices (B) and (D) because there are no "half" computers. If $x = 1$, the inequality isn't true. However, if $x = 2$, it is. So Donna must sell at least 2 computers to reach her goal.

18. **(D)**, 4

Since $\frac{6}{x} = 2$ and $\frac{12}{y} = 24$, then $x = 3$ and $y = \frac{1}{2}$. Thus,

$$\frac{3x+1}{y+2} = \frac{10}{2.5} = 4.$$

19. **(E)**, 22

When two parallel lines are cut by a transversal, the angles formed are either equal (corresponding angles or vertical angles) or supplementary. $\angle 3$ and $\angle 6$ are supplementary, which means they total 180 degrees: $\angle 3 + \angle 6 = 180$, so

$$6x + 48 = 180$$
$$6x = 132$$
$$x = 22$$

20. **(D)**, Both the 41–60 age group and over 60 age group

The 21–40 age group had $25 + 20 + 5 = 50$ respondents; the 41–60 age group had $20 + 35 + 20 = 75$ respondents; and the over 60 age group had $55 + 15 + 5 = 75$ respondents.

21. **(D)**, $\frac{1}{3}$ of 500,000

All of the other answer choices are equivalent, and since $\frac{1}{3}$ is less than 35%, answer choice (D) is the smallest.

22. **(A)**, $b = 2g$; $b + g = 60$

No trick to this. Just "translate" the words into algebra, and right away you get answer choice (A).

23. **(B)**, $6.40

Three miles equals 12 quarter miles, so after the first quarter mile, there are 11 quarter miles left. The cost is thus $2.00 + 11(.40) = \$6.40$.

24. 90

The equation for the average, or mean, is $\frac{\text{sum of items}}{\text{number of items}}$, or in this case with x being Jim's score on the last exam, $\frac{75 + 85 + 90 + x}{4} \geq 85$. Multiply both sides by 4, to get $340 = 250 + x \geq 340$, or $x \geq 90$.

25. **(B)**, 100

Do not include *BD* because the perimeter is the sum of the *outside* distances. The perimeter is thus five segments, each equal to 20, so $p = 5 \times 20 = 100$.

26. **(E)**, There are three modes

The mode is the value with the highest frequency. In this group of numbers, there are three numbers with a frequency of 2: 6, 12, and 15, so there are three modes.

27. **(C)**, 21%

Note that successive discounts are on the price being discounted, not on the original price. Each successive price can be figured by multiplying by the percentage to pay rather than the discount percentage. In other words, a discount of 40% means the price will be 60% of the original. If the original price is X, the first discount of 40% means a price of .60X, the next discount of 30%

means a price of .70 (.60X) = .42X, and the last discount of 50% means a price of (.50)(.42X) = .21X, or 21% of the original price. The important thing here is that the question is about the price, so use the discounted price, not the percentage discount, in all calculations: (.60)(.70)(.50) = .21.

28. (D), $\dfrac{7}{72}$

This is actually easier than it looks. Multiply the top and bottom of the main fraction by 12 (the LCM of 3, 4, and 6) to get

$$\frac{12}{12}\left(\frac{\frac{1}{3}+\frac{1}{4}}{6}\right)$$

$$=\frac{4+3}{72}=\frac{7}{72}$$

29. (C)

The steps are: $4x - 6 = 2x - 2$

Add 6 to both sides of the equation: $4x = 2x + 4$

Subtract 2x from both sides $2x = 4$

Divide both sides by 2 $x = 2$

The signs in the other answer choices are incorrect.

30. (D), $\dfrac{4b+15a}{5ab}$

The lowest common denominator (LCD) of these fractions is the product of their denominators, $5ab$. Multiply the expression by $\dfrac{5ab}{5ab}$, which equals 1, so it doesn't change the expression—it just simplifies it.

$$\frac{5ab}{5ab}\left(\frac{4}{5a}+\frac{3}{b}\right)=\frac{4b}{5ab}+\frac{3(5a)}{5ab}=\frac{4b+15a}{5ab}.$$

31. (B), (1, 5)

Translation simply means to move horizontally and/or vertically, but the triangle doesn't change orientation—it doesn't rotate or "flip." If a translation problem involves the location of only one point on the triangle, just concentrate on that one point, A here. In this problem, the information about point B just tells what the translation is. B is moved from (–2, 6) to (4, 6), or (4 –(–2)) = 6 spaces to the right, which can also be figured out from the grid. Then point A must also be moved 6 spaces to the right, which would place it at (1, 5), which can be determined visually on the graph. Note that since the y value of B hadn't changed, the y value of A also shouldn't change, which eliminates answer choices (A), (C), and (D) right away.

32. $\dfrac{1}{12}$

If the wheel is honest, every spin is independent of any other spin, so the probability of any outcome on each spin is 1 out of 12, or $\dfrac{1}{12}$.

33. (A), 16

When the bases are the same in division, simply subtract the exponents, so $2^7 \div 2^3 = 2^{7-3} = 2^4 = 16$. Or just use $128 \div 8 = 16$. Note that answer choice (C) is incorrect because the bases shouldn't be divided.

34. (A), 457,920

Eliminate answer choices (B), (D), and (E) because for the number to be divisible by both 2 and 5, the number must end in a 0. So the problem narrows down to which of two choices is divisible by 9, and answer choice (A) is divisible by 9, so answer choice (C) doesn't even have to be checked. Alternatively, instead of dividing by 9, you could have used the not-too-well-known fact that if the digits of a number add to a multiple of 9 (you can add the digits in any order), the number is divisible by 9. In answer choice (A), the digits are 4, 5, 7, 9, 2, and since $4 + 5 = 9$, $9 = 9$, and $7 + 2 = 9$, the number is divisible by 9 without even having to add $4 + 5 + 7 + 9 + 2$.

35. (D), $x - 6$

If Makena will be x years old in 5 years, she must be $x - 5$ years old now. Last year, she was one year younger, or $(x - 5) - 1 = x - 6$.

36. 10

Kevin scored 24 points, which was 40% of Team A's score. The equation to find the team's score x is $24 = .40x$, or $x = 60$ points. Team B's score was 70 points. The question asks for the difference, which is $70 - 60 = 10$ points, so even though Kevin did a fine job, his team lost.

37. (B), 15 miles

From the graph, Stacey rode 45 miles by 2:00 p.m. and 60 miles by 2:30 p.m., so the number of miles she rode in that half hour is $60 - 45 = 15$ miles.

38. (D), 180

When two parallel lines are cut by a transversal, the angles formed are either equal (corresponding angles or vertical angles) or supplementary. Here, x and y are supplementary, so their sum equals 180°.

39. (D), 24

Let x = the number of red crayons. The probability that a crayon is red is

$$\frac{1}{3} = \frac{\text{number of red crayons}}{\text{total number of crayons}} = \frac{x}{6 + 5 + 5 + x}$$

$$\frac{1}{3} = \frac{x}{16 + x}$$

$$3x = 16 + x$$

$$2x = 16$$

$$x = 8 \text{ red crayons}$$

So the total number of crayons is $16 + 8 = 24$.

40. (D), 60

This is the same as asking which of the numbers squared equals 3600. Therefore, answer choices (A), (B), and (E) are eliminated. Answer choice (C) would have four zeroes under the radical, and answer choice (D) would have only two, so that is the correct answer.

41. (D), $6.50

On Monday, the jacket cost $100 - $35 = $65. On Friday, this price was reduced by another 10%, or $.10($65) = 6.50, so she saved $6.50 from Monday's price. Answer choice (A) is the total savings on Friday; answer choice (B) is the savings if she had bought the jacket on Monday; answer choice (C) is 10% off the original price, not Monday's sale price; and answer choice (E) is 10% of the savings, not the cost, of the coat from Monday's price.

42. B , C , and E

These answer choices all show y as a function of x. The function criterion is that for every x there is only one value of y. Also the graph of a function must pass the vertical line test (no vertical line passes through the graph more than once). This is not true for answer choice

$\boxed{A}$, which is the equation of a circle and thus doesn't pass the vertical line test, nor for answer choice $\boxed{D}$, which has an infinite number of values for y for each value of x.

43. (C), $y = 2x - 4$

Notice that all answer choices are in slope-intercept form except the last one. Notice also that the y-intercept is given as -4 in the table (it is the value when $x = 0$). So eliminate all answers except (A) and (C). (Eliminate (E) because even though the constant term is -4, the equation is not in slope intercept form, and once it is put in that form, the -4 will change—you don't even have to figure out what it will be, just that it won't remain as -4.) To choose between (A) and (C), substitute another pair of points to eliminate which one isn't correct. In this case, since a value for x when $y = 0$ is given, try $x = 2$ first in both equations because you only have to check whether the value of the equation is positive or negative (and therefore not 0) to eliminate an equation—you don't even have to evaluate the equation.

44. $\boxed{D}$

Only $\boxed{D}$ is false because we don't know anything about the angles formed in the figure. All of the other statements are true because lines OA, OB, OC, and OD are all radii of circle O and therefore are all equal.

45. (C), 20

According to the formula for the mean, $\dfrac{s + (-8)}{2} = 6$, which becomes $s + (-8) = 12$, and $s = 20$. Alternatively, eliminate all of the answer choices except (B) and (C) because the mean must be between the two values, and 6 is outside of the range for the other answer choices. Since the mean should be equidistant between the two values, 10 won't work, but 20 will.

46. (A), $<$

If the two fractions are changed to fractions with the same denominator (42), they would be $\dfrac{1}{6} = \dfrac{6}{42}$ and $\dfrac{4}{7} = \dfrac{24}{42}$, so $\dfrac{1}{6} < \dfrac{4}{7}$. In some cases, such as this one, the relative sizes of two fractions is obvious and can be answered right away, but this method works in all cases.

47. (A), 2 feet

The dimensions are two numbers whose sum is half of the perimeter, or 12, and whose product is 20. By trial and error, the sides are 10 and 2, so the shorter side is 2 feet.

48. (B), both 4 and -4

Change the equation into an equation with the absolute value alone on one side:

$$|n| + 3 = 7$$
$$|n| = 4$$

$$n = 4 \qquad\qquad\qquad n = -4$$

Answer choices (D) and (E) are incorrect due to an error in solving the original equation by adding 3 rather than subtracting it.

49. (A), 40°

When two parallel lines are cut by a transversal, the angles formed are either equal (vertical angles or corresponding angles). or supplementary. Therefore,

$$(2x + 60) + x = 180$$
$$3x = 120$$
$$x = 40°$$

Therefore, $y = x = 40°$.

50. (A), 6

This equation is in slope-intercept form, $y = mx + b$, so the y-intercept, b, can be read directly from the equation with no figuring or graphing necessary. If an equation is presented that is not in slope-intercept form, the y-intercept can be found by setting $x = 0$ and solving for y.

51. (D), 48.6

The mean is the total divided by the number of inputs:

$$\frac{18 + 5 + 34 + 87 + 99}{5}$$

$$= \frac{243}{5} = 48.6$$

52. (B), 4

Multiply all terms in the equation by 2 to clear the fraction:

$$3x + 4 = 16$$
$$3x = 12$$
$$x = 4$$

All of the other answer choices didn't multiply every term by 2 or made an arithmetic error.

53. (B), 50°

Angles m and n are supplementary, and $\angle m = 65°$. So $\angle n = 180° - 65° = 115°$. Therefore, $\angle n - \angle m = 115° - 65° = 50°$.

54. (B), $a > c > b$

The sides of a triangle are named by the lowercase letter of the opposite angle. Thus, side a is opposite angle A. From the figure, the sizes of the angles in order are $A > C > B$. The relative lengths of the sides are ordered by the sizes of the angles opposite them. Therefore, $a > c > b$.

55. 72

There are 25 data points, so count from either end of the graph to determine where the middle (13th) data point lies. It is within the dots of a pulse of 72.

56. (A), $\frac{7}{15}$

These are mutually exclusive events and the question is an "or" problem, so the two probabilities are multiplied. Since there is no replacement for the second selection, there are only 6 red balls left and only 9 balls total. The probability of the second event therefore changes from $\frac{7}{10}$ to $\frac{6}{9}$. The probability is

$$\frac{7}{10} \times \frac{6}{9} = \frac{42}{90} = \frac{7}{15}$$

Praxis Core
Reading Practice Test 1

Also available at the online REA Study Center (*www.rea.com/studycenter*)

The Praxis Core Reading (5712) test is computer-based, so we strongly recommend that you take our online practice tests to simulate test-day conditions and to receive these added benefits:

- **Timed testing conditions**—Gauge how much time you can spend on each question.

- **Automatic scoring**—Find out how you did on the test, instantly.

- **On-screen detailed explanations of answers**—Learn not just the correct answer but also why the other answers are wrong.

- **Diagnostic score reports**—Pinpoint where you're strongest and where you need to focus your study.

Praxis Core
Reading Practice Test 1 Answer Sheet

1. Ⓐ Ⓑ Ⓒ Ⓓ Ⓔ   20. Ⓐ Ⓑ Ⓒ Ⓓ Ⓔ   39. Ⓐ Ⓑ Ⓒ Ⓓ Ⓔ

2. Ⓐ Ⓑ Ⓒ Ⓓ Ⓔ   21. Ⓐ Ⓑ Ⓒ Ⓓ Ⓔ   40. Ⓐ Ⓑ Ⓒ Ⓓ Ⓔ

3. Ⓐ Ⓑ Ⓒ Ⓓ Ⓔ   22. Ⓐ Ⓑ Ⓒ Ⓓ Ⓔ   41. Ⓐ Ⓑ Ⓒ Ⓓ Ⓔ

4. Ⓐ Ⓑ Ⓒ Ⓓ Ⓔ   23. Ⓐ Ⓑ Ⓒ Ⓓ Ⓔ   42. Ⓐ Ⓑ Ⓒ Ⓓ Ⓔ

5. Ⓐ Ⓑ Ⓒ Ⓓ Ⓔ   24. Ⓐ Ⓑ Ⓒ Ⓓ Ⓔ   43. Ⓐ Ⓑ Ⓒ Ⓓ Ⓔ

6. Ⓐ Ⓑ Ⓒ Ⓓ Ⓔ   25. Ⓐ Ⓑ Ⓒ Ⓓ Ⓔ   44. Ⓐ Ⓑ Ⓒ Ⓓ Ⓔ

7. Ⓐ Ⓑ Ⓒ Ⓓ Ⓔ   26. Ⓐ Ⓑ Ⓒ Ⓓ Ⓔ   45. Ⓐ Ⓑ Ⓒ Ⓓ Ⓔ

8. Ⓐ Ⓑ Ⓒ Ⓓ Ⓔ   27. Ⓐ Ⓑ Ⓒ Ⓓ Ⓔ   46. Ⓐ Ⓑ Ⓒ Ⓓ Ⓔ

9. Ⓐ Ⓑ Ⓒ Ⓓ Ⓔ   28. Ⓐ Ⓑ Ⓒ Ⓓ Ⓔ   47. Ⓐ Ⓑ Ⓒ Ⓓ Ⓔ

10. Ⓐ Ⓑ Ⓒ Ⓓ Ⓔ   29. Ⓐ Ⓑ Ⓒ Ⓓ Ⓔ   48. Ⓐ Ⓑ Ⓒ Ⓓ Ⓔ

11. Ⓐ Ⓑ Ⓒ Ⓓ Ⓔ   30. Ⓐ Ⓑ Ⓒ Ⓓ Ⓔ   49. Ⓐ Ⓑ Ⓒ Ⓓ Ⓔ

12. Ⓐ Ⓑ Ⓒ Ⓓ Ⓔ   31. Ⓐ Ⓑ Ⓒ Ⓓ Ⓔ   50. Ⓐ Ⓑ Ⓒ Ⓓ Ⓔ

13. Ⓐ Ⓑ Ⓒ Ⓓ Ⓔ   32. Ⓐ Ⓑ Ⓒ Ⓓ Ⓔ   51. Ⓐ Ⓑ Ⓒ Ⓓ Ⓔ

14. Ⓐ Ⓑ Ⓒ Ⓓ Ⓔ   33. Ⓐ Ⓑ Ⓒ Ⓓ Ⓔ   52. Ⓐ Ⓑ Ⓒ Ⓓ Ⓔ

15. Ⓐ Ⓑ Ⓒ Ⓓ Ⓔ   34. Ⓐ Ⓑ Ⓒ Ⓓ Ⓔ   53. Ⓐ Ⓑ Ⓒ Ⓓ Ⓔ

16. Ⓐ Ⓑ Ⓒ Ⓓ Ⓔ   35. Ⓐ Ⓑ Ⓒ Ⓓ Ⓔ   54. Ⓐ Ⓑ Ⓒ Ⓓ Ⓔ

17. Ⓐ Ⓑ Ⓒ Ⓓ Ⓔ   36. Ⓐ Ⓑ Ⓒ Ⓓ Ⓔ   55. Ⓐ Ⓑ Ⓒ Ⓓ Ⓔ

18. Ⓐ Ⓑ Ⓒ Ⓓ Ⓔ   37. Ⓐ Ⓑ Ⓒ Ⓓ Ⓔ   56. Ⓐ Ⓑ Ⓒ

19. Ⓐ Ⓑ Ⓒ Ⓓ Ⓔ   38. Ⓐ Ⓑ Ⓒ Ⓓ Ⓔ

Praxis Core
Reading Practice Test 1

Time: 85 minutes for 56 selected-response questions

> **Directions:** Each statement or passage in this practice test is followed by a question or questions based on its content. After reading each statement or passage, choose the best answer to each question from among the five choices given. (Note that in limited cases, when you're asked to "select *all* that apply," there may be as few as three choices presented.) Answer all questions following a statement or passage based on what is stated or implied in that statement or passage; you are not expected to have any previous knowledge of the topics treated in the statements and passages. Remember to answer every question and mark the corresponding letter on the answer sheet.

To our readers: Answer choices in this practice test are designated by letters. Such labeling allows you to more easily follow our answer explanations both in print and with our online content. On the actual Praxis Core test, which is computerized, you will click on unlabeled ovals or squares.

Acupuncture practitioners, those who use the placement of needles at strategic locations under the skin to block pain, have been tolerated by Amer-
Line ican physicians since the 1930s. This form of Chi-
(5) nese treatment has been used for about 3,000 years and until recently has been viewed suspiciously by Western medicine. New research, however, indicates that acupuncture might provide relief for sufferers of chronic back pain, arthritis, and even pain
(10) experienced by alcoholics and drug abusers as they kick the habit.

1. According to the passage, acupuncture has been found to help people suffering from all of the following EXCEPT

   (A) arthritis

   (B) recurring back pain

   (C) alcoholics in withdrawal

   (D) liver disease

   (E) drug addicts in withdrawal

> **Questions 2 and 3 are based on the following passage, which is excerpted from Dr. Martin Luther King's "I Have a Dream" speech, delivered in Washington, D.C., in 1963.**

Five score years ago, a great American, in whose symbolic shadow we stand today, signed the Emancipation Proclamation. This momentous
Line decree came as a great beacon light of hope to mil-
(5) lions of Negro slaves who had been seared in the flames of withering injustice. It came as a joyous daybreak to end the long night of their captivity.

But one hundred years later, the Negro is still not free; one hundred years later, the life of the
(10) Negro is still sadly crippled by the manacles of segregation and the chains of discrimination; one hundred years later, the Negro lives on a lonely island of poverty in the midst of a vast ocean of material prosperity; one hundred years later, the Negro is
(15) still languished in the corners of American society and finds himself an exile in his own land.

So we've come here today to dramatize a shameful condition. . . .

2. Why does King begin by referencing the "great American" Lincoln and the Emancipation Proclamation, which Lincoln signed in 1863?

(Select all that apply.)

A He is standing on the steps of the Lincoln Memorial.

B He implies that he was inspired by Lincoln's example.

C He says that discrimination and segregation are finally over.

D He says one hundred years after emancipation was promised, the Negro is free.

E He suggests that the effort to obtain this freedom and equality for black Americans through Lincoln's Emancipation Proclamation has not been realized.

3. By beginning his speech with the phrase "five score years ago" instead of "a hundred years ago," King seeks to invoke

(A) the assassination of President Lincoln

(B) the end of the Civil War

(C) the signing of The Emancipation Proclamation

(D) the election of President Lincoln

(E) Lincoln's Gettysburg Address

Questions 4 through 6 refer to the following excerpt:

For Hush Puppies—the classic American brushed-suede shoes with the lightweight crepe sole—the Tipping Point came somewhere between
Line late 1994 and early 1995. The brand had been all
(5) but dead until that point. . . . But then something strange happened. At a fashion shoot, two Hush Puppies Executives—Owen Baxter and Geoffrey Lewis—ran into a stylist from New York who told them that the classic Hush Puppies had suddenly
(10) become hip in the clubs and bars of downtown Manhattan. Baxter and Lewis were baffled at first. It made no sense to them that shoes that were so obviously out of fashion could make a comeback. . . . By the fall of 1995, things began to happen in a
(15) rush. First the designer John Bartlett called. He wanted to use Hush Puppies in his spring collection. Then another Manhattan designer, Anna Sui, called, wanting shoes for her show as well. . . . "It was total word of mouth," [Los Angeles designer
(20) Joel] Fitzgerald remembers. In 1996, Hush Puppies won the prize for best accessory at the Council of Fashion Designers awards dinner at Lincoln Center, and the president of the firm stood up on the stage with Calvin Klein and Donna Karan and accepted
(25) an award for an achievement that—as he would be the first to admit—his company had almost nothing to do with. Hush Puppies had suddenly exploded, and it all started with a handful of kids in the East Village and Soho.

From The Tipping Point: How Little Things Can
Make a Big Difference. Copyright © 2000, 2002
by Malcolm Gladwell. Used by permission
of Little, Brown and Company.

4. In the context of Lines 26–28 of the passage, the word "exploded" is most nearly synonymous with which of the following word groups?

(A) Debunk, repudiate, invalidate

(B) Assess, decipher, decode

(C) Proliferate, disseminate, popularize

(D) Transform, metamorphose, convert

(E) Exhibit, flaunt, showcase

5. In the passage, the author is primarily concerned with presenting which of the following?

    (A) An analysis of the American corporate world

    (B) A case study of the sociological phenomenon of trends

    (C) An argument about the resuscitation of a failing company

    (D) An explanation of successful marketing and advertising strategy

    (E) An exploration of significant designers in the fashion world

6. Which of the following is an untrue statement about the passage?

    (A) Hush Puppies employed a very successful marketing strategy in order to revive the brand.

    (B) Without the interest in the brand shown by Manhattan trendsetters, Hush Puppies would not have made a comeback.

    (C) The events described in the passage are examples of how high fashion is often influenced by popular culture.

    (D) In the years directly previous to 1994, Hush Puppies shoes were commonly considered passé.

    (E) Hush Puppies are commonly made of soft leather with rubber soles.

Questions 7 through 9 refer to the following passage:

The thousand injuries of Fortunato I had borne as I best could, but when he ventured upon insult I vowed revenge. You, who so well know the nature
Line of my soul, will not suppose, however, that gave
(5) utterance to a threat. At length I would be avenged; this was a point definitely settled—but the very definitiveness with which it was resolved precluded the idea of risk. I must not only punish, but punish with impunity. A wrong is unredressed when ret-
(10) ribution overtakes its redresser. It is equally unredressed when the avenger fails to make himself felt as such to him who has done the wrong.

It was about dusk, one evening during the
Line supreme madness of the carnival season, that I
(15) encountered my friend. He accosted me with excessive warmth, for he had been drinking much. The man wore motley. He had on a tight-fitting parti-striped dress, and his head was surmounted by the conical cap and bells. I was so pleased to see him
(20) that I thought I should never have done wringing his hand. I said to him—"My dear Fortunato, you are luckily met. How remarkably well you are looking to-day. But I have received a pipe of what passes for Amontillado, and I have my doubts."

(25) "How?" said he. "Amontillado? A pipe? Impossible! And in the middle of the carnival!"

"I have my doubts," I replied; "and I was silly enough to pay the full Amontillado price without consulting you in the matter. You were not to be
(30) found, and I was fearful of losing a bargain."

Source: Poe, Edgar Allan. "The Cask of Amontillado." *Edgar Allan Poe: The Dover Reader*. New York: Dover Publications, 2014. (1846)

7. Which group of words best describes the author's manner toward Fortunato?

    (A) Tranquil, serene, and placid

    (B) Cajoling, coaxing, and persuasive

    (C) Lecherous, leering, and repulsive

    (D) Saccharine, contradictory, and irrational

    (E) Candid, astute, and judicious

8. Which of the following best describes the meaning of the word "surmounted" in the context of the underlined sentence?

    (A) Crowned, topped, crested

    (B) Accented, emphasized, underscored

    (C) Heightened, increased, enhanced

    (D) Reduced, degraded, undermined

    (E) Softened, toned down, mellowed

9. The main idea of the passage is which of the following?

    (A) Heritage

    (B) Family

    (C) Knowledge of wine

    (D) Revenge

    (E) Cannot be determined

Questions 10 and 11 refer to the following passage:

Teachers should be cognizant of the responsibility they have for the development of children's competencies in basic concepts and principles of
Line free speech. Freedom of speech is not merely the
(5) utterance of sounds into the air; rather, it is couched in a set of values and legislative processes that have developed over time. These values and processes are a part of our political conscience as Americans. Teachers must provide ample opportunities
(10) for children to express themselves effectively in an environment where their opinions are valued. Children should have ownership in the decision-making process in the classroom and should be engaged in activities where alternative resolutions to problems
(15) can be explored. Because teachers have such tremendous power to influence in the classroom, they must be careful to refrain from presenting their own values and biases that could "color" their students' belief systems. If we want children to develop their
(20) own voices in a free society, then teachers must support participatory democratic experiences in the daily workings of the classroom.

10. The title that best expresses the ideas in the passage is

    (A) "The Nature of the Authoritarian Classroom"

    (B) "Concepts and Principles of Free Speech"

    (C) "Management Practices That Work"

    (D) "Exploring Freedom in American Classrooms"

    (E) "Developing Children's Competencies in Free Speech"

11. It can be inferred from the passage that instructional strategies that help children in the development of citizenship competencies include all of the following EXCEPT:

    (A) Participation in rule-making

    (B) Promotion of self-esteem

    (C) Indoctrination in societal principles

    (D) Consideration of cultural and gender differences

    (E) Education in conflict management

Questions 12 and 13 refer to the following passage:

The remarks I have made will suffice to display the character of Anglo-American civilization in its true light. It is the result (and this should be
Line constantly present to the mind of two distinct ele-
(5) ments), which in other places have been in frequent hostility, but which in America have been admirably incorporated and combined with one another. I allude to the spirit of Religion and the spirit of Liberty. The settlers of New England were at the
(10) same time ardent sectarians and daring innovators. Narrow as the limits of some of their religious opinions were, they were entirely free from political prejudices. Hence arose two tendencies, distinct but not opposite, which are constantly discernible
(15) in the manners as well as in the laws of the country.

It might be imagined that men who sacrificed their friends, their family, and their native land to a religious conviction were absorbed in the pursuit of the intellectual advantages which they purchased
(20) at so dear a rate. The energy, however, with which they strove for the acquirement of wealth, moral enjoyment, and the comforts as well as liberties of the world, is scarcely inferior to that with which they devoted themselves to Heaven.

(25)   –Alexis de Tocqueville

Source: Tocqueville, Alexis de. *Democracy in America.*
Translated by Henry Reeve. (1835) From Chapter 2:
"The Origins of the Anglo-Americans"

12. Based on the passage, the author would agree with which of the following statements?

    (Select all that apply.)

    ☐ A The land in America is not suitable for aristocracy.

    ☐ B The land in America is not fertile enough.

    ☐ C New Englanders epitomized the spirit of innovation.

    ☐ D The settlers devoted at least as much energy to accumulate wealth as they did to reach heaven.

    ☐ E Americans abandoned materialism in favor of political freedom.

13. Which of the following words, if substituted for "purchased" (Line 19), would MOST change the meaning of the sentence?

    (A) Acquired

    (B) Obtained

    (C) Earned

    (D) Forfeited

    (E) Gained

Questions 14 and 15 refer to the following image:

Copyright © Del Monte Food, Inc.

---

14. Which implied conclusion is best supported by the information in the image?

    (A) Based on the woman's hair and her attire, we can assume it is an ad for ketchup taken from what looks like the 1980s.

    (B) The expression on the woman's face indicates innocence mixed with surprise that she can accomplish this task.

    (C) She is demure and proper with her pressed blouse buttoned to the top.

    (D) Her skin, makeup, and nails are "perfect."

    (E) Since they are "weaker" when it comes to physical strength, women usually need to ask a man for help in tasks like opening the ketchup.

15. Who is the intended audience for this ad?

    (A) Male consumers

    (B) Female consumers

    (C) Children

    (D) Ad executives

    (E) Supermarket owners

Questions 16 through 21 are based on the following passages:

Passage 1

According to the fifth edition of the *Diagnostic and Statistical Manual of Mental Disorders* (DSM-5), there are two major forms of bipolar disorder—
Line bipolar I and II, which are separate diagnoses. The
(5) most important distinction between bipolar I and II is that a person with bipolar I has one or more manic episodes or mixed (mania and depression) episodes not otherwise explained by a medical condition or substance abuse, while someone with
(10) bipolar II has at least one hypomanic episode. The main difference between mania and hypomania is a matter of severity. The DSM defines mania as a "distinct period during which there is an abnormally and persistently elevated, expansive (grand,
(15) superior), or irritable mood." The episode must last at least a week. The mood includes symptoms such

as inflated self-esteem, little need for sleep, pressure of speech (talking constantly), flight of ideas, easily distracted, excess pursuit of goal-directed
(20) activities or psychomotor agitation (pacing, hand-wringing, etc.), and/or an excess pursuit of pleasure with a high risk of danger. The hypomania of bipolar II is a milder form of mania that is never accompanied by delusions or hallucinations.

Passage 2

(25)   Jim is exceptionally cheerful, sometimes needs only three hours sleep instead of his usual seven, spends more money than he safely should, speaks far more rapidly than usual, has delusions, and hallucinates. His behavior is noticeably different from
(30) his own stable mood. On the other hand, Bill has decreased energy, feelings of worthlessness, and thoughts of suicide.

16. According to Passage 1, what key word does <u>not</u> express an aspect of mania?

    (A) Sustained

    (B) Irritable

    (C) Calm

    (D) Abnormal

    (E) Elevated

17. According to Passage 1, which of the following statements best describes the similarities between mania and hypomania?

    (A) Individuals imagine things that never happened.

    (B) Individuals have episodes with abnormal mood changes.

    (C) Addiction to gambling is prevalent.

    (D) Extreme hallucinations persist.

    (E) A tendency to go on spending binges.

18. As used in Line 7, "manic" most nearly means

    (A) aversion

    (B) disgust

    (C) hysteria

    (D) hatred

    (E) serenity

19. According to Passage 1, the main difference between mania and hypomania is

    (A) severity

    (B) rage

    (C) calmness

    (D) rigidity

    (E) stringency

20. In considering Passage 1 as it relates to Passage 2, it can be inferred that Jim most likely suffers from

    (A) hypomania

    (B) depression

    (C) mania

    (D) rage disorder

    (E) obsessive-compulsive disorder

21. Which of the following best describes the attitude of the author of Passage 1?

    (A) Informative and objective

    (B) Opinionated and rash

    (C) Subjective and easily influenced

    (D) Hostile and defeated

    (E) Apathetic and uncaring

I.P. Pavlov provided the most famous example of classical conditioning. During his research on the physiology of digestion in dogs, Pavlov noticed
Line that, rather than simply salivating in the presence of
(5) food, the dogs began to salivate in the presence of the lab technician who normally fed them. Pavlov called this anticipatory salivation *psychic secretion*. From this observation he predicted that, if a particular stimulus in the dog's surroundings was
(10) present when the dog was given food, then this stimulus would become associated with food and cause salivation on its own. In his initial experiment, Pavlov used a bell to call the dogs to their food and, after a few repetitions, the dogs started
(15) to salivate in response to the bell. Pavlov called the bell the *conditioned* (or *conditional*) *stimulus* (CS) because its effect depended on its association with food. He called the food the *unconditioned stimulus* (US) because its effect did not depend on previ-
(20) ous experience.

Source: T.L. Brink (2008) Psychology: A Student Friendly Approach, *"Unit 6: Learning." pp. 97–98.*

22. The passage supports which of the following inferences?

(Select *all* that apply.)

A Pavlov did not like dogs.

B Before the experiment, the dogs did not salivate.

C Because Pavlov noticed that dogs salivated in the presence of the lab technician, he devised an experiment using a bell to train them to know food was coming.

D If they had heard the bell, the dogs would have barked.

E The dogs connected the noise of the bell ringing with the idea that food was coming.

One of many tragedies of the Civil War was the housing and care of prisoners. The Andersonville prison, built by the Confederates in 1864 to accom-
Line modate 10,000 Union prisoners, was not completed
(5) when prisoners started arriving. Five months later, the total number of men incarcerated had risen to 31,678.

The sounds of death and dying were not diminished by surrender of weapons to a captor.
(10) Chances of survival for prisoners in Andersonville were not much better than in the throes of combat. Next to overcrowding, inadequate shelter caused unimaginable suffering. The Confederates were not equipped with the manpower, tools, or sup-
(15) plies necessary to house such a population of captives; prisoners themselves gathered lumber, logs, anything they could find to construct some sort of protection from the elements. Some prisoners dug holes in the ground, risking suffocation from cave-
(20) ins, but many were left exposed to wind, rain, cold, and heat.

Daily food rations were exhausted by the sheer numbers they had to serve, resulting in severe dietary deficiencies. The overcrowding, mea-
(25) ger rations, and deplorable unsanitary conditions resulted in rampant disease and a high mortality rate. The consequences of a small scratch or wound could result in death in Andersonville. During the prison's 13-month existence, more than 12,000
(30) prisoners died and were buried in the Andersonville cemetery. Most of the deaths were caused by diarrhea, dysentery, gangrene, and scurvy that could not be treated due to inadequate staff and supplies.

23. The main idea of the passage is best summarized by which statement?
    (A) The major problem for the Confederates was finding burial spaces for the cemetery.
    (B) The prison was never completed.
    (C) Prison doctors were ill-equipped to handle emergencies.
    (D) Andersonville prison was adequate to care for three times as many prisoners as it could hold.
    (E) Many prisoners died as a result of their stay in Andersonville.

24. From this passage, the author's attitude toward the Confederates is one of
    (A) approval
    (B) impartiality
    (C) contempt
    (D) indifference
    (E) denial

25. The first sentence of the second paragraph of this passage can best be described as which of the following?
    (A) A tribute
    (B) A digression
    (C) A hypothesis
    (D) An exposé
    (E) An example of irony

Questions 26 through 29 refer to the following passage:

The Inventory categorizes plants as High, Moderate, or Limited, reflecting the level of each species' negative ecological impact in California. Other factors, such as economic impact or difficulty of management, are not included in this assessment. It is important to note that even Limited species are invasive and should be of concern to land managers. Although the impact of each plant varies regionally, its rating represents cumulative impacts statewide. Therefore, a plant whose statewide impacts are categorized as Limited may have more severe impacts in a particular region. Conversely, a plant categorized as having a High cumulative impact across California may have very little impact in some regions. . . . The Inventory categorizes "invasive non-native plants that threaten wildlands," according to [set definitions]. Plants were evaluated only if they invade California wildlands with native habitat values. The Inventory does not include plants found solely in areas of human-caused disturbance such as roadsides and cultivated agricultural fields.

Source: California Invasive Plant Council, "California Invasive Plant Inventory," accessed Aug. 15, 2014, at http://www.cal-ipc.org

26. The passage implies that the categories assigned to certain plant species are
    (A) based on their regional impact
    (B) representative of environmental impact on the entire state of California
    (C) applicable to the impacts of included plants in all regions
    (D) determined by the species' economic impact
    (E) derived from federal Environmental Protection Agency guidelines

27. The tone of the passage is best described as

    (A) agitated and incensed

    (B) alluring and enthralling

    (C) malevolent and vindictive

    (D) informative and objective

    (E) salubrious and wholesome

28. The plant inventory covered in the passage excludes botanical species that are

    (A) found only in areas of human-spurred disruption like roadsides and farmland

    (B) causing an invasive environmental impact on native habitats

    (C) encroaching upon agricultural areas of cultivation

    (D) difficult to manage or impact residents economically

    (E) invasive limited species

29. The passage suggests that plants in the "Limited" category

    (A) are evaluated only if they grow along roadsides or agricultural fields

    (B) have the same environmental impact regardless of regional specificity

    (C) are measured by evaluating the positive ecological impact the species has on the state

    (D) have some minimal impact on native habitats and still require monitoring

    (E) are constrained by land management

Questions 30 through 35 refer to the following excerpt from a speech by Elie Wiesel.

It is with a profound sense of humility that I accept the honor—the highest there is—that you have chosen to bestow upon me. I know your choice transcends my person.

Line

(5)   Do I have the right to represent the multitudes who have perished? Do I have the right to accept this great honor on their behalf? I do not. No one may speak for the dead, no one may interpret their <u>mutilated</u> dreams and visions. And yet, I sense

(10)   their presence. I always do—and at this moment more than ever. The presence of my parents, that of my little sister. The presence of my teachers, my friends, my companions. . . .

This honor belongs to all the survivors and

(15)   their children and, through us to the Jewish people with whose destiny I have always identified.

I remember: it happened yesterday, or eternities ago. A young Jewish boy discovered the Kingdom of Night. I remember his bewilderment, I

(20)   remember his anguish. It all happened so fast. The ghetto. The deportation. The sealed cattle car. The fiery altar upon which the history of our people and the future of mankind were meant to be sacrificed.

I remember he asked his father: "Can this be

(25)   true? This is the twentieth century, not the Middle Ages. Who would allow such crimes to be committed? How could this world remain silent?"

And now the boy is turning to me. "Tell me," he asks, "what have you done with my future, what

(30)   have you done with your life?" And I tell him that I have tried. That I have tried to keep memory alive, that I have tried to fight those who would forget. Because if we forget, we are guilty, we are accomplices.

Line
(35)   And then I explain to him how naïve we were, that the world did know and remained silent. And that is why I swore never to be silent whenever human beings endure suffering and humiliation. We must take sides. Neutrality helps the oppres-
(40) sor, never the victim. Silence encourages the tormentor, never the tormented. Sometimes we must <u>interfere</u>. When human lives are endangered, when human dignity is in jeopardy, national borders and sensitivities become irrelevant. Wherever men and women are persecuted because of their race, religion, or political views, that place must—at that moment—become the center of the universe.

Source: Wiesel, Elie. "Hope, Despair and Memory."
In *Nobel Lectures in Peace 1981–1990*. Singapore:
World Scientific, 1997. (1986)

30. What does Wiesel mean when he says in Lines 44–45, ". . . national borders and sensitivities become irrelevant. . ."?

(A) Nations should remain neutral when human lives are endangered.

(B) Nations should intervene when human lives are endangered.

(C) Nations should help the oppressor when human lives are in jeopardy.

(D) Nations should help men and women in their own borders who are persecuted.

(E) Nations should speak softly and carry a big stick.

31. How should the use of "mutilated" be interpreted in the sentence, "No one may speak for the dead, no one may interpret their mutilated dreams and visions" (Lines 7–9)?

(A) The dreams of the Jewish people were destroyed.

(B) The dreams of the Jewish people were difficult.

(C) The dreams of the Jewish people were emotionally charged.

(D) The dreams of the Jewish people were realized.

(E) The dreams of the German soldiers were dashed.

32. What would be a good alternate title for the passage?

(A) "Humility and Honor"

(B) "The Denial of a Young Jewish Boy"

(C) "Moving on from Sadness"

(D) "The Causes of World War II"

(E) "Remembering the Courage of the Jewish People in a Time of Crisis"

33. Which of the following morals is implied by the passage?

(A) Inaction can make people accomplices in persecution.

(B) Good people cannot overcome evil.

(C) Tell the truth regardless of the consequences to yourself.

(D) Turn someone in even if he or she is a friend.

(E) Familiarity breeds contempt.

34. In the context of the passage, "interfere" (Line 42) most nearly means

(A) delay the war

(B) get involved to take a stand

(C) lead the nations of the world

(D) speak out

(E) witness the brutality

35. On what occasion is the author presenting his remarks?

(A) A re-examination of the Holocaust

(B) An award ceremony

(C) A speech at the United States Holocaust Memorial Museum

(D) A speech at the John F. Kennedy Presidential Library & Museum

(E) A rally for human rights

Questions 36 and 37 refer to the following passage:

Most Americans assume that English is the language of the United States, but they are naïve to imagine that every American speaks it fluently.
Line In 2000, non-English households made up 17.9
(5) percent of the population. By 2007, it was 19.7 percent. As of the latest data, from the 2011 American Community Survey, the share is now 20.8 percent—fully one-fifth of all people living in the U.S.

Non-English speakers reside in 50 states. In
(10) some 23 states, the non-English-speaking minority makes up 10% or more of the total population. All of American history is characterized by the language phenomenon. For those misguided Americans who believe that their country is and always
(15) has been a monolingual country, the facts just do not support their claim.

36. Which of the following characterizes the author's attitude toward a belief that America is a monolingual country?

(A) Impartiality

(B) Indifference

(C) Criticism

(D) Anger

(E) Optimism

37. Which of the following statements can be inferred from the information given?

(A) Non-English languages are found primarily along the East and West coasts.

(B) No indicators suggest that the percentage of non-English speaking populations will decrease.

(C) This language situation is relatively new to the United States.

(D) In the next decade, the United States should become primarily monolingual.

(E) The United States is comparable to Great Britain in percentage of non-English speakers.

38. How does the word "naïve" as used in Line 2 influence the author's tone?

(A) It reveals that the author is hypercritical.

(B) It shows that she or he is pejorative.

(C) It reveals his or her condemnation.

(D) It supports the fact that the author is critical of the idea that the United States is a monolingual nation.

(E) It is complimentary and forgiving of the false beliefs held by Americans.

39. Which of the following is a claim set forth by the author?

(Select *all* that apply.)

A   Non-English-speaking households are rising.

B   Non-English-speaking households are declining.

C   English-speaking households are rising.

D   English-speaking households are declining.

E   The facts support the claim that America is a monolingual country.

Question 40 is based on the following graphic representation:

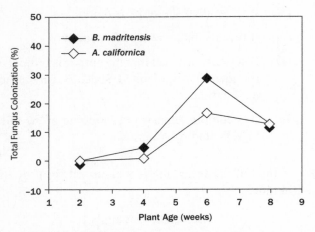

Progress of fungus colonization in *Bromus madritensis* and *Artemisia californica* over 8 weeks in soil with typical N (nitrogen) amount. (Colonization is the successful occupation of a new habitat by a species not found there before.)

40. Which conclusion about fungus colonization at the eight-week mark is best supported by the data presented in the graph?

(A) *B. madritensis* was colonized more rapidly by the fungus than *A. californica*.

(B) During colonization, nitrogen deposits around the *B. madritensis* root system dissipated at a higher rate than with *A. californica*.

(C) The fungus colonized *A. californica* at half the percentage rate of *B. madritensis*.

(D) *B. madritensis* was colonized by the fungus at about 15 percentage points higher than *A. californica*.

(E) The fungus colonized *B. madritensis* at the same percentage as it colonized *A. californica*.

Question 41 refers to the following statement:

The funnel cloud appeared capricious with its destruction, darting from one street to another, obliterating any object in its path.

41. In this context the word "capricious" most nearly means

(A) unpredictable

(B) intense

(C) threatening

(D) adaptable

(E) belligerent

Questions 42 and 43 refer to the following passage:

Many times different animal species can inhabit the same environment and share a common food supply without conflict, because each species
Line occupies a separate niche defined by its specific
(5) physical adaptations and habits. For example, the little green heron, equipped with legs too short to do much wading, fishes from shore for its food. The Louisiana heron wades out a little further into the shallows during the daytime hours, while the
(10) yellow-crowned night heron stalks the same shallows after dark. Diet also varies in size and amount, according to the size of the bird.

42. According to the passage, which one of the following basic assumptions can be made about how a bird's diet varies according to size?

(A) Small birds can eat twice their weight.

(B) The larger birds can swallow larger fish and water snakes.

(C) Birds have to adapt their diets according to what is available within their environment.

(D) Fishing from shore is difficult for smaller birds.

(E) The type of bill is an adaptation for the type of food the animal eats.

43. The title that best expresses the ideas of this passage is

    (A) "The Heron Family"

    (B) "Diet Variations of Birds"

    (C) "A Separate Niche at the Same Pond"

    (D) "Long-Legged Fishing"

    (E) "Fishing Habits of the Heron"

Questions 44 through 46 refer to the following passage:

The Indians of California had five varieties of acorn which they used as their principal source of food. This was a noteworthy accomplishment in
Line technology since they first had to make the acorn
(5) edible. A process had to be developed for leaching out the poisonous tannic acid. They ground the acorns into a meal and then filtered it many times with water. This had to be done through sand or through tightly woven baskets. Early Indian camp-
(10) sites reveal the evidence of the acorn-processing labor necessary to provide enough food for their subsistence. The women patiently ground acorns into meal with stone pestles. The result, a pinkish flour that was cooked into a mush or thin soup,
(15) formed the bulk of their diet.

44. The central idea of the passage is the early Indians of California

    (A) had ample food sources

    (B) left evidence of their meal processing at ancient campsites

    (C) differed from other Indians in their use of natural resources

    (D) contributed distinctive talents and technological expertise in providing food sources

    (E) produced finely crafted woven baskets

45. According to the passage, which of the following was a technological innovation developed by the early California Indians in the production of food?

    (A) Irrigation of crops

    (B) Grinding meal

    (C) Filtration system

    (D) Dams

    (E) Removal of tannic acid

46. Inferentially, what would be a major problem the early Indians faced in their production of food?

    (A) They needed many pounds of acorns to produce enough meal.

    (B) Acorns had to be carried a great distance to their campsites for grinding.

    (C) The acorn grinding took many hours of hard labor.

    (D) Acorns were scarce.

    (E) It was difficult to filter the meal without losing it.

Questions 47 through 49 refer to the following passage:

Beginning readers, and those who are experiencing difficulty with reading, benefit from assisted reading. During assisted reading the teacher
Line orally reads a passage with a student or students.
(5) The teacher fades in and out of the reading act. For example, the teacher lets his or her voice drop to a whisper when students are reading on their own at an acceptable rate and lets his/her voice rise to say the words clearly when the students are having
(10) difficulty.

Students who are threatened by print, read word-by-word, or rely on grapho-phonemic cues will be helped by assisted reading. These students are stuck on individual language units which can be
(15) as small as a single letter or as large as phrases or sentences. As Frank Smith (1977) and other reading educators have noted, speeding up reading, not slowing it down, helps the reader make sense of a passage: This strategy allows students to concen-
(20) trate on meaning as the short-term memory is not overloaded by focusing on small language units. As the name implies, assisted reading lets the reader move along without being responsible for every language unit; the pressure is taken off the student.
(25) Consequently, when the reading act is sped up, it sounds more like language, and students can begin to integrate the cueing systems of semantics and syntax along with grapho-phonemics.

47. As a strategy, assisted reading is best for

   (A) beginning readers who are relying on grapho-phonemic cues

   (B) learning-disabled readers who are experiencing neurological deficits

   (C) beginning readers who are relying on phono-graphic cues

   (D) remedial readers who are experiencing difficulty with silent reading

   (E) beginning readers who are experiencing difficulty with silent reading

48. Language units as presented in the passage refer to

   (A) individual letters, syllables, or phrases

   (B) individual letters, syllables, or sentences

   (C) individual letters, phrases, or paragraphs

   (D) individual letters, phrases, or sentences

   (E) individual letters, sentences, or paragraphs

49. According to the passage, to make sense of a passage a reader must

   (A) focus on small language units

   (B) overload short-term memory

   (C) slow down when reading

   (D) read word-by-word

   (E) speed up the reading act

Questions 50 through 53 refer to the following passage:

   New health research shows that regular vigorous exercise during the middle and late years of life not only keeps the heart healthy, but also may pro-
Line tect against colon cancer, one of the major killers in
(5) the U.S. The researchers in the study compared the rate of colon cancer among those who were physically inactive with those who were either active or highly active.

   Seventeen thousand one hundred forty-eight
(10) men, ages 30 to 79, were covered in the study. Among men judged to be inactive there were 55 cases of colon cancer; among those moderately active, there were 11; and only 10 cases of colon cancer were found among the very active ones.

50. Which of the following makes an appropriate title for the passage?

   (A) "New Health Research on Colon Cancer"

   (B) "Colon Cancer: A Major Killer in the U.S."

   (C) "Regular Vigorous Exercise May Prevent Colon Cancer"

   (D) "Results of Research on Colon Cancer"

   (E) "A Prescription for Preventing Colon Cancer"

51. Based on the result of the research, what generalization regarding colon cancer for men and women can be made?

   (A) Women are more susceptible to disease than are men.

   (B) Women are more likely to participate in surveys.

   (C) Young men are more susceptible to colon cancer than are all women.

   (D) Men are more inactive than women.

   (E) Regular exercise is highly beneficial for older men and women.

52. What important message did you get from the passage?

   (A) Regular exercise is good for the health.

   (B) Only middle-aged men get colon cancer.

   (C) Women need not worry about colon cancer.

   (D) Regular exercise is needed only by older people.

   (E) Children are too young to exercise.

53. What is the major limitation of the study?

    (A) It did not explain "vigorous exercise."

    (B) It did not include children.

    (C) It did not include men below 30.

    (D) It did not include women of the same age group.

    (E) It did not include a large enough sample.

Questions 54 through 56 refer to the following chart:

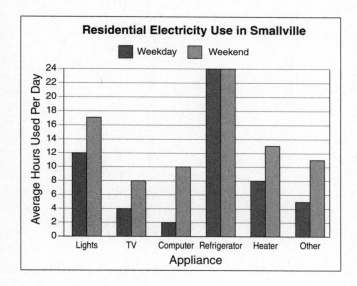

54. The data in the graph would be MOST likely to support which of the following scenarios?

    (A) On average, household members use the refrigerator more on weekdays and weekends.

    (B) On average, household members prefer using the computer to watching television.

    (C) On average, household members are around the house more on the weekend.

    (D) On average, refrigerators have low efficiency ratings.

    (E) On average, home energy use is generally growing.

55. The graph provides information about

    (A) the amount of electricity used by appliances

    (B) the types of appliances that use electricity by hours per day

    (C) the types of appliances that use electricity by hours per year

    (D) the types of appliances that use electricity by hours per month

    (E) the cost to run household appliances per kilo-watt-hour

56. Based on the data presented in the graph, which of the following conclusions may be drawn?

    (Select *all* that apply.)

    A   On weekdays, the refrigerator motor was on twice as long as the lights.

    B   The heater is 61% more efficient on weekdays than weekends.

    C   The computer was on five times as long on the weekends as the weekdays.

Praxis Core
Reading Practice Test 1 Answer Key

1.	(D)	20.	(C)	39.	A and D
2.	B and E	21.	(A)	40.	(E)
3.	(E)	22.	C and D	41.	(A)
4.	(C)	23.	(E)	42.	(B)
5.	(B)	24.	(B)	43.	(C)
6.	(A)	25.	(E)	44.	(D)
7.	(B)	26.	(B)	45.	(C)
8.	(A)	27.	(D)	46.	(E)
9.	(D)	28.	(A)	47.	(A)
10.	(E)	29.	(D)	48.	(D)
11.	(C)	30.	(B)	49.	(E)
12.	C and D	31.	(A)	50.	(C)
13.	(D)	32.	(E)	51.	(E)
14.	(E)	33.	(A)	52.	(A)
15.	(B)	34.	(B)	53.	(D)
16.	(C)	35.	(B)	54.	(C)
17.	(B)	36.	(C)	55.	(B)
18.	(C)	37.	(B)	56.	A and C
19.	(A)	38.	(D)		

1. (D)

Choice (D) is correct. This is a supporting detail question. "Liver disease" is not mentioned in the passage as benefiting from acupuncture, whereas all of the other choices are.

2. [B] and [E]

The correct responses are [B] and [E], the former because this is implicit in King's remarks, and the latter because he states it directly. While choice [A] is a true statement on its own, it doesn't address the question. Choices [C] and [D] are not true. Choice [E] is the most comprehensive answer, and it addresses what King says has not happened "one hundred years later."

3. (E)

Choice (E) is the best response. King echoes a phrase from one of Lincoln's most memorable speeches, the Gettysburg Address, which begins with the sentence, "Four score and seven years ago our fathers brought forth, upon this continent, a new nation, conceived in liberty, and dedicated to the proposition that 'all men are created equal.'" Hearkening to Lincoln's speech with an unusual reference to "score" adds poignancy to King's prose as it underlines the inequality that remains a century (or "five score years") later.

4. (C)

Choice (C) is correct. The first string of words means "to discredit." The second string of words (B) means "to make sense of or interpret." The fourth string of words (D) means "to change." And the last set (E) means "to show off." In the context of the passage, we see that Hush Puppies became popular because of the club scene, which is why they spread (proliferated) in their distribution (dissemination).

5. (B)

Choice (B) is correct, although choice (A) may initially look like a strong contender. Look closer, however, and you'll see that the passage does not analyze the corporate world (A), nor does it explain marketing and advertising strategies (D). It isn't an argument (C) but instead an analysis, or case study, about the comeback that Hush Puppies experienced. While fashion designers (E) are mentioned, they are not the passage's prime focus. The excerpt concerns how societal trends can contribute to a brand's revival. Thus, choice (B) is the best response.

6. (A)

Choice (A) is the untrue choice and thus is the correct answer. Hush Puppies didn't use a marketing strategy: The revival was a result of individuals in the clubs popularizing the shoes with young people and designers. The rest of the statements in the passage are true. We can infer that the passage discusses the fallen popularity of Hush Puppies in 1994 and before (which (D) explains). Choice (E) describes the shoes and is explained in Lines 2 and 3 of the passage.

7. (B)

The correct answer is (B). This passage from a short story is challenging—it was written by Edgar Allan Poe in the mid-1800s. The language is precise and ornate and reflects the period. The narrator's tone, though, is removed and conniving. If you look at the emotional impact of the first paragraph, such words as "revenge," "unredressed retribution," and "impunity" convey that the narrator wants revenge. He then meets with Fortunato, who is drunk. He begins to speak with him about Amontillado (which we can infer is an alcoholic beverage) and he is up to no good. He acts happy to meet him, yet in the first paragraph we learn that he could hardly bear the "thousand injuries" he had borne from this man. Choice (B) fits best because the narrator seeks to sweet-talk Fortunato as a diabolical part of how he edges closer to achieving his revenge.

8. (A)

The correct answer is (A). The cap and bells are on his head, which is made clear in the context of the full sentence (Lines 17–19). The other choices are not applicable in the context of the sentence.

9. (D)

The correct answer is (D). In the first paragraph, the narrator talks about his anger towards Fortunato. In the second paragraph, he is trying to engage him in conversation. It is a story about how the narrator wants to get back at Fortunato. Heritage (A) and family (B) are not discussed in the passage. For choice (C), wine is discussed only offhandedly in that Amontillado is wine; however, the central idea of the story is revenge.

10. (E)

The correct answer is choice (E). The first and last sentences of the passage support this choice. Choice (A) contradicts information in the passage, and choices (B), (C), and (D) go beyond the scope of the passage.

11. (C)

Choice (C) is the correct answer. Reviewing the author's discussion of developing children's competencies in citizenship, we may conclude that indoctrination is contradictory to the passage.

12. C and D

The correct responses are choices C and D. While choices A and B are ideas the author presents later in the totality of the work excerpted for this question, he does not cover them here. Choice E, which contradicts Choice D, is incorrect because the passage makes it clear that the settlers devoted considerable energy toward achieving material gain.

13. (D)

The correct answer is (D) because "forfeited" is the near-opposite of "purchased." The other words are synonymous with "purchased," which means "acquired" (A), "obtained" (B), "earned" (C), or "gained" (E).

14. (E)

The correct answer is (E). (A) is not true because the ad actually ran in the early to mid-1950s. While the other choices are observations a viewer can make, these answers do not represent an "implied conclusion." Only choice (E) does.

15. (B)

The correct answer is (B). The simple reason for this is that in the time period in which the advertisement ran, women did the majority of the food shopping. Male consumers might like the ad, but based on the pitch it is safe to say that it isn't primarily intended for them.

16. (C)

The correct answer is (C). The word "abnormal" (D) is used with respect to mania as are all the other words. "Calm" is the opposite of what mania looks like, so that choice is definitely not expressing an aspect of mania.

17. (B)

Choice (B) is correct. Both conditions are episodic with abnormal mood changes which are accompanied by "abnormal mood changes." While the answers in choices (A), (C), and (D) describe situations associated with mania, none of these characteristics is mentioned in the text as being indicative of hypomania. In fact, the passage describes only the type of episodes that do not occur with hypomania: delusions and hallucinations. While spending sprees (E) actually are characteristic of both mania and hypomania, this is not mentioned in the passage and thus choice (E) cannot be correct.

18. **(C)**

The correct answer is (C). Mania is not being opposed to, sickened by, or hateful of one's surroundings (A), (B), and (D). It is also not characterized by calmness (E). "Mania" is a form of hysteria.

19. **(A)**

The correct answer is choice (A) because mania isn't as severe as hypomania (see Lines 11–12). While people with bipolar disorder may experience rage (B), and they might exhibit rigidity (D) and/or stringency (E) about certain things, these choices are not mentioned in the passage because they are not characteristic of the disorder. As a distractor, "calmness" (C) seeks to play off the idea of severity but is not addressed directly in the passage and thus is not the best answer.

20. **(C)**

The correct answer is (C). Passage 2 says Jim is "noticeably different" in behavior and mood. In addition, the passage notes that he has delusions and hallucinations, which are uncharacteristic of hypomania (A). Bill is described as having depression (B), which is actually not the focus of this passage. Rage disorder (D) and obsessive-compulsive disorder (E) are also not the focus of Passage 1, so we can eliminate these choices because we are analyzing only where the two passages intersect.

21. **(A)**

The correct answer is the first choice. The other choices have negative connotations. The author of this passage begins by saying a new edition of the diagnostic manual was the source, so he or she is knowledgeable about the field. The tone is instructive and objective, so the first choice is the best.

22. $\boxed{\text{C}}$ **and** $\boxed{\text{E}}$

The correct responses are choices $\boxed{\text{C}}$ and $\boxed{\text{E}}$. Choice $\boxed{\text{A}}$ is incorrect because Pavlov used dogs in his experiment. Dogs have always salivated, so choice $\boxed{\text{B}}$

is out. Choice $\boxed{\text{D}}$ is incorrect because nothing was said about the dogs' previous response to a bell.

23. **(E)**

Choice (E) is correct. The passage states that housing of prisoners was "one of many tragedies of the Civil War" (Line 1), and that "overcrowding, meager rations . . . resulted in rampant disease and a high mortality rate" (Lines 24–28), implying that the prison facility was inadequate for the number of prisoners. All other choices are discussed, but the main issue was overcrowded conditions.

24. **(B)**

Choice (B) is correct. The author emphasized there was a lack of supplies and manpower to care for the prisoners, not a lack of interest in doing so by the Confederates. Hence, choices (C), (D), and (E) are not appropriate. Choice (A) is not suggested by the text.

25. **(E)**

Choice (E) is correct. It is ironic that although weapons were surrendered, death was still undiminished. Irony is the opposite of what might be expected or appropriate. The passage implies that being captured was not a guarantee of survival in Andersonville. This choice is supported by the second sentence of the second paragraph (Lines 10–11). That line is not a tribute (an acknowledgment), nor is it a digression (off topic), or a hypothesis (guess). While the author might be exposing something, it is not an exposé. So choice (E) is the best.

26. **(B)**

The correct answer is (B). This is an inference question. We see from the question that the three categories of plants are categorized based on "cumulative impacts statewide" (Lines 9–10). Therefore, choices (A) and (C) are incorrect. Neither economic factors (D) nor EPA guidelines (E) are cited in the passage—by either allusion or implication. Thus, Choice (B) is the best answer.

27. (D)

The correct answer is (D). The passage is intended to inform and illustrate ideas objectively. It is not distressed (A), nor is it bad or ill-intentioned (C). It is also not glamorous or fascinating (B); the voice is technical. Choice (E) is incorrect because salubrious means healthful, and that idea does not apply here.

28. (A)

The correct answer is (A), which is synonymous with the last sentence of the passage, which says: "The Inventory does not include plants found solely in areas of human-caused disturbance such as roadsides and cultivated agricultural fields" (Lines 19–22). Choice (C), "encroaching upon agricultural areas of cultivation," while plausible in a casual scan of the answer options, is less straightforward than choice (A).

29. (D)

The correct answer is (D). This is a supporting-detail question, and the answer is found in this line: "It is important to note that even Limited species are invasive and should be of concern to land managers" (Lines 6–8). The word "roadside" makes choice (A) incorrect. It is not included in the Inventory, according to the passage. Choice (B) is wrong because we know from the passage that the "Limited" category has less of an ecological impact on California, even though it may still have a significant impact. This explanation also discounts choice (C). Choice (E) states that even plants in the "Limited" category are regarded as invasive, and advises that such plants should be "of concern to land managers"; the passage does not reveal how the plants' spread might be constrained by land management.

30. (B)

The correct answer is (B). The author says borders do not matter because countries should intervene or get involved. The other choices indicate neutrality (A), helping the oppressor (C), helping only themselves (D), or resorting to scare tactics (E), none of which is indicated in, or connects with the context of, the passage.

31. (A)

The correct answer is (A). "Mutilated" conveys brutality and destruction. The meaning of "mutilated" does not equate with "difficult" (B) or "emotionally charged" (C). Choice (D), in using "realized," renders the antonym, or opposite, of "mutilated." Choice (E), German soldiers, can be cast aside since the text is silent on German soldiers. Therefore, the first choice is the best answer.

32. (E)

The best answer is choice (E). While the passage discusses humility and honor, a title simply pairing those two terms is too broad. Conversely, choice (B) is too specific. Choice (C) is too general, and choice (D) is irrelevant to the passage. Therefore, the last choice is the best. It parallels the actual title and expresses the thematic dimensions of the text.

33. (A)

The best answer choice is (A). Choice (B) contradicts Wiesel's idea as described in the passage. Choice (C) applies to the ideas in the passage but the writer does not address truth as a topic, so there is no moral to be drawn about it. Likewise, choices (D) and (E) may be good morals, but they are not mentioned here. Thus, the best answer is choice (A).

34. (B)

Choice (B) is correct. "Interfere" has a positive connotation here, in that Wiesel says people must take a stand against the forces that perpetrate evil. The other choices either don't say enough, as we see in choice (D), "speak out," or they mention ideas that are not expressed in the passage, as we see in choices (E), "witness the brutality," (C), "lead the nations of the world," and (A), "delay the war."

35. (B)

The correct answer is choice (B). The question requires you to identify the occasion of Wiesel's remarks, not the subject of those remarks. We know Wiesel is receiving an award for which he expresses his gratitude because he says so in Lines 1–4. He takes the opportunity to tell the story of the terrible events that define the Holocaust (A), but this is a consequence of being at the award ceremony, not the occasion itself. While such a speech hypothetically could be given at the Holocaust Museum (C), the Kennedy Library (D), or at a human rights rally (E), there is no evidence in the passage to support any of these choices.

36. (C)

Choice (C) is correct. The author criticizes the belief that America is a monolingual country. She or he is more than impartial (A), as indicated by words such as "misguided" (Line 13) and "facts just do not support their claim" (Lines 15–16). Nothing in the passage indicates anger (D) or an optimistic attitude (E). "Indifference" (B) would mean that the author doesn't care, but the characterizations the author uses (e.g., branding as "naïve" those who assume all Americans are fluent in English) establish that this is not the case.

37. (B)

Choice (B) is correct. Choices (A), (C), and (E) generalize beyond the information in the passage, and choice (D) contradicts information provided by the passage.

38. (D)

The correct answer is choice (D). The author is critical but maintains a professional tone. Choices (A), (B), and (C) use words with too strong a connotation. Choice (E) is inaccurate by definition. Calling someone naïve is not a compliment.

39. A and D

The correct responses are choices A and D. Although the author does not explicitly say these words, this is the claim set forth in the first paragraph. Choice B is untrue based on the evidence. The evidence also

contradicts choice C, proving that non-English-speaking households are rising. Choice D, as a corollary to choice (A), says the same thing from the other side of the coin. The purpose of the passage is to debunk the myth that is restated as choice E. Therefore, that is not a correct answer either.

40. (E)

The correct answer is choice (E). This is a comparison-over-time chart. You are asked to find what's measured at the end of the eight-week period covered by the chart. The chart happens to be gauging the impact of a fungus on a coastal sage scrub species called *Artemisia californica* and an exotic grass called *Bromus madritensis*. But it could just as easily be showing the relative market penetration over time of two competing consumer products (e.g., Chevrolet Volt versus Nissan LEAF electric cars). The chart's *x*-axis, running horizontally, shows the age of the plants in weeks. Choices (A) and (C) can be eliminated because the relative pace with which colonization took place is not germane to the question. Choice (D) cannot be correct because the status it describes exists only at the six-week mark, not at eight weeks. Choice (B) is not addressed by the chart – which says only that the soil had a "typical" amount of nitrogen – and is therefore irrelevant. The graph clearly shows that *B. madritensis* and *A. californica* ended up colonized by the fungus at the same percentage rate (about 12%) at the end of eight weeks, so the correct answer is choice (E).

41. (A)

"Capricious" means unpredictable, so choice (A) must be the correct response. None of the other choices fit this definition.

42. (B)

Choice (B) is supported as the best response by the last sentence in the passage: "Diet also varies in size and amount, according to the size of the bird."

43. (C)

Choice (C) is the best answer because the author specifically discusses how the birds share the same food supply but occupy different areas of the pond. Each of the other choices is too broad and general.

44. (D)

Choice (D) is supported in the second sentence. All other choices are subsidiary ideas.

45. (C)

The passage states, as choice (C) indicates, that the filtration system was a "noteworthy accomplishment in technology" (Lines 3–4).

46. (E)

The passage emphasizes the complicated process of filtering the meal through sand or tightly woven baskets. Choices (A), (B), and (C), while true, are not the most difficult problem. Choice (D) contradicts information given in the text.

47. (A)

Choices (D) and (E) are incorrect as the strategy is for oral reading, not silent reading. Choices (B) and (C) are not supported by the passage—thus choice (A) is correct.

48. (D)

Choices (A), (B), (C), and (E) include syllable and paragraph elements, which are not supported by the passage. The passage states " . . . individual language units which can be as small as a single letter or as large as phrases or sentences" (Lines 14–16).

49. (E)

Choices (A), (B), (C), and (D) are not supported by the passage. The passage states that "speeding up reading, not slowing it down, helps the reader make sense of a passage" (Lines 17–19).

50. (C)

A title is supposed to synthesize the main idea of a passage. In this passage the best synthesis is (C); hence, it is the correct answer.

51. (E)

Regular exercise, according to research, is highly beneficial. Choices (A), (B), (C), and (D) are illogical and incorrect.

52. (A)

Answer choice (A) is sound and is the best and correct answer. Choice (B) is an incorrect answer; choice (C) is an incorrect implication; the same can be said of choices (D) and (E).

53. (D)

The study covered only men, hence, a major limitation is the fact that it did not include women of the same age group. The correct answer, therefore, is (D). Choice (A) may not be an essential in the study, hence, definitely not a major limitation; choice (B), while a limitation, cannot be considered "major." Besides, "children" could include babies through young adolescents—a rather wide age range. Choice (C) is also a limitation, but it does not state the precise age range. Choice (E) is incorrect since more than 17,000 men were included in the study.

54. (C)

Because more household electricity is consumed on weekends than weekdays for every category, choice (C) seems logical. The other answer choices are not shown on the chart.

55. (B)

The correct answer is (B). While (A) is generally what is being measured, it is not the best choice. The graph looks at average hours used per day (indicated on the vertical axis). Therefore, (C) and (D) are not correct. Choice (E) cannot be correct because neither cost nor kilowatt-hours are addressed by the graph. An answer such as Choice (E) is a reminder to you that graph-prompted questions are as exacting as those hinging on verbal-text stimuli. Unless you're being asked to draw an inference, the answer must literally be in the stimulus.

56. [A] **and** [C]

The correct responses are choices [A] and [C]. [A] is correct because the refrigerator motor ran 24 hours—twice the time the lights were used. Of course, most refrigerators in real life would shut off occasionally because they're insulated, but we have to use only the information we're given. Choice [C] is also correct because the weekend hourly total for the computer's usage equaled 10, five times the weekday total. Choice [B] requires a bit of care to eliminate. While it's true that the heater used 61% more electricity on the weekend versus the weekdays, this has nothing to do with efficiency [B], which is defined as the ratio of the output power divided by the input power. Efficiency is not mentioned in the graph, so choice [B] should not be selected.

Praxis Core
Reading Practice Test 2

Also available at the online REA Study Center (*www.rea.com/studycenter*)

The Praxis Core Reading (5712) test is computer-based, so we strongly recommend that you take our online practice tests to simulate test-day conditions and to receive these added benefits:

- **Timed testing conditions**—Gauge how much time you can spend on each question.

- **Automatic scoring**—Find out how you did on the test, instantly.

- **On-screen detailed explanations of answers**—Learn not just the correct answer but also why the other answers are wrong.

- **Diagnostic score reports**—Pinpoint where you're strongest and where you need to focus your study.

Praxis Core
Reading Practice Test 2 Answer Sheet

1. Ⓐ Ⓑ Ⓒ Ⓓ Ⓔ   20. Ⓐ Ⓑ Ⓒ Ⓓ Ⓔ   39. Ⓐ Ⓑ Ⓒ Ⓓ Ⓔ

2. Ⓐ Ⓑ Ⓒ Ⓓ Ⓔ   21. Ⓐ Ⓑ Ⓒ Ⓓ Ⓔ   40. Ⓐ Ⓑ Ⓒ Ⓓ Ⓔ

3. Ⓐ Ⓑ Ⓒ Ⓓ Ⓔ   22. Ⓐ Ⓑ Ⓒ Ⓓ Ⓔ   41. Ⓐ Ⓑ Ⓒ Ⓓ Ⓔ

4. Ⓐ Ⓑ Ⓒ Ⓓ Ⓔ   23. Ⓐ Ⓑ Ⓒ Ⓓ Ⓔ   42. Ⓐ Ⓑ Ⓒ Ⓓ Ⓔ

5. Ⓐ Ⓑ Ⓒ Ⓓ Ⓔ   24. Ⓐ Ⓑ Ⓒ Ⓓ Ⓔ   43. Ⓐ Ⓑ Ⓒ Ⓓ Ⓔ

6. Ⓐ Ⓑ Ⓒ Ⓓ Ⓔ   25. Ⓐ Ⓑ Ⓒ Ⓓ Ⓔ   44. Ⓐ Ⓑ Ⓒ Ⓓ Ⓔ

7. Ⓐ Ⓑ Ⓒ Ⓓ Ⓔ   26. Ⓐ Ⓑ Ⓒ Ⓓ Ⓔ   45. Ⓐ Ⓑ Ⓒ Ⓓ Ⓔ

8. Ⓐ Ⓑ Ⓒ Ⓓ Ⓔ   27. A B C D E   46. Ⓐ Ⓑ Ⓒ Ⓓ Ⓔ

9. Ⓐ Ⓑ Ⓒ Ⓓ Ⓔ   28. Ⓐ Ⓑ Ⓒ Ⓓ Ⓔ   47. Ⓐ Ⓑ Ⓒ Ⓓ Ⓔ

10. Ⓐ Ⓑ Ⓒ Ⓓ Ⓔ   29. Ⓐ Ⓑ Ⓒ Ⓓ Ⓔ   48. Ⓐ Ⓑ Ⓒ Ⓓ Ⓔ

11. Ⓐ Ⓑ Ⓒ Ⓓ Ⓔ   30. Ⓐ Ⓑ Ⓒ Ⓓ Ⓔ   49. Ⓐ Ⓑ Ⓒ Ⓓ Ⓔ

12. Ⓐ Ⓑ Ⓒ Ⓓ Ⓔ   31. Ⓐ Ⓑ Ⓒ Ⓓ Ⓔ   50. Ⓐ Ⓑ Ⓒ Ⓓ Ⓔ

13. Ⓐ Ⓑ Ⓒ Ⓓ Ⓔ   32. Ⓐ Ⓑ Ⓒ Ⓓ Ⓔ   51. Ⓐ Ⓑ Ⓒ Ⓓ Ⓔ

14. Ⓐ Ⓑ Ⓒ Ⓓ Ⓔ   33. Ⓐ Ⓑ Ⓒ Ⓓ Ⓔ   52. Ⓐ Ⓑ Ⓒ Ⓓ Ⓔ

15. Ⓐ Ⓑ Ⓒ Ⓓ Ⓔ   34. Ⓐ Ⓑ Ⓒ Ⓓ Ⓔ   53. Ⓐ Ⓑ Ⓒ Ⓓ Ⓔ

16. Ⓐ Ⓑ Ⓒ Ⓓ Ⓔ   35. A B C D E   54. Ⓐ Ⓑ Ⓒ Ⓓ Ⓔ

17. Ⓐ Ⓑ Ⓒ Ⓓ Ⓔ   36. Ⓐ Ⓑ Ⓒ Ⓓ Ⓔ   55. Ⓐ Ⓑ Ⓒ Ⓓ Ⓔ

18. A B C D E   37. Ⓐ Ⓑ Ⓒ Ⓓ Ⓔ   56. Ⓐ Ⓑ Ⓒ Ⓓ Ⓔ

19. Ⓐ Ⓑ Ⓒ Ⓓ Ⓔ   38. Ⓐ Ⓑ Ⓒ Ⓓ Ⓔ

Praxis Core
Reading Practice Test 2

Time: 85 minutes for 56 selected-response questions

> **Directions:** Each statement or passage in this practice test is followed by a question or questions based on its content. After reading each statement or passage, choose the best answer to each question from among the five choices given. (Note that in limited cases, when you're asked to "select *all* that apply," there may be as few as three choices presented.) Answer all questions following a statement or passage based on what is stated or implied in that statement or passage; you are not expected to have any previous knowledge of the topics treated in the statements and passages. Remember to answer every question and mark the corresponding letter on the answer sheet.

To our readers: Answer choices in this practice test are designated by letters. Such labeling allows you to more easily follow our answer explanations both in print and with our online content. On the actual Praxis Core test, which is computerized, you will click on unlabeled ovals or squares.

Questions 1 through 5 refer to the following passage:

Recently, I was made keenly aware of the different Englishes I do use. I was giving a talk to a large group of people, the same talk I had already given to half a dozen other groups. The nature of the
Line
(5) talk was about my writing, my life, and my book, *The Joy Luck Club*. The talk was going along well enough, until I remembered one major difference that made the whole talk sound wrong. My mother was in the room. And it was perhaps the first time
(10) she had heard me give a lengthy speech, using the kind of English I have never used with her. I was saying things like, "The intersection of memory upon imagination" and "There is an aspect of my fiction that relates to 'thus-and-thus'—a speech
(15) filled with carefully wrought grammatical phrases, burdened, it suddenly seemed to me, with nominalized forms, past perfect tenses, conditional phrases, all the forms of standard English that I had learned in school and through books, the forms of English I did not use at home with my mother.

Source: *Tongue Tied: The Lives of Multilingual Children.* Otto Santa Anna., ed. Rowman & Littlefield, 2004, p. 169.

---

1. The author's main purpose in writing this selection is

   (A) to explain the difference between her and her mother's English skills

   (B) to discuss the intricacies of the English language

   (C) to promote her new book, *The Joy Luck Club*

   (D) to show the different ways the author uses English

   (E) to show how being raised Asian-American has influenced the author's English

2. According to the passage, the reader can infer that

   (A) the author feels uncomfortable speaking in English with her mother

   (B) the mother has never heard her daughter give a book talk before

   (C) the mother cannot understand English

   (D) the audience does not approve of the English the author uses around her mother

   (E) the author has never given a book talk

3. Which of the following best describes the tone of the passage?

   (A) Informal and opinionated

   (B) Formal and subjective

   (C) Formal and objective

   (D) Overzealous and biased

   (E) Informal and introspective

4. Which of the following is the best meaning of the word "wrought" as it is used in Line 15 of the passage?

   (A) Shaped through artistry

   (B) Elaborately embellished

   (C) Manufactured

   (D) Beaten into shape with tools

   (E) Deeply stirred and excited

5. Which of the following would be the best title of the passage?

   (A) "The Joy Luck Club"

   (B) "A Variety of English"

   (C) "How to Give a Speech"

   (D) "Mothers and Daughters"

   (E) "My Heritage, My English"

6. Based on this passage, the reader can most likely infer that

   (A) the narrator is describing an arsonist

   (B) the narrator enjoys fire

   (C) the narrator lives in a dystopian world

   (D) the narrator is doing something illegal

   (E) the fire was an accident

7. All of the following words and phrases are metaphors in the passage EXCEPT

   (A) great python

   (B) fireflies

   (C) brass nozzle

   (D) conductor

   (E) symphonies

8. Which of the following best illustrates the narrator's opinions?

   (A) Lines 1–3

   (B) Lines 3–4

   (C) Lines 5–9

   (D) Lines 6–7

   (E) Lines 7–8

Questions 6 through 8 refer to the following passage:

It was a pleasure to burn. It was a special pleasure to see things eaten, to see things blackened and changed. With the brass nozzle in his fists, with this
Line great python spitting its venomous kerosene upon
(5) the world, the blood pounded in his head, and his hands were the hands of some amazing conductor playing all the symphonies of blazing and burning to bring down the tatters and charcoal ruins of history. With his symbolic helmet numbered 451 on
(10) his stolid head, and his eyes all orange flame with the thought of what came next, he flicked the igniter and the house jumped up in a gorging fire that burned the evening sky red and yellow and black. He strode in a swarm of fireflies.

(Ray Bradbury, *Fahrenheit 451*. New York: Random House, 1953)

Questions 9 through 12 refer to the following passage:

Emily: (softly, more in wonder than in grief) I can't bear it. They're so young and beautiful. Why did they ever have to get old? Mama, I'm here. I'm
Line grown up. I love you all, everything.—I can't look
(5) at everything hard enough. (pause, talking to her mother who does not hear her. She speaks with mounting urgency) Oh, Mama, just look at me one minute as though you really saw me. Mama, fourteen years have gone by. I'm dead. You're a grand-
(10) mother, Mama. I married George Gibbs, Mama. Wally's dead, too. Mama, his appendix burst on a camping trip to North Conway. We felt just terrible about it—don't you remember? But, just for a moment now we're all together. Mama, just for
(15) a moment we're happy. Let's look at one another.

Line
(20) (pause, looking desperate because she has received
no answer. She speaks in a loud voice, forcing herself to not look at her mother) I can't. I can't go
on. It goes so fast. We don't have time to look at
one another. (she breaks down sobbing, she looks
around) I didn't realize. All that was going on in
(25) life and we never noticed. Take me back—up the
hill—to my grave. But first: Wait! One more look.
Good-by, Good-by, world. Good-by, Grover's Corners? Mama and Papa. Good-bye to clocks ticking?
and Mama's sunflowers. And food and coffee. And
(30) new-ironed dresses and hot baths? and sleeping and
waking up. Oh, earth, you're too wonderful for anybody to realize you. (she asks abruptly through her
tears) Do any human beings ever realize life while
they live it?—every, every minute? (she sighs) I'm
(35) ready to go back. I should have listened to you.
That's all human beings are! Just blind people.

Our Town: A Play in Three Acts by Thornton Wilder.
New York: HarperCollins, 2003, p. 105.

9. In Lines 1 and 2, which word most nearly means "sadness from loss"?

   (A) Young

   (B) Beautiful

   (C) Bear

   (D) Grief

   (E) Wonder

10. Emily complains that "human beings" are

   (A) thoughtless people

   (B) old people

   (C) blind people

   (D) dead people

   (E) young people

11. What does Emily say about the earth?

   (A) It is acceptable but sad.

   (B) It's too wonderful for people to realize.

   (C) It's where she wants to be.

   (D) It's something she despised.

   (E) It's a disappointment.

12. How many years have passed since Emily died?

   (A) 20

   (B) 10

   (C) 14

   (D) 7

   (E) 3

Questions 13 through 15 refer to the following passage:

He lay in bed with one of his sisters. She must
have kicked him or muscled her way into the majority of the bed-space, because he was on the very
Line edge with his arm around her. The boy slept. His
(5) candlelit hair ignited the bed, and I picked both him
and Bettina up with their souls still in the blanket.
If nothing else, they died fast and they were warm.
The boy from the plane, I thought. The teddy bear
boy. Where was Rudy's comfort? Who was there to
(10) soothe him as life's rug was snatched from under
his sleeping feet?

There was only me.

And I'm not too great at that sort of comforting
thing, especially when my hands are cold and the
(15) bed is warm. I carried him softly through the broken street, with one salty eye and a heavy, deathly
heart. With him I tried a little harder. I watched the
contents of his soul for a moment and saw a black-
painted boy calling the name Jesse Owens as he ran
(20) through an imaginary tape. I saw him hip-deep in
some icy water chasing a book, and I saw a boy
lying in bed, imagining how a kiss would taste from
his glorious next door neighbor. He does something
to me, that boy. Every time. He steps on my heart.
(25) He makes me cry.

Source: Markus Zusak, *The Book Thief.*
New York: Random House (2007), pg. 531.

13. What is the main purpose of the passage?

   (A) To describe the boy's death

   (B) To show the many horrors of Nazi Germany

   (C) To show how fleeting life is

   (D) To reveal how inconsiderate human beings can be

   (E) To bear witness to the effects of war

14. What is the tone of the passage?

   (A) Helpless and pessimistic

   (B) Somber and regretful

   (C) Mellifluous and inevitable

   (D) Mournful and introverted

   (E) Removed and optimistic

15. Who is most likely narrating this passage?

   (A) A child

   (B) An Italian soldier

   (C) Death

   (D) Time

   (E) A dentist

16. Based on the passage, which of the following statements would the narrator most likely agree with?

   (A) The road to hell is paved with good intentions.

   (B) There is no such thing as a happy ending.

   (C) Death is inevitable.

   (D) The world will always keep turning.

   (E) Beauty is in the eye of the beholder.

17. What does the statement "There was only me" (Line 12) imply?

   (A) No one else had survived.

   (B) The narrator is the only person who can do this.

   (C) Rudy's parents were away.

   (D) The narrator often sees these types of situations.

   (E) The narrator feels ill equipped for his or her job.

18. What is most likely the purpose of providing flashbacks of Rudy's life? (Select *all* that apply.)

   A ☐ To flesh out Rudy's sister's character

   B ☐ To evoke sympathy from the reader

   C ☐ To flesh out Rudy's character

   D ☐ To excite anger

   E ☐ To evoke contentedness

> **Questions 19 through 22 are based on the following passage:**

   Among the revolutionary processes that transformed the nineteenth-century world, none was so dramatic in its human consequences or far-reaching
Line in its social implications as the abolition of chat-
(5) tel slavery. Whether accomplished by black revolution, legislation, or civil war, emancipation not only eliminated an institution increasingly at odds with the moral sensibility of the age, but raised intractable questions about the system of economic
(10) organization and social relations that would replace slavery. Especially in the Western Hemisphere, plantation slavery was simultaneously a system of labor, a mode of racial domination and a foundation upon which arose a distinctive ruling class.
(15) As a result, its demise threw open the most fundamental questions of economy, society, and polity. And in all post-emancipation societies, the pivot on which social conflict turned was the new status of the former slaves.

Source: Eric Foner, *Nothing But Freedom: Emancipation and Its Legacy*. Baton Rouge: Louisiana State University Press (1983)

19. The main idea of this passage is best described by which of the following?

    (A) Human consequences outweigh freedoms.

    (B) Slavery was a revolutionary process that transformed the nineteenth century.

    (C) Plantation slavery only occurred in the Western Hemisphere.

    (D) The abolition of plantation slavery made blacks equal to whites on all accounts.

    (E) Regardless of the emancipation, slavery still held power over economic, social, and political organization in society.

20. The author's tone can best be described as

    (A) indifferent

    (B) sardonic

    (C) concerned

    (D) righteous

    (E) sinister

21. Which of the following could be argued to be a short-term positive result stemming from the abolition of chattel slavery?

    (A) Congress ratified the Thirteenth, Fourteenth, and Fifteenth Amendments to the Constitution, which prohibited slavery, guaranteed all citizens equal protection under the law, and granted universal suffrage to men.

    (B) Jim Crow Laws legalized the segregation between blacks and whites and further continued slavery even after emancipation.

    (C) The Supreme Court ruled in 1896 in *Plessy v. Ferguson* that separated facilities for whites and blacks were constitutional, which encouraged the passage of discriminatory laws that wiped out the gains made by blacks during Reconstruction.

    (D) Black southerners were forced to comply not simply with state policies and city codes, but with unwritten "Negro laws" as well.

    (E) The states ratified the 19th Amendment, granting women the right to vote.

22. According to the passage, the abolition of chattel slavery did which of the following?

    (A) Ended the Civil War

    (B) Created fairness between blacks and whites

    (C) Made it easy for former slaves to gain economic independence

    (D) Gave former slaves voting rights

    (E) Created a new economic and social class in society

> **Questions 23 and 24 refer to the following passage:**

The United States' final offer on a lease agreement for the Subic Bay Naval Base in the Philippines was rejected by the Philippine Senate. Hence,
Line for the first time in nearly a century, U.S. military
(5) strategy for the Asia-Pacific region will no longer be centered on the Philippines, and the nation's economic survival and development will no longer rely on U.S. dependency. Somehow, this dependency on the U.S. has served as an impediment to the Philip-
(10) pines' ability to join East Asia's economic boom.

23. Which of the following best summarizes what the passage is about?

    (A) Philippine-U.S. military relations have come to an end.

    (B) The Philippines' economic dependency on the U.S. ended with its Senate's rejection of the U.S. lease offer.

    (C) The U.S. lease offer for the Subic Bay Naval Base was rejected by the Philippine Senate; hence the U.S. will no longer have its military base in the Asia-Pacific region.

    (D) The Philippines is now on its own in its economic survival and development.

    (E) The U.S. military strategy for the Asia-Pacific region will no longer be focused on the Philippines following the Philippine Senate's rejection of the U.S. lease offer.

24. The U.S. military's pullout from Subic Bay would mean

    (A) fewer jobs for Filipinos

    (B) fewer Americans in the Philippines

    (C) a chance for the Philippines to survive on its own

    (D) weakening of U.S.-Philippine relations

    (E) less protection for the Philippines

Questions 25 through 29 are based on the following excerpt from "The Rape of the Lock" by Alexander Pope.

> One speaks the glory of the British Queen,
> And one describes a charming Indian screen;
> A third interprets motions, looks, and eyes;
> *Line* At every word a reputation dies.
> *(5)* Snuff, or the fan, supply each pause of chat,
> With singing, laughing, ogling, and all that.
> Meanwhile, declining from the noon of day,
> The sun obliquely shoots his burning ray;
> The hungry judges soon the sentence sign,
> *(10)* And wretches hang that jurymen may dine;

25. The last two lines suggest that this society

    (A) takes pride in its justice system

    (B) hurriedly administers justice for the wrong reasons

    (C) sentences the wrong people to death

    (D) sentences people for humanitarian reasons

    (E) has no problem with the death penalty

26. The juxtaposition of Lines 1 and 2 suggests that the people

    (A) talk of trivia

    (B) revere the monarchy and Indian screens equally

    (C) are Imperialists

    (D) are Royalists

    (E) have divergent interests

27. Which of the following DO NOT properly capture the meaning or describe the function of "obliquely" in the context of Line 8? (Select *all* that apply.)

    A "perpendicularly"

    B "at a steep angle"

    C a pun on hidden meanings

    D a pun on "stealth"

    E a nautical reference

28. The change in voice from the first half of the excerpt into the second is best described as one from

    (A) light to dark

    (B) critical to amused

    (C) sarcastic to lighthearted

    (D) amused to sad

    (E) sarcastic to bleak

29. The form of this writing is

    (A) haiku

    (B) rhyme

    (C) prose

    (D) limerick

    (E) riddle

Questions 30 through 34 refer to the following passage:

Frederick Douglass was born Frederick Augustus Washington Bailey in 1817 to a white father and a slave mother. Frederick was raised by his *Line* grandmother on a Maryland plantation until he was *(5)* eight. It was then that he was sent to Baltimore by his owner to be a servant to the Auld family. Mrs. Auld recognized Frederick's intellectual acumen and defied the law of the state by teaching him to read and write. When Mr. Auld warned that educa- *(10)* tion would make the boy unfit for slavery, Frederick sought to continue his education in the streets.

When his master died, Frederick was returned to the plantation to work in the fields at age 16. Lat-
Line er, he was hired out to work in the shipyards in Bal-
(15) timore as a ship caulker. He plotted an escape but was discovered before he could get away. It took five years before he made his way to New York City and then to New Bedford, Massachusetts, eluding slave hunters by changing his name to Douglass.

(20) At an 1841 anti-slavery meeting in Massachu-setts, Douglass was invited to give a talk about his experiences under slavery. His impromptu speech was so powerful and so eloquent that it thrust him into a career as an agent for the Massachusetts
(25) Anti-Slavery Society.

Douglass wrote his autobiography in 1845 pri-marily to counter those who doubted his authentic-ity as a former slave. This work became a classic in American literature and a primary source about
(30) slavery from the point of view of a slave. Douglass went on a two-year speaking tour abroad to avoid recapture by his former owner and to win new friends for the abolition movement. He returned with funds to purchase his freedom and to start his
(35) own anti-slavery newspaper. He became a consul-tant to Abraham Lincoln and throughout Recon-struction fought doggedly for full civil rights for freedmen; he also supported the women's rights movement.

30. According to the passage, Douglass's prime moti-vation in writing his autobiography stemmed from a(n)

    (A) desire to make money for his anti-slavery movement

    (B) desire to start a newspaper

    (C) interest in authenticating his life as a slave

    (D) desire to educate people about slavery

    (E) desire to promote the Civil War

31. The central idea of the passage is that Frederick Douglass

    (A) was influential in changing the laws regarding the education of slaves

    (B) was one of the most eminent human rights leaders of the 19th century

    (C) was a personal friend and confidant to a presi-dent

    (D) wrote a classic in American literature

    (E) supported women's rights

32. According to the author of this passage, Mrs. Auld taught Frederick to read because

    (A) Frederick wanted to learn like the other boys

    (B) she recognized his natural ability

    (C) she wanted to comply with the laws of the state

    (D) he needed to read to work in the home

    (E) she obeyed her husband's wishes in the matter

33. The title that best expresses the ideas of this pas-sage is

    (A) "The History of the Anti-Slavery Movement"

    (B) "The Dogged Determination of Frederick Douglass"

    (C) "Reading: Window to the World"

    (D) "Frederick Douglass's Contributions to Free-dom"

    (E) "The Oratorical and Literary Brilliance of Frederick Douglass"

34. As used in Line 22, "impromptu" most nearly means

    (A) unprepared

    (B) quiet

    (C) forceful

    (D) boisterous

    (E) embellished

Questions 35 through 38 refer to the following passage:

The price of cleaning up the environment after oil spills is on the increase, especially after the recent spill off the U.S. Gulf Coast that created
Line miles of sludge-covered beach. While numerous
(5) smaller spills have occurred along the coast of California, none have been as disastrous as the spills in Alaska and the Gulf Coast. Tides and prevailing winds carried much of this oil to shore in a matter of days. Workers tried to contain the oil with weight-
(10) ed, barrel-shaped plastic tubes stretched along the sand near the water. They hoped to minimize the damage. Generally, the barriers were successful, but there remained many miles of oil-covered sand. Cleanup crews shoveled the oil-covered sand into
(15) plastic bags for removal.

Coastal states are responding to the problem in several ways. California is considering the formation of a department of oceans to oversee protection programs and future cleanups. Several states called
(20) for a commission of independent experts to recommend solutions, while other states have suggested training the National Guard in cleanup procedures. Other states are calling for the creation of an oil-spill trust fund large enough to cover the costs of a
(25) major spill. Still other states are demanding federal action and funding. Regardless of the specific programs that may be enacted by the various states or the federal government, continued offshore drilling and the shipping of oil in huge tankers creates a
(30) constant threat to the nation's shoreline.

35. The passage mentions which of the following potential actions? (Select *all* that apply.)

    [A] Establishing of a state agency to supervise ocean protection

    [B] Equipping oil tankers with double hulls

    [C] Erecting a sea wall to protect the Gulf Coast from an accidental oil spill

    [D] Training the National Guard in cleanup procedures

    [E] Creating an oil-spill trust fund

36. What was the purpose of the barrel-shaped plastic tubes?

    (A) To keep sightseers away from the oil

    (B) To keep oil-soaked animals off the beach

    (C) To force the oil to soak into the sand

    (D) To keep the remaining water-borne oil spillage from coming ashore

    (E) To clean the oil-saturated water

37. The passage directly supports which of the following assertions about oil spills?

    (A) Cleaning up after a spill is a race against time.

    (B) The federal government has no stake in cleanups.

    (C) The oil companies are doing nothing to prevent spills.

    (D) The National Guard's charter prevents it from acting to contain spills.

    (E) A federal blue-ribbon commission should be appointed by the president to recommend oil-spill prevention methods.

38. What is the author's opinion of the hazards created by oil spills?

    (A) Oil spills must be expected if the present methods of production and shipment continue.

    (B) Oil spills are the result of untrained tanker crews.

    (C) Oil spills would not be a problem if the government was better prepared to clean up.

    (D) Oil spills are the responsibility of foreign oil producers.

    (E) Oil spills are just part of the cost of doing business.

America's national bird, the mighty bald eagle, is being threatened by a new menace. Once decimated by hunters and loss of habitat, this new-
Line est danger is suspected to be from the intentional
(5) poisoning by livestock ranchers. Authorities have found animal carcasses injected with restricted pesticides. These carcasses are suspected to have been placed to attract and kill predators such as the bald eagle in an effort to preserve young grazing ani-
(10) mals. It appears that the eagle is being threatened again by the consummate predator, humans.

39. One can conclude from this passage that

(A) the pesticides used are detrimental to the environment

(B) the killing of eagles will protect the rancher's rangeland

(C) ranchers must obtain licenses to use the pesticides

(D) the poisoning could result in the extinction of the bald eagle

(E) pesticides have been obtained illegally

40. The author's attitude is one of

(A) detached observation

(B) concern

(C) informed acceptance

(D) suspicion

(E) unbridled anger

To the Shakers, perfection was found in the creation of an object that was both useful and simple. Their Society was founded in 1774 by Ann Lee,
Line an Englishwoman from the working classes who
(5) brought eight followers to New York with her. "Mother Ann" established her religious community on the belief that worldly interests were evil. To gain entrance into the Society, believers had to remain celibate, have no private possessions, and
(10) avoid contact with outsiders. The order came to be called "Shakers" because of the feverish dance the group performed.

Another characteristic of the group was the desire to seek perfection in their work. Shaker
(15) furniture was created to exemplify specific characteristics: simplicity of design, quality of craftsmanship, harmony of proportion, and usefulness. While Shakers did not create any innovations in furniture designs, they were known for fine crafts-
(20) manship. The major emphasis was on function, and not on excessive or elaborate decorations that contributed nothing to the product's usefulness.

41. The passage indicates that members of the religious order were called "Shakers" because

(A) they shook hands at their meetings

(B) they did a shaking dance at their meeting

(C) they took their name from the founder

(D) they were named after the township where they originated

(E) they developed a shaking disorder

42. Which of the following is the most appropriate substitute for the use of the term "innovations" (Line 18)?

(A) Corrections

(B) Colors

(C) Changes

(D) Functions

(E) Brocades

43. The passage suggests which of the following about the Shakers?

    (A) Shaker furniture is well-proportioned and ornate in design.

    (B) Shakers believed in form over function in their designs.

    (C) Shaker furniture has seen a surge in popularity.

    (D) Shakers appeared to believe that form follows function.

    (E) Shaker furniture is noted for the use of brass hardware.

Questions 44 through 46 refer to the following passage:

Benjamin Franklin began writing his autobiography in 1771, but he set it aside to assist the colonies in gaining independence from England. After a
Line hiatus of 13 years, he returned to chronicle his life,
(5) addressing his message to the younger generation. In this significant literary work of the early United States, Franklin portrays himself as benign, kindhearted, practical, and hardworking. He established a list of ethical conduct and recorded his transgres-
(10) sions when he was unsuccessful in overcoming temptation. Franklin wrote that he was unable to arrive at perfection, "yet I was, by the endeavor, a better and happier man than I otherwise should have been if I had not attempted it."

44. Which of the following is the least appropriate substitute for the use of the term "ethical" in Line 9?

    (A) Moral

    (B) Depraved

    (C) Virtuous

    (D) Honorable

    (E) Qualifiable

45. The passage suggests which of the following about Franklin's autobiography?

    (A) It was representative of early American literature.

    (B) It fell short of being a major work of literary quality.

    (C) It personified Franklin as a major political figure.

    (D) It was a notable work of early American literature.

    (E) It was directed toward his enemies.

46. Which of the following slogans best describes Franklin's assessment of the usefulness of attempting to achieve perfection?

    (A) Cleanliness is next to godliness.

    (B) Nothing ventured, nothing gained.

    (C) Ambition is its own reward.

    (D) Time is money.

    (E) Humility is everything.

Questions 47 through 50 refer to the following passage:

As noted by Favat in 1977, the study of children's stories has been an ongoing concern of linguists, anthropologists, and psychologists.
Line The past decade has witnessed a surge of inter-
(5) est in children's stories from researchers in these and other disciplines. The use of narratives for reading and reading instruction has been commonly accepted by the educational community. The notion that narrative is highly structured and
(10) that children's sense of narrative structure is more highly developed than expository structure has been proposed by some researchers. Early studies of children's stories followed two approaches for story analysis: the analysis of story content or
(15) the analysis of story structure. Early research on story structure focused on formal models of structure, such as story grammar and story schemata. These models specified basic story elements and formed sets of rules similar to sentence grammar for ordering the elements.

(20) The importance or centrality of narrative in a child's development of communicative ability has been proposed by Halliday (1976) and Hymes (1975). Thus, the importance of narrative for language communicative ability and for reading and reading *(25)* instruction has been well documented. However, the question still remains about how these literacy abilities interact and lead to conventional reading.

Story content analysis has centered primarily on examining motivational and psychodynamic aspects *(30)* of story characters as noted in the works of Erikson and Pitcher and Prelinger in 1963 and Ames in 1966. These studies have noted that themes or topics predominate and that themes change with age.

47. This passage is most probably directed at which of the following audiences?

(A) Reading educators

(B) Linguists

(C) Psychologists

(D) Reading researchers

(E) Anthropologists

48. According to the passage, future research should address

(A) how story structure and story schema interact with comprehension

(B) how children's use and understanding of narrative interacts and leads to conventional reading

(C) how basal texts and literature texts differ from children's story structure

(D) how story content interacts with story comprehension

(E) how narrative text structure differs from expository text structure

49. The major distinction between story content and story structure is that

(A) story content focuses on motivational aspects whereas story structure focuses on rules similar to sentence grammar

(B) story content focuses on psychodynamic aspects whereas story structure focuses on formal structural models

(C) story content and story structure essentially refer to the same concepts

(D) story content focuses on themes and topics whereas story structure focuses on specific story elements

(E) story content focuses primarily on characters whereas story structure focuses on story grammar and schemata

50. Which of the following is the most complete and accurate definition of the term "surge" (Line 3) as used in the following sentence?

The past decade has witnessed a surge of interest in children's stories from researchers in these and other disciplines. (Lines 2–4)

(A) A heavy swell

(B) A slight flood

(C) A sudden rise

(D) A sudden increase

(E) A sudden rush

Questions 51 to 53 refer to the following chart:

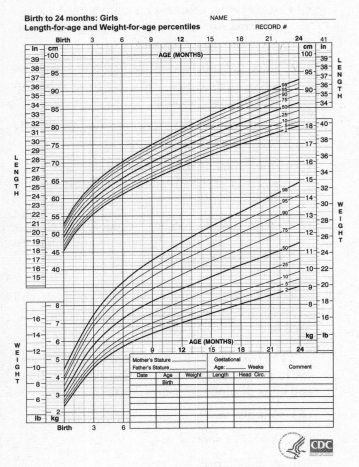

Source: Published by the Centers for Disease
Control and Prevention, November 1, 2009.
WHO Child Growth Standards
(*www.who.int/childgrowth/en*)

51. It can be inferred from the chart that it is important to make careful measurements of weight and height at which of the following intervals?

(A) Every month, from birth to 2 years

(B) Every year, from birth to 1 year

(C) Every 3 years, up to 5 years of age

(D) Every 24 months

(E) Every 3 years through adolescence

52. The implied use of the chart is which of the following?

(A) The trend of growth becomes precisely predictable.

(B) Length for age and weight for age can be measured over time.

(C) People can spot variations and faltering growth by using the chart.

(D) Centimeters are converted into inches throughout.

(E) Age can be estimated by growth when the age of the child is not known.

53. Which of the following conclusions is supported by the chart?

(A) Without the aid of a growth chart, it is virtually impossible to detect changes in the rate of growth, such as sudden loss of weight or halt in gain.

(B) Each baby should have more than one growth chart.

(C) The height of an individual is influenced both by genetic and environmental factors.

(D) The maximum growth potential of an individual is decided by hereditary factors

(E) Only height is affected by long-term nutritional deprivation.

HAWK ON A FRESHLY PLOWED FIELD

My Lord of the Field, proudly perched on the sod,
You eye with disdain
Line And mutter with wings
(5) As steadily each furrow I tractor-plod.
"Intruder!" you glare, firmly standing your ground,
Proclaim this fief yours
By Nature so willed—
Yet bound to the air on my very next round.
(10) You hover and soar, skimming close by the earth,
Distract me from work
To brood there with you
Of changes that Man wrought your land—for his
       worth.
(15) In medieval days, lords were god over all:
Their word was the law.
Yet here is this hawk
A ruler displaced—Man and Season forestall.
My Lord of the Field, from sight you have flown
For purpose untold,
(20) When brave, you return
And perch once again, still liege-lord—but Alone.

54. Which of the following is the most complete and accurate definition of the term "liege-lord" (Line 21) as used in the poem?

(A) Monarch

(B) King

(C) Owner

(D) Sovereign

(E) Master

55. Which of the following best describes the author's attitude toward the hawk?

(A) Whimsical

(B) Romantic

(C) Pensive

(D) Intimidating

(E) Fearful

56. Which of the following is the most complete and accurate definition of the term "medieval" (Line 15) as used in the poem?

(A) Antiquated

(B) Feudal

(C) Old

(D) Antebellum

(E) Antediluvian

Praxis Core
Reading Practice Test 2 Answer Key

1. (D)	20. (C)	39. (D)
2. (B)	21. (A)	40. (B)
3. (E)	22. (E)	41. (B)
4. (B)	23. (E)	42. (C)
5. (E)	24. (C)	43. (D)
6. (A)	25. (B)	44. (B)
7. (C)	26. (B)	45. (D)
8. (A)	27. A and E	46. (B)
9. (D)	28. (D)	47. (D)
10. (C)	29. (B)	48. (B)
11. (B)	30. (C)	49. (B)
12. (C)	31. (B)	50. (D)
13. (A)	32. (B)	51. (A)
14. (B)	33. (D)	52. (C)
15. (C)	34. (A)	53. (A)
16. (C)	35. A and D	54. (E)
17. (D)	36. (D)	55. (C)
18. B and C	37. (A)	56. (B)
19. (E)	38. (A)	

READING PRACTICE TEST 2: ANSWERS

1. (D)

The correct answer is choice (D). She and her mother do have different English skills (A), and she is there to promote her book (C). She was raised Asian-American, and this undoubtedly made a difference (E). But these choices do not bear on the purpose of the passage. We can find the purpose in the first line: it is to show the different ways the author uses English (or, more precisely, the idea that there is more than one type of English that she uses). The passage doesn't describe the intricacies of the English language (B) in that it doesn't talk about all of the small grammatical rules that make English difficult to learn.

2. (B)

The correct answer is choice (B). This is an inference question. There is no evidence in the passage that choice (A) is true, and we do not know whether choice (C) is true based on the passage. We also can't say how the audience might evaluate a situation (D). From the context, we can see that the author has given talks before but, as she says, "it was perhaps the first time she had heard me give a lengthy speech, using the kind of English I have never used with her" (Lines 10–11). Therefore, we can assume that to the author's recollection, her mother has never heard her give a speech or use that type of English. Choice (B) is the best answer.

3. (E)

Choice (E) is the best answer. The passage is couched in straightforward language and hints that the writer is sharing information with us that she has reflected upon. This question challenges us to find the correct pairing. We can easily discard a choice once we determine just one of the two terms is a bad match with the author's tone. Thus, we can remove choice (A) from consideration by establishing that the passage is not opinionated, or conceited—the author's expression of empathy toward her mother characterizes quite the

opposite: open-mindedness. Choices (B) and (C) should be eliminated because the passage is conversational, not formal. Choice (D) would make the author "overzealous" (overly enthusiastic), when in reality she strikes a calming, thoughtful note.

4. (B)

Choices (A), (B), and (C) are close contenders. Choice (A) isn't the best because there is no artistry going on in the type of language the author uses. Choice (C) means "artificial," and that isn't exactly what the author is saying. She is explaining that the language is sophisticated and highly structured as opposed to the other English she speaks at home. Choice (D) cannot be correct because there is no literal tool-shaping taking place, and choice (E) likewise asks us to consider another actual meaning of "wrought" that does not fit the context of the passage. Therefore, choice (B) is the best answer.

5. (E)

Choice (E) is the correct answer. Choice (A) is not the best because it names the book the author speaks of having written in the passage. Choice (B) is bland and non-specific. Choices (C) and (D) are too broad. "My Heritage, My English" is the best answer because it speaks to the author's theme more closely than any of the other response options.

6. (A)

The best answer is choice (A). The question asks the reader to understand a point of view. The speaker or narrator is describing someone who gets pleasure from setting fires (namely, an arsonist). The narrator discusses a "he" in the story who we read is a firefighter. We do not know if the speaker himself enjoys fire (B) or if he himself is doing something illegal (D). While the passage is "dystopian" (having to do with an imaginary wretched scenario) in that it features firefighters who set fires, choice (C) is not the best answer because the passage literally describes arsonous behavior. Choice (E) is at odds with the passage because we know that the fire was not an accident ("he flicked the igniter and the house jumped").

7. (C)

The correct answer is choice (C), which is literal, not metaphorical, since the person being described is a firefighter who is holding a hose with a nozzle. All the other choices draw metaphorical comparisons: The "great python" (A) is the hose, the "fireflies" (B) are the flames that ignite when he sets the fire, the allusion to "conductor" (D) and "symphonies" (E) liken his actions to someone leading an orchestra.

8. (A)

Choice (A) is correct. This question again asks the reader to distinguish point of view. In the first three lines, we hear the narrator make a statement about burning. Then, he describes the firefighter. The entire passage indirectly tells us something about the narrator's opinions, but the most direct communication of his opinions occurs in the beginning of the passage.

9. (D)

The correct answer is choice (D). "Grief" means "sadness from loss." This is a supporting-detail question. The other choices are vocabulary words in the first two lines, but they do not correlate with the definition we need to match.

10. (C)

The correct answer is choice (C). The answer is in the last line of the monologue. This is a supporting-detail question.

11. (B)

The correct answer is choice (B). Emily might want to go back (C), but we do not know this from the passage. Choices (D) and (E) are incorrect because in the monologue, she expresses her love for life. Choice (A) doesn't describe her passion with the word "acceptable."

12. (C)

The correct answer is choice (C). Lines 8–9 answer this supporting-detail question.

13. (A)

The correct answer is choice (A). The passage describes a young boy's death. While this is a horrific result, the passage doesn't show other implied "horrors," just the particular horror of Rudy's death. Indeed, life is fleeting (C), but again, showing that is not the goal of this text, nor is it to show how inconsiderate people can be (D) or how war (a much larger topic) creates such accounts (E). Choice (A) is the best answer provided.

14. (B)

The second choice is best. The narrator is "somber," reflecting on this boy's life, and he is "regretful" because the boy has no future. In the first choice, the words aren't strong enough for the description. It isn't "mellifluous" (sounding smooth), nor is it "introverted" (withdrawn) and certainly not "optimistic."

15. (C)

The correct answer is choice (C). The way to answer the question is to work backwards from the answers. Choices (A) and (E) are out because the voice we hear is not a child's, and we get no indication from the text that the narrator is a dentist. It might be an Italian soldier but it's unlikely that a soldier would be on the side of a victim like this. So we are left with two abstract concepts— "Time" (D) and "Death" (C). The key to the answer lies in the line "There was only me." Here, we see Death, or the "grim reaper," coming to get the boy. So choice (C) is correct. We can infer the answer from the text.

16. (C)

The correct answer is choice (C) because this passage is primarily about death, not beauty, persistence (D), extreme pessimism (B), or right actions of any form (A).

17. (D)

The best answer is choice (D). Again, "Death" is the only one who sees these situations, and Death alone takes in these situations.

18. B and C

The correct responses are both B and C . We do not get a sense of Rudy's sister from the passage, so choice A can be eliminated. Both B and C are correct in that the passage evokes sympathy in the reader and lets us know about Rudy.

19. (E)

Choice (E) is the correct response. The last five lines of the passage speak of this multi-dimensional impact. Choice (A) isn't related to the passage. Choice (B) is just a statement of fact. Choices (C) and (D) are not true.

20. (C)

The best answer is choice (C). The author is concerned about slavery. He is not uncaring (A), sarcastic (B), virtuous (D), or threatening (E).

21. (A)

Choice (A) is the best answer because it provides positive Constitutional outcomes for liberated slaves.

Choices (B), (C), and (D) continued discriminatory practices against African Americans. While it's true that woman suffrage (E) was vigorously debated in the wake of the Civil War, owing to the efforts of Elizabeth Cady Stanton, Susan B. Anthony, and Lucy Stone, those efforts failed. In fact, a Kansas state referendum saw both black and woman suffrage voted down. Meanwhile, black male suffrage, while becoming a federal constitutional reality via the Fifteenth Amendment would come to be severely hobbled for another century by state and local poll taxes, literacy tests, and other means devised to disenfranchise African Americans. Woman suffrage (E) would not be granted under the U.S. Constitution until the 19th Amendment was adopted in 1920, which, while historically linked to black suffrage, is not a short-term result, as the question asks.

22. (E)

The correct answer is choice (E). The purpose of the passage is to discuss economic and social implications of the abolition of chattel slavery. The other choices are incorrect because the abolition didn't end the Civil War (A), nor did it create fairness between blacks and whites (B). While it was easier for slaves to gain economic independence, it was still difficult for them to do so (C). Slaves got voting rights through the Constitution, not through the abolition of chattel slavery, so (D) is incorrect.

23. (E)

The most complete summary of the passage is stated in (E); hence, this is the correct answer. Choice (A) is not true, so it is incorrect; choice (B) is too broad—the U.S. pullout is not the only issue related to the Philippine economy. The passage doesn't say there won't be a U.S. base in the Philippines, so choice (C) isn't what the passage is about. Choice (D) is incorrect because the Philippines will not be completely on its own, as it will pursue trade relations with the U.S. and other trading partners.

24. (C)

The passage explicitly says the U.S. presence in the Philippines has been an impediment to the nation's ability to participate in East Asia's "economic boom"; hence, the correct answer is choice (C). Choices (A), (B), (D), and (E) are all possible consequences but are all quite debatable outside the framework of the passage.

25. (B)

The prisoners are speedily sentenced because the judges and the jurymen are hungry and want to go home for supper as the day ends—the prisoners may be guilty, but the wrong reasons determine their choice of sentence (B). The last two lines don't address the pride of the people in the justice system, so (A) is incorrect. The sarcasm of the piece suggests that this society uses the system for personal selfish benefits—certainly not a humanitarian society (D). And, while it may be true that the wrong people are sentenced to death (C) and that "society has no problem with the death penalty" (E), these answers do not adequately appreciate the scope of Pope's sarcasm, which satirizes all manner of hasty, imprudent verdicts.

26. (B)

The question wants you to analyze the clash or conflict of two very different and specific concepts in conversation: the glory of the Queen in one breath and a fire screen (or room divider) in another. The juxtaposition is not so much to suggest trivia (A) or seriousness (the Queen's glory is serious but the furniture is not), but that this society holds both in equal reverence (B). No real evidence is given that the people are Imperialists (C) or Royalists (D). The poem may imply, in the first two lines, that people are interested in different things (E), but again, there is no real evidence; at issue is the clash of two distinct ideas.

27. $\boxed{\text{A}}$ **and** $\boxed{\text{E}}$

There is a clever use of the language in the adverb "obliquely." It stands for the angle of the sun as it declines toward sunset at a steep angle $\boxed{\text{B}}$ but also for the hidden meanings behind the word as it refers to this society's inappropriate conduct: the deceit, the amorality, and the stealth in choices $\boxed{\text{C}}$ and $\boxed{\text{D}}$. It certainly does not mean that the sun is at a perpendicular angle, choice $\boxed{\text{A}}$, nor does it imply anything about the sea $\boxed{\text{E}}$.

28. (D)

The move is light to dark (A) in the physical movement of the day but not specifically in the voice. The author undergoes a shift in mood from initial amusement at the trivial chitchat of the day to sadness that the judicial system sends men to the gallows willy-nilly. Thus, the best answer is choice (D).

29. (B)

Succeeding lines end with like sounds, so this is a rhyme (B). This is not true for the other forms of writing.

30. (C)

Douglass was interested in raising social consciousness about slavery. The passage stresses his interest in refuting those who doubted his claim to have been a slave.

31. (B)

Even though Douglass's love of education is clear in the passage, the assertion of choice (A) that he influenced laws affecting the education of slaves is not supported by the text. None of the other choices, though true, are cited in the text. For the record, Douglass, after being a wary critic of Lincoln, actually did become friendly with the president (C), did write an American classic (D), and did support women's rights (E).

32. (B)

This choice is supported by the statement, "Mrs. Auld recognized Frederick's intellectual acumen." Choices (C) and (E) contradict information in the passage. The passage does not support choices (A) and (D).

33. (D)

Choices (A), (B), and (C) are either too broad or too general. Choice (E) is too specific and limited to cover the information in the passage.

34. (A)

An "impromptu" speech is given without preparation.

35. A **and** D

Choices A and D are correct because the passage specifically mentions these possible initiatives to prevent and control oil spills. While tankers are mentioned B, only the threat they pose, not a way in which they could be built to help prevent spills in the first place, is mentioned. As for C, while the Gulf Coast is mentioned, there is no reference to a sea wall, only to an after-the-fact coastal barrier composed of "weighted, barrel-shaped plastic tubes."

36. (D)

Choice (D) is correct because workers were trying to keep the oil in the water and away from the beach. Choices (A) and (B) are incorrect because neither sightseers nor animals are discussed in the passage. Choice (C) is incorrect because the cleanup crews wanted to remove the oil, not let it soak into the sand. The tubes are used to contain the oil, not clean the water, so choice (E) is incorrect.

37. (A)

Choice (A) is correct. In Lines 7–9, the author says that after spills off Alaska and the Gulf Coast, "tides and prevailing winds" carried the oil ashore "in a matter of days." Choice (B) is incorrect since the passage contradicts it. Choice (C) is incorrect because there is no claim made in the passage that the oil companies have done nothing. Choice (D) is incorrect since the passage actually suggests training National Guardsmen in clean-up procedures. As for choice (E), neither the president nor a blue-ribbon commission is mentioned.

38. (A)

The last sentence of the passage specifically states that spills will remain a threat so long as offshore drilling and the shipment of oil in "huge" tankers continue. Choice (B) is incorrect because the passage does not discuss tanker crews or training programs for them—only for the National Guard. Although the passage does imply that the government should be better prepared to stage a cleanup, the author does not state that oil spills would cease to be a problem if the government were better prepared. Therefore, choice (C) is incorrect. Choice (D) is incorrect because foreign oil producers are not mentioned. Choice (E) is incorrect because the passage never says that the oil companies consider oil spills part of the cost of doing business.

39. (D)

It is implied that the poisoning of animal carcasses in the habitat of bald eagles presents a new danger of extinction for America's symbol. Choices (A), (C), and (E) are not mentioned in the passage. Choice (B) suggests a possible reason for the poisoning, but the passage is silent on this point.

40. (B)

The author's use of words such as "mighty bald eagle" and "threatened by a new menace" bespeaks concern for the topic. Therefore, choices (A) and (C) are not applicable. The author appears for the most part to be objective. Given the tone and substance of the passage, choices (D) and (E) are too strong to be correct.

41. (B)

This choice is supported by the first paragraph of the passage. All other choices are irrelevant to information contained in the passage.

42. (C)

"Innovations" require new or novel changes to be made.

43. (D)

The passage discusses the importance of utility as well as simplicity to the Shakers; therefore, the function of the piece of furniture would be more important than the particular form. Choices (A), (B), and (E) are contradictory to the information given, and choice (C) goes beyond information given in the text.

44. (B)

"Depraved" means corrupted or perverted. All other choices have to do with accepted standards of conduct.

45. (D)

The author states in Lines 6–7 that Franklin's work was a "significant work of the early United States." None of the other choices is supported by the text.

46. (B)

The final sentence of the paragraph supports this choice. Choice (C) might apply, but choice (B) is closest to the overall mood of the passage. Choices (A), (D), and (E) are not relevant to the question.

47. (D)

As the passage presents information by various researchers on children's stories, Lines 25–27 present an unanswered question that still needs to be addressed by reading researchers, as provided in choice (D).

48. (B)

Although more information may be needed about story content and story structure as indicated in choices (A), (C), (D), and (E), the main question that remains to be answered is choice (B).

49. (B)

Each choice provides partially correct information about story content and story structure; choice (B) provides the most complete response.

50. (D)

Each choice is a possible definition. However, choice (D) is most appropriate as there was an increased interest by researchers in these and other areas even though it has been an ongoing concern of some researchers.

51. (A)

The correct answer is choice (A). The chart measures length and weight each month up to 24 months. Measuring at longer intervals (every 24 months, every year, or every 3 years) would not provide careful measurements during this critical growth time in a child's life.

52. (C)

The correct answer is (C). Choice (A) is not right because growth trends are not precise. Choice (B) is the overall purpose of the chart, which is not the same as the implied use. Choice (D) is true but not a use for the chart. Choice (E) is a way that the chart could be used but the situation described is not as common as (C) and thus not the best answer.

53. (A)

The correct choice is (A). Choice (B) is illogical and unhelpful since it would suggest there's multiple growth charts to follow, which runs counter to the idea of judging against a standardized set of data. While choices (C), (D), and (E) happen to be true in the world, they are not conclusions that could be drawn from this chart.

54. (E)

Choices (A), (B), and (D) suggest rights either by heredity or supreme authority, whereas choice (C) indicates rights just by possession. The hyphenated term "liege-lord" connotes both entitled rights and power to command respect. Thus choice (E), "master" (one who assumes authority and property rights through ability and power to control), best represents the hawk.

55. (C)

Choices (A), (D), and (E) are not supported by the passage. Choice (B) represents a possible conclusion, but because there is only one best choice for this question, go with (C), which suggests thoughtful consideration of the hawk.

56. (B)

Choices (D) and (E) are incorrect by definition. While choices (A) and (C) offer possible definitions, "feudal" (B) most clearly denotes an association with the Middle Ages, also known as medieval times.

Praxis Core
Writing Practice Test 1

Praxis Core
Writing Practice Test 1 Answer Sheet

1. Ⓐ Ⓑ Ⓒ Ⓓ Ⓔ   15. Ⓐ Ⓑ Ⓒ Ⓓ Ⓔ   29. Ⓐ Ⓑ Ⓒ Ⓓ Ⓔ

2. Ⓐ Ⓑ Ⓒ Ⓓ Ⓔ   16. Ⓐ Ⓑ Ⓒ Ⓓ Ⓔ   30. Ⓐ Ⓑ Ⓒ Ⓓ Ⓔ

3. Ⓐ Ⓑ Ⓒ Ⓓ Ⓔ   17. Ⓐ Ⓑ Ⓒ Ⓓ Ⓔ   31. Ⓐ Ⓑ Ⓒ Ⓓ Ⓔ

4. Ⓐ Ⓑ Ⓒ Ⓓ Ⓔ   18. Ⓐ Ⓑ Ⓒ Ⓓ Ⓔ   32. Ⓐ Ⓑ Ⓒ Ⓓ Ⓔ

5. Ⓐ Ⓑ Ⓒ Ⓓ Ⓔ   19. Ⓐ Ⓑ Ⓒ Ⓓ Ⓔ   33. Ⓐ Ⓑ Ⓒ Ⓓ Ⓔ

6. Ⓐ Ⓑ Ⓒ Ⓓ Ⓔ   20. Ⓐ Ⓑ Ⓒ Ⓓ Ⓔ   34. Ⓐ Ⓑ Ⓒ Ⓓ Ⓔ

7. Ⓐ Ⓑ Ⓒ Ⓓ Ⓔ   21. Ⓐ Ⓑ Ⓒ Ⓓ Ⓔ   35. Ⓐ Ⓑ Ⓒ Ⓓ Ⓔ

8. Ⓐ Ⓑ Ⓒ Ⓓ Ⓔ   22. Ⓐ Ⓑ Ⓒ Ⓓ Ⓔ   36. Ⓐ Ⓑ Ⓒ Ⓓ Ⓔ

9. Ⓐ Ⓑ Ⓒ Ⓓ Ⓔ   23. Ⓐ Ⓑ Ⓒ Ⓓ Ⓔ   37. Ⓐ Ⓑ Ⓒ Ⓓ Ⓔ

10. Ⓐ Ⓑ Ⓒ Ⓓ Ⓔ   24. Ⓐ Ⓑ Ⓒ Ⓓ Ⓔ   38. Ⓐ Ⓑ Ⓒ Ⓓ Ⓔ

11. Ⓐ Ⓑ Ⓒ Ⓓ Ⓔ   25. Ⓐ Ⓑ Ⓒ Ⓓ Ⓔ   39. Ⓐ Ⓑ Ⓒ Ⓓ Ⓔ

12. Ⓐ Ⓑ Ⓒ Ⓓ Ⓔ   26. Ⓐ Ⓑ Ⓒ Ⓓ Ⓔ   40. Ⓐ Ⓑ Ⓒ Ⓓ Ⓔ

13. Ⓐ Ⓑ Ⓒ Ⓓ Ⓔ   27. Ⓐ Ⓑ Ⓒ Ⓓ Ⓔ

14. Ⓐ Ⓑ Ⓒ Ⓓ Ⓔ   28. Ⓐ Ⓑ Ⓒ Ⓓ Ⓔ

Praxis Core
Writing Practice Test 1

Time: 40 minutes for 40 multiple-choice items
     60 minutes for two essays

USAGE

Directions: Each question consists of a sentence that contains four underlined portions. Read each sentence and decide whether any of the underlined parts contains a grammatical construction, a word use, or an instance of incorrect or omitted punctuation or capitalization that would be inappropriate in carefully written English. If so, select the underlined portion that must be revised to produce a correct sentence. If there are no errors in the sentence as written, select "No error." No sentence has more than one error. Remember to answer every question.

1. Despite an effort to encourage participation, there is many students who still do not go to student activities. No error.
   A   B   C   D   E

2. The basketball coach met the player to work at him. No error.
             A   B   C   D   E

3. Over the last year, their extended family had growed. No error.
   A   B   C   D   E

4. The teacher and his aide join the principal and I for lunch every Tuesday. No error.
        A   B   C   D   E

5. Tuna, salmon, and halibut are among the many types of fish that is especially popular in sushi restaurants. No error.
                                  A   B   C   D   E

6. Jasmine learns math much easier than most people. No error.
        A   B   C   D   E

7. The sound that a functioning wind turbine makes does not come from its gear box but because of the movement of
           A   B   C   D

its blades through the air. No error.
                   E

8. Some of the people <u>with whom</u> the witness <u>worked</u> <u>were engaged</u> in covert activities <u>on behalf of</u> the United States
                  A   B   C   D

   government. <u>No error</u>.
              E

9. The <u>bad</u> storm that passed <u>through the Philippines</u> <u>caused</u> wind, flooding, and storm surges. <u>No error</u>.
       A   B   C D   E

10. I <u>stopped</u> drinking <u>energy drinks</u> at night <u>before</u> bedtime <u>unless</u> they kept me awake. <u>No error</u>.
      A   B   C   D   E

11. <u>We</u> <u>forgot</u> <u>to sing</u> "Happy Birthday" before <u>we ate</u> the cake. <u>No error</u>.
     A   B   C   D   E

12. <u>Of all</u> the important contributions to history that he <u>might have made</u>, John Montagu, the fourth Earl of Sandwich,
      A   B

    is <u>better</u> known for a lunch of meat inserted <u>between</u> two slices of bread. <u>No error</u>.
       C   D   E

13. *Huckleberry Finn*, by <u>general consensus</u> Mark Twain's <u>greatest</u> work, is not <u>only</u> an American classic <u>but also</u> one
                             A   B   C   D

    of the great books of the world. <u>No error</u>.
                                 E

14. Mama, the narrator of Alice Walker's short story "Everyday Use," <u>speaks</u> fondly of her daughter <u>upon her return</u>
                                                       A   B

    home after a long absence <u>like</u> Mama is <u>proud</u> of her. <u>No error</u>.
                               C   D   E

15. <u>When</u> Dr. Martin Luther King, Jr., wrote his famous letter from the Birmingham jail, he advocated neither evading
      A

    <u>or</u> defying the <u>law;</u> but he accepted the idea that a penalty <u>results from</u> breaking a law, even an unjust one. <u>No error</u>.
     B   C   D   E

16. <u>Because some</u> people believe <u>strongly</u> that channeling, the <u>process by which</u> an individual goes into a trance-like
         A   B   C

    state and communicates the thoughts of an ancient warrior or guru to an audience, helps them cope with modern

    problems, but others condemn the whole idea <u>as</u> mere superstition. <u>No error</u>.
                                                   D   E

17. The reason <u>a large percentage</u> of American college students <u>located</u> Moscow in California is <u>because</u> they <u>were not</u>
                A   B   C   D

    <u>required</u> to learn the facts of geography. <u>No error</u>.
      A   E

SENTENCE CORRECTION

Directions: Each item presents a sentence. In every case, either a portion of the sentence or the entire sentence is underscored. You will be given five ways of writing the underscored portion. Choice (A) always repeats the original; the other four choices offer other options. If you believe the original should be left alone, select choice (A); otherwise you should select another choice that you think produces the best version of the sentence. This section tests correctness and effectiveness of expression. In selecting your answers, you should be guided by the structural and grammatical conventions of standard written English. Remember to answer every question.

18. Siblings growing up in a family do not necessarily have equal opportunities to achieve, <u>the difference being their placement in the family, their innate abilities, and their personalities</u>.

    (A) the difference being their placement in the family, their innate abilities, and their personalities.

    (B) because of their placement in the family, their innate abilities, and their personalities.

    (C) and the difference is their placement in the family, their innate abilities, and their personalities.

    (D) they have different placements in the family, different innate abilities, and different personalities.

    (E) their placement in the family, their innate abilities, and their personalities being different.

19. Two major provisions of the United States Bill of Rights <u>is freedom of speech and that citizens are guaranteed a trial by jury</u>.

    (A) is freedom of speech and that citizens are guaranteed a trial by jury.

    (B) is that citizens have freedom of speech and a guaranteed trial by jury.

    (C) is freedom of speech and the guarantee of a trial by jury.

    (D) are freedom of speech and that citizens are guaranteed a trial by jury.

    (E) are freedom of speech and the guarantee of a trial by jury.

20. Poets of the nineteenth century tried <u>to entertain their readers but also with the attempt of teaching them</u> lessons about life.

    (A) to entertain their readers but also with the attempt of teaching them

    (B) to entertain their readers but also to attempt to teach them

    (C) to both entertain their readers and to teach them

    (D) entertainment of their readers and the attempt to teach them

    (E) both to entertain and to teach their readers

21. Although most college professors have expertise in their areas of specialty, <u>some are more interested in continuing their research than in teaching undergraduate students</u>.

    (A) some are more interested in continuing their research than in teaching undergraduate students.

    (B) some are most interested in continuing their research rather than in teaching undergraduate students.

    (C) some prefer continuing their research rather than to teach undergraduate students.

    (D) continuing their research, not teaching undergraduate students, is more interesting to some.

    (E) some are more interested in continuing their research than to teach undergraduate students.

22. <u>Whether adult adoptees should be allowed to see their original birth certificates or not</u> is controversial, but many adoptive parents feel strongly that records should remain closed.

    (A) Whether adult adoptees should be allowed to see their original birth certificates or not

    (B) Whether adult adoptees should be allowed to see their birth certificates or not

    (C) The fact of whether adult adoptees should be allowed to see their original birth certificates

    (D) Allowing the seeing of their original birth certificates by adult adoptees

    (E) That adult adoptees should be allowed to see their original birth certificates

23. <u>Having studied theology, music, along with medicine,</u> Albert Schweitzer became a medical missionary in Africa.

    (A) Having studied theology, music, along with medicine

    (B) Having studied theology, music, as well as medicine

    (C) Having studied theology and music, and, also, medicine

    (D) With a study of theology, music, and medicine

    (E) After he had studied theology, music, and medicine

24. When the Mississippi River threatens to flood, sandbags are piled along its banks, <u>and they do this to keep its waters from overflowing</u>.

    (A) and they do this to keep its waters from overflowing.

    (B) to keep its waters from overflowing.

    (C) and then its waters won't overflow.

    (D) and, therefore, keeping its waters from overflowing.

    (E) and they keep its waters from overflowing.

25. <u>Because of the popularity of his light verse</u>, Edward Lear is seldom recognized today for his travel books and detailed illustrations of birds.

    (A) Because of the popularity of his light verse

    (B) Owing to the fact that his light verse was popular

    (C) Because of his light verse, that was very popular

    (D) Having written light verse that was popular

    (E) Being the author of popular light verse

26. China, <u>which ranks third in area and first in population between the world's countries</u>, also has one of the longest histories.

    (A) which ranks third in area and first in population among the world's countries

    (B) which ranks third in area and has the largest population among the world's countries

    (C) which is the third largest in area and ranks first in population among the world's countries

    (D) in area ranking third and in population ranking first among the world's countries

    (E) third in area and first in the number of people among the world's countries

27. <u>The fewer mistakes one makes in life</u>, the fewer opportunities you have to learn from your mistakes.

    (A) The fewer mistakes one makes in life

    (B) The fewer mistakes you make in life

    (C) The fewer mistakes he or she makes in life

    (D) The fewer mistakes there are in one's life

    (E) The fewer mistakes in life

28. Although the word "millipede" means one thousand feet, millipedes have no more than 115 pairs of legs <u>that are attached to the segments of their bodies</u>.

    (A) that are attached to the segments of their bodies.

    (B) , which are attached to segments of their bodies.

    (C) attaching themselves to segments of their bodies.

    (D) whose attachment is to the segments of their bodies.

    (E) the attachment of which is to the segments of their bodies.

REVISION IN CONTEXT

Directions: The following passage is a draft of an essay. Some portions of the passage need to be strengthened through editing and revision. Read the passage and choose the best answers for the questions that follow. Some questions ask you to improve sentences or portions of sentences. In some cases, the indicated portion of the passage will work best as it is and thus will require no changes. In choosing answers, consider development, organization, word choice, style, and tone, and follow the requirements of standard written English. Remember to answer every question.

[1] Having composed one of the most popular and well-known ballet pieces of the 20ᵗʰ century, a Spanish folk dance inspired French composer Maurice Ravel. [2] Therefore, the full work, which lasts about 15 minutes, is said to be played somewhere in the world roughly every 15 minutes. [3] To some extent, *Bolero* owes its place in pop culture to Hollywood for the music's memorable role in the eponymously named motion picture *Bolero* in 1934 and, then, nearly a half-century later, in *Ten*.

[4] Throughout the piece, the theme is repeated 18 times, which may do nothing so much as point to the fact that Ravel was suffering from Alzheimer's disease while composing the piece. [5] Ravel was confident he had a hit, exulting, "I have written a masterpiece: Unfortunately, there is no music in it." [6] The sister of the legendary Russian dancer Vaslav Nijinksy choreographed this classic ballet created by Ravel.

[7] What is it about the *Bolero* that draws us in? [8] Perhaps it's the sense of anticipation we experience during the studious build-up, as we move ever closer to the crescendo, when a frenzied burst of energy brings to bear the full force and majesty of the orchestra. [9] The center and driving force of it is a snare drum. [10] The percussionist begins by playing *pianissimo* in a steady pattern lasting two measures and six beats, as quietly as possible. [11] The first flute evidently introduces the melody, while instruments such as the clarinet, bassoon, and piccolo contribute individual parts. [12] As more instruments join in, each player also begins to play steadily louder. [13] For most of the performance, *Bolero* is played unrelentingly in C major. [14] The end of the piece is signaled by a brief shift to E major and then the audience is whipped back to C major after just eight bars.

29. In context, which sentence provides the best revision for Sentence 1 (reproduced below)?

    Having composed one of the most popular and well-known ballet pieces of the 20ᵗʰ century, a Spanish folk dance inspired French composer Maurice Ravel.

    (A) (As it is now)

    (B) A popular Spanish folk dance inspired French composer Maurice Ravel to create one of the best-known ballet pieces of the 20ᵗʰ century.

    (C) As a popular French composer, a Spanish folk dance inspired Maurice Ravel to create one of the most popular ballet pieces of the 20ᵗʰ century.

    (D) As a popular Spanish folk dance, Maurice Ravel was inspired to create one of the most popular ballet pieces of the 20ᵗʰ century.

    (E) Maurice Ravel, a French composer inspired by a Spanish folk dance to create one of the most popular ballet pieces of the 20ᵗʰ century.

30. In context, which is the best version of the underlined portion of Sentence 2 (reproduced below)?

    <u>Therefore</u>, the full work, which lasts about 15 minutes, is said to be played somewhere in the world roughly every 15 minutes.

    (A) (As it is now)

    (B) Yet

    (C) Equally important

    (D) Accordingly

    (E) In fact

31. In context, which is the best version of the underlined portion of Sentence 4 (reproduced below)?

    Throughout the piece, the theme is repeated 18 times, <u>which may do nothing so much as point to the fact that Ravel was suffering from Alzheimer's disease while composing the piece.</u>

    (A) (As it is now)

    (B) which, in other words, could indicate that Ravel was in a confused state when he composed the piece.

    (C) by which it is clear that, significantly, Ravel was suffering from Alzheimer's disease.

    (D) which some say is proof Ravel was suffering from Alzheimer's disease when he wrote it.

    (E) so clearly, Alzheimer's disease was on the march.

32. In context, which revision to Sentence 10 (reproduced below) is most needed?

    The percussionist begins by playing pianissimo in a steady pattern lasting two measures and six beats, as quietly as possible.

    (A) Replace "pattern" with "tempo"

    (B) Delete "as quietly as possible"

    (C) Replace "begins" with "starts"

    (D) Replace "playing" with "performing"

    (E) Replace "lasting" with "encompassing"

33. In context, which is the best revision of the underlined portion of Sentence 6 (reproduced below)?

    The sister of the legendary Russian dancer Vaslav Nijinksy choreographed <u>this classic ballet created by Ravel</u>.

    (A) (As it is now)

    (B) this classic ballet

    (C) this classic ballet of Ravel's

    (D) this classic ballet that Ravel created

    (E) this classic ballet from Ravel's oevre

34. Which of the following sentences is LEAST valuable to advancing the passage's main theme?

    (A) Sentence 1

    (B) Sentence 2

    (C) Sentence 3

    (D) Sentence 6

    (E) Sentence 8

35. In context, which is the best revision of the underlined portion of Sentence 9 (reproduced below)?

> The center and driving force of <u>it</u> is a snare drum.

(A) (As it is now)

(B) this musical composition

(C) the folk dance

(D) them

(E) Nijinsky

36. In context, the deletion of which word or phrase in Sentence 11 (reproduced below) would make the passage clearer?

> The first flute evidently introduces the melody, while instruments such as the clarinet, bassoon, and piccolo contribute individual parts.

(A) first

(B) evidently

(C) instruments such as

(D) such as the clarinet, bassoon, and piccolo

(E) individual

RESEARCH SKILLS

Directions: The following questions test your familiarity with basic research skills. For each question, choose the best answer. Remember to answer every question.

37. When doing Internet research, which of the following determinations about a website is paramount?

(A) Whether it is commercial or not-for-profit

(B) Whether it has links to other reputable sites

(C) Whether its information is credible and timely

(D) Whether the site's information is contradictory

(E) Whether the site has multiple authors

38. The sentence below appears in the introduction of a student's research paper. What is its function?

> When one considers injuries—some of which have been fatal—along with short- and long-term neurological damage, it becomes clear that the "sport" known as mixed martial arts should change its guidelines.

(A) This is a thesis statement with claims the writer will prove.

(B) This is logical reasoning that proves the claims.

(C) These are examples the writer will use in the second paragraph.

(D) This is a thesis statement, which is a guideline for every research paper.

(E) This is the development of a counterclaim.

39. What form of information should a writer initially give the reader in the introduction of a research paper if he or she is presenting the audience with a new or unfamiliar concept?

(A) Statistics

(B) Anecdote

(C) Quotation

(D) Definition

(E) Questions

40. Sue is writing a research paper in favor of eutha-
nasia. She uses Internet sources and has a lot of
relevant information. However, when outlining the
paper, she can't find the sources of many of the
facts and statistics she plans to use. What is Sue's
problem?

   (A) She forgot to cite or record full citations on
   her sources when she was writing the paper.

   (B) She should have made an annotated bibliography.

   (C) She forgot to write a sentence outline.

   (D) There is no problem because students don't
   need to cite statistics and facts from the
   Internet.

   (E) There is no problem because she can say
   where she got the information without providing an in-text citation in her paper.

SOURCE-BASED ESSAY

On the actual test, you will see the essay question at the top of the computer screen and space will be provided at the bottom
for you to write your essay. For this assignment, however, we suggest you open a text document on your computer or laptop,
or write in longhand in a notebook.

Time: 30 minutes

Directions: In the following section you will read two short passages on a topic and then plan and write an essay on
that topic. Your essay will be an informative essay based on the two sources that are provided. Read the topic and
sources carefully. Spend some time considering the topic and organizing your thoughts before you begin writing.
Do not write on a topic other than the one specified. Essays on topics of your own choice will not be accepted. Your
response must be in English. Write clearly and effectively, using concrete examples where appropriate. How well you
write is more important than how much you write, but to cover the topics adequately, you will probably need to write
more than one paragraph.

Assignment: Both of the following sources address the ways in which television has an impact on daily life. Read the
two passages carefully and then write an essay in which you identify the most important concerns regarding the issue.
Your essay must draw on information from both of the sources and explain the issue. In addition, you may draw on
your own experiences, observations, or reading. Be sure to cite the sources whether you paraphrase or quote directly.

Source 1

Adapted from: Robinson, John P. "Television and Leisure Time: A New Scenario." In *Measuring Media
Influence, Journal of Communication*, Vol. 31, Issue 1,
pp. 120–130. March 1981.

The impact of television on daily life remains a topic of
continual interest and speculation. While most concern
among academics and in the popular press has centered
on television's influence on societal violence, sexual
mores, or drug dependency, there also has been interest in its impact on more routine and mundane behavior
including the public's leisure activities.

Source 2

Adapted from: Comstock, G. *The Evolution of American
Television*, Thousand Oaks, Calif.: SAGE Publications,
1989, pg. 312.

There is no more clearly documented way in which television has altered U.S. life than in the expenditure of
time. It has not only changed the way the hours of the day
are spent, but the choices available for the disposal of
those hours. In so doing, television has brought the age
of the mass media to maturity. Television is neither simply entertainment nor simply news, but an institution that
encompasses both at all times, and which influences our
lives. It achieves this influence by the time it consumes,
by the incursion of that time on other activities and competing media, and by the content of what it disseminates.

ARGUMENTATIVE ESSAY

On the actual test, you will see the essay question at the top of the computer screen and space will be provided at the bottom for you to write your essay. For this assignment, however, we suggest you open a text document on your computer or laptop, or write in longhand in a notebook.

Time: 30 minutes

Directions: You will plan and write an argumentative essay on the topic presented. The essay will be based on your own reading, experience, or observations. Read the topic carefully. You will probably find it best to spend a little time considering the topic and organizing your thoughts before you begin writing. Do not write on a topic other than the one specified. Essays on topics of your own choice will not be acceptable. In order for your test to be scored, your responses must be in English.

Read the opinion stated below:

"There is a wonderful, mystical law of nature that the three things we crave most in life—happiness, freedom, and peace of mind—are always attained by giving them to someone else."

Assignment: Discuss the degree to which you agree or disagree with this opinion. Use support from your own reading, observation, and personal experience.

Praxis Core
Writing Practice Test 1 Answer Key

1.	(C)	15.	(B)	29.	(B)
2.	(C)	16.	(A)	30.	(E)
3.	(D)	17.	(C)	31.	(D)
4.	(B)	18.	(B)	32.	(B)
5.	(C)	19.	(E)	33.	(B)
6.	(C)	20.	(E)	34.	(D)
7.	(D)	21.	(A)	35.	(B)
8.	(E)	22.	(E)	36.	(B)
9.	(D)	23.	(E)	37.	(C)
10.	(D)	24.	(B)	38.	(A)
11.	(E)	25.	(A)	39.	(D)
12.	(C)	26.	(E)	40.	(A)
13.	(A)	27.	(B)		
14.	(C)	28.	(B)		

Usage

1. (C)

"Students" is the subject, so the verb must be the plural, "are." The use of "despite" (A) properly sets up consideration of how efforts "to encourage participation" (B)—a verb phrase correctly used as an infinitive—have fallen short. Choice (D) has no problem because "many" requires a plural subject, "students."

2. (C)

The correct idiomatic phrasing would have the coach "work with" the player. The preposition "with" serves to indicate participation in an action, transaction, or arrangement. "Work at" means "to exert effort" and is applied to a task, not a person. For example, a politician might "work at" winning over voters.

3. (D)

"Had growed" is the wrong verb tense. Since the process of the family's growth began last year and is still continuing, the present participle is needed in the sentence. The verb phrase should read "has grown."

4. (B)

Here, we see a compound noun phrase as a subject, and then another compound noun phrase, which is the object of the verb "join." The pronoun "I" is incorrect and should be changed to "me." One way to attack this is to isolate the "I." Would you say, "Join I for lunch"? The sentence misconstrues pronoun case. Don't make the mistake of treating the pronouns "principal and I" as the subjects of the sentence when they're actually the objects. Similarly, you wouldn't say, "He gave the gift to Pedro and I." After all, would you say, "He gave the gift to I"? The correct statement would be, "He gave the gift to Pedro and me."

5. (C)

Don't be thrown by the relative clause (a clause beginning with a relative pronoun—in this case, "that"). Although "fish" by itself can be singular or plural, you should be guided by the compound antecedent ("Tuna, salmon, and halibut"), which is plural, and you should use "that are." You wouldn't say, "Tuna, salmon, and halibut is popular." Note that choice (D), in underlining the "s" in *sushi*, asks you to judge whether that letter needs to be capitalized. Because *sushi* is neither a proper noun nor starting the sentence, the lowercase "s" is correct.

6. (C)

An adverb is needed to describe how Jasmine learns math. Thus, "easily" should be used instead of the adjective "easier" and, to correct the sentence at hand, would be part of the phrase "more easily."

7. (D)

The correct word would be "from" instead of "because of" to match the "come from," a phrase integral to drawing a contrast. The sentence seeks to call attention to a fact that's different than expectations would have it. The sentence must maintain parallel structure, which means not mixing grammatical forms.

8. (E)

This sentence contains no grammatical, idiomatic, logical, or structural errors. It conforms with standard written English. Choice (A), "with whom," introduces an adjective clause modifying the word "people." The relative pronoun "whom" is in the objective case because it serves as the object of the preposition "with." The simple past tense "worked," choice (B), is appropriate. Choice (C), "were engaged," is plural to agree with its subject, "some." Choice (D) is an appropriate idiomatic phrase that also means "for."

9. (D)

Commas are needed to separate items in a series. "Wind" is the first in a series of types of bad weather. It needs to be separated by a comma from the next item in the series. The other choices are acceptable: "bad" (A) is used appropriately as an adjective, "through the Philippines" (B) is an appropriate prepositional phrase; "caused" (C) is conjugated in the past tense, which correlates with the verb "passed."

10. (D)

"Unless" signals an exception, but we know from the rest of the sentence we're looking for the reason why the speaker of the sentence gave up energy drinks before bedtime. This means the sentence needs a term that means "for this reason" (e.g., "because"). The other answer choices do not reveal any errors in standard written English. Running down the list, the verb "stopped" (A) is conjugated appropriately; the adjective "energy" (B) modifies the noun "drinks," and the preposition "before" (C) is logical.

11. (E)

This sentence contains no grammatical, idiomatic, logical, or structural errors, so choice (E) is the correct answer. The sentence indicates two actions, both now stopped, taking place in sequence: "We forgot to sing . . . before we ate the cake." Both actions, the singing and the eating, are in the past and, accordingly, the correct tense is used in the sentence as presented.

12. (C)

"Better," the comparative form of "good," is faulty in the sentence because no direct comparison is being drawn between the extent to which the Earl of Sandwich is known for inventing the sandwich versus anything else. (To consider the distinction, suppose you encountered this sentence: "The fourth Earl of Sandwich is *better* known for inventing the sandwich than for commanding the British Navy.") Since the original sentence makes it clear that the renown of this member of the British peerage rests squarely on one particular thing, only the superlative, "best," fits.

13. (A)

The underlined portion of the sentence is redundant. "Consensus" means "general agreement," so replace "consensus" with "agreement."

14. (C)

While "like" is sometimes used as a conjunction in casual conversation, it still does not pass muster in standard written English. The conjunction we need is either "as if" or "as though."

15. (B)

When making comparisons, "either" is twinned with "or" and "neither" with "nor." Note that choice (C), which shows an underlined semicolon, asks you to decide whether the punctuation is correct. It is.

16. (A)

"Because" serves no purpose. The sentence is easily fixed by dropping "Because" and starting with "Some."

17. (C)

The error in this sentence lies in choice (C). It should say "that" instead of "because." This is an example of faulty predication, which can take several forms, but which here involves the redundancy created by the pairing of "the reason" with "is because." First, notice that "the reason" and "is because" basically mean the same thing. To fix the predication error in the original sentence, substitute the relative pronoun "that" for "because."

Sentence Correction

18. (B)

The best answer to correct this sentence is choice (B); this answer shows the causal relationship between sibling opportunities and their placement in the family, their innate abilities, and their personalities, and retains the subordination of the original sentence. Choices (A) and (E) use dangling phrases. Choice (C), with its use of the coordinating conjunction "and," treats the lack of opportunity and its cause as if they are of equal weight and does not show the causal relationship between them. Choice (D) creates a run-on sentence.

19. (E)

Only choice (E) corrects the two major problems in the sentence, the lack of subject–verb agreement and the lack of parallelism. In choices (A), (B), and (C), the verb "is" does not agree with its plural subject, "provisions." Choices (A) and (D) have unlike constructions serving as predicate nominatives, the noun "freedom" and the clause "that citizens are guaranteed a trial by jury." Choice (E) correctly uses the plural verb "are" to agree with the plural subject, and the predicate nominative is composed of two parallel nouns, "freedom" and "guarantee."

20. (E)

The errors found in the original sentence, choice (A), involve parallelism and redundancy. Choice (E) uses the parallel infinitives "to entertain" and "to teach" as direct objects and eliminates the repetition created in the use of both "tried" and "attempt" in the original sen-

tence. Choices (B) and (C) provide parallel construction, but choice (B) retains the redundancy and choice (C) incorrectly splits the infinitive "to entertain"; although choice (D) provides parallelism of the nouns "entertainment" and "attempt," the redundancy still remains, and the word order is not idiomatic.

21. (A)

The given sentence is acceptable in standard written English. Each of the alternate choices introduces a problem. Choice (B) uses the superlative form of the adjective, "most interested," when the comparative form, "more interested," is correct for the comparison of two options; choices (C) and (E) introduce a lack of parallelism; and choice (D) is not idiomatic.

22. (E)

The noun, or nominal, clause in choice (E) is idiomatically acceptable, functioning as a noun phrase. The use of "Whether" in choices (A) and (B) is paired with "or not," a phrase that is merely extra baggage, contributing nothing to the meaning and complicating construction. In choice (C), "the fact of whether" is not idiomatic. Choice (D) uses an awkward gerund phrase that is also not idiomatic.

23. (E)

This sentence presents two problems, namely use of a preposition instead of a coordinating conjunction to join the objects of the participle "having studied" and failure to show a time relationship. Choice (E) corrects both problems. Choice (B) simply replaces the preposition "along with" by "as well as"; choice (C) unnecessarily repeats the conjunction "and" rather than using the quite appropriate series construction. Also hindering choices (B) and (C), as well as (A) and (D), is that they do not correctly show the time relationship.

24. (B)

This sentence contains the ambiguous pronoun "they," for which there is no antecedent, and therefore fails to show the relationship of the ideas expressed. Choice (B) eliminates the clause with the ambiguous pronoun and correctly expresses the reason for the sandbag placement. Choice (C), by joining the first and second clauses with "and," fails to show the subordinate relationship of the second to the first. Choice (D) introduces a dangling phrase with a coordinating conjunction, "and," that suggests the joining of equals; and choice (E) retains both errors from the original sentence.

25. (A)

This sentence suffers no problem in structure or logic, so you should have decided to accept the underlined portion as it is (A). Choice (B) introduces awkward, wordy phrasing (i.e., "Owing to the fact that"). Choice (C) is not only awkward but misuses "that" when "which" is the relative pronoun required to signal a nonrestrictive relative clause. Choices (D) and (E) do not establish that the popularity of Lear's light verse over-shadows his other accomplishments—a causal link that binds the sentence's two clauses together.

26. (E)

This sentence misconstrues the use of "between" versus "among." "Between" is correct if the comparison being drawn is between either just two entities or if the nature of the relationship hinges on a head-to-head comparison (e.g., "The competition *between* Nokia and every other smartphone maker is fierce."). Choices (B) and (C) lack parallelism and are wordy. Choice (D), while featuring parallel structure, is idiomatically awkward with its participial phrases "ranking third" and "ranking first."

27. (B)

This sentence lacks both consistent pronoun use and parallel construction. Because the non-underscored portion of the sentence uses the pronouns "you" and "your," the first part of the sentence must also use the second-person pronoun. Choice (B) provides that consistency and also retains parallel construction.

28. (B)

The last clause is independent of the beginning of the sentence, so it should be separated by a comma and begin with "which" (B). None of the possible revisions makes any real improvement. Moreover, choice (B) adds an error in subject-verb agreement. Choice (C) creates confusion in pronoun reference with the addition of "themselves," and choices (D) and (E) are not idiomatic.

Revision in Context

29. (B)

Choice (B) is the correct answer. This is a grammatically correct, concise statement using active voice. The sentence as it appears in the given text has two problems: First, it has a dangling modifier the "French composer" mistakenly modifying "Spanish folk dance," and, second, it has the redundancy of "popular" and "well-known." A modifier should describe, clarify, or give greater detail about a person or concept. Be sure the sentence names the doer of the action clearly. All the other response options eliminate the redundancy but have other issues. As in the original sentence, choices (C) and (D) fail to avoid dangling modifiers. Choice (E) is a sentence fragment.

30. (E)

Choice (E) is the correct answer. The prior sentence sets the table for emphatic phrasing to crystallize the extent of *Bolero*'s popularity. "Therefore," the transition word used in the text as it is, is typically used either to show sequence or to summarize or conclude. We're looking to do neither but rather to emphatically offer a supporting detail or example. "In fact" gives us just that by stressing the truth of the assertion of the piece's popularity. This is a good example of how transitions function as the glue that holds ideas together in writing—and how transitions must be chosen with care. Choice (B), "Yet," would show exception. Choice (C), "Equally important," could be used to add an unrelated thought that the writer wants to convey as carrying equal weight to the idea(s) just presented. Choice (D), "Accordingly," like "Therefore" (the transition that incorrectly appears in the original text), is used to summarize or conclude.

31. (D)

Choice (D) is the correct answer, as it results in a direct, cogent statement within the boundaries of the estab-

lished context. Choice (B) alters the meaning of the sentence. We know Alzheimer's disease is specifically in play, and should be cited, because it's part of the context of the text as presented. Choice (C) is needlessly wordy and leaves out a valuable fact—that Ravel may have been afflicted by Alzheimer's while he was composing *Bolero*. As for choice (E), a quick glance might make this choice appealing, but only if you hadn't read the passage. Even though it references Alzheimer's, the revision is not idiomatic.

32. (B)

The correct answer is (B). Key to ensuring the sentence's soundness is to avoid the redundancy created by "as quietly as possible," an idea already conveyed earlier in the sentence by "pianissimo." Even if you didn't know what "pianissimo" (a direction in music to play very softly) means, Sentences 7 and 11 create a context from which you can deduce the meaning. None of the other choices, all essentially synonyms, is necessary to enhance the sentence's structure or precision.

33. (B)

Choice (B) is the correct answer. Every other choice needlessly mentions Ravel's composition of the work, something already established.

34. (D)

Choice (D) is the correct answer. Sentence 6, while offering an interesting historical fact, does little to propel the passage's main theme, which centers on the music's popularity. This theme is extended or buttressed by choices (A), (B), (C), and (E).

35. (B)

Choice (B) is the correct answer. In this sentence, "it" lacks a clear antecedent. Choice (C), "the folk dance," is incorrect because the sentence is clearly addressing Ravel's piece, not the folk dance. Choice (D) is an incorrect pronoun, and choice (E) incorrectly associates the drum with Nijinksy, which represents a fundamental misunderstanding of the passage.

36. (B)

The correct answer is (B). The use of "evidently" is misguided because the author is neither trying to prove a case involving the flute nor wondering aloud about the flute's contribution as it engages the melody. "Evidently" can be read as calling into question the flute's role rather than simply stating it as fact. The author is simply describing the piece's instrumentation. We know we're dealing with a concrete fact that does not require any qualifier. Deleting "evidently" solves the problem.

Research Skills

37. (C)

The correct answer is choice (C). The main question to ask is how credible, or believable, a website is. Whether it's a commercial or not-for-profit site (A) does not in itself have any bearing on its credibility as a source. While links to other reputable sites (B) could be helpful in making your evaluations, and anything the website says that's self-contradictory (D) would be important to note, both of these issues are secondary to an overall credibility assessment. The number of authors behind a web resource (E) does not inherently affect its value to a researcher. What matters more is the authors' credibility in the subject matter on which they're holding themselves out as experts. This again points to choice (C) as the best answer.

38. (A)

The correct answer is choice (A). The writer is previewing the claims for which proof will be offered in the body of the paper. By establishing the extent of the problem (injury, neurological damage, and death), the writer will offer support for the larger argument that guidelines for this sport should be changed. The other choices are incorrect. Choice (D), while a true statement, is too general. This isn't the making of a counterclaim (E) because it sets out the structure and sequence of the paper. Therefore, the best answer is choice (A).

39. (D)

The correct answer is choice (D). The most important information a writer can offer when presenting an unfamiliar concept is a definition. The other ideas are all good things to do along the way in a paper, but, in the specific context governing this question, giving a definition needs to come first when explaining unfamiliar concepts. Once the reader is rooted in the new idea, the author should elaborate with statistics (A), anecdotes (B), and/or quotations (C). The paper should also highlight questions (E) around which the research was designed and pose its own questions to suggest areas of further study.

40. (A)

The best answer is choice (A). Sue didn't follow the rule "cite as you write." As a result, she doesn't know where she got the information because she didn't include in-text citations in her notes and then in her paper. Neither an annotated bibliography (B) nor a sentence outline (C) would help fix the problem. Because we know this really would present a problem in preparing a bona fide research paper, neither choices (D) nor (E) are suitable answers.

SCORING GUIDE FOR SOURCE-BASED ESSAY

Use these objective criteria to score your essay. Then compare your essay to the sample essays that follow.

Score of 6

A 6 essay shows a high degree of competency. An essay in this category:

- Is both well organized and well developed

- Uses information from both sources to discuss the issue and creates meaningful connections between these sources

- Organizes and develops ideas coherently

- Varies syntax and expression

- Is nearly free from errors in syntax, structure, grammar, usage, and mechanics

- Correctly cites both sources when paraphrasing or quoting

Score of 5

A 5 essay shows a high degree of proficiency but may have minor errors. An essay in this category:

- Discusses the matter clearly, creating solid connections between the two sources and offering pertinent support

- Includes information from both sources to discuss the issue

- Is organized and clear

- Shows some sentence variety and ease in the use of language

- Is virtually free from errors in grammar, usage, and mechanics

- Cites both sources when paraphrasing or quoting directly

Score of 4

A 4 essay responds to the assignment and shows some degree of deeper understanding of the assignment. An essay in this category:

- Shows adequate organization, support, development, and connections between the two sources

- Sufficiently explains the issue

- Uses and cites information from both sources when paraphrasing and quoting to explain the issue

- Displays satisfactory use of language, grammar, usage, and mechanics, but may have some errors

Score of 3

A 3 essay shows some degree of understanding, but its response to the topic is deficient. An essay in this category reveals one or more of the following limitations:

- Is inadequate in explaining the issue

- May incorporate only one source or incorporates two sources ineffectively; may fail to cite sources that are paraphrased or quoted directly

- Has incomplete support and a weak connection between sources

- Has insufficient organization and development of ideas

- Has consistent repetition of syntactical or structural errors

Score of 2

An essay receiving a score of 2 shows limited understanding, and its response to the topic is seriously deficient. An essay in this category reveals one or more of the following weaknesses:

- Shows weak organization or development

- Incorporates only one source and does so inadequately

- Fails to clearly and thoroughly discuss the issue

- Has limited support and connections between sources

- Has consistent and serious errors in grammar, usage, syntax, and word choice

- Does not cite quoted or paraphrased information

Score of 1

An essay receiving a score of 1 exhibits a lack of basic writing skills. An essay in this category:

- Contains serious and persistent writing errors

or

- Is disorganized and undeveloped, contains consistent repetition of errors, and is incomprehensible

Sample Source-based Essay 1

Score range: 5 to 6
Word count: 455

In the past 30 years, television has become a very popular pastime for almost everyone. From the time the mother places the baby in his bouncy seat in front of the television so that she can relax and have a second cup of coffee until the time the senior citizen in the retirement home watches Vanna White turn the letters on "Wheel of Fortune," Americans spend endless hours in front of the "boob tube." I believe that television can become an addiction that provides an escape from the problems of the world.

When my mother was a little girl, what did children do to entertain themselves? They played. Their games usually involved social interaction with other children as well as imagitively creating entertainment for themselves. They also developed hobbies like woodworking and sewing. Today, few children really know how to play with each other or entertain themselves. Instead, they sit in front of the television, glued to cartoons that are senseless and often violent. Robinson is correct when he explains that most scholars and writers see how television has affected society in terms of violence (120). Even if children watch educational programs like "Sesame Street," they don't really have to do anything except watch and listen to what the answer to the question is.

Teenagers, also, use television as a way of avoiding doing things that will help them mature. How many kids do much homework anymore? Why not? Because they come home from school tired and relax in front of the television. Television has become "an institution," as Comstock explains. It is more than just a source of information or entertainment: it is actually an entity unto itself that "encompasses both at all times" (Comstock, 312). Even if teenagers watch a controversial program about some problem in the world like AIDS or the wars in Afghanistan and Iraq, they don't usually do anything about it. Television keeps them inactive and unresponsive for the most part.

In addition, young mothers use television to escape their problems. The terrible woes of the people on the soap operas make their problems seem less important. This means that they don't need to solve their own problems.

Although it may seem as if television is really great for older people, I think even my grandmother would have more fun if she had more interests rather than just watching quiz shows. I know she has blotted out the "real world" and that she expects us to act like children she has seen on old television shows like "The Brady Bunch."

In conclusion, I believe that television really can become an addiction that allows people of all ages to avoid facing their own problems and lose themselves in the problems of other people.

Analysis of Source-based Essay 1

Essay 1 merits a score in the range of 5 to 6. It has a traditional structure that lends solidity to the writing. The first paragraph introduces the issue, even suggesting the chronological organization of the essay. Each subsequent paragraph has a clear topic sentence and details to develop it. Some paragraphs are more developed than others, and the conclusion could use more than one sentence. Nevertheless, the conclusion effectively restates the thesis. The writer makes claims that contrast confidently with the sources. He or she also incorporates the ideas from the sources into his or her own ideas. The essay is unified around the writer's opinion. It is logical and effectively uses transitional words to connect main ideas. The syntax varies, and the vocabulary works to advance the writer's points. Although the writer misspells a word ("imagitively," in Paragraph 2) uses the colloquial "kids," and has some problems with parallelism, repetition, and pronoun usage, the essay is well-written considering the 30-minute time limit.

Sample Source-based Essay 2

Score range: 3 to 4
Word count: 296

I disagree with John P. Robinson when he says that "most concern among academics and in the popular press has centered on television's influence on societal violence, sexual mores, or drug dependency" (Robinson, 120). I think that instead of being bad for people, television not only does not blot out the real world but, instead, gives the person watching it a chance to experi-

ence the real world, even places he can't possibly go and may never get a chance to go.

For instance, I've learned a lot about history, like the Vietnam War, by watching TV: I heard things about it, about how some of the veterans didn't feel as if they were welcomed right when they came back from that war. I didn't understand what was the matter. Then, they build a special memorial in Washington for the veterans that didn't come back. Since then I have seen a lot of programs that showed what went on in Vietnam, and I've heard Vietnam vets talk about what happened to them. I think that that war became very real to me because of TV.

Television educates us about the dangers of growing up in America today. I've seen good programs about the dangers of using drugs, about teenage pregnancy and what happens if you try to keep the baby, about eating too much cholesterol (that doesn't matter to me yet, but my dad needs to watch that!), and also anorexia. These are things we all need to know about, and TV has told about them so we know what to do.

I really am convinced that television brings the real world into your house. I think us kids today know a lot more about the real world than our grandparents did who grew up without television.

Analysis of Source-based Essay 2

Essay 2 has a score range of 3 to 4, meaning it's a competent effort. The writer takes a position and develops it. The first paragraph provides a clear introduction, and paragraphs two and three develop the claims that support the thesis. General examples are provided. The second paragraph doesn't start with a claim. Rather, it begins with an example. The final paragraph concludes the essay by restating the writer's point. The essay contains some problems with correct usage, colloquial words like "kids" in the last paragraph, and a lack of specific, concrete examples. For example, what, specifically, did the writer learn about the Vietnam War? We read sort of a list of ideas but not a real lesson. Sentences lack variety in length and construction, with several beginning with "I." Ideas are not always clearly related to each other. There is also unnecessary repetition as well as errors in pronoun use and spelling.

Sample Source-based Essay 3

Score range: 1 to 2
Word count: 165

I get really upset when someone says they don't think we should watch television. Us students learn a lot more from television than whats in a lot of classes in school. Iv'e even leart stuff from the commertials they show the best way to clean a house or the best kind of car to buy right now I wouldn't have no idea what to get my sister for her birthday if I hadn't of seen it on television and said to mysself, "Sally'd love one of these"!

If no one watched television, can u just think about how much crime there would be because kids would be board and would have to get excitement somewheres else than his own living room where the TV set is on. I like to watch TV shows on my phone.

There's also educational television with shows that ask questons and see if you know any answers. That's where I learned a whole lot of stuff about the world and everything.

Analysis of Source-based Essay 3

Essay 3 would earn a score in the range of 1 or 2. Numerous deficiencies bring the score down. The writer digresses from the sources and makes no reference to them. Although he or she has a clearly stated opinion, the writer fails to develop it in a logical, united fashion. There is no clear introduction; claims are not developed with support. The logic is flawed, as shown by the last sentence in the second paragraph, which comes out of nowhere. There are careless spelling errors. The paper lacks a conclusion. There is a huge run-on and other problems in pronoun reference and case, as well as misspelled words and idiomatic errors. The language is imprecise, and the ideas are undeveloped.

SCORING GUIDE FOR ARGUMENTATIVE ESSAY

Use these objective criteria to score your essay. Then compare you essay to the sample essays that follow.

Score of 6

A 6 essay demonstrates a high degree of skill in response to the assignment but may have a few minor errors. An essay in this category:

- Has a clear thesis

- Organizes and develops ideas logically and coherently

- Develops claims and counterclaims by supplying sufficient evidence and describing the strengths and weaknesses of both sides of an argument

- Explains ideas clearly with good reasons

- Demonstrates effective sentence variety

- Clearly displays facility in the use of language

- Is generally free from errors in grammar, usage, and mechanics

Score of 5

A 5 essay demonstrates clear proficiency in response to the assignment but may have minor errors. An essay in this category:

- Has a clear or implied thesis

- Makes claims and considers both sides of the argument

- Organizes and develops ideas clearly, making connections between them

- Explains key ideas, supporting them with applicable reasons, examples, or details

- Displays some sentence variety

- Displays capacity in the use of language

- Is by and large free from errors in grammar, usage, and mechanics

Score of 4

A 4 essay establishes competency in response to the assignment. An essay in this category:

- Has a thesis

- Shows control in the organization and development of ideas although claims may or may not consider both sides of the argument

- Explains some key ideas, supporting them with acceptable reasons and support

- Displays passable use of language

- Shows some control of grammar, usage, and mechanics, but may display errors

Score of 3

A 3 essay demonstrates some competence in response to the assignment but is obviously flawed. An essay in this category reveals one or more of the following weaknesses:

- Has an inadequate thesis

- Shows inadequate organization and development of ideas

- Presents inadequate reasons, examples, or details

- Has errors in language, grammar, usage, and mechanics

Score of 2

A 2 essay is very inconsistent. An essay in this category reveals one or more of the following errors:

- Has no clear position or thesis

- Presents no claims or entertainment of the opposing viewpoint

- Shows weak organization or very little development

- Has few or no relevant reasons or support

- Contains recurrent serious errors in the use of language, grammar, usage, and mechanics

Score of 1

A 1 essay demonstrates fundamental deficits in writing skills. An essay in this category:

- Contains serious and persistent writing errors, is incomprehensible and/or underdeveloped.

Sample Argumentative Essay 1

Score range: 5 to 6
Word count: 488

Happiness, freedom, and peace of mind are goals that everyone wants in life. Yet they are very abstract and difficult to measure. Happiness is a frame of mind that means we enjoy what we do. Freedom is the ability to do what we want, although it is limited to not doing anything that takes away freedom from other people. Peace of mind is a feeling that we are all right and that the world is a good place. How does one achieve these important goals? They can best be acquired when we try to give them to other people rather than when we try to get them ourselves.

The people who feel happiest, experience freedom, and enjoy peace of mind are most often people who are concentrating on helping others. In 1997, Mother Theresa of Calcutta died, but she remains an example for me today. Because she took care of homeless people and was so busy, she probably didn't have time to worry about whether she was happy, free, and peaceful. She always looked cheerful in her pictures.

There are other people in history who seem to have attained the goals we all want by helping others. Jane Addams established Hull House in the slums of Chicago to help other people, and her life must have brought her great joy and peace of mind. She gave to the mothers in the neighborhood freedom to work and know that their children were being taken care of; and Jane Addams apparently had the freedom to do what she wanted to help them.

On the other hand, there are people in literature who directly tried to find happiness, freedom, and peace of mind; and they were often miserable. The two people who come to mind are Scrooge and Silas Marner. Scrooge had been selfish in the past, and he wouldn't give anything for the poor. He wasn't a bit happy even at Christ-mas. Later, when he began helping others, he became happy. Silas Marner was very selfish, hoarding his money and thinking it would make him happy. Only when he tried to make little Eppie happy was he able to be happy, too, even without his stolen money.

Critics may take an opposing view, holding that there are people who do not help others who find happiness. They may claim that we don't need anyone else's joy or even their permission to be happy. Giving is a choice, and very often people who don't give and take care of themselves are happy. I concede that very often, as soon as you stop making everyone else happy, the happier and more free you'll be. However, I still claim that true happiness comes from helping others: especially those in need. There is always someone who isn't doing as well as you are, and I believe we are here on earth to reach out to others. That is how we find joy and peace.

Analysis of Argumentative Essay 1

Essay 1 introduces a precise, knowledgeable argument, establishes claims, and distinguishes an alternative or opposing claim. The organization is logical. The claims and counterclaim are thorough and look at the strengths and limitations of each side. The essay displays keen audience awareness and is well organized. The opening paragraph serves as the introduction with a thesis. There is a central coherent argument and a conclusion. Sentence structure is varied. Support is more than adequate. There are few errors in sentence construction, usage, or mechanics. Although the essay would benefit from some minor revisions, it is well done considering the 30-minute time limit.

Sample Argumentative Essay 2

Score range: 4 to 5
Word Count: 289

I think there is a basic problem in this quotation. I do not think that anyone can give happiness, freedom, or peace of mind to anybody. Those things have to come from inside the person, not from someone else, no matter how hard they try to give them to him. That means that the person trying to make someone else happy, free, and peacefull will be frusterated because he really can't do what he wants to do. And if he is frustrated, he won't be happy, free, and peacefull himself.

I think an example of this in history is when the missionaries went to Oregon in early United States history and tried to help the Indians, and the Indians got smallpox and then killed the missionaries. So no one was happy, free, or had a peaceful mind. That's happened with other missionaries in China and other places, too. It just wasn't possible to give happiness, freedom, and peace of mind to anyone else, and the people giving it often lost it themselves.

I know an example from my own life. My parents have tried very hard to make my little sister happy. They have done everything for her and, I'll tell you, she's so spoiled that nothing makes her happy. When they gave her a new bicycle, she was unhappy because she didn't like the color. I'd think she'd be glad just to have a nice bike. I know they never gave me one as nice as they gave her.

So I really think that whoever said the quotation was not right at all. You can't give happiness, freedom, and peace of mind to someone else at all, so you can't get those qualities by giving them.

Analysis of Argumentative Essay 2

Essay 2 has a score range of 4 to 5. It is organized clearly, with an introduction in the first paragraph, a clear statement of thesis, and a conclusion in the last paragraph. Although a few sentences are not relevant to the topic being discussed, the writer attempts to maintain one focus and to support his or her position with specific details. Paragraphing is solid. However, the use of "I think" and "I know" weakens the essay, and pronouns without clear antecedents occur repeatedly, further sapping the essay of clarity. Sentence patterns and vocabulary lack variety

and there are some errors in spelling (e.g., "peacefull" and "frusterated"), usage, and sentence construction. Transitions are also largely lacking. Still, the writer manages to achieve a competent piece of writing.

Sample Argumentative Essay 3

Score range: 3 to 4
Word count: 150

I agree with the idea that you don't get happiness without trying to make other people happy. But I'm not sure that you always get happiness when you give it to someone else, you may try to make someone else happy and you're miserable even though you do it.

For instance, I've tried many times to make my grandmother happy. No matter what I do, she complains about me and tells my mother I should do everything different. She didn't even act like she liked my Christmas present last year, and she sure didn't make me happy either. Its just the opposite when you let someone else be free he takes away from your freedom and you don't feel free at all.

So, all in all, I think maybe sometimes you get happiness and freedom when you give it to others but most of the time things just get worse.

Analysis of Argumentative Essay 3

Essay 3 would earn a score in the range of 3 to 4. The writer attempts to introduce his or her topic in the first paragraph, but the thesis is not stated precisely. Although the last paragraph serves as a conclusion, it, too, lacks clarity and singleness of purpose. Paragraph 2 gives a specific illustration to develop the theme, but Paragraph 3 lacks specific detail. Although there are some transitional words, the essay rambles with words and ideas repeated. In addition, the essay contains errors in usage, sentence construction, and mechanics.

Sample Argumentative Essay 4

Score range: 1 to 2
Word count: 178

I don't think you can give happiness or piece of mind to anyone maybe you can give freedom. My folks are giving me more freedom now that I useta have, so you can give that to someone else. But nobody knows what makes me happy so I can be happy only if I decide what it is I want and go out and get it for myself. And then I'll have piece of mind, too.

Happiness don't come much but I'm happyest when I'm with a bunch of friends and we are having fun together. That's what friends like being together with other people. but nobody gives me that kind of happiness I have to find a bunch of friends I like and than be with them. And thats real freedom, too, but nobody gave it to any of us. My folks think they can make me happy by giving me gifts but usually I don't like what they give me, and there idea of going for a ride or eating together isn't my idea of being happy.

Analysis of Argumentative Essay 4

Essay 4 would receive a score in the range of 1 to 2. The writer states the thesis in the first sentence and maintains a consistent position, but fails to use an introductory paragraph. There is no conclusion. The writer tries to give some specific details but rambles, failing to marshal the details effectively to support his thesis. In addition, there are serious errors in sentence construction, including the run-on sentence at the beginning. There are also major problems with spelling (e.g., "useta" and "piece of mind" in Paragraph 1, and "happyest" in Paragraph 2), usage, and mechanics.

Praxis Core
Writing Practice Test 2

Praxis Core
Writing Practice Test 2 Answer Sheet

1. Ⓐ Ⓑ Ⓒ Ⓓ Ⓔ

2. Ⓐ Ⓑ Ⓒ Ⓓ Ⓔ

3. Ⓐ Ⓑ Ⓒ Ⓓ Ⓔ

4. Ⓐ Ⓑ Ⓒ Ⓓ Ⓔ

5. Ⓐ Ⓑ Ⓒ Ⓓ Ⓔ

6. Ⓐ Ⓑ Ⓒ Ⓓ Ⓔ

7. Ⓐ Ⓑ Ⓒ Ⓓ Ⓔ

8. Ⓐ Ⓑ Ⓒ Ⓓ Ⓔ

9. Ⓐ Ⓑ Ⓒ Ⓓ Ⓔ

10. Ⓐ Ⓑ Ⓒ Ⓓ Ⓔ

11. Ⓐ Ⓑ Ⓒ Ⓓ Ⓔ

12. Ⓐ Ⓑ Ⓒ Ⓓ Ⓔ

13. Ⓐ Ⓑ Ⓒ Ⓓ Ⓔ

14. Ⓐ Ⓑ Ⓒ Ⓓ Ⓔ

15. Ⓐ Ⓑ Ⓒ Ⓓ Ⓔ

16. Ⓐ Ⓑ Ⓒ Ⓓ Ⓔ

17. Ⓐ Ⓑ Ⓒ Ⓓ Ⓔ

18. Ⓐ Ⓑ Ⓒ Ⓓ Ⓔ

19. Ⓐ Ⓑ Ⓒ Ⓓ Ⓔ

20. Ⓐ Ⓑ Ⓒ Ⓓ Ⓔ

21. Ⓐ Ⓑ Ⓒ Ⓓ Ⓔ

22. Ⓐ Ⓑ Ⓒ Ⓓ Ⓔ

23. Ⓐ Ⓑ Ⓒ Ⓓ Ⓔ

24. Ⓐ Ⓑ Ⓒ Ⓓ Ⓔ

25. Ⓐ Ⓑ Ⓒ Ⓓ Ⓔ

26. Ⓐ Ⓑ Ⓒ Ⓓ Ⓔ

27. Ⓐ Ⓑ Ⓒ Ⓓ Ⓔ

28. Ⓐ Ⓑ Ⓒ Ⓓ Ⓔ

29. Ⓐ Ⓑ Ⓒ Ⓓ Ⓔ

30. Ⓐ Ⓑ Ⓒ Ⓓ Ⓔ

31. Ⓐ Ⓑ Ⓒ Ⓓ Ⓔ

32. Ⓐ Ⓑ Ⓒ Ⓓ Ⓔ

33. Ⓐ Ⓑ Ⓒ Ⓓ Ⓔ

34. Ⓐ Ⓑ Ⓒ Ⓓ Ⓔ

35. Ⓐ Ⓑ Ⓒ Ⓓ Ⓔ

36. Ⓐ Ⓑ Ⓒ Ⓓ Ⓔ

37. Ⓐ Ⓑ Ⓒ Ⓓ Ⓔ

38. Ⓐ Ⓑ Ⓒ Ⓓ Ⓔ

39. Ⓐ Ⓑ Ⓒ Ⓓ Ⓔ

40. Ⓐ Ⓑ Ⓒ Ⓓ Ⓔ

Praxis Core
Writing Practice Test 2

Time: 40 minutes for 40 multiple-choice items
       60 minutes for two essays

USAGE

Directions: Each question consists of a sentence that contains four underlined portions. Read each sentence and decide whether any of the underlined parts contains a grammatical construction, a word use, or an instance of incorrect or omitted punctuation or capitalization that would be inappropriate in carefully written English. If so, select the underlined portion that must be revised to produce a correct sentence. If there are no errors in the sentence as written, select "No error." No sentence has more than one error. Remember to answer every question.

1. The <u>firewood</u> <u>are</u> too <u>wet</u> to light the fireplace at night. <u>No error</u>.
        A   B   C   D   E

2. School policy says <u>either</u> your father or mother <u>have</u> to attend the parent-teacher conference at Jefferson School
            A   B   C
    <u>this month</u>. <u>No error</u>.
        D   E

3. <u>At some future point in time</u>, I <u>will be going</u> to <u>the orthodontist</u> <u>for further treatment</u>. <u>No error</u>.
            A   B   C   D   E

4. Ramón y Cajal's 1904 monograph <u>on</u> the human nervous system, <u>still</u> considered a seminal work in neurobiology,
                                     A   B
    <u>infers</u> that neural connections <u>in the brain</u> are highly structured. <u>No error</u>.
       C   D   E

5. After the child disappeared, the police <u>search</u> <u>every inch</u> of the neighborhood <u>to find her</u>. <u>No error</u>.
                                    A   B   C   D   E

6. <u>The supermarket</u> does a <u>terrible</u> job <u>of lighting</u> <u>their</u> parking lot. <u>No error</u>.
        A   B   C   D   E

7. The mother <u>asked</u> <u>her</u> toddler <u>to stop interrupting</u> <u>and</u> the child refused. <u>No error</u>.
                  A   B   C   D   E

8. <u>Although he</u> is one of the <u>luminances</u> of world literature, Kafka published <u>very</u> little <u>during his lifetime</u>. <u>No error</u>.
    A   B   C   D   E

9. <u>After downsizing, they</u> are looking into redistributing the work <u>among</u> the employees <u>who</u> remain. <u>No error</u>.
    A   B   C   D   E

10. <u>Cathy read</u> the <u>article</u> <u>about poverty in India</u> <u>quick</u>. <u>No error</u>.
     A   B   C   D   E

11. The doctor warned <u>Ellis</u>, "<u>if</u> you don't stop smoking<u>,</u> you will eventually get lung <u>cancer."</u> <u>No error</u>.
                   A   B   C   D   E

12. <u>Julie's parents</u> walked <u>down the street</u> and <u>held</u> hands <u>as if</u> they had just met. <u>No error</u>.
     A   B   C   D   E

13. <u>At</u> the uptown ballfield, the natural turf <u>never stops</u> growing, <u>yet</u> <u>the grounds crew</u> never stops working. <u>No error</u>.
    A   B   C   D   E

14. <u>Living in the city</u> <u>is</u> expensive; <u>to live</u> in the suburbs is also <u>costly</u>. <u>No error</u>.
     A   B   C   D   E

15. Hawks and owls can be seen <u>more frequent</u> in <u>populated</u> areas than <u>most people suppose</u>, and it is <u>possible</u> to hear
                                   A   B   C   D

screech owls at night when the adult birds feed their chicks. <u>No error</u>.
                                                            E

16. The grass was <u>growing over</u> the curb and the oak tree had a branch hanging almost <u>to</u> the ground, so we decided to
                   A   B

trim <u>it</u> before the neighbors became <u>annoyed with us</u>. <u>No error</u>.
    C   D   E

17. <u>Inertial</u> navigation is a guidance system of navigation employed in submarines when <u>they are</u> under water, in
   A
                                                                                       B

missiles used <u>for</u> defense purposes, in aircraft, and <u>to get humans to the moon in the Apollo exploration series</u>.
               C   D

<u>No error</u>.
  E

18. To stay cool <u>during the summer</u>, Americans <u>not only</u> are using ceiling fans, but they are also using devices
                      A   B

<u>to add humidity</u> to the air in <u>particularly</u> arid climates such as Arizona. <u>No error</u>.
    C   D   E

SENTENCE CORRECTION

Directions: Each item presents a sentence. In every case, either a portion of the sentence or the entire sentence is underscored. You will be given five ways of writing the underscored portion. Choice (A) always repeats the original; the other four choices offer other options. If you believe the original should be left alone, select choice (A); otherwise you should select another choice that you think produces the best version of the sentence. This section tests correctness and effectiveness of expression. In selecting your answers, you should be guided by the structural and grammatical conventions of standard written English. Remember to answer every question.

19. The new store manager proved herself to be not only capable and efficient but also a woman who was adept at working in a hectic, high-traffic environment.

    (A) to be not only capable and efficient but also a woman who was adept

    (B) not only to be capable or efficient but also a woman who was adept

    (C) not only to be capable and efficient but also a woman who was adept

    (D) to be not only capable and efficient but also adept

    (E) to be not only capable and efficient but also an adept woman

20. Hunting, if properly managed and carefully controlled, can cull excess animals, thereby producing a healthier population of wild game.

    (A) Hunting, if properly managed and carefully controlled,

    (B) Managing it wisely, carefully controlled hunting

    (C) Managed properly hunting that is carefully controlled

    (D) Properly and wisely controlled, careful hunting

    (E) If properly managed, hunting, carefully controlled,

21. In spite of my reservations, I agreed on the next day to help her put up new wallpaper.

    (A) I agreed on the next day to help her put up new wallpaper.

    (B) I agreed on the next day to help put up her new wallpaper.

    (C) I agreed to help her put up new wallpaper on the next day.

    (D) I, on the next day, agreed to help her put up new wallpaper.

    (E) I agreed to, on the next day, help her put up new wallpaper.

22. We saw many of, though not nearly all, the existing Roman ruins along the Mediterranean coastline of Africa.

    (A) We saw many of, though not nearly all, the existing Roman ruins

    (B) We saw many, though not nearly all, of the existing Roman ruins

    (C) Seeing many, though not nearly all, of the existing Roman ruins

    (D) Having seen many of, though not nearly all, the existing Roman ruins

    (E) Many of, though not nearly all, the existing Roman ruins we saw

23. The horned owl is a carnivore who hunts a diversity of creatures, like hares, grouse, and ground squirrels.

    (A) The horned owl is a carnivore who hunts a diversity of creatures, like

    (B) The horned owl, a carnivore who hunts a diversity of creatures like

    (C) A hunting carnivore, the horned owl likes a diversity of creatures

    (D) The horned owl likes a diversity of carnivorous creatures, such as

    (E) The horned owl is a carnivore who hunts a diversity of creatures, such as

24. In many of his works, Tennessee Williams, <u>about whom much has been written</u>, has as main characters drifters, dreamers, and those who are crushed by having to deal with reality.

    (A) about whom much has been written

    (B) about who much has been written

    (C) about whom much has been written about

    (D) about him much having been written

    (E) much having been written about him

25. The world history students wanted to know <u>where the Dead Sea was at and what it was famous for</u>.

    (A) where the Dead Sea was at and what it was famous for.

    (B) where the Dead Sea is at and for what it is famous.

    (C) where the Dead Sea is located and why it is famous.

    (D) at where the Dead Sea was located and what it was famous for.

    (E) the location of the Dead Sea and what it was famous for.

26. Literary historians <u>cannot help but admit that they do not know</u> whether poetry or drama

    is the oldest form of literature.

    (A) cannot help but admit that they do not know

    (B) cannot admit that they do not admit to knowing

    (C) cannot help admitting that they do not know

    (D) cannot help but to admit that they do not know

    (E) cannot know but admit that they do not

27. Getting to know a person's parents will <u>often provide an insight to</u> his personality and behavior.

    (A) will often provide an insight to

    (B) will often provide an insight into

    (C) will often provide an insight for

    (D) will provide often an insight for

    (E) often will provide an insight with

28. Upon leaving the nursery, Mr. Greene, together with his wife, <u>put the plants in the trunk of the car they had just bought</u>.

    (A) put the plants in the trunk of the car they had just bought.

    (B) put in the plants to the trunk of the car they had just bought.

    (C) put into the trunk of the car they had just bought the plants.

    (D) put the plants they had just bought in the trunk of the car.

    (E) put the plants into the trunk of the car

29. <u>Having command of color, symbolism, as well as technique</u>, Georgia O'Keeffe is considered to be a great American painter.

    (A) Having command of color, symbolism, as well as technique

    (B) Having command of color, symbolism, and her technical ability

    (C) Because of her command of color, symbolism, and technique

    (D) With her command of color and symbolism and being technical

    (E) A commander of color, symbolism, and technique

30. <u>Whether the ancient ancestors of the first Americans actually migrated or did not</u> across a land bridge now covered by the Bering Strait remains uncertain, but that they could have has not been refuted by other theories.

    (A) Whether the ancient ancestors of the first Americans actually migrated or did not

    (B) Deciding if the ancient ancestors of the first Americans actually migrated or did not

    (C) That the ancient ancestors of the first Americans actually did migrate

    (D) Whether in actuality the ancient ancestors of the first Americans migrated or not

    (E) That the ancient ancestors of the first Americans may actually have migrated

REVISION IN CONTEXT

Directions: The following passage is a draft of an essay. Some portions of the passage need to be strengthened through editing and revision. Read the passage and choose the best answers for the questions that follow. Some questions ask you to improve sentences or portions of sentences. In some cases, the indicated portion of the passage will work best as it is and thus will require no changes. In choosing answers, consider development, organization, word choice, style, and tone and follow the requirements of standard written English. Remember to answer every question.

Tony Hawk: Master Skateboarder

[1] In 1983, Tony Hawk, a fifteen-year-old from San Diego, California, won his first professional skateboarding contest. [2] Two years later, he landed the first "720," a 720-degree spin, or two full revolutions. [3] Considered a pioneer in the world of extreme sports, Tony Hawk's determination and drive helped transform his hobby of skateboarding into a profitable business, yet also a way in which to make a positive difference in the world. [4] So successful would Tony become that by age 17, his annual income eclipsed that of his high school teachers.

[5] In his childhood, Tony had lofty ambitions and a lot of energy, but he was hard on himself when he did not succeed at the gamut of things he attempted. [6] Regardless, his mom, Nancy, describes young Tony as "challenging" because he had so much liveliness but no outlet for it. [7] However, when Tony was just nine years old, his older brother finally found something that Tony could devote his attention to: a skateboard.

[8] Frank Hawk, Tony's father, contributed to his son's success by being supportive of his interest. [9] While everyone else in the family was too busy to drive Tony to competitions, Frank made himself more available than he or she was, and drove him across California to participate. [10] In the family's backyard, he built skate ramps, half pipes, and areas for Tony to refine his talent. [11] Disappointed with the privation of skateboarding sponsoring organizations for his young son, Frank founded both the California Amateur Skateboard League and the National Skateboard Association. [12] He was so involved that some skateboarding officials commented that it was increasingly difficult to determine who had the most zeal for the sport: Tony or his father.

[13] At the 1999 X Games, Tony landed a "900": a two-and-a-half rotation midair flip above the lip of a vertical ramp. [14] Not long after the X Games, with many victories to his name, he retired from competitive skateboarding. [15] He had been practicing the trick for a decade during his attempts to master it, time after time he fell horribly, suffering four injuries that included broken ribs and compressed vertebrae. [16] Although he no longer competes, Tony still performs on his board in front of large audiences.

31. Which answer choice is the best grammatical replacement for the underlined portion of Sentence 3 (reproduced below), taking into account the context of the sentence?

    Considered a pioneer in the world of extreme sports, Tony Hawk's determination and drive helped transform his hobby of skateboarding into a profitable business, yet also a way in which to make a positive difference in the world.

    (A) Tony Hawk had

    (B) Tony Hawk along with his determination and drive

    (C) Tony Hawk

    (D) Tony Hawk's extreme ability to use his determination and drive

    (E) Tony Hawk would have

32. In the context of the passage, which of the following is the best version of the underscored portion of Sentence 6 (reproduced below)?

> <u>Regardless</u>, his mom, Nancy, describes young Tony as "challenging" because he had so much liveliness but no outlet for it.

   (A) (As it is now)

   (B) Granted

   (C) Perhaps

   (D) That is to say

   (E) Indeed

33. The writer is considering deleting Sentence 7. If the writer were to make the deletion, the essay would mainly lose which of the following?

   (A) An explanation of how Tony Hawk was first introduced to the sport of skateboarding

   (B) An indication of where Tony Hawk's talent came from

   (C) A revelation about Tony Hawk's rise to fame and how he uses his talents to this day

   (D) Impertinent detail that distracts the reader from the central point of the essay

   (E) A vague inference about Tony's character

34. In the context of the passage, which revision is best in Sentence 9 (reproduced below)?

> While everyone else in the family was too busy to drive Tony to competitions, Frank made himself <u>more available than he or she was</u>, and drove him across California to participate.

   (A) (As it is now)

   (B) more available than them

   (C) available

   (D) more available than him or her

   (E) more scarce

35. Which one of the following revisions in the underlined portion of Sentence 11 (reproduced below) best reflects the tone of the essay?

> <u>Disappointed with the privation of skateboarding sponsoring organizations for his young son,</u> Frank founded both the California Amateur Skateboard League and the National Skateboard Association.

   (A) (As it is now)

   (B) Unhappy with the lack of skateboarding sponsors,

   (C) Annoyed with the ridiculous lack of skateboarding groups for his talented son,

   (D) Disheartened by his attempts to find appropriate skateboarding groups for his son,

   (E) Dissuaded by the hidebound attitude of the skateboarding clubs,

36. Which of the following is the best way to revise the underlined portion of Sentence 12 (reproduced below) without altering the meaning of the text?

> He was so involved that some skateboarding officials <u>commented that it was increasingly difficult to determine</u> who had the most zeal for the sport: Tony or his father.

   (A) (As it is now)

   (B) said it was tough to say

   (C) were quoted as saying it was hard to figure

   (D) said it was easy to see

   (E) wondered

RESEARCH SKILLS

Directions: The following questions test your familiarity with basic research skills. For each question, choose the best answer. Remember to answer every question.

37. All of the following are questions writers should ask themselves in selecting a topic for a research paper EXCEPT:

    (A) Is the topic too broad?

    (B) Is the topic too limited?

    (C) Is the topic contemporary?

    (D) Is the topic debatable?

    (E) Is the topic one-sided?

38. To perform a keyword search for information using a library database, a writer should do which of the following?

    (A) Develop a working bibliography

    (B) Ask special services what resources they have available

    (C) Consult with the card catalog

    (D) Search for words related to the topic, using the title, author, and subject for direction

    (E) Distinguish between primary and secondary sources

39. All of the following are parts of the editing and proofreading stage of the research paper writing process EXCEPT:

    (A) Checking spelling, capitalization, and punctuation

    (B) Reviewing grammar and usage

    (C) Reorganizing the paper based on a new outline and thesis

    (D) Checking list of references

    (E) Citing Internet sources correctly

40. Which of the following should be used to indicate an undated source in a bibliographic entry?

    (A) doi

    (B) ibid.

    (C) et al.

    (D) s.v.

    (E) n.d.

SOURCE-BASED ESSAY

On the actual test, you will see the essay question at the top of the computer screen and space will be provided at the bottom for you to write your essay. For this assignment, however, we suggest you open a text document on your computer or laptop, or write in longhand in a notebook.

Time: 30 minutes

Directions: In the following section you will read two short passages on a topic and then plan and write an essay on that topic. Your essay will be an informative essay based on the two sources that are provided. Read the topic and sources carefully. Spend some time considering the topic and organizing your thoughts before you begin writing. Do not write on a topic other than the one specified. Essays on topics of your own choice will not be accepted. Your response must be in English. Write clearly and effectively, using concrete examples where appropriate. How well you write is more important than how much you write, but to cover the topics adequately, you will probably need to write more than one paragraph.

Assignment: Both of the following sources address different aspects of heroism. Read the two passages carefully and then write an essay in which you identify the most important concerns regarding the issue. Your essay must draw on information from both of the sources and explain the issue. In addition, you may draw on your own experiences, observations, or reading. Be sure to cite the sources whether you paraphrase or quote directly.

Source 1

When the first *Superman* movie came out, I was frequently asked, "What is a hero?" My answer was that a hero is someone who commits a courageous action without considering the consequences. Now my definition is completely different. I think a hero is an ordinary individual who finds strength to persevere and endure in spite of overwhelming obstacles.

—Christopher Reeve, actor who was paralyzed
in an equestrian competition

Source 2

Hundreds of spectators gathered outside the jailhouse, shouting encouragement as the boycotters walked inside to be booked, cheering and applauding when they left. The act of being arrested, which for so long had terrified the black community, had become a badge of honor. People who had once trembled before the law were now proud to be arrested for the cause of freedom. As the exuberant crowd of onlookers laughed and cheered, waving and hugging boycott leaders as the passed in and out, some of the white sheriff's deputies began to enjoy themselves too, laughing and trading jokes with the crowd, until the sheriff himself stormed outside to shout, "This is no vaudeville show!"

Freedman, Russell. *Freedom Walkers:
The Story of the Montgomery Bus Boycott.*
New York: Holiday House, 2006.

ARGUMENTATIVE ESSAY

On the actual test, you will see the essay question at the top of the computer screen and space will be provided at the bottom for you to write your essay. For this assignment, however, we suggest you open a text document on your computer or laptop, or write in longhand in a notebook.

Time: 30 minutes

Directions: You will plan and write an argumentative essay on the topic presented above. The essay will be based on your own reading, experience, or observations. Read the topic carefully. You will probably find it best to spend a little time considering the topic and organizing your thoughts before you begin writing. Do not write on a topic other than the one specified. Essays on topics of your own choice will not be acceptable. In order for your test to be scored, your responses must be in English.

Read the opinion stated below:

"I'm against the draft. I believe we should have a professional military; it might be smaller, but it would be more effective."—Jesse Ventura, professional wrestler, actor, veteran, and American politician

Assignment: Discuss the degree to which you agree or disagree with this opinion. Use support from your own reading, observation, and personal experience.

Praxis Core
Writing Practice Test 2 Answer Key

1.	(B)	15.	(A)	29.	(C)
2.	(C)	16.	(C)	30.	(C)
3.	(A)	17.	(D)	31.	(C)
4.	(C)	18.	(B)	32.	(E)
5.	(B)	19.	(D)	33.	(A)
6.	(D)	20.	(A)	34.	(C)
7.	(D)	21.	(C)	35.	(B)
8.	(B)	22.	(B)	36.	(B)
9.	(B)	23.	(E)	37.	(C)
10.	(D)	24.	(A)	38.	(D)
11.	(B)	25.	(C)	39.	(C)
12.	(E)	26.	(C)	40.	(E)
13.	(C)	27.	(B)		
14.	(C)	28.	(D)		

Usage

1. (B)

This sentence contains an error in choice (B), "are," which should be replaced with "is" because the subject, "firewood," is singular, not plural. Note that in underscored choice (D), the item asks you to judge whether some mark of punctuation is required. Since no pause is necessary, no comma should be inserted.

2. (C)

The error is in choice (C), "have." Two singular subjects connected by "or, either/or, or neither/nor" take a singular verb, which in this case would be "has." Note that the first underscored choice, (A), asks you to consider whether the lowercase *p* in "policy" needs to be capitalized. It's correct as it stands because it's not a proper noun.

3. (A)

The error is found in choice (A), at some future point in time. It's superfluous and can be deleted because the future tense of the remaining sentence already tells us the action will take place at some unspecified point in the future. Had choice (A) instead provided, say, a day or date, it would be giving valuable information. The other choices are correct: "I will be going" (B) is a correctly conjugated future tense verb; "the orthodontist" (C) is a direct object upon which the verb phrase "will be going" is acting; and "for further treatment" (D) functions well as a prepositional phrase.

4. (C)

The sentence contains an error in choice (C), "infers." This verb is incorrectly used. An author can "imply," "indicate," "reveal," or otherwise present an idea. A published work leaves it to the reader to infer or deduce.

5. (B)

The sentence contains an error in choice (B), "search." The error occurs with the use of the wrong verb tense. Since the process began in the past, a past tense verb is needed. The verb phrase should read "searched." The other choices are acceptable. Choice (A) is an introductory phrase set off by a comma; "every inch" (C) is an appropriate idiomatic phrase; and choice (D) is an infinitive verb.

6. (D)

The sentence contains an error in choice (D), "their." Agreement is needed here between the pronoun and its antecedent. Since "supermarket" is singular, the pronoun should be "its" instead of "their." Pronouns must agree in number with the words to which they refer. While one can often hear "their" used to refer to a singular thing in casual speech, this is not standard written English. The other choices are acceptable since "supermarket" (A) is a noun with an article in front of it, "terrible" (B) functions as an adjective, and "of lighting" (C) is a prepositional phrase.

7. (D)

The sentence contains an error in choice (D), the coordinating conjunction "and." "But" is needed to draw the contrast between the mother's command and the reaction it elicits.

8. (B)

The sentence contains an error in choice (B), "luminances." This should be revised to say "luminaries." "Luminance" means the quality or state of being luminous, or bathed in light. "Luminary" means a person of distinction.

9. (B)

The sentence contains an error in choice (B), "they," which is vague. Because the sentence stands alone, it should specifically identify who the doer of the action is. "After downsizing" (A) is an introductory phrase set off by a comma, so it is correct. "Among" (C) is correct because work gets distributed collectively to employees. "Who" is also correct because it modifies "employees."

10. (D)

The sentence contains an error in choice (D), "quick." An adverb is needed to describe how Cathy read the article. Thus, "quickly" should be used instead of "quick," and it would go before "read," the verb it modifies. The subject and verb are conjugated correctly, so choice (A) is acceptable. "Article" (B) is a noun functioning as a direct object in the sentence. The prepositional phrase "about poverty in India" (C) describes the article.

11. (B)

The sentence contains an error in choice (B), the *i* in "if." The first letter of a direct quotation must be capitalized when the quoted material is a full sentence. A person's name must also be capitalized, as it is in this case (A). A comma is needed to set off the introductory part of the quote (C). The period is correctly placed inside the quotation marks (D), as befits standard written American English.

12. (E)

You should have selected choice (E), No error. The sentence contains no grammatical, idiomatic, logical, or structural errors. Choice (A), "Julie's parents," is the subject. The prepositional phrase "down the street" (B) is correct. "Held" (C) is conjugated in accordance with the other past tense verb, "walked." Choice (D), "as if," is an appropriate idiomatic phrase.

13. (C)

The sentence contains an error in choice (C), "yet." The use of "yet" strikes a note of contrast, but flies in the face of the strong parallel being drawn ("never stops . . . never stops"). The correct coordinating conjunction would be "and."

14. (C)

The sentence contains an error in choice (C), "to live." The sentence pairs two corresponding ideas that should be expressed with the same grammatical form. Because "living" is a gerund, the infinitive "to live" should be replaced with "living" to make the construction parallel. The rest of the sentence is in good grammatical form. Choice (B), "is," agrees with its subject "living" in number. Choice (D) is an adjective that is synonymous with "expensive."

15. (A)

The sentence contains an error in choice (A), "more frequent." The adverbial form, "frequently," should be used to modify the verb. Choices (B) and (D) are correct subject-verb combinations. The adjective form, "possible," of choice (C) correctly follows the linking verb "is."

16. (C)

This sentence contains an error in choice (C). The antecedent for "it" is unclear because "it" can refer to either the grass or the branch. Choice (A), "over the curb," is a complete prepositional phrase and choice (B), "to," is correctly used as a preposition in the phrase "to the ground." Choice (D) is idiomatically correct because we become "annoyed *with*" people but "annoyed *at*" things or situations.

17. (D)

The preposition "in" has three objects: "submarines," "missiles," and "to get" (D), which must be made parallel to the two nouns before it, so that's where this sentence's one error lies. Choice (D) could be revised this way: "in space vehicles, even playing a role in the Apollo exploration series." It's a long sentence but now it parses. Choice (A), "Inertial," is an adjective modifying "navigation." Choice (B), "they are" is a part of a subordinate clause modifying "submarines." Choice (C) is a preposition used correctly.

18. (B)

Choice (B) marks this sentence's error. This sentence is not parallel. Two actions are mentioned, connected by "not only" and "but also." The sentence should read, "not only are Americans…but they are also…" Choices (A), "during the summer," and (C), "to add humidity," contain a properly used prepositional phrase and infinitive, respectively. Choice (D), "particularly," is an adverb modifying the adjective "arid" to indicate the unusual degree to which Arizona's climate is characterized by aridness, or dryness.

Sentence Correction

19. (D)

The conjunction "not only . . . but also" must be properly placed to indicate which qualities are being discussed and to maintain proper parallelism. Choice (D) contains three adjectives to follow the verb "to be": "capable and efficient" and "adept." Choices (A), (B), (C), and (E) are not parallel. In addition, choices (B) and (C) have "to be" after the conjunction, and this construction would require another verb after the second conjunction, "but also."

20. (A)

This sentence contains two concepts, proper management and careful control. In choice (A) these two concepts are concisely worded and appear in parallel form. Choice (B) has no noun for "Managing" to modify. Choice (C) would be acceptable with the addition of commas to set off the introductory phrase. Choice (D) mangles the concepts, and the wording in choice (E) is poor.

21. (C)

Choice (A) is a "squinting" modifier: it is unclear if "on the next day" tells when "I agreed" or when "to put up." Choice (B) does not clarify this problem. Choice (D) unnecessarily splits the subject and the verb, and choice (E) unnecessarily splits an infinitive.

22. (B)

In standard written English, the interrupter (aka parenthetical element) should not come between a preposition and its object. Choices (A), (D), and (E) are all incorrect because they all misplace the interrupter. Choices (C) and (D) produce a fragment because the subject, "we," is missing.

23. (E)

To mean "for example," the expression "like" is incorrect; the correct usage is "such as." Therefore, choices (A) and (B) are incorrect. Choices (C) and (D) incorrectly use "likes" as a verb, thereby changing the intent of the sentence.

24. (A)

Choice (A) correctly uses the object pronoun "whom" to follow the preposition "about." Choice (B) uses the wrong pronoun. Choice (C) inserts an extraneous preposition "about" that has no object. Choice (D) is awkward wording; choice (E) is also poor wording, especially with the pronoun "him" so far away from its antecedent.

25. (C)

Choice (C) clearly and simply deals with the location and the fame of the Dead Sea. Since the Dead Sea still exists, the verbs should be in the present tense, which eliminates the original sentence (A) and choices (D) and (E). In choice (B), where we see the phrase "where the Dead Sea is at," the word "at" is redundant; it is sufficient to write "where the Dead Sea is," but you're not given this as a response option, making choice (C) the best selection.

26. (C)

The phrase "cannot help" should be followed by a gerund, not by "but." Choice (C) follows "cannot help" with the gerund "admitting." Choices (A) and (D) are incorrect because they follow "cannot help" with "but." The wording of choice (B), "cannot admit," and choice (E), "cannot know," twists the meaning of the sentence.

27. (B)

Idiomatic usage calls for "into" to follow "insight." The proper usage is found only in choice (B).

28. (D)

The dependent clause ("Upon leaving the nursery,") makes it clear that the Greenes have just purchased plants. The modifying phrase, "they had just bought," should be carefully placed in the sentence to clearly modify "plants" and not "car." Choice (D) has the modifying phrase immediately following "plants," and the meaning is clear. The wording of choices (A), (B), and (C) makes the reader think the car has just been purchased. Choice (E) omits the concept that a purchase has taken place by deleting the phrase "they had just bought."

29. (C)

Choice (C) is the best answer. This is the only response option that coherently links O'Keeffe's artistic mastery to the high regard in which she is held. The original sentence (A) suffers from two problems: failing to create the aforementioned correlation and using mixed forms in series. Choice (B) compounds the problems in choice (A) by adding a superfluous pronoun ("her"). Choice (D)'s diction disqualifies it from consideration; the verbal "being technical" veers from the intended discussion of the artist's masterful *technique*. Choice (E) misuses the noun "commander." In this form, the term can only mean someone in an official position of command or control, typically in law enforcement or the military, which hardly fits the context.

30. (C)

Choice (C) is the correct answer, eliminating both imbalanced structure and redundancy, the dual issues that should have had you looking for ways to improve the original sentence (A). Choice (B)'s gerund creates a subtle example of faulty predication, meaning that the sentence's subject cannot carry out the action that the sentence's verb depicts: It's not the deciding that remains uncertain, it's proof of the *act of crossing* the land bridge that does. Choice (D) is virtually a carbon copy of the original, and fails to remedy what ails the original. Choice (E) pointlessly hedges ("*may* actually *have* migrated"), making the sentence wordier.

Revision in Context

31. (C)

This question tests parallelism and logic. The first clause should have you looking for the "pioneer." Tony Hawk is that person, *not* "his determination and drive." So the correct answer is choice (C). Choice (A) introduces the past perfect, which means the sentence would have to be stating an action that was completed at some point in the past before something else happened. But the transformation to which the sentence alludes is a single action. Choices (B) and (D) only magnify the error in the original sentence. Choice (E), "would have," would be used to refer to the past to talk about things that did not happen. Be careful. Any grammatical change you make must support the established logic of the passage. We know that Tony actually did make skateboarding financially viable because the passage says he "helped transform his hobby of skateboarding into a profitable business"; don't revise the sentence in any way that would undermine or lose sight of meaning drawn from context.

32. (E)

The correct answer is choice (E). The second paragraph's lead-off sentence raises the implicit prospect of frustration in Nancy's son Tony trying but not succeeding at a "gamut" of things. Sentence 6 reinforces, or emphasizes, the struggle to find a sustained way to channel her son's high energy. Choice (E) fits this context well because it provides the necessary intensification. "Regardless" (A), in the given sentence, draws a contrast. "Granted" (B) would signal a concession. "Perhaps" (C) would mark a qualification. "That is to say" (D) would indicate a clarification.

33. (A)

Choice (A) is the best answer; in explaining how Tony was introduced to the sport, the sentence captures a pivotal moment. Thus, deleting it would actually impair the essay's logical progression. The sentence says nothing about talent (B) or Tony's rise to fame (C), is hardly impertinent (D), and, given the centrality of the event and the simple directness of the sentence, choice (E) is incorrect as well.

34. (C)

The correct answer is choice (C). Only "available" itself is necessary in the underscored portion of the sentence. In fact, the intended contrast between Frank and other members of the family is set up in the dependent (first) clause with the dependent marker "while." Choices (B) and (D) perpetuate the problem instead of solving it. Choice (E), "more scarce," is a near antonym to the correct answer.

35. (B)

Choice (B) is the correct answer. This question hinges on your command of contextual vocabulary—a critical underlying facet of the Praxis Core tests. The Praxis Core is designed to test your vocabulary skills, but not directly. The key word in this sentence is *privation,* not often heard in daily affairs; it means "the act of depriving." Even if you didn't know the meaning, however, the sentence goes on to say that Frank founded sponsoring organizations for his son's sport. Choice (B) highlights that skateboarding amateurs like his son lacked a broader web of support to pursue their sport. Choice (B) has the added benefit of being more economically phrased than the original sentence. Choice (C) strikes a petulant tone inconsistent with the rest of the essay. Choice (D) puts the onus on Frank himself, which again does not fit the context. Finally, there is no sign that other skateboarders were "hidebound," or inflexible (E), nor does this notion jell with the tone of the essay as a whole.

36. (B)

Choice (B) is the correct answer, precisely and succinctly conveying the intended meaning. Watch for the test to challenge you to respond with answers that are not only error-free but also concise. Choice (C) replaces one wordy phrase with another. Choice (D) gainsays the passage, making this response option easy to dismiss. Choice (E) underplays the gusto shared by father and son, as embodied in "zeal."

Research Skills

37. (C)

The correct answer is choice (C). The rest of the choices are appropriate questions to ask, but a topic need not be contemporary to be acceptable for a research paper.

38. (D)

The correct answer is choice (D), which explains how to conduct a keyword search. The other choices are aspects of the research process but not related to conducting a keyword search.

39. (C)

Choice (C) is correct because it describes an aspect of the revision process. The other choices describe tasks that are done in the editing phase.

40. (E)

The correct answer is choice (E). Researchers use *n.d.,* the abbreviation for "no date," to indicate that no date is available for a source. The other choices are other types of bibliographic designations: *doi* is short for digital object identifier, the character string that uniquely identifies an electronic resource; *ibid.* is the abbreviation for the Latin term *ibidem* (literally "the same place"), which is used to show that a citation refers to the immediately preceding source; *et al.* is short for the Latin *et alia* (literally "and others") and is used to indicate additional authors; and *s.v.* is the abbreviation for the Latin *sub voce* (literally "under the word"), which is used to refer to a particular section of a bibliographic entry (e.g., a research paper on sustainable urban design in an encyclopedia article would give the bibliographic details for the encyclopedia followed by "*s.v.* Sustainable urban design").

SCORING GUIDE FOR SOURCE-BASED ESSAY

Use these objective criteria to score your essay. Then compare your essay to the sample essays that follow.

Score of 6

A 6 essay shows a high degree of competency. An essay in this category:

- Is both well organized and well developed

- Uses information from both sources to discuss the issue and creates meaningful connections between these sources

- Organizes and develops ideas coherently

- Varies syntax and expression

- Is nearly free from errors in syntax, structure, grammar, usage, and mechanics

- Correctly cites both sources when paraphrasing or quoting

Score of 5

A 5 essay shows a high degree of proficiency but may have minor errors. An essay in this category:

- Discusses the matter clearly, creating solid connections between the two sources and offering pertinent support

- Includes information from both sources to discuss the issue

- Is organized and clear

- Shows some sentence variety and ease in the use of language

- Is virtually free from errors in grammar, usage, and mechanics

- Cites both sources when paraphrasing or quoting directly

Score of 4

A 4 essay responds to the assignment and shows some degree of deeper understanding of the assignment. An essay in this category:

- Shows adequate organization, support, development, and connections between the two sources

- Sufficiently explains the issue

- Uses and cites information from both sources when paraphrasing and quoting to explain the issue

- Displays satisfactory use of language, grammar, usage, and mechanics, but may have some errors

Score of 3

A 3 essay shows some degree of understanding, but its response to the topic is deficient. An essay in this category reveals one or more of the following limitations:

- Is inadequate in explaining the issue

- May incorporate only one source or incorporates two sources ineffectively; may fail to cite sources that are paraphrased or quoted directly

- Has incomplete support and a weak connection between sources

- Has insufficient organization and development of ideas

- Has consistent repetition of syntactical or structural errors

Score of 2

An essay receiving a score of 2 shows limited under-standing, and its response to the topic is seriously defi-cient. An essay in this category reveals one or more of the following weaknesses:

- Shows weak organization or development

- Incorporates only one source and does so inad-equately

- Fails to clearly and thoroughly discuss the issue

- Has limited support and connections between sources

- Has consistent and serious errors in grammar, usage, syntax, and word choice

- Does not cite quoted or paraphrased information

Score of 1

An essay receiving a score of 1 exhibits a lack of basic writing skills. An essay in this category:

- Contains serious and persistent writing errors

or

- Is disorganized and undeveloped, contains con-sistent repetition of errors, and is incomprehen-sible

Sample Source-based Essay 1

Score range: 5 to 6
Word count: 348

As a child, I remember seeing heroes depicted in television and movies. Now that I am older, I am all too well aware that heroes are in high demand but can rarely be found. To accomplish heroic acts, all individuals need is an open mind and a willing heart. Ancient heroes like Oedipus and Beowulf as well as modern heroes like Chris-topher Reeve and the freedom walkers demonstrate that heroes embody idealized virtues and strength to

carry on in spite of huge challenges. Collectively, their lives show how individuals can achieve extraordinary feats and make a difference in the lives of others.

The ancient hero possessed many romanticized vir-tues such as physical strength, honesty, courage, and intelligence. Oedipus saved his people from pestilence by solving the riddle of the Sphinx. As leader, he was sworn to find the murderer of the previous king; Oedipus' brave pursuit of justice was conducted with honesty and integrity. Beowulf, another famous ancient hero, existed at a time when life was wild, dangerous, unpredictable.

Modern society also demonstrates evidence of heroes. Men have been decorated for fighting in the Civil War, in World War I, and in World War II. Even the actor who portrayed Superman, Christopher Reeve, became a hero when he fell from a horse and, as a quadriplegic, fought hard for research to help people.

Actors like John Wayne and Clint Eastwood reveal what heroism look like. They are larger than life on the theatre screen, and their vices are at least predict-able and reasonably innocuous. But the real heroes we find in everyday people who do extraordinary things. For instance, the freedom riders proudly got themselves arrested in the larger struggle for civil rights in the Unit-ed States. It is these ordinary heroes that are most impressive. They stood up for what was right in the face of death threats and persecution.

In the final analysis, heroism is something that has been with us since ancient times. In the 21st century, we need to look closer to home to see everyday heroes who are persevering in spite of many obstacles.

Analysis of Source-based Essay 1

Essay 1 has a score in the range of 5-6. It is the stron-gest of the four essays. It is not perfect but it shows a good command of the English language as well as depth of thought. The writer uses a traditional essay structure: The first paragraph is the introduction and ends with the thesis statement; the second and third paragraphs discuss traditional and contemporary heroes, as stated in the last sentence of the thesis paragraph. The fourth paragraph discusses heroes who transcend the representations in television and film. Each of the body paragraphs has a clear topic sentence. The writer gives several distinct examples from the sources to support his or her ideas. The vocabulary works, and the syntax is varied.

Sample Source-based Essay 2

Score range: 3 to 4
Word count: 301

Heroes are people who perform the extraordinary and who are highly regarded by society. These outstanding people have characteristics that are desirable to everyone, but the ways in which heroes use their talents glorify them even more. A true hero will do anything in his power to help others.

Two heroes from modern literature exhibit the quality of self-sacrifice. In Remarque's novel All Quiet on the Western Front, Paul Baumer is a German ground soldier who endures many disappointments and difficulties while fighting for his country. Paul does not shirk his duties as a soldier of the German people. Moreover, Paul goes out of his way to train the raw recruits and to care for a soldier suffering from shell shock. Another hero, Willy Loman in Death of a Salesman, makes all the everyday sacrifices a father makes for children and a husband makes for a wife. Willy drives long distances in order to make a living. When Willy feels he is hindering his family, he makes the ultimate sacrifice of suicide to get out of the way.

The true heroes of today are the common people, not unlike Willy and Paul. Stories regularly appear in the newspaper of everyday heroes. The woman with knowledge of CPR saves a drowning child from certain death. A neighbor saves two children from an apartment fire. Teachers take the extra time to listen to a student's

personal problem. Parents stand tough against their child's unreasonable demands. Even the freedom fighters in the Civil Rights movement were ordinary people who took an extraordinary stand against discrimination. All of these people are heroes in their own way.

Every day they stand behind their ideals, living up to their moral standards, in order to help others. It is the day-to-day dedication that makes these twentieth-century heroes extraordinary.

Analysis of Source-based Essay 2

Essay 2 would merit a score range of 3–4. It is competent. The writer takes one position and develops it. The first paragraph provides a clear introduction, and paragraphs two and three develop the claims that support the thesis. Examples support the essay, but the syntax does not vary enough. In addition, the body of the essay alludes to only one of the sources. The last sentence of the third paragraph is especially weak.

Sample Source-based Essay 3

Score range: 1 to 2
Word count: 150

It is not true that there are no heroes nowadays. Everywhere you look, a person see heroes to believe in.

When you go to the movie theater, many movies are about good guys versus bad guys. Not just Westerns. Sometimes the good cop gets killed. But he usually kills a few criminals for himself before he dies. In many movies, justice wins when the villain is defeated. No matter who wins, people in the audience know what is right and what is defeated. No matter who wins, the people in the audience know what is right and what is wrong because the heroes kill because he needs to defend themselves or because the wrong guy needed to be killed. Rambo would not kill anyone except the enemy. This teaches good values about heroes and their motives since people like to go to the movies, they see a lot of heroes.

Analysis of Source-based Essay 3

Essay 3 would earn a score in the range of 1–2. The ideas are inexact, and the sentences are poorly structured. The essay mixes informal voice and slang. There is an agreement error, a fragment, a shift in person, a lack of paragraphs, and a failure to use either source. The most serious concern is the lack of specific examples and the use of sweeping generalizations. The concluding two sentences are vague and poorly worded.

SCORING GUIDE FOR ARGUMENTATIVE ESSAY

Use these objective criteria to score your essay. Then compare you essay to the sample essays that follow.

Score of 6

A 6 essay demonstrates a high degree of skill in response to the assignment but may have a few minor errors. An essay in this category:

- Has a clear thesis

- Organizes and develops ideas logically and coherently

- Develops claims and counterclaims by supplying sufficient evidence and describing the strengths and weaknesses of both sides of an argument

- Explains ideas clearly with good reasons

- Demonstrates effective sentence variety

- Clearly displays facility in the use of language

- Is generally free from errors in grammar, usage, and mechanics

Score of 5

A 5 essay demonstrates clear proficiency in response to the assignment but may have minor errors. An essay in this category:

- Has a clear or implied thesis

- Makes claims and considers both sides of the argument

- Organizes and develops ideas clearly, making connections between them

- Explains key ideas, supporting them with applicable reasons, examples, or details

- Displays some sentence variety

- Displays capacity in the use of language

- Is by and large free from errors in grammar, usage, and mechanics

Score of 4

A 4 essay establishes competency in response to the assignment. An essay in this category:

- Has a thesis

- Shows control in the organization and development of ideas although claims may or may not consider both sides of the argument

- Explains some key ideas, supporting them with acceptable reasons and support

- Displays passable use of language

- Shows some control of grammar, usage, and mechanics, but may display errors

Score of 3

A 3 essay demonstrates some competence in response to the assignment but is obviously flawed. An essay in this category reveals one or more of the following weaknesses:

- Has an inadequate thesis
- Has an inadequate organization and development of ideas
- Presents inadequate reasons, examples, or details
- Has errors in language, grammar, usage, and mechanics

Score of 2

A 2 essay is very inconsistent. An essay in this category reveals one or more of the following errors:

- Has no clear position or thesis
- Presents no claims or entertainment of the opposing viewpoint
- Shows weak organization or very little development
- Has few or no relevant reasons or support
- Contains recurrent serious errors in the use of language, grammar, usage, and mechanics

Score of 1

A 1 essay demonstrates fundamental deficits in writing skills. An essay in this category:

- Contains serious and persistent writing errors, is incomprehensible and/or underdeveloped.

Sample Argumentative Essay 1

Score range: 5 to 6
Word count: 394

The cynic in me wants to react to the idea of a military draft by looking at what critics have had to say. These complaints suggest that wars might never be fought in the first place if people drafted were the adult leaders and lawmakers (as well as the children of such people). Still, I believe the draft is a good thing because I see everywhere—not just in the youth—the effects of a selfish and self-indulgent culture.

One reads and hears constantly about young people who do not care about the problems of our society. These youngsters seem interested in money and the luxuries money can buy. They do not want to work from the minimum wage up, but want instead to land a high paying job without "paying their dues." An informal television news survey of high school students a few years ago suggested that students had the well entrenched fantasy that with no skills or higher education they would not accept a job paying less than $20 an hour. Perhaps military service would instill a sense of caring for the community.

The shiny gleam of a new expensive sports sedan bought on credit by a recent accounting student reflects self indulgence that might be toned down by military service. That self-indulgence may reflect merely a lack of discipline, but it also may reflect a lack of purpose in life. Philosophers, theologians, and leaders of all types suggest throughout the ages that money and objects do not ultimately satisfy. Helping others—service to our fellow human beings—often does. Critics may argue that there are many ways individuals can be of service and that it does not have to be through the military. True enough, but someone needs to stand up and protect the freedoms we have been afforded as a nation. Military services gives people experiences in responsibility and the real world and takes away the desire many people have to acquire material things.

In short, the military draft may help young people restore their faith in their nation and what it means to them. Yet, this is the land of opportunity, but it is also a land of forgotten people, and it is a land that faces threats from the outside. A military draft would remind young people of their past and of their collective responsibility to the future.

Analysis of Argumentative Essay 1

The essay introduces a precise and knowledgeable argument, establishes claims, and distinguishes an opposing claim. The organization is logical and clean. To ensure a top score, the writer would take a deeper look at the strengths and limitations of each side of the argument. The writer has good awareness of audience. There is a coherent central argument and a conclusion. Syntax varies. Although the essay would benefit from some minor revisions, it is well done, considering the 30-minute time limit.

Sample Argumentative Essay 2

Score range: 3 to 4
Word count: 349

If we were to have the draft today, he would be obligated, by law, to register for the military draft. This is done so that in case of a war or something catastrophic, these boys and men can be called on for active duty in the military. It is good to know that we will have the manpower in case of a war but my opinion on the military draft is negative. I don't like the idea of forcing someone to sign up at a certain age for something that they don't want to happen. Of course, I know that we need some sort of military manpower on hand just in case, but it would be so much better if it was left to the individual to decide what area to serve in and what time.

When a boy turns 18, he's a rebel of sorts. He doesn't want someone telling him what to do and when to do it; he's just beginning to live. In Switzerland, when a boy turns 18, he goes into some branch of the military for a

time of training. He is given his gun, uniform, and badge number. Then, once a year for about two weeks he suits up for retraining. He does this unitl he is about 65 years old. Now in a way this is like a draft but the men love it and feel that it is honorable. I think that they like it because it does not discriminate and their jobs pay them for the time away. Switzerland seems to give the 18 year old somewhat of a choice what division to go in and whether or not to join. They're not as strict on joining as we are so it's more of an honorable thing to do.

Of course, I'd love to see it as strictly up to the individual but it can't be that way. We have too many enemies that we might go to war with and we would need a strong military. Switzerland has nothing to worry about as long as they have their banks.

Analysis of Argumentative Essay 2

Essay 2 merits a score of about 3 or 4. It displays competent thinking, but it does not state its topic as well as Essay 1. The extended example of Swiss military conscription is the main strength of the essay. The writer hedges a bit but conveys an opinion. Sentences vary, and the vocabulary is competent. Some spelling and grammatical errors interfere with the communication.

Sample Argumentative Essay 3

Score range: 1 to 2
Word count: 120

Feeling strongly against the draft, as I could not agree with the idea of requiring young people to serve in the military. I agree with Jesse Ventura that we should have no draft. I feel this would say something about the world situation. I believe the leaders and people would have to give up the idea of peace totally. Which would evetually lead to our own destruction.

Although I do believe young people should serve their country in a peaceful more useful way. They should be more politically aware of what the government is trying to do. They should work in a peaceful way to try and make changes that work for the good of all people of the world.

Analysis of Argumentative Essay 3

Essay 3 would earn a grade of not more than a 1 or 2. It has many problems. It not only fails to present a coherent argument, but it also shows a fundamental lack of understanding of syntax. There are many sentence-level errors, including run-ons and misspellings. The concluding statement comes out of nowhere. There also is no structure for an argumentative essay. It lacks a thesis, claims, counterclaims, and a developed conclusion.

Index

Math Practice Test 1: Self-Assessment Guide

Check the boxes for each question you answered correctly. Items are sorted by question number under each content category.

Number and Quantity

6	10	14	16	19	21	22	26	28

31	35	41	42	46	50	54

Algebra and Functions

3	7	11	15	17	20	23	27	29

32	36	40	43	47	51	55	56

Geometry

1	5	9	13	25	30	34	38

45	49	53

Probability and Statistics

2	4	8	12	18	24	33	37

44	48	52

Math Practice Test 2: Self-Assessment Guide

Check the boxes for each question you answered correctly. Items are sorted by question number under each content category.

Number and Quantity

1	2	8	9	15	16	21	23	27

28	33	34	36	40	41	46	48

Algebra and Functions

3	4	5	11	12	13	17	18	22

29	30	35	37	42	43	50	52

Geometry

6	10	19	25	31	38	44	47

49	53	54

Probability and Statistics

7	14	20	24	26	32	39	45

51	55	56

Reading Practice Test 1: Self-Assessment Guide

Check the boxes for each question you answered correctly. Items are sorted by question number under each content category.

Key Ideas and Details

1	2	4	5	7	9	10	23	29	30

32	35	37	42	43	44	46	47	49	50

Craft, Structure, and Language Skills

3	8	13	16	18	19	21	24	25	27

31	34	36	38	41	45	48

Integration of Knowledge and Ideas

6	11	12	14	15	17	20	22	26	28

33	39	40	51	52	53	54	55	56

Reading Practice Test 2: Self-Assessment Guide

Check the boxes for each question you answered correctly. Items are sorted by question number under each content category.

Key Ideas and Details

1	2	6	13	19	24	26	31	32	33

35	36	38	41	46	47	48	49

Craft, Structure, and Language Skills

3	4	5	7	8	9	10	11	14	20

27	29	34	40	42	44	50	54	55	56

Integration of Knowledge and Ideas

12	15	16	17	18	21	22	23	25

28	30	37	39	43	45	51	52	53

Writing Practice Test 1: Self-Assessment Guide

Check the boxes for each question you answered correctly. Items are sorted by question number under each content category.

Usage

1	2	3	4	5	6	7	8	9	10

11	12	13	14	15	16	17

Sentence Correction

18	19	20	21	22	23	24	25	26	27

28

Revision in Context

29	30	31	32	33	34	35	35	36

Research Skills

37	38	39	40

Writing Arguments

Rate yourself on a 6-point scale (see scoring guide, pg. 505)

Writing Informative/Explanatory Texts

Rate yourself on a 6-point scale (see scoring guide, pg. 508)

Writing Practice Test 2: Self-Assessment Guide

Check the boxes for each question you answered correctly. Items are sorted by question number under each content category.

Usage

1	2	3	4	5	6	7	8	9	10

11	12	13	14	15	16	17	18

Sentence Correction

19	20	21	22	23	24	25	26	27	28

29	30

Revision in Context

31	32	33	34	35	36

Research Skills

37	38	39	40

Writing Arguments

Rate yourself on a 6-point scale (see scoring guide, pg. 505)

Writing Informative/Explanatory Texts

Rate yourself on a 6-point scale (see scoring guide, pg. 508)